# Four Britons and Nationalism

# Four Britons and Nationalism

Henry Wickham Steed, Robert William Seton-Watson,
Arnold Joseph Toynbee and Carlile Aylmer Macartney
in/on East-Central Europe and Beyond
(1903–1978)

ÁGNES BERETZKY

H P

Helena History Press

©2024 Ágnes Beretzky
All rights reserved
Published in the United States by: Helena History Press LLC

H P

A division of KKL Publications LLC, Reno, NV USA
www.helenahistorypress.com

Publishing scholarship about and from Central and East Europe


ISBN: (hardback) 978-1-943596-41-6
ISBN: (ebook) 978-1-943596-42-3

Graphic Designer: Sebastian Stachowski

*To László Péter (1929-2008)*
*Emeritus Professor of Hungarian History, University College*
*London School of Slavonic and East European Studies*

# Table of Contents

Note on Terminology   ix

Preface   xi

Introduction   1

Chapter 1. Steed, Seton-Watson and Toynbee on National Self-Determination in East-Central Europe and Turkey (1903–1920)   15

Chapter 2. "This new order has come to stay": From Versailles to Paris (1920–1947)   55

Chapter 3. In a Bipolar World 1947–78   235

Conclusion   257

Bibliography   271

Index   289

Gallery   297

# Note on Terminology

The term Central-Europe, that is, Middle-Europe, or the Lands between Germany and Russia, has been geopolitically as well as historically controversial. In 1915 Friedrich Naumann's concept of *Mitteleuropa* envisaged a German-dominated area in the heart of Europe, which was confronted by rival theories either from the *New-Europe*-group (Seton-Watson or Lewis Namier) to create a "zone of small nations," or, for example, by Tomáš Garrigue Masaryk (1850–1937), who described Central-Europe as the territory "East of Germany, Austria-Hungary, the Balkans and the Eastern part of Russia (Poland)" in his 1916 memorandum „At the Eleventh Hour." Throughout this book, the term East-Central Europe is used to denote the area between Germany and Russia/the Soviet Union until 1945. After the end of World War II, all these countries forcefully incorporated into the Soviet sphere will be referred to as Eastern Europe. (Since the Ottoman Empire ruled over European territories for part of the period under study, and not the least because of Arnold J. Toynbee's interest in the subject, Turkey and the Armenian minority are also included in the analysis.)

As many places in East-Central Europe have two or three names, it is attempted in each case to use the currently official version, followed by the alternative(s) in brackets or hyphenated. So, for instance, the great Transylvanian city is referred to Kolozsvár (Cluj, Klausenburg) prior to 1920 and from 1940–45 and otherwise as Cluj (Kolozsvár, Klausenburg). However, there are a few exceptions: the island southeast of the present Slovak capital is referred to as Grosse Schütt (Csallóköz, Veľký Žitný ostrov) throughout, despite its ethnic composition or official status, as this has been most commonly used in English texts. In the case of monolingual, mono-ethnic place names, the alternative in brackets is omitted, e.g. Ružomberok.

All names denoting individuals appear in the original, with the cyrillic alphabet latinized (e.g. Nikola Pasić).

# Preface

This book has been in the making for a quarter of a century. It started in a university canteen with Professor László Péter from the School of Slavonic and East European Studies (since 1999, University College, London); the food was forgettable, but not the conversation. On the invitation of Miklós Lojkó, my then supervisor, the grand old man was in Budapest for a visit, and after a lecture at university, he took my piece of writing on Robert William Seton-Watson for a read. After sharing his remarks and explaining his corrections to my rudimentary creation at the canteen the next day, all this quite mercifully, he put forward the idea that the topic of Seton-Watson on Hungary was quite incomplete without Carlile Aylmer Macartney, his former student and admirer, yet another British historian with unpronounceable first and middle names that no Hungarian could/can easily recall.

In the following years, owing to a generous Soros-grant and through recommendations by my then professor and current academician, Ignác Romsics, I spent some months reading the Seton-Watson and Macartney papers and correspondence in the Bodleian Library, Oxford, and the library of the School of Slavonic and East European Studies, London. As well I read some relevant materials in the Public Records Office and the BBC archives in Reading. The research was finished, or rather terminated, and published in 2005, and I look at it as "juvenilia" today. Though the basic conclusion(s) have since remained unaltered, a feeling of incompleteness lingered in the air, so after some fifteen years (and four kids), I took up the storyline again and included Henry Wickham Steed. Doing so seemed especially relevant after having read Andre Liebich's pioneering study of his life, published in 2018, which I found and still find essential, but as it is with practically all books, it seemed also lacking in major themes that appeared indispensable. Thus, during the Covid-ridden and difficult times, I took to travelling again, this time owing to a research grant generously provided by Károli Gáspár University of the Reformed Church, Budapest. I went to London and worked my way through the vast collection of Steed's papers and correspondence, Macartney's LNU-documents in the British Library as well as his Chatham House Speeches and correspondence in the Library of the Royal Institute of International Affairs (RIIA). In the meantime, some minor research took place at the Library of the University of New Hampshire, as well as in the National Széchényi Library, Budapest (OSZK).

Third time's a charm, so soon another trip to Oxford and one to London followed. Taking Professor Géza Jeszenszky's advice, who has been researching British–Hungarian relations for half a century, I embarked upon the ever-more-vast legacy of the long-neglected Arnold Joseph Toynbee, a historian and director of the RIIA. Although he had had a thousand ties to both Seton-Watson and Steed, and also to Macartney, involving him in the project not only deepened its findings, but necessarily also broadened its focus: as we will see, Toynbee untiringly practiced his craft as a writer throughout his long life and even by the application of the strict principle of selection, no work on him or including him (and nationalism) could be undertaken without at least outlining his ideas on the very ideology together with his activity in South-Eastern-Europe and the Near-East: Greece and Turkey.

Apart from archival sources, the present book draws upon a huge number of printed books and articles as well as the support of many people getting me along the way. Besides the aforementioned late László Péter, Miklós Lojkó, Ignác Romsics and especially Géza Jeszenszky, I am greatly indebted to librarians, the always kind and helpful David Bates at Chatham House library and Dóra Kőszegi at OSZK, whom I could approach with my questions any time. The support and help I received during my first stay in Oxford from Valerie and Robert de Newtown, and during the second from Balázs Vedres, Katalin Dancsi as well as their three wonderful kids is also invaluable.

But writing a book also implied time taken away from other things; my otherwise magnificent duties as a wife and mother. Thus, profound gratitude goes out most of all to my husband and children, not only for the maturity and willingness to do without me for many long hours, but also to effectively assisting me with what they could: checking data or books, offering advice, comments, a powerful neck massage or a tasty lunch.

Finally, I am grateful to Ignác Romsics and Miklós Zeidler for the maps, Krisztina Kós for proofreading the text, and in particular to Katalin Kádár

Lynn of Helena History Press for her dedicated support. The contributions to this book are thus shared by many; however, the responsibility for its conclusions is fully mine.

# Introduction

"Dear friend, you belong today not only to yourself, your family, and your people, but also to us. In our history, and in our schools, yes even also on our street signs your name will be immortalised." Thus wrote the Slovak Anton Štefánek to the historian-publicist Robert William Seton-Watson[1] upon the unveiling of his, Seton-Watson's, bust at Ružomberok City Hall in 1937. Between the two world wars, Seton-Watson was awarded honorary doctorates by the Universities of Prague, Zagreb, Belgrade and Cluj (Kolozsvár), and the same title was also offered to Seton-Watson's life-long comrade in arms, probably the greatest journalist of the twentieth century, Henry Wickham Steed.[2] He "has and always will have a place of honour in the history of our liberation,"[3] stressed the Czechoslovak minister of foreign affairs, Edvard Beneš, and the Romanian diplomat Dimitrie Ciotori was equally full of praise, calling him "the leader of the Caravan."[4]

As we will see, another eminent British historian, Carlile Aylmer Macartney, had addressed Hungarian audiences 186 times in his BBC broadcasts over three years and, as an expert for the British Foreign Office, he produced 143 memoranda on the Danube Basin, and Hungary in particular. As a professor of history, he wrote four books on East-Central Europe and five more on Hungary—

---

1 J. Rychlík, T. Marzik, M. Bielik (eds.), *R. W. Seton-Watson and His Relations with the Czechs and Slovaks, Documents 1906–1951*, Prague, Martin, Ústav, T.G. Masaryka and Matica Slovenská, 1995, I/433.
2 The "deeply touched" Steed to Rector of Cluj University, April 24, 1929. Correspondence and Papers of Henry Wickham Steed, British Library, Archives and Manuscripts [hereafter: Steed Papers] MS 74 128. In 1929, after a lavish ceremony, the University of Cluj bestowed upon him the honorary doctorate and made him also an honorary citizen of the city.
3 Edouard Benes, *Souvenirs de guerre et de révolution*, Paris, 1928, I/174–175.
4 N. Ciotori to Steed, December 30, 1951. Steed Papers MS 74 134. Between 1923 and 1936, Dimitrie N. Ciotori was press attaché at the Romanian Legation in London, where he befriended, among others, Nicolae Titulescu and Ion Antonescu, the future Marshall.

the most by any English-language author after Seton-Watson. However, he did not receive the same recognition, if any, in Hungary as either Seton-Watson or, to a certain extent, Steed did in the pre-1945 successor states.

Posterity is often harsh in its criticism, or worse, it often turns annoyingly ignorant. With the possible exception of Seton-Watson, none of the three Britons is a household name any more in Britain. As we will see, the historian and former director of the Royal Institute of International Affairs, Arnold Joseph Toynbee, has been practically side-lined since the 1960s, and even worse, no biography of Steed was published until 2018 (and that in Switzerland), and no biography of Macartney has ever appeared in any language.[5]

If we look at their legacies in today's East-Central Europe, we find that forty-five years of communism largely wiped them out, and only Seton-Watson returned after 1990— to Slovakia as a celebrated figure[6] in academic circles, and to Hungary, somewhat misleadingly, as an antithesis of Macartney, "the gravedigger of the Dual Monarchy," or most recently as "Mr. Trianon, the greatest enemy of Hungarians."[7] Despite his staunch support for a united South Slav state, or perhaps because of this, Steed is not much remembered in any of the Successor States of Yugoslavia, nor anywhere else in particular. He could not become outdated, as, apart from a few years after 1920, he never was quite "in mode." The most burning question for the historian is always why it is worth researching or writing about a particular topic, in this case about the four once so active Britons. Why not give them a well-earned final rest?

Unlike the fading memory of Steed, Toynbee, Macartney and, to some extent, Seton-Watson, nations in East-Central Europe and beyond have survived

---

5   The only monograph being Ágnes Beretzky's *Scotus Viator és Macartney Elemér: Magyarország-kép változó előjelekkel*, Akadémiai, 2005, followed by Róbert Barta's publications, the most comprehensive of which is his long overdue collection of the selected works by Macartney in Hungarian: *A magyarság vonzásában. Válogatás Carlile Aylmer Macartney írásaiból és beszédeiből* [Attracted by the Hungarians: A selection of Carlile Aylmer Macartney's writings and speeches], Debrecen, 2011. In English so far the most comprehensive are Robert William Seton-Watson's son Hugh's obituary, Carlile Aylmer Macartney 1895-1978. In: Proceedings of The British Academy, LXVII. London 1981, 411-432; Miklós Lojkó's C.A. Macartney and Central Europe. European Review of History 6, 1999, 37-57, and the comparative essay by László Péter, The Political Conflict between R. W. Seton-Watson and C.A. Macartney over Hungary.(In: László Péter, Martyn Rady, *British-Hungarian Relations Since 1848*, London, Hungarian Cultural Centre and School of Slavonic and East European Studies, University College London, 2004, 167-193.)
6   In addition to several international conferences, his memorial was re-erected in Ružomberok, a commemorative stamp was issued in 2007 and an exhibition was opened in Kežmarok (Késmárk).
7   Ernő Raffay, *Mr. Trianon, Scotus Viator a magyarok legnagyobb ellensége* [Mr. Trianon. Scotus Viator, the Greatest Enemy of Hungarians], Budapest, Kárpátia Stúdió, 2023. This title seems to be shared with Steed. See Hungarian historian Henrik Marczali's daughter Paula [Póli] Marczali on Steed. In: *Apám [Marczali Henrik] pályája, barátai* [My father's Career, and Friends], Auróra könyvek, München, 1973, 53-54.

into and even thrive in the twenty-first century, while their nationalism has remained quite incomprehensible to the West. This is despite the fact that East-Central Europe has been a hotbed of ethnic conflict, the place where two world wars have started, and where even today (in 2024) there is no peace. Indeed, our four Britons were among the few Westerners who took pains to make sense of the region's history, with all its underlying socio-cultural complexities. They lived among us and learned our languages(s). Therefore, it seems essential to tell of their lives and interpret their ethnic-related writings about the region from as many angles as possible.

Moreover, Steed, Seton-Watson, Toynbee or Macartney, as foreign correspondent, newspaper editor, publicist, historian, director and academic, had a vast store of knowledge and network of connections, and were employed at one point by the British Foreign Office as experts/advisers. They could assist us Central and Eastern Europeans, too, in our difficult journey of self-scrutiny. The more so, given that the same Great War and especially the subsequent treaties that, we, Hungarians here together with some of our friends would say "scattered Hungary across the map"[8], are both hailed by our neighbours as precipitating the crumbling of Austria-Hungary and the emergence of the new states of Czechoslovakia, Yugoslavia and enlarged Romania. The former two in the meantime have ceased to exist, however, in the latter 450 public events were scheduled in 2018 to celebrate the centennial of "the Day of Unification." The most important of these, with the biggest parade ever, took place in Alba Iulia (Gyulafehérvár), where the union of Transylvania with Romania was proclaimed on December 1, 1918.[9] Given these celebrations, the writings of the four influential Britons, as experts in East-Central-European history (and much more), may offer the successor states of Czechoslovakia, Yugoslavia and also Romania some food for thought, as well. Particularly, as the once leading authorities' disagreements and conflicts are rooted not so much in their assessments of pre- or mid-war Hungarian nationalism, but in that of the Successor States. As Macartney once remarked: "Seton-Watson saw through the Hungarians, but I see through the Czechs, Slovaks and the Croats, *too.*"[10] Having read his books and papers, the Romanians should be included as well.

---

8  John O'Sullivan, Making a Virtue of Nationalism, *Hungarian Review*, Vol. XI, No. 3, May 2020, 3.
9  https://www.rri.ro/en_gb/december_1_2018-2590418
10 Carlile Aylmer [C.A.] Macartney to Géza Jeszenszky via personal communication on November 14, 1969. Qtd. in Géza Jeszenszky, *Lost Prestige: Hungary's Changing Image in Britain 1894–1918*, Helena History Press, 2020, 390 fn.

Writing a book is essentially a balancing act between elaboration and confinement. What is attempted on the following pages is a focus on the nations and nationalism of the Successor States of Austria-Hungary from 1920-1947, that is from Versailles to Paris, with an outline of the pre-1918 events, supplemented by the relevant Turkish and Armenian aspects. All this is done from the perspective of the four influential British figures: Henry Wickham Steed (1871-1956), Robert William Seton-Watson (1879-1951), Arnold Joseph Toynbee (1889-1975) and Carlile Aylmer Macartney (1895-1978).

Henry Wickham Steed's biographer, Andre Liebich, is right in claiming that his protagonist's life "deserves to be told."[11] The doyen of the four, he was indeed an interesting blend of the genuine cosmopolitan with the quintessentially English, though second-rate primary and secondary education. Unlike, Seton-Watson, Toynbee or Macartney, he never earned an English, let alone Oxbridge degree, having left England at a young age and studying economics, philosophy, history and several other subjects at German and French universities. Spending twenty-one years abroad, however, had one essential advantage: Steed obtained an amazing, almost unparalleled linguistic confidence in German, French, and to a certain extent, Italian.[12] Interestingly, mastering German was coupled with an acute and unconventional Germanophobia from the very beginning of his career, directed not so much against the people, but rather at the German-Prussian Imperial system, "the omnipotent and deified state," and its militarism.[13]

It soon turned out that journalism was Steed's calling, and between 1896 and 1913 he became the correspondent of the *Times* in Berlin, Rome and eventually, Vienna, which was a prestigious position to hold. The Settlement of 1867 between Austria and Hungary had seemed to stabilize the Monarchy for decades as one of the key players in the European balance of power game.[14] The leading

---

11  Andre Liebich, *Henry Wickham Steed, Greatest Journalist of His Times*, Peter Lang AG, 2018, 10.
12  Ibid., 22-23.
13  Henry Wickham Steed [hereafter: Steed], *Through Thirty Years 1892-1922*, London, William Heinemann Ltd, 1924, I/11. It is reviewed in Géza Jeszenszky, A történelmi Magyarország egyik sírásója: H.W. Steed [One of the gravediggers of historical Hungary: H.W. Steed], *Emlékirat és Történelem*, Budapest, Magyar Történelmi Társulat Nemzetközi Magyarságtudományi Társaság [Memoirs and History, Hungarian Historical Society International Society for Hungarian Studies], 2012, 18-35.
14  During a debate on Hungary in the House of Commons on July 21, 1849, Palmerston declared: "Austria is a most important element in the balance of European power. [...] The political independence and liberties of Europe are bound up, in my opinion, with the maintenance and integrity of Austria as a great European Power, and therefore anything which tends by direct, or even remote, contingency to weaken and to cripple Austria, but still more to reduce her from the posi-

daily newspapers all employed a permanent correspondent in Vienna, nevertheless the correspondent for the *Times* was considered the person of utmost significance. Partly due to his prodigious command of languages, Steed's network of connections grew truly impressive: Edward Goschen, the British minister in Vienna (1905-08) fully trusted him,[15] as did other ministers, British, French, Italian politicians, King Edward VII,[16] King George VI and Clemenceau. "A good journalist looks upon his work as a kind of ministry, a vocation, not merely as trade or profession, and often has to go through moral crisis. A good journalist prefers losing his job rather than give way in real issues of right or wrong."[17]

Unlike Steed's, Seton-Watson's family background shaped his career in many ways. His father, a successful businessman in a Scottish firm, amassed a considerable fortune, which for many years provided a stable background for his son's travels in Germany and Italy and his historical and political studies. Seton-Watson attended New College, Oxford, and, inspired by his history tutor, H. A. L. Fisher, he spent the summer of 1901 in Germany: the result of his stay, an essay titled "Maximilian, Holy Roman Emperor," won him the Stanhope Historical Essay Prize.[18] "The old order changeth, yielding place to new"[19] was one of the first sentences young Seton put down in print as a future historian, quite unaware of its prophetic nature.[20] The same year his first book appeared, 1902, he sent his first political letter to the *Spectator*, arguing, quite unlike Steed, that English-German good relations were the key to European peace. After his father's sudden death, and with an ample fortune in hand, Seton-Watson gave the Scottish Bar a wide berth and went on to pursue historical studies on the Con-

tion of a first-rate Power to that of a secondary State, must be a great calamity to Europe and one which every Englishmen ought to depreciate, and to try to prevent." Jeszenszky 2020, 42.

15  Sir Edward Goschen, the new British minister to Austria-Hungary, remained strongly under the journalist's influence throughout his time in Vienna. The Foreign Office in this period got into the habit of informing itself about Austro-Hungarian affairs mainly from the *Times*. Jeszenszky 2020, 209-210. See also Christopher Henry Durham Howard (ed.), *Diary of Edward Goschen*, London, Offices of the Royal Historical Society, 1980, 171.
16  Steed claimed to have had at least ten political talks with him between 1906 and 1909. Steed to J. P. Gooch, April 20, 1954. Steed Papers MS 74134.
17  Steed, "Journalist III," December 1945. British Broadcasting Corporation [BBC] West African Service. Steed Papers 74 183.
18  Harry Hanak, *Great Britain and Austria-Hungary during the First World War*, London, 1962, 21. Hugh and Christopher Seton-Watson, *The Making of a New Europe, Robert W. Seton-Watson and the Last Years of Austria-Hungary*, London, 1981, 15.
19  Seton-Watson, *Maximilian, Holy Roman Emperor, (Stanhope Historical Essay 1901)*. London, A. Constable & Co. Ltd., 1902, 4.
20  Hugh and Christopher Seton-Watson [H. & C.], *The Making of a New Europe, Robert W. Seton-Watson and the Last Years of Austria-Hungary*, University of Washington Print, 1981, 18.

tinent—in Berlin, Paris and Vienna. In retrospect, the guiding hand of Providence was unmistakably there.[21]

With his studied mildness of demeanour, Arnold Joseph Toynbee differed both from the "always shy and diffident"[22] Seton-Watson and the eccentric and even narcissistic Steed. Toynbee was raised by a middle-class English Protestant family. His father as well as his grandfather were ear, nose, and throat specialists, the latter having successfully treated Queen Victoria. But young Arnold developed a passion for the humanities after having been inspired by the tales of his wise mother, herself once a student at Cambridge.[23] When Toynbee was twelve, he spent an entire semester with pneumonia, lying amidst maps of the Great Persian Empire and that of Rome. The Armenians, Georgians, Turks, and Arabs that followed Alexander piqued young Arnold's interest,[24] and owing to his superb memory and extensive vocabulary he quickly excelled at Winchester, winning five out of the seven school-leaving prizes.[25] Naturally, Balliol College, Oxford, followed and Toynbee was proud to state that he had belonged to the last generation in England that had received a full traditional Western education in Greek and Latin classics.[26] Much later, he even confessed in a private letter: "I am in many ways more familiar with the classical World that with the one in which we are living, and when I want to express my deep feelings, I do this more naturally and easily in Greek than in any form of English."[27]

Another Winchester student with a talent for the classics, and the youngest of the four, Carlile Aylmer Macartney was the fifth child of a well-to-do Northern Irish-born lawyer. In 1914 he was awarded a scholarship at Trinity College, Cambridge, but, unlike the other three, he volunteered to go to war and was listed as a Second Lieutenant shortly after its outbreak.[28] He fought for two years, was wounded, healed, and was sent back to the front in France. Seven

---

21 *Spectator*, June 21, 1902. H & C Seton-Watson 1981, 13-15.
22 Marion Esther [May] Seton-Watson to Steed, October 22, 1954. Steed Papers MS 74134
23 Edith Toynbee wrote a child's history of Scotland and tested each chapter with his son as bedtime readings.
William H. McNeill, *Arnold J. Toynbee: A Life*, Oxford, Oxford University Press, 1989, 7. See also Toynbee Correspondence and Papers, Western Manuscripts Bodleian Library, Oxford [hereafter: Toynbee Papers] MS. 13967/68 Family correspondence 1915-1923 and MS 13967/69/2. Correspondence between Toynbee and his mother, 1912-1917.
24 McNeill, Toynbee Revisited, *Bulletin of the American Academy of Arts and Sciences*, Vol. 41, No. 7 (Apr., 1988), 13-27, 17.
25 McNeill 1988, 13-27, 14.
26 Toynbee, Outline of My Life and Work Up To Date: Autobiography, September 22, 1948. Toynbee Papers MS 13967/40.
27 Toynbee to David Morgan Esq., April 25, 1945, MS 13967/83/2 Correspondence.
28 "Navy and Military News from London Gazette," *Birmingham Daily Post*, November 7, 1914, 5.

out of the fifteen scholars in his year perished, but he survived.²⁹ Despite returning to Trinity after the armistice, however, Macartney never earned a degree. His first published work, modestly titled *Poems*, was written in 1915 and the preceding years. But unlike Toynbee's prize-winning Latin verse about Giuseppe Garibaldi, the hero of Italian unification, or Seton-Watson's *Scotland Forever!*, Macartney's poems had little to do with a romantic love of freedom or national self-determination, but rather with conservative themes of loyalty and perseverance, as in his Ballade of Cathedral Close:

> *Before me on the crown*
> *Of yonder hilltop high*
> *The stark howitzers frown*
> *Remorseless cruelty.*
> *A sullen shell screams by-*
> *I heed not how it goes,*
> *Seeing in memory*
> *The old Cathedral close.*
> *[...]ENVOIE.*
> *So I must still defy*
> *The menace of our foes,*
> *And save, if I should die,*
> *The old Cathedral close.*³⁰

## On the Wrong Side of History? Nations and Nationalism

Whether one likes it or not, to this day nationalism has remained a powerful and durable phenomenon. As is well known, after the Enlightenment dynastic loyalty was shifted to the language, culture and traditions of the various ethnic-linguistic communities, and the end of the First World War ushered in the increase of sovereign states, especially in East-Central Europe. National self-determination soon became a fundamental tenet of international law. Moreover,

---

29  At Ypres and his life was saved by his comrade Horace Brown (a civilian miner), with whom he remained in contact for the rest of his life, despite their different social status. Hugh Seton-Watson, "Carlile Aymler Macartney 1895–1978," The Proceedings of the British Academy, London, LXVII (1981), 411. Lojkó 1999, 38. Róbert Barta 2011,13. Beretzky 2005, 11.
30  Leutenant C.A. Macartney, *Poems*, London, Erskine Macdonald, 1915, 11.

since the end of World War II[31] nationality has become a basic human right and the number of independent nation-states has doubled. In 1991, the end of the Soviet Union witnessed yet another high peak in the formation of nation-states.

It would take a separate monograph to analyse even the most recent scholarship on the theory of nationalism, which is clearly outside the scope of the present book. One can sum up the two most contrasting concepts on the origins of nations as "inscribed in the natural order" as against "ex nihilo created,"[32] highlighting the two schools of discussion: the primordialist and the radical evolutionist. However, in practice, all scholars of the field have agreed to disagree, and there has been no universally accepted definition of the term *nation*, and consequently, of nationalism either. One reason for the lack of consensus might be the Janus-faced[33] nature of nationalism: on the one hand the magnetic dominant ideology with a quasi-sacred character behind national awakening, that is, cultural nationalism, and, simultaneously, political nationalism as a prime destroyer of (semi-)great empires, the Ottoman realm, as well as Austria-Hungary, the Soviet Union or the British Empire.

Are nation and the related ideology of nationalism "something psychological and sacred,"[34] as argued by Seton-Watson, or emotionally aversive, like the "world's poison"[35] put forward by Arnold Toynbee some two decades later? Is the nation-state the central pillar of stability that still dominates world politics today? Or is it outmoded or even pathological, and thus we are compelled to look a level beyond to the global scale? True, countless obituaries for the nation state have already been drafted by communists and cosmopolitans in global corporations and supranational institutions, and one might feel that we, in the

---

31 Article 15 in the United Nations Declaration puts forward the twin ideas that "Everyone has the right to a nationality" and "No one shall be arbitrarily deprived of his nationality nor denied the right to change his nationality," thus further increasing the "prestige of nationhood."
32 Radical creationists, like Gellner argue that nations were fathered by modernity, a radical cultural break with the past. The result could be the creation of a high culture, dispersed by an effective mass education system. Gellner's disciple and later critic, A.D. Smith, although maintaining the claims for creationism, denied "ex nihilo creation" and argued for the role played by cultural continuity and shared historical memories. He gave himself the label "ethno-symbolist" within the modernist camp and was convinced that the differences between nationalism across periods and continents were too great to be embraced by a single theory. Anthony D. Smith, Memory and Modernity: Reflections On Ernest Gellner's Theory of Nationalism, *Nations and Nationalism*, 3, 1996, 371-388. 372. http://fbemoodle.emu.edu.tr/pluginfile.php/44356/mod_resource/content/1/A. percent20d. percent20Smith-memory percent20and percent20modernity percent201994, percent20NN.pdf Accessed March 23, 2023.
33 Furthermore, nationalism can be both strong and weak, universal and particular, old and new at the same time.
34 Seton-Watson, *Treaty Revision and Hungarian Frontiers*, London, Eyre & Spottiswoode Ltd., 1934, 70.
35 Toynbee, *Change and Habit, The Challenge of our Time*, London, Oxford University Press, 1966, 87.

twenty-first century, are just expecting the body to topple into its grave. But it will not. What we have witnessed, especially after the peculiarly unusual years of Covid-19, is the still lingering power of the nation-state, which might be attributed to the fact that it is large enough to resist imperial power but small enough to call upon the loyalty of its members.[36]

"A nation is a society united by a delusion about its ancestry and by a common hatred of its neighbours."[37] This might be one plausible but generally never endorsed definition, as put forward by William Ralph Inge, an Anglican priest and professor of divinity at Cambridge. True, national identities often emerge out of antagonism between neighbouring countries[38]—being English is a matter of not being Irish, and vice versa, and similarly, being Hungarian might be defined as not being Slovak, Croat, Serb or Ruthene, and certainly, the other way round. Therefore, any study of one particular nation and its related ideology (nationalism) in East-Central Europe must contain various references to the other neighbouring nations and their ideologies. The more so, as since the nineteenth century the peaceful coexistence of the various national awakenings (cultural nationalisms) has long been jeopardized by the overlapping territorial aspirations that transformed several multi-ethnic territories into hotbeds of fierce conflict.

Benedict Anderson, undoubtedly one of the most original theorists of the topic, defined nation as a collective act of imagination, creating limited but not imaginary communities in which national identity serves important purposes.[39] He formulated three paradoxes of nationalism, one of which entails the "objective modernity" of nations as against their "subjective antiquity" in the eyes of nationalists. As we will see, especially in the case of more recent nations, the search for evidence of historical right or precedence constituted and still constitutes a significant part of their national consciousness, aided in particular by Seton-Watson, and to a lesser extent Steed as well as (the young) Toynbee.

However, the post-1920 Toynbee, as well as Seton-Watson's son, Hugh, came increasingly to regard (extreme) nationalism as "a crude substitute religion, replacing withered faith by fanatical hatreds."[40] It needs to be emphasized, nevertheless, that before the Enlightenment, *religio* meant religiousness or piety,

---

36 David Miller, *Political Philosophy, A Very Short Introduction*, Oxford, Oxford University Press, 115-120.
37 William Ralph Inge, *The End of an Age: and Other Essays*, Putnam, 1948, 127.
38 "Geography gives us our neighbours, but history gives us our enemies." – goes the similar Irish saying.
39 Benedict Anderson, *Imagined Communities*, London, Verso, 2006, 5.
40 Hugh Seton-Watson, *Nations and States An Enquiry into the Origins of Nations and the Politics of Nationalism*, London, Methuen, 1977, 12.

referring to the practice of religion by people of faith, as against a more modern definition of religion in the abstract sense as a "communally embedded system of belief."[41] Furthermore, by the twentieth century, the very concept of religion had become hopelessly elusive or vague, and the criteria to differentiate between "religions proper" or "revealed" religions and "political," "secular," "pseudo," "quasi," "substitute" or "counter" religions were in most cases missing, or were themselves highly ideological.[42] But more on this this in a subsequent chapter.

## Liberalism and Nationalism Intertwined: Steed and Seton-Watson

At the beginning of the nineteenth century, individual and national self-determinations seemed to go hand in hand, to be two sides of the same coin: independence. The anti-dynastic revolutions of 1848 led by an educated elite united liberalism and nationalism even more strongly. Yet the new matrimony did not last long, as the power of the elite started to be increasingly challenged by working class demands and also by nationalist agendas.

Two formidable nineteenth-century British prime ministers, Benjamin Disraeli and William Ewart Gladstone, clashed several times over Britain's Balkan strategy, most notably on the policy to be followed regarding the emerging nationalism in the area. Conservative Disraeli saw the situation as a matter of British imperial and strategic interests; that is, in line with Palmerston's policy of supporting the Ottoman Empire against Russian expansion. Liberal Gladstone, on the other hand, assessed the situation from a moral starting point: as Bulgarian Christians had been massacred by the Turks, it was immoral to support the perpetrators. Until 1907, traditional British foreign political orientation remained pro-Turk and definitely anti-Russian, and Steed as well as Seton-Watson inherited much both from Gladstone, but also from Disraeli.

In fact, Steed identified himself as a Gladstonian liberal against any kind of state oppression. This is best highlighted by an entry in his memoir, *Through Thirty Years*: "I have ever been partisan [...] A partisan of England, [...] of ordered freedom as against tyranny or licence; of reality against humbug and pretence

---

41 Wilfred Cantwell Smith, *The Meaning and End of Religion*, First Fortress Press Edition, 1991, vii.
42 These pseudo or quasi etc. religions are also called political theologies based on the systematic analogy of their concepts with theological ones. See Tamás Nyirkos, The Proliferation of Secular Religions: Theoretical and Practical Aspects, *Pro Publico Bono, Public Administration*, 2021/2, 68–85. • DOI: 10.32575/ppb. 2021.2.4.

[...] of men whom I thought honest."[43] This liberal stance was indoctrinated by his father[44] and by Madame Clémence Rayer-Rose, the former *Morning Post* correspondent in Italy, a woman twenty-two years his senior with whom he shared a joint household for four decades.[45]

As with Gladstone, the metaphysical character of Henry Wickham Steed's nationalism originated in his religious stance. Having grown up in a strict congregationalist family, he abandoned the devout religiosity of the family as a young adult. However, he retained a moral sensibility, which he described as a protestant inclination "to apply moral standards to matters which [he] thought ethically colourless."[46] In 1893, he wrote: "The only escape from littleness and selfishness–the only road to true happiness lies in reaching that we too have our task of redeeming and ennobling mankind [...] everyone must get to work on the individual cases which are ready to hand and which he is peculiarly fitted to handle because he more or less understands them."[47]

Nevertheless, Steed was equally, if not more motivated by imperial and strategic considerations. He put forward in 1907:

> We are not, or ought not to be bound up with any 'isms', save Imperialism, i.e. care for the Empire in the right sense; we are not, or ought not to be identified with any 'vested interest'; economic, political or religious, save with one interest of the Empire in good and just government and the welfare of its citizens."[48]

Throughout his life, this pragmatic liberal imperialist attitude dominated his thinking; he was convinced that any sound British policy had to be based on British interests.[49] His stance was further strengthened by the various po-

---

43 Steed 1924, I/XI. See also Steed's answer to R. Jordet, (from Bergen, Norway) March 23, 1929: "I am certainly not a socialist [...] my own preferences are broadly liberal." Steed Papers MS 74 128.
44 Obituary of William [sic] Wickham Steed, *Manchester Guardian*, January 14, 1956, 3.
45 Clémence Rayer-Rose de Corps-Billoux (1849–1937) was born in an old Savoyard family, thus becoming Italian by upbringing and temperament, but soon acquired French citizenship by an early marriage to French Savoyard, Rayer; she was fluent in English, due to her long residence in England after the death of husband in 1867, as well as in French and Italian, but neither was her native tongue. Scholars tend to agree that the—at least—quadrilingual woman had an unspecified South-Slav origin. Steed Papers, MS 74139 and Liebich 2018, 42.
46 Steed, 1923, I/ XI.
47 Steed to his brother Robert, January 21, 1893. Steed Papers MS 74138.
48 Steed to Chirol, July 24, 1907, PHS Papers. Steed Papers. See also Steed 1924, I/271-2.
49 Steed to Austen Chamberlain, April 6, 1925. Steed Papers MS 74126. A month later, in another letter, interestingly, he referred to Europe as "a wicked continent" as against the "virtuous island." Steed to Simonds Frank, May 19, 1925. Steed Papers MS 74126.

sitions he held at the prestigious British daily the *Times* and often manifested itself in his counselling the various competing nationalisms from a supranational position. Steed strongly believed in the evolution of nations and even in the creation of one where it did not exist—as we will see, he became the "spiritual godfather" of the post-Habsburg new states and nations. His room at the *Times* office–as he recalled–became a point of pilgrimage for "alien friends" in London. On entering it, his colleagues "would sometimes look under the table to see if no 'Czechoslavs' or 'Yugoslovaks' [sic] were hidden there."[50]

As regards Seton-Watson's attitude to the various nationalisms, there were also two forces at work. As is usually noted, from his early years up to the end of his career, his Scottish ancestry played a part. In fact, his slender volume *Scotland for Ever!*, and especially the first poem with the same title both reveal his admiration and interest in his Scottish forbears. However, the book contains much more than that: other verses reveal that Seton-Watson's interest in small nations was fuelled not so much by his (narrow) Scottish national feeling as by a Byronic love of freedom, that is, a passionate (universal) philanthropy very much in line with the prevailing Gladstonian liberal credo, the "higher and broader" traditional policy of the "sympathy with suffering weakness."[51] This is best unveiled in his poem *Ambition's Height*:

> *I love not the eventless life and death*
> *That still content unnumbered multitudes;*
> *That living grave, where callous care intrudes,*
> *Treating creation like a little breath.*
> *Must I slave on in dull monotony,*
> *With sweat of brow through labour lone and long?*
> *No; let me soar at once above the throng -*
> *A blood-red meteor on the evening sky!*
> *Let me rouse nations with my thrilling song,*
> *Then with one flash sink suddenly and die!*
> *Die? my frail body! — but my soul should live,*
> *And fire the lives of thousands o'er the world,*

---

50  Steed 1924, II/130-131. See also: Steed to Harold Williams February 9, 1928. Steed Papers MS 74103.
Steed retained his creationist attitude to nationhood: in 1934 he summarized the year 1918 as follows: "Old nations reborn, new nations created." Steed, The Great War 1914-1918. In: Stirling Taylor (ed.), *Great Events in History*, London, Cassell and Company, Ltd., 1934, 825.

51  James Joll (ed.), *Britain and Europe, Pitt to Churchill, 1790-1940*, Oxford, Oxford University Press, 1967, 174. See also Cornwall 2017, 329-333.

> *Till Fortune from her pedestal was hurl'd,*
> *And sank submissive, never to revive.*[52]

In accordance with the German romantic tradition, throughout his life Seton-Watson interpreted nationalism as a metaphysical phenomenon akin to religion: as "something psychological and sacred."[53] However, the preface in his 1898 book is also sincere in its assertion that it does not wish to cast a shadow over England by (over)exalting Scotland,[54] and he in fact regarded the relationship between the two countries—England and Scotland—as an ideal to be followed by Czechs and Slovaks or by Croats and Serbs, etc. As László Péter aptly put it, Seton-Watson's passionate philanthropy, that is, his idealist liberalism, had other limits: he was never simply "pleading the cause of the weak," but rather his arguments and concerns about particular national conflicts were shaped by general perceptions of the European political background, a conventional balance of power principle with strategic interests and stability as its highest aims.[55]

Between 1905 and 1918, liberal imperialist Steed and the more idealist Seton-Watson worked tirelessly for the self-determination of East-Central European nations as will be elaborated on in the next chapter.

---

52  Seton-Watson 1898, 45.
53  Seton-Watson, *Treaty Revision and Hungarian Frontiers*, London, 1934, 70.
    This coincides with a typical evolutionist, primordialist concept. For more see: Mark Cornwall, R.W. Seton-Watson And Nation-Building Clashes in Late Habsburg Space, *The Slavonic and East European Review*, 100 (1), 2022, 9–10.
54  "My praise of Scotland must not be taken to imply any shadow of slight or dislike towards England." Seton-Watson 1898, Preface.
55  Péter 2004, 677–678.

# 1. Steed, Seton-Watson and Toynbee on National Self-Determination in East-Central Europe and Turkey (1903–1920)

This chapter covers the time period between Steed's arrival in Vienna as foreign correspondent of the *Times* and the peace treaties after the Great War. In addition to the archival materials and the six volumes of Seton-Watson's correspondence with the Yugoslavs, Romanians, Czechs and Slovaks, I have been able to draw on three indispensable, masterly written biographies: *The Making of a New Europe* (1981) contains a detailed account of Seton-Watson's early years by his sons, both historians, Hugh and Christopher; the more recent and equally essential *Wickham Steed - Greatest Journalist of his Times* by Andre Liebich from 2018; and finally, the all-important *Arnold J. Toynbee: A Life* by William McNeill, published in 1989.

With the exception of during the Cold War, Seton-Watson's impact on East-Central European nation-building between 1905–1919 has been acknowledged and recognised although often coming to diametrically opposite conclusions: his changing attitude toward Germany and Hungary, together with the various manifestations of his interest in the small peoples in the Dual Monarchy have been the subject of monographs, as well as countless articles or conference papers. The most insightful of these might be László Péter's "R.W. Seton-Watson's Changing Views on the National Question of the Habsburg Monarchy and the European Balance of Power," and the superb and far most detailed is Géza Jeszenszky's *Lost Prestige: Hungary's Changing Image in Britain 1894–1918*, published in 2020. The latter all the more so, as it devotes a worthy space to Steed, who is otherwise generally neglected, and also to Toynbee, who has been generally overlooked in his relation to the nation-building in East-Central Europe. Thus, owing to the abundance of materials on Seton-Watson's pre-1920-perspective, it is not the purpose of this chapter to reach any definitive new conclusions. It rather aims to bring to light his early motivations, ideas and activities, in parallel with those of Steed and Toynbee, in favour of national self-determination in or even beyond East-Central Europe.

## 1.1. "Worn-out Fairytales": Seton-Watson, Steed and Austria-Hungary (1903–1907)

A study of Steed's and Seton-Watson's early encounters with/in East-Central Europe, above all Austria-Hungary, is a study of parallels. While stationed in Vienna as foreign correspondent of the *Times* from 1903, Steed maintained regular contacts with several influential people[1] and even confessed that he found the Austrian capital "hideous after Pest. Cold and grey and wet and stiff." It made him angry to hear fellows in the Reichsrat talk of "washing the heads of Magyars." He felt that he had been bitten by a "Transleithanian" microbe, admitting: "I haven't felt so much at home since I left my pagan friends in the Tiber."[2] Many years later he still remembered how "refreshing" he had found the Hungarian society of men and women who "spoke freely and had ideas of their own."[3]

Good impressions of Magyar patriotism, however were soon mixed with a "drop of bitterness in the cup." Steed was the first to grow suspicious about the conduct of Hungarian politicians, first and foremost Count Albert Apponyi, an aristocrat, also the president of the House of Representatives, whom Theodore Roosevelt had described as "an advanced Liberal in matters political but also in matters ecclesiastical" and "like an American Liberal of the best type."[4] The *Times* correspondent had a different opinion. Upon their first encounter in 1902, the count assured Steed "in perfect English" that he, Steed, "should never be able to understand Hungarian affairs since they could not be comprehended without full knowledge of Hungarian Constitutional Law," and thus it would be a mistake to persist in dealing with matters Hungarian.[5] Apponyi's

---

[1] Steed regularly met among others, the historian Henrik Marczali and Ármin Vámbéry, the orientalist and professor at Budapest University, also a paid agent of the British political establishment. He also had a regular contact with the Hampel-Pulszky family, too; with Polyxéna Pulszky (1857–1921), who had been born in England while her father, Ferenc Pulszky, was in exile there. She married József Hampel (1849–1913), a noted archaeologist, and kept up with the family friends of her childhood. Steed's and Madame Rose's letters to the Hampel-Pulszky family: Országos Széchényi Könyvtár KT [OSZK KT] FOND VIII/2698 and 2346. See also Jeszenszky 2020, 89–90.
[2] Steed to Ferenc Hampel, March 17 1903. OSZK KT FOND VIII/2698.
[3] Steed 1924, I/97.
[4] Zoltán Peterecz, The visit of the most popular American of the day: Theodore Roosevelt in Hungary, *Hungarian Studies*, 28 (2), 2014, 235–254. doi:10.1556/HStud.28.2014.2.
[5] Steed 1924, I/197.

patronising attitude backfired: from then on Steed multiplied his efforts to learn enough to "break the neck of the language in about six months." In a letter to the manager of the *Times*, Moberly Bell, he argued that it would be "a great pull" to be able to read the Hungarian press and "deal with the Magyars at first hand"[6], which he did accomplish quite soon. During the years to come, Steed's opinion of Apponyi deteriorated further. He wrote early 1903: "I know Apponyi well, [ ...] he is one of the cleverest, vainest, worst-balanced, and most dangerous men I have ever met."[7]

Steed's opinion of the leading Hungarian politicians further deteriorated during the unfolding constitutional crisis, that is, the fundamental conflict between the constitutional aspirations of the devoted followers of the 1848–49 Hungarian freedom fighter, Lajos Kossuth, and the foreign political interests of the Dual Monarchy. When in 1902–3 the common Ministry of Defence worked out a plan to increase the annual contingent of recruits to correspond to the population growth, the staff increase was obstructed in the Hungarian Parliament by the (Kossuthist) Independence Party, which demanded national reform of the army in exchange. It wanted the introduction of Hungarian as the language of command (some seventy words) in all the regiments of Hungary. This claim touched upon the royal prerogatives and therefore implied the revision of the Settlement, which Franz Joseph resisted.[8] The crisis was further aggravated in November 1904, when Hungarian prime minister István Tisza wanted to put an end to the opposition's obstruction. When Tisza hastily called elections, for the first time in almost forty years, his Liberal Party lost its majority. Steed happened to be at hand and recalled:

> I went often to Budapest in those stormy days and was actually with Tisza on the evening of January 26, 1905, when the election returns came in. As the evening wore on it became clear that he had suffered a defeat unprecedented in Hungarian politics. Yet he showed no emotion, nor did a word of criticism of the Coalition or of the electorate escape his lips. He had done what he thought right and was prepared to abide by the consequences whatever they might be.[9]

---

6 Steed to Bell, August 6, 1903. Steed Correspondence, *Times* Archive, New Printing House Square [PHS Papers]. Steed Papers.
7 Steed to Bell, January 5, 1903. PHS Papers. Steed Papers.
8 László Péter, The Army Question In Hungarian Politics 1867–1918, *Central Europe*, Vol. 4, No. 2, November 2006, 84–110, 97–98.
9 Steed 1924, I/ 222

## 1. Steed, Seton-Watson and Toynbee on National Self-Determination

The crisis ended in April 1906 when the Coalition was finally willing to form a government after having dropped the army issue. Nevertheless, up until the outbreak of the First World War, the constitutional question, the extent to which Hungary had rights to legal independence, divided the House of Representatives more than any other political issue. It grew to become an obsession, in Steed's formulation, "a barren constitutional quibbling."[10] As László Péter aptly stated, Hungary came to be viewed as a destabilizing factor: the maintenance of Austria-Hungary's great-power status would have required a larger and better equipped army. But for over a decade the Hungarian parliament nevertheless rejected even the Army's modest request for more recruits, as no other elected assembly in Central and Eastern Europe had done at any time before the Great War. As a result, the Dual Monarchy was rapidly falling behind its rivals, and its ragtag army was fully dependent on the German high command during the Great War.[11]

Steed followed the governmental crisis of 1905–1906 and offered constructive criticism through his reports to the *Times*,[12] soon realizing that an internally weakened Austria-Hungary was unable to fulfil its historic mission to be a stronghold against Russian expansion, the Pan-Slav movements, and the rapidly increasing power of Bismarckian Germany. He became convinced that the constitutional crisis tarnished Hungary's reputation as a liberal state and that the short-sighted politicians of the Party of Independence and '48 were to be blamed: the old generation of Magyars, he explained to the foreign editor of the *Times*, Valentine Chirol,[13] "has been replaced by a hybrid crew, half brigands, half pettifoggers and wholly corrupt."[14]

By enfeebling the Dual Monarchy, the constitutional crisis also "unmasked the policy of Magyarization."[15] As a permanent resident in the region, Steed, too, became aware of the oppression of nationalities and gradually made himself an expert on the nationality problem of Austria-Hungary. In a letter to the proprietor of the *Times*, Moberly Bell,[16] he confessed that it had taken him five or six thousand miles of travelling within the Monarchy "to get the grip of

---

10 Steed, *Times*, September 5, 1905.
11 Péter 2006, 108.
12 *Times*, January 30, February 1, 8, 15, March 6, 14, 23, April 7, 10, 1906.
13 Valentine Chirol (1852–1928): English journalist, Times' Foreign editor between 1899 and 1912.
14 Steed to Chirol, September 12, 1907, PHS Papers. Steed Papers.
15 Péter 2004, 674. Jeszenszky 2000, 251.
16 Charles Frederic Moberly Bell (1847–1911) joined the *Times* in 1891, when it was in dire financial straits, managing to restore administrative and business order while exerting influence on the political line in a spirit of support for Pax Britannica. The History of the *Times*, Vol. 3. *The Twentieth Century Test, 1884–1912*, London, The Macmillan Company, 1947, 113. Jeszenszky 2020, 57.

the situation."[17] He toured the Slovak-inhabited regions, the Southern Slav districts, and Galicia as well as Transylvania. Wherever he went, he established strong personal ties with the local national leaders, including the Croat journalist, Frano Supilo and the Dalmatian Ante Trumbić, but most important of all, Tomáš Garrigue Masaryk.[18] He met the latter in May 1907, and the two became life-long friends: "Some people impress by Personal magnetism," he wrote three decades later, characterising the Czech leader as someone in possession of "a rather mystic greatness," "a lay saint," like John Hus; there was "no other figure like his in modern History."[19]

Steed's rapprochement with the leading politicians of the nationalities was greatly facilitated by his mysterious companion, the *Morning Post* correspondent Madame Clémence Rose.[20] In addition to her origins, the nature of their relationship has always remained a matter of controversy; a few scholars, contemporaries and relatives define it as that of "a mother and son," "aunt and nephew,"[21] or one "limited to their friendship as comrades and running the joint household."[22] The fact is that up until her death in 1937 Madame Rose had an unusually strong influence on Steed.; Her salons in London with its regular Saturday afternoon gatherings, and in 1919 in Paris, too, were greatly valued, and there Steed would meet several anti-Habsburg émigrés such as Edvard Beneš, Trumbić, or Masaryk, who had come to discuss the most burning issues.[23] "When she was in a room with celebrated statesmen, she made them unessential," Masaryk remembered. "Everyone respected and loved her, as she was the one who ensures the intimate, almost family atmosphere at our gatherings,"[24] another frequent guest recalled.

---

17  Steed to Bell, May 24, 1908. PHS Papers. Steed Papers.
18  Tomáš Garrigue Masaryk (1850–1937), a half-Slovak philosopher, political activist and later the founding father as well as the first president of Czechoslovakia. In 1878, while studying in Leipzig, he married the Brooklyn-born Charlotte Garrigue and took her name.
19  Steed, The Obituary of Masaryk 1937. Steed Papers MS 74 104.
20  Liebich 2018, 42.
21  Liebich 2018, 43. Jeszenszky 2020, 61 fn.
22  István Koszta, "*Nemcsak Erdély volt a tét*"- *Kései tudósítás a párizsi konferenciáról: Alexandru Vaida-Voevod levelei, feljegyzései, levéltári okmányok, emlékezések, naplórészletek a párizsi békekonferenciáról* ["It was not only Transylvania at stake" - Late coverage of the Paris Conference: letters, notes, archival documents, memoirs, diary excerpts of Alexandru Vaida-Voevod from the Paris Peace Conference], Budapest, Miercurea Ciuc-Csíkszereda, 2010, 238–239.
23  Liebich 2018, 42. In exile after 1920, Mihály Károlyi, too, was among the regular guests at Steed's Holland House Saturday afternoon teas. He called Madame Rose „the boss." Mihály Károlyi, *Faith without Illusion*, London, Jonathan Cape, 1956, 202.
24  Koszta 239.

It is quite probable that the intimacy was not confined to the gatherings, as Steed's letters reveal affections far beyond filial piety.[25] This was resented by many of his contemporaries —even closing the door to several representatives of Viennese and Hungarian high-society. As his contemporary Heinrich Friedjung recalled:

> A most unusual couple [...] A scoffer thinks she is aging to cover her relationship with Steed, and that might be the greatest sacrifice a woman could make. [...] She evidently controls him through the power of her stronger personality, she speaks for him, she thinks of his future [...] She spoke incessantly, he just made comments, I listened in amazement as the intimate partner shared the most dangerous confidences with Steed.[26]

But it was not only Steed and Madame Rose who made an odd couple. As Robert William Seton-Watson recorded: "One day there entered my room in a pension near the *Votivkirche* a man of about 34, tall, slight, alert, well-groomed, with a trimmed auburn imperial, wearing a fur coat [...]": Wickham Steed. He was the antithesis of the "little Scotchman, hesitating in speech and insignificant in appearance,"[27] yet, in Seton-Watson's words, "one of the most fruitful friendships"[28] of his entire life had begun.

Like Steed, in the beginning Seton-Watson also shared the "conventional admiration" for Lajos Kossuth's nation that generally existed among the British. He saw a nation "which had made great sacrifices for the cause of liberty and also

---

25   "Si jeune/jeine et si devouré," Steed to MR, September 14, 1929: "P.H. eui t'aime comme tojours," Steed to MR, April 13, 1930; "In unchanging love and friendship, as we have done these 34 years, your own P.H," Steed to MR September 4, 1931; "Je vous embrasse/embiasse bien tendrement et je vous aime," Steed to MR, September 26, 1932; "Always the same constant love," Steed to MR, September 28, 1932. Steed Papers MS 74139.
    To further uncover the mystery of this relationship it is enough to add that within two months of Clémence Rose's death, Steed married Violet Mason (1896-1970), whom he had known and loved for sixteen years, and whose existence he had kept secret from his family, including his own mother, until Madame Rose's death. The same silence surrounded his earlier relationship with Clémence Rose: despite the fact that the two shared a household for forty years, Steed's niece complained in 1986 that among the Steed Papers there was no obituary of Madame Rose, as "any references or publicity re [her] were taboo" since 1937. Joan Stephenson to Christopher Seton-Watson'(?), July 14, 1986. Steed Papers MS 74139. See also Liebich 2018, 41-44 and 259-266.
26  Friedjung's Diary entry on February 11, 1909. Heinrich Friedjung, *Geschichte in Gesprächen, Aufzeichnungen 1898-1919*, Band II, 1904-1919, Wien, Böhlau Verlag, 1997, 200.
27  Charles Seymour, *Letters from the Paris Peace Conference*, (Harold B. Whiteman, ed.), Yale University Press, 1965, 124.
28  Hugh and Christopher Seton-Watson 1981, 30.

had traditional links with Britain."²⁹ The Hungarian Calvinism that had much in common with the Presbyterian culture of Scotland also attracted him. The culmination of his devotion was a self-compiled genealogical chart that traced his ancestors back to a Scottish king, then through the French Philip the Brave and the Hungarian Andrew II back to Árpád. Again, like Steed, he also started learning Hungarian. However, very much unlike him, initially Seton-Watson stood up for the righteousness of the Hungarian language of command, which he regarded as an integral precondition of Hungarian independence. The Compromise, he explained, could be regarded as a temporary historical document until it was capable of fulfilling national demands. As Hungary had outgrown it, revision of the Settlement was inevitable. He repeated the same line of reasoning in the *Scottish Review* in March 1906, closing his article with dignified praise: "Let us hope that this phoenix among the nations will once more rise triumphant over every obstacle."³⁰

At the end of April 1906 Seton-Watson finally set out on his long-awaited journey to Hungary and arrived in Budapest towards dusk, "when all the hills of Buda were breaking into specks of light creating an impression of fairyland."³¹ The aim of his visit was twofold: collecting data for a historical monograph on Hungarian Calvinism and being on the spot to study the situation after the constitutional crisis. Right after his arrival, he had a long conversation with Count Apponyi, whom he praised for his eloquence, fluent and faultless English. When, however, Seton-Watson suggested that granting a certain extent of local government control would be practicable in Hungary, Apponyi reacted: "Croatia [...] is a nation with its own distinctive rights and position, which we fully recognize [...] but in the rest of Hungary there is only one nation in the state, namely the Hungarian." Upon being asked what result he expected from the prevailing policy of Magyarization, Seton-Watson's next host, Professor Lajos Láng,³² proved to be even more short-sighted: "We shall just keep on at it until there is not a Slovak left."³³ Unfortunately, and again like Steed, those whom Seton-Watson met belonged to the worst set of politicians, both in the capital and in the countryside. No wonder he drew the following conclusion: "The most striking feature

---

29   Hugh Seton-Watson, Robert William Seton-Watson and the Trianon Settlement, in Bela K. Király Peter Pastor, Ivan Sanders (eds.), *War and Society in East-Central Europe, Essays on Word War I.: Total War and Peacemaking, A Case Study on Trianon*. New York, 1982, 4.
30   *Scottish Review*, March 12, 1906.
31   H. & C. Seton-Watson 1981, 31.
32   Minister of Commerce in the former Széll-Government (1902–03).
33   H. & C. Seton-Watson 1981, 32–33.

## 1. Steed, Seton-Watson and Toynbee on National Self-Determination

of all my conversations is that the Magyars try to keep back the truth from me by making vague and general admissions to save their central position."[34]

Again very much in line with Steed, Seton-Watson also took great pains to get acquainted with Austria-Hungary, earning the pseudonym *Scotus Viator*, or "Wandering Scot." During his journeys to Transylvania, Vasile Goldis, the leader of the Romanian National Party, explained to him in detail how the Nationality Law of 1868 was being perverted and falsified. This was "the most useful lesson to Seton-Watson, who later used the same method in his arguments with the Magyars."[35] At the end of June 1906, he met a Slovak journalist, Anton Štefánek,[36] who introduced him to the plight of the Slovaks, "a most neglected of the Slav races."[37] It was also Štefánek's introductory letters that led the "Wandering Scot" to Slovak leaders in all significant towns from the Vág Valley to Ruthenia in the spring of 1907. During this journey, Seton-Watson felt increasingly at home—the Slovaks reminded him of the people of the Scottish Highlands, and their folk-art so enchanted him that he always maintained that "of all the nations he had known, [the Slovaks] had the most profound and unspoilt sense of beauty in colour and sound."[38] In the following years he worked hard to make Europe realize "the innate genius"[39] of the Slovak peasantry.

Seton-Watson summarised the results of his travels in "Political Prospects in Austria-Hungary," a long article published in the *Spectator* in June 1907. Unsurprisingly, the Hungarian government was labelled "reactionary," with no safeguards for the right of assembly; and the author was quick to highlight that despite the 48.6 percent non-Magyar population, only nineteen percent of Hungary's schoolchildren received instruction in their own language.[40] Thus, by the

---

34 Ibid., 49.
35 H. & C. Seton-Watson 1981, 38. See also Lajos Arday, *Térkép csata után, Magyarország a brit külpolitikában (1918–1919)* [Map after the Battle: Hungary in British Foreign Policy (1918–1919)], Budapest, Magvető, 1990, 114–115.
36 Anton Štefánek (1877–1964), a Slovak journalist, politician and a promoter of Czechoslovakism.
37 As Mark Cornwall observed, Seton-Watson generally used "race" to describe peoples on the continent or beyond and always "nation" to refer to the - more progressed - peoples of the United Kingdom. Cornwall, Robert William Seton-Watson and Nation-Building Clashes in Late Habsburg Space, *Slavonic and East European Review*, Vol. 100, Number 1, January 2022, 65–94, 69.
38 H. & C. Seton-Watson 1981, 54. Somewhat contradicts this Seton-Watson's letter to his Croat friend from 1909: "No one hates more than I do a priest-ridden and superstitious people." Although in the rest of the letter he softened this statement somewhat when explaining that it was better for an underdeveloped nation to be bigotedly religious than communist. Seton-Watson to Lupis-Vukić, October 17, 1909. Ljubo Boban (ed.), *R. W. Seton-Watson i Jugoslaveni: korespondencija 1906–1941 [Korespondencija]*, Sveučilište u Zagrebu, Institut za hrvatsku povijest, 1976, I/53.
39 Europe and the Slovak Question. Seton-Watson Papers, SEW 1/1.
40 H. & C. Seton-Watson 1981, 53.

summer of 1907, Seton-Watson had joined Steed, as not only had his support for the Coalition and its pro-independence arguments vanished, so too had his support for the Hungarian ruling elite.

The 1905–06 constitutional crisis brought too much publicity to Hungarian politics, which the 1907 tragedy of Csernova-Černová only reinforced. In October of that year, a conflict about the consecration of a newly built church in that Slovak-inhabited northern Hungarian village was ended by gendarme's bullets, which took the lives of fifteen locals. Steed quickly travelled to the spot but was not allowed into the Rózsahegy (Ružomberok) court. The next morning, he received a warning from the *Times* foreign editor, Chirol, that it was "neither necessary nor wise to mix ourselves up too much in these internal affairs."[41] Yet the tragedy proved to be everything but internal, as a few days later, highly critical reports appeared in major Western European papers, especially after the forty accused villagers received a total of thirty-six years' imprisonment. Among others the *Times, Spectator,* liberal *Daily News,* conservative *Morning Post, Manchester Guardian, Lo Spettatore* of Rome, the Viennese *Neue Freie Presse* and the *Frankfurter Zeitung* published repudiating articles, primarily authored by Steed,[42] Seton-Watson[43] or the Norwegian Nobel-laurate, Bjørnstjerne Bjørnson.[44]

---

41  Chirol to Steed, November 27, 1907. PHS Papers. Steed Papers.
42  Steed wrote to Moberly Bell on July 14, 1908, the following: "The Magyars, if working harmoniously with the other Hungarian races and the Austrian Slavs, will be strong enough to act as an effectual barrier against France and us in a European war. If, on the contrary, the Magyars are at loggerheads with one half of the Hungarian population, they will not only be reduced to impotence at the critical moment, but will suffer, as they now suffer under the enmity of the 20 million Austro-Hungarian Slavs, who, as opponents of Pan-Germanism, are on our side, but who, without the Magyars are as sheep without a shepherd. If we associate ourselves with Magyar chauvinism in its endeavour to Magyarize the non-Magyars by force, we shall produce an exactly similar impression upon the Slav world as if we praised the Prussian persecution of the Poles." PHS Papers. Steed Papers.
43  Scotus Viator, "A Monster Trial in Hungary," *Spectator*, March 28, 1908. See also his *Political Persecution in Hungary: An Appeal to British Public Opinion*, A. Constable, 1908, which was simultaneously published in German and French.
44  On Norwegian Nobel-laurate Bjørnstjerne Bjørnson's campaign see Ágnes Beretzky, "Twin Champions of the Slovak Cause: Bjørnstjerne Bjørnson and Robert William Seton-Watson," *Central Europe*, 2023, 1–15. Both Bjørnson and Seton-Watson, as well as most commemorators ignore the fact that the head of the gendarmerie together with four other gendarmes (i.e., five out of seven) were of Slovak nationality, as were the replacement priests who had been sent to carry out the consecration. Although Csernova-Černová has been cited in Slovak and Norwegian literature as a textbook example of ethnic oppression in Hungary, it is important to stress that (Slovak) Catholic peasant anger was equally inflamed by Hungarian liberal reforms (1895) such as equality for the Jews and easier divorces. The irony of the tragedy is that Father Hlinka and the villagers condemned the Hungarian government not only for the oppression of nationalities, but also for being far too liberal. See also Miroslav Szabó, National Conflict and Anti-Semitism at the Beginning of The Twentieth Century. The Case of the Czech Slovakophiles, Karel Kálal and Eduard Lederer, *Judaica Bohemiae*, Vol. XLIV, 2009/1, 49–81.

## 1.2 Seton-Watson's *Racial Problems*—Effects on Contemporaries

As already noted, by the end of 1907, partly as a result of the tragedy in Csernova (Černová), not only Steed but also Seton-Watson wrote off the Hungarians altogether. This was all the more unfortunate, as in December 1908, the latter's compendium of his earlier travels and the collected source material on the minority problems in the Danube Basin, *The Racial Problems in Hungary*, exploded onto the Christmas book market. With this six hundred plus page door stopper, Seton-Watson immediately became *the* expert on Hungarian history.

Jeszenszky characterizes the book as a polemic rather than a factual, scientific analysis, and in this respect one quite unworthy of an academic historian.[45] However, the program outlined in Chapter XXI of *The Racial Problems* does not recommend any radical standpoint. By leaving the territorial integrity of the country untouched, it contained the reforms considered essential for the future: the extension of the right to vote, the reorganization of counties by nationality, the lifting of all restrictions on the right of association and assembly, and the extension of mother tongue education to universities.[46]

Seton-Watson's passionate piece of polemical writing had a long-lasting effect in Britain. Although, as the *Times* correspondent in Vienna, Steed had been earlier acquainted with Hungary and became more fluent in the language, it was Seton-Watson who pioneered unveiling the oppression of nationalities and became the authority on anything connected to minority problems or politics in the Danube basin. Steed was not stingy with his praise: "The Magyars," he argued, "will be forced to buy [Racial Problems] *bon gré mal gré*. It is the first serious study of the non-Magyar question that has as yet appeared in any language, and, unless I am quite mistaken, it will go on selling for a long time to come."[47] In this he was quite right.

In 1909, while an undergraduate student at Oxford, Arnold Toynbee's eye, too, was caught by a book lying on his tutor Alfred Zimmern's desk. In his *Acquaintances* many years later, he recalled borrowing and reading what he claimed to be "a landmark" in his education.[48] Some six years later, during the Great War, Toynbee's first book, *Nationality and the War* appeared with the following acknowledgement:

---

45 Jeszenszky 2020, 279–280.
46 Seton-Watson 1908, 409–411.
47 Steed to Bell, June 4, 1908, PHS Papers. Steed Papers
48 Toynbee, *Acquaintances*, Oxford University Press, 1967, 50.

For what I have written on Hungary I am likewise in debt [...] above all to the work of Dr. Seton-Watson. So far as I deal with his subjects, my information is taken at second hand: I have learnt all I know about Magyarization from his *Racial Problems in Hungary*, and all I know about modern Croatia from his *Southern Slavs*. I can do no better than refer the reader to these two books for the substantiation of my indictment against the Magyar nation.[49]

Toynbee's complaints included the distortion of Hungarian statistics by "census-officials," which, he continued, was insignificant compared to "the gross perversions of truth perpetrated by Hungarian officialdom in 1910." "A demoralised" nation "succumbed to chauvinism" was his final verdict on Hungary,[50] a perspective taken almost verbatim from Seton-Watson.

Almost three decades after *Racial Problems* appeared, Seton-Watson's student and by then opponent, C.A. Macartney also spoke about the book in a tone of appreciation: "To Magyar writers, Professor Seton-Watson is anathema. [...] I can, however, find no work from the other side to set against his; since his opponents either ignore or deny the problems of which he treats, instead of explaining them."[51]

Macartney accurately described the reception of *Racial Problems* in Hungary. Although it stirred the Hungarian public, it was not thoroughly read or discussed, let alone translated; the selective map[52] or the author's one-sided analyses[53] were ignored. Probably the most important shortcoming was that Seton-

---

49  Toynbee 1915, ix.
50  Ibid.
51  Macartney 1937, 24.
52  The book ends with a "racial map of Hungary" the data of which, apart from the southern frontier, are generally unreliable: Nagyvárad-Oradea, Kolozsvár-Cluj and Temesvár-Timisoara are exclusively Romanian, as well as 40 percent of county Csík and 66 percent of county Maros-Torda; Munkács-Mukachevo is completely Ruthene, as well as Kassa-Košice, Eperjes-Prešov, Balassagyarmat, Vác and Pozsony-Bratislava are Slovak, etc. Interestingly enough, the book itself comprises data concerning the proportion of the nationalities in the Hungarian counties (p. 468) and cities (p. 13) which are fully in accordance with the Hungarian statistics: Nagyvárad-Oradea (91.3 percent Hungarian), Kolozsvár-Cluj (85 percent), Kassa- Košice (63.4 percent), County Csík (86.4 percent) and County Marostorda (57.8 percent). In: *A Magyar Korona országainak 1900. évi népszámlálása, I. rész, A népszámlálás leírása községenként* [The 1900 Census of the Countries of the Hungarian Crown, Part I, Description of the Census by Municipality], Budapest, 1902. 21*. 22*. It is indeed difficult to believe that Seton-Watson could make such a mistake.
53  A lot can be revealed by the fact that three chapters were added to the book on Slovak culture written by Slovak authors and all forty-two illustrations and photos are exclusively of Slovak purport. Esme Howard, Consul General in Budapest, explained in his "Annual Report for the Foreign Office": "Mr. Seton-Watson has taken the Slovaks under his special protection, and endeavours to endow them with many gifts and qualities which perhaps they do not really possess. But the truth probably lies somewhere between his rhapsodies over their literature and art, and

Watson made no distinction between forced and spontaneous "Magyarization"; the latter has recently been called by Pieter Judson "event-driven" or "situational" nationalism.⁵⁴ Instead of explaining, for example, that at around 1900 the ordinary person's level of commitment to a nation was often unreliable and unpredictable, a significant portion of the Hungarian reactions took the form of aggressive attacks on the author himself. Seton-Watson was labelled the "perfidious Scot," indeed a "paid agent" of Vienna, who "has fastened himself on the skin of the Hungarian state like a tick, [an] unpleasant parasite."⁵⁵ This is even more unfortunate because constructive criticism could still have had an impact in 1908–09: Seaton-Watson himself highlighted that "everybody who points out the misinterpretations and exaggerations in my book (in the spirit of genuine criticism and not chauvinistic slander) will be welcome, and the remarks will be included in the following Czech and German publications."⁵⁶

Seton-Watson had always had the reputation of being a difficult person to convince, and as time progressed, his selective sensitivity became more and more marked, giving way to several unbalanced conclusions. Moreover, owing to the general lack of constructive criticism from the Hungarian side, the distance between Seton-Watson and proponents of the Hungarian standpoint proved unbridgeable. "I don't care a brass farthing what the Magyar press writes about me. It is merely scurrilous,"⁵⁷ the offended publicist-historian wrote, and believed till the end of his life.

## 1.3. From Bosnian Crisis to Sarajevo: 1908–1914

In the same year as the publication of Seton-Watson's heavy-hitter, the Bosnian Crisis, also known as the Annexation Crisis or the First Balkan Crisis broke out when Austria-Hungary declared its intention to annex Bosnia-Herzegovina, which it had governed since 1878 but had previously been under the control of the Ottoman Empire. Unlike during 1903–08, the period afterwards until the

---

the intolerant and the rather stupid contempt of most Magyars, who deny that the Slovaks ever have or ever can produce anything." Qtd. in Jeszenszky 2020, 297.
54 Pieter Judson, *The Habsburg Empire: A New History*, Belknap Press: An Imprint of Harvard University Press, 2016, 309.
55 Ferenc Herczeg, Scotus Viator és a budapesti radikálisok [Scotus Viator and the Budapest radicals], *Magyar Figyelő*, December 15, 1911, 523.
56 Oszkár Jászi, Scotus Viator Magyarországról [Scotus Viator on Hungary], *Huszadik Század* 2 (1909-II): 60–72. Jeszenszky 2020, 285.
57 Zimmern Papers, MSS. Eng. Box 12, fols 129, Western Manuscripts, Bodleian Library, Oxford.

## 1.3. From Bosnian Crisis to Sarajevo: 1908–1914

outbreak of war was marked by some differences in perception between Steed and Seton-Watson. In line with Hungary's Wekerle Government, but against His Majesty's, Seton-Watson approved of the annexation, since in his opinion it immediately restored the prestige of the Monarchy.[58] Steed, on the other hand, held a completely different view: he regarded Bosnia's annexation as "the first link of Berlin–Bagdad, Germany's drive to the East."[59] Many years later, he even described the event as the prelude to the crisis of July 1914.[60] Thus, he became convinced that it was impossible for Austria-Hungary to pursue an independent foreign policy, and he began to support the national movements within the Monarchy in an attempt to resist German expansion.

Regarding the Austro-Hungarian monarch, Franz Joseph, there was also a detectable difference between Seton-Watson and Steed. The latter expected the ruler to practice Slavophile policy as a result of the increasing German danger, and as it turned out to be a chimera, distrusted him. Seton-Watson, on the other hand, believed the "Kaiser-König" and held the view that "instinct had guided Francis Joseph into trusting his people in Austria and was even now guiding him to the same course in Hungary."[61]

By the time the Coalition broke up and the government resigned in 1909, it had long lost Hungary's remaining credit not only with Steed and Seton-Watson, but with the British public, too. The fundamental reason was the incompetent Coalition's four years in power, a time of the grand illusion that the defeat in the conflict with Franz Joseph could ever be mitigated by a policy of violence against nationalities, coupled with chauvinistic, sword-wielding rhetoric. The British Consul General reported, "No wonder the other 'nationalities' are up in arms."[62] The Croatian parliamentarians' change in attitude offers great proof for this: owing to co-operation with the ruling Liberal Party prior to 1905, they only requested to speak in the Hungarian Parliament seventeen times before 1905, and even then, they did so in Hungarian despite having the legal right to do so in their mother tongue. During the coalition government, 1906–10, on the other hand, it was striking that ninety-five of their one hun-

---

58   Péter László, Scotus Viator és a magyar kérdés az első világháború előtt [Scotus Viator and the Hungarian Question before the First World War]. In: Éva Saáry, Judit Steinmann (eds.), *Gesta Hungarorum III*, Zurich, Swiss Hungarian Literature and Fine Arts Society, 1990, 104. Hanak 1962, 17.
59   Ibid. In his *Through Thirty Years* Steed recalled: "The course of the Bosnian annexation crisis had already proved [Austria-Hungary] to be bound, hand and foot, to Germany." Steed 1924, II/390.
60   Steed to I.M. Stephens, February 24, 1931. Steed Papers MS 74 130. See also Steed, *The Doom of the Hapsburgs*, Arrowsmith, 1936, 120. Qtd. in Liebich 2018, 61. Jeszenszky 2020, 269.
61   H. & C. Seton-Watson 1981, 53.
62   Dispatch by Frederick S. Clarke, British Consul General in Budapest, March 11, 1907. PHS Papers. Steed Papers. Jeszenszky 2000b, 244.

dred and twenty-four speeches were delivered in Croatian.[63] Despite putting a halt to chauvinistic rhetoric as well as making improvements in nationality policy, István Tisza's government[64] of the newly-formed Party of National Work (*Nemzeti Munkapárt*) could not restore the country's damaged image. The failure was partly owing to Steed's and Seton-Watson's books and articles,[65] which, by the end of the 1900s, had succeeded in convincing most of the British public that Hungary's veil of liberalism concealed political oppression, above all of the non-Hungarian minorities.

The year 1911 saw the publication of another significant book by Seton-Watson: his *Southern Slav Question and the Habsburg Monarchy* contained the plan of the reorganisation of Austria-Hungary's dualist structure into a trialist system. This system posited the creation of a third centre within the Monarchy, i.e., the Kingdom of Croatia uniting Croatia, Slavonia, Dalmatia, Istria and Bosnia-Herzegovina. "The Southern Slav territory is a natural geographical unit," according to Seton-Watson, "with homogeneous population and a single language that has been split up to artificial fragments [...]."[66] In supporting trialism, i.e., a tripartite state, Seton-Watson was both utopistic and realistic: on the one hand, he clearly downplayed both the historical and religious divide between the peoples, while, quite naively, counting on Austrian support. On the other hand, he rightly believed that trialism would end Hungarian dominance once and for all.

In reality, the regions inhabited by the South Slavs were politically fragmented territories characterised by a highly complex ethno-religious and linguistic mosaic, which gave rise to several ethnic nationalism in the region. Such a mix of

---

63 András Cieger, Horvát képviselők a magyar országgyűlésben (1868–1918) [Croatian Representatives in the Hungarian Parliament]. In: Pál Fodor-Dénes Sokcsevits, *A horvát–magyar együttélés fordulópontjai. Intézmények, társadalom, gazdaság, kultúra* [The Turning Points of Croatian-Hungarian Coexistence. Institutions, Society, Economy, Culture], Budapest, MTA Bölcsészettudományi Kutatóközpont Történettudományi Intézet, Horvát Történettudományi Intézet [Centre for Humanities Research Institute of History, Croatian Institute of History], 2015, 426–435, 426–428.

64 In 1930 Steed, described Tisza as a "Calvinist to the backbone, preferred to break rather than bend, intense and narrow patriotism, but it was impossible not to respect his sincerity. He understood that power of Magyar oligarchy, [...] depended upon preventing anything in the shape of universal suffrage [and] would not admit that non-Magyar nationalities had any effective political rights as such. Despite his piety he was an ardent duellist and steeple chaser, fought more than 30 duels always wounded opponents." Steed added: "I always thought that Tisza was the biggest man not merely in Austria-Hungary and, indeed, the only statesman on the enemy side during the war. None of the Germans were comparable to him in moral force and driving power." Steed to Rev. James R. Johnston, Edinburgh, November 29, 1930. Steed Papers MS 74130.

65 Steed, *Times*, June 14, 1910. Seton-Watson, *Corruption and Reform. A Study of Electoral Practice*, London, Constable and Co., 1911, 158–161.

66 Seton-Watson 1911, 337. On page 2 he stated boldly: "Linguistic unity has already been achieved; for the Croat language is Serb written with Latin, the Serb language, Croat written with Cyrillic characters."

populations made it impossible to draw ethnic-based boundaries without triggering hostilities. Therefore, the civic idea of political unification seemed the ideal solution to the problem of competing ethno-national cultural aspirations: the idea of South Slavism, or Yugoslavism (with "yugo" meaning "south"), established common political principles and a vision of state organization as the criterion for belonging to a nation. Its antecedents were the Illyrian movement of the Croatian linguist Ljudevit Gaj (1809–1872) as well as the federal Habsburg Monarchy scheme of Croatian Roman Catholic bishop Josip Juraj Strossmayer (1815–1905), which were both marginalised by the 1867 Compromise. In order to stabilise the Monarchy, Seton-Watson thus reinvigorated the Yugoslav idea, which he nevertheless based on a non-existent, idealistic geographical-national-linguistic uniformity.

Of course, in the background of Seton-Watson's pro-Slav turn there lay not only his sensitivity towards the small and oppressed nations, but two other factors as well: on the on hand was the 1907 Anglo-Russian treaty, which was brokered by the French; British foreign policy, which had hitherto been distrustful of the Slavs, was replaced by a pro-Russian public mood and a growing interest in the South Slavs in general. The other factor that triggered Seton-Watson's trialist-turn was the (Agram) Zagreb trial of fifty-three Austro-Hungarian Serbs charged with treason and the subsequent Friedjung trial of 1909, which examined the credibility of the evidence used in the prior trial. The majority of documents, it was revealed, had been forged. Not only Seton-Watson became disappointed in the Monarchy, especially in the political methods of its foreign minister, Baron von Aerenthal, the disillusionment was widespread. His friend Steed attended every session at court, where he was amazed by the Austrian historian's primary opponent: T. G. Masaryk.[67]

Steed's book *The Hapsburg Monarchy* was based on his decade-long experience in his position as the *Times* correspondent, only to cause considerable indignation. By 1913 the author regarded the Dualist setting as outdated, as in his opinion real power was vested in the dynasty and the institutions it controlled, whose survival depended on its strength to carry out the required democratic reforms. Steed's brilliance of expression could not hide his periodic prejudices against certain persons and groups. He devoted only a few pages to Hungary, stating: "The present generation of Magyars has been so steeped in chauvinism as to have lost all sense of their real position in Europe, [...] the future may reserve for them trials as severe as any they have experienced during their che-

---

67  Liebich 2018, 61. H. & C. Seton-Watson 1981, 76–78.

## 1. Steed, Seton-Watson and Toynbee on National Self-Determination

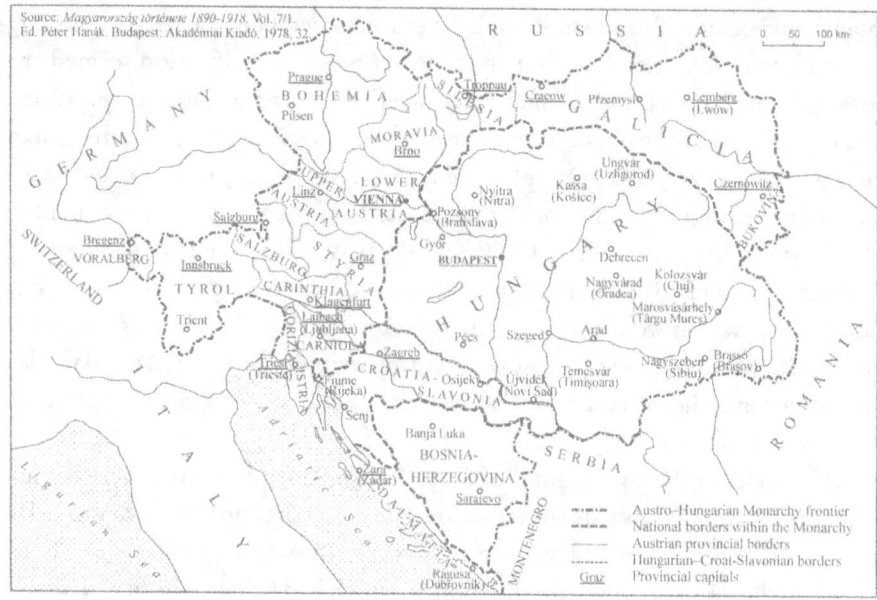

The Countries and Provinces of the Austro-Hungarian Monarchy in 1913. Source: Ignác Romsics, *Hungary in the Twentieth Century*, Budapest, Corvina-Osiris, 1999, 10..

quered history." Having identified Jews with Germans and with German interests, *The Habsburg Monarchy* offered a highly prejudiced discussion on the role of the Jews, as well, but that in no fewer than fifty pages.[68]

In 1913 Steed left Vienna for good. Having won the confidence of Lord Northcliffe, the new proprietor of the *Times*, he was able to assert his views far more effectively. After his appointment as foreign editor at the onset of 1914, he became one of the most effective spokesmen for the exiled national movements working to break up Austria-Hungary. Backed by Clémence Rose as his unpaid political secretary and advisor, and together with Seton-Watson, they soon formed the "London trio" and after the outbreak of the war offered a friendly refuge and home for, among others, Masaryk. Masaryk was able to set forth his aims in the papers controlled by Lord Northcliffe and get access to the most influential quarters in London.[69]

---

[68] Steed, *The Hapsburg Monarchy*, London, Constable and Company, 1913, 321 and 145–194. Interestingly, it was the rise of the Nazi dictator that finally turned the editor into a philosemite, and after 1933-1934 he extended his advocacy of statehood for various Eastern European nationalities to the Jewish national cause. More on this in Andre Liebich, *The Antisemitism of Henry Wickham Steed*, *Patterns of Prejudice*, Vol. 46, 2012, 180–208.

[69] Masaryk, *The Making of a State*, London, George Allen and Unwin Ltd, 1927, 96. The English version was arranged and prepared with an introduction by Steed.

Toynbee was eighteen and ten years younger than Steed and Seton-Watson, respectively: when the latter's *Southern Slav Question in the Habsburg Monarchy* appeared, Toynbee had just finished his studies in Oxford. Then he spent a year travelling and studying archaeology in Greece and then Turkey as preparation for a post in Balliol College as tutor of Greek and Roman History. His stay coincided with the First Balkan War of 1912, which established his interest in the history of modern Eastern Europe and beyond.

As a result of that conflict, the Ottoman Empire lost 37 percent of its territory and 21 percent of its population; in fact, it was squeezed out of Europe. With such loss of territory, the multi-ethnic and pluralistic religious character of the empire was lost, and the Christian communities, with the exception of the Armenians, disappeared. At the same time, the Balkan victories provided Serbia and the Slavs within the Monarchy with even more confidence and made them a much more significant factor than ever before.

## 1.4. The Three Britons and the Great War 1914-1916

In June 1914, Archduke Franz Ferdinand was assassinated in Sarajevo, and exactly one month later the Monarchy declared war on Serbia. The armed conflict soon escalated into a world war with unprecedented military machinery: Belgium was invaded and plundered by the Germans, becoming a symbol of the Kaiser's brutality.

As Toynbee put it in retrospect, 1914 had been the "watershed date" in history; "the world I grew up in as a child went down, [...] all of a sudden, the curtain was pulled away, affecting my whole life."[70] Though at the age of twenty-five when the hostilities broke out, Toynbee was never conscripted, having been declared "medically unfit" due to the dysentery he suffered from after drinking polluted water during his 1912 visit to Greece.[71] Interestingly, his paper revealing that this infection would and could return was signed by a (pacifist) Quaker

---

[70] "Geschichte und Gegenwart"- Gespräch mit Sven Hasselblatt in Londoner Wohnung, 21.30-22.40, Mai 31, 1970, Sendung Norddeutscher Rundfunk. Toynbee Papers, MS 13967/7 Broadcasts 1929-1955.

[71] Toynbee to Major E.B. Ferres, June 28, 1916. Toynbee referred to a copy of Army Form B 2512 A, "Not accepted, medically unfit," signed F.P. Irench, Dec 9 1915. Toynbee Papers MS 13 967/39 General Miscellaneous Correspondence 1911-1956.
A year later, on September 30, 1916, Toynbee received a certificate of exemption from the Foreign Office, due to being engaged "on work of national importance." Toynbee to Colonel H. Dawson, R.O. Kensington Town Hall, April 19, 1917. Toynbee Papers MS 13 967/39 General Miscellaneous Correspondence 1911-1956.

doctor who also happened to be a family member on his wife's side. Therefore, Toynbee definitely would have been accepted for active duty if he had not revealed his former sickness, which haunted him till the end of his life.

The outbreak of war shocked Seton-Watson, too. In August 1914, he wrote to his wife: "The solution I have advocated for years—South Slav, Hungarian—died rather a most unnatural death at midnight before last. From now onwards the Great Serbian State is inevitable and we must create it. I find Steed and Strachey absolutely atone with me in this. [...] Dalmatia, Bosnia, Croatia, Istria must be united to Serbia. Roumania must have all her kinsmen."[72]

The Monarchy's declaration of war against Serbia, in Seton-Watson's opinion, was evidence that it had become a tool for Pan-German plans. Thus, Austria-Hungary had given up its position as a significant independent player in the balance of power in Europe. This was exactly the same view Steed had held ever since the annexation crisis and the Agram trial. In October 1914, upon receiving a telegram from Masaryk urging him "to hear what is going on, not only on the battlefields, but in the heads of those who will shape the future, perhaps the future map of Europe"[73] and then following Steed's instructions, Seton-Watson travelled to the Netherlands undercover as a temporary courier. In Rotterdam he met Masaryk, whose "moral stature" deeply affected him. The meeting signalled the onset of a life-long friendship and yielded the first statement of Czechoslovakism: in a memorandum sent to Steed, Masaryk put forward his idea of an Independent Bohemia comprising the historic lands of Bohemia and Moravia, Silesia together with the Slovak districts of Northern Hungary down the river Ipoly to the Danube, including Pressburg-Pozsony (Bratislava). He also described the Slovaks as "Bohemians in spite of their using their dialect as their literary language" together with emphasizing the united country's role in a new

---

72  H. & C. Seton-Watson 1981, 101. Prior to July 1914, Seton-Watson was no enemy of the Monarchy, which is clearly demonstrated by his statements after the assassination in Sarajevo. He wrote the following to *Contemporary Review* in the middle of July 1914: "The man may perish, but the idea cannot die. The mission of the Habsburgs in Europe is more obvious than ever, and if the young Archduke [Charles] be willing to take up his uncle's legacy, all men of every creed, race and party, at home or abroad, must stand by him and endeavour in their own way to help him prove his mettle." See also H. & C. Seton-Watson 1981, 101.
In the same vein, Seton-Watson was still regretful, writing to former consul general in Egypt Lord Cromer a year after the declaration of war: "Though the events of the war have driven me to abandon my belief in Trialism and to advocate the dissolution of the Dual Monarchy - alike in the interest of a majority of its own races and as the only sure means of defeating Germany - still I can never cease to regret the lost hopes which I had centred upon the late Archduke and his genuine determination to work for internal reform." Seton-Watson to Lord Cromer, September 12, 1915. *Korespondencija* I/150.

73  Masaryk to Seton-Watson, September 17, 1914. Rychlík, Marzik, Bielik (eds.) 1995, I/201.

"cordon sanitaire" to defend British interests against the Monarchy, the "vassal of Berlin after 1866."[74]

From the outbreak of the war, the British authorities regarded Steed as an aide who helped clarify whether the Aliens Restriction Act would be applied to political emigrants from the Monarchy, which would have resulted in their imprisonment and/or deportation. It was through his intervention, among others, that the two best-known figures of political emigration from the Dual Monarchy in Britain—Masaryk and the Dalmatian-born journalist Frano Supilo, a Hungarian citizen—were allowed to enter the United Kingdom in autumn 1914.[75] In his Memorandum of January 7, 1915, Supilo laid down the foundation of British pro-Slav propaganda: as the role of "anti-German buffer state" would not be fulfilled either by autonomy or by the small, separate South Slav states, whether Croatian, Slovene or Serb, the unification of the Southern Slavs was indispensable.[76]

As put forward in Jeszenszky's *Lost Prestige*, a special cooperation pattern evolved among exiles arriving from the Monarchy and their friends in Britain. Apart from arguing for the dissolution of the Monarchy, the former provided inside news and information recognized as useful to the Entente; while the latter conveyed such views and information to the British press and to Whitehall in forms tailored to the British taste and frame of mind. Thus, it became possible to present Czech, Croatian, Serbian and Romanian interests and war aims as simultaneously British strategic, political and economic interests."[77]

In the meantime, Turkey's entry into the war on the side of the Central Powers sealed the fate of the Armenian community in the empire. The most influ-

---

74 Masaryk to Steed May 5, 1915. Steed Papers MS 74103.
75 Calder 1976, 19–21. Frano Supilo (1870–1917), a journalist and editor from Fiume, until his death an émigré leader of the South Slav unity movement, was described by Seton-Watson as "one of the most gifted political minds." *New Europe*, October 4, 1917, 366. Supilo is said to have nicknamed Seton-Watson "Ja-aber" because he was usually hard to persuade, so stubbornly adherent to his views. In G.H. Bolsover: R. W. Seton-Watson, 1879–1951, From the Proceedings of the British Academy, Vol. XXXVII, London, 1952, 344.
76 Frano Supilo, Memorandum to Sir Edward Grey, January 7, 1915. The Italian original was translated by Henry Wickham Steed. In Vangelis Kechriotis-Maciej Górny-Ahmet Ersoy (eds.), *Discourses of Collective Identity in Central and Southeast Europe*, Vol. 3/1: *Modernism: The Creation of Nation-States*, CEU Press, 2009, 250–257.
cf. Steed's letter to Noel Buxton: "Our only chance of creating an effective barrier to the pressure of the German block in Central-Europe lies in the creation of a compact "Yugoslavia" to include Slovenes, Croats and Serbs. Fusion of these various elements into a united State will be a matter of some difficulty, but the work is essential to a satisfactory settlement." Steed to Noel Buxton, January 29, 1915, McGill Library Archival Collections Catalogue, https://archivalcollections.library.mcgill.ca/index.php/w-Steed Accessed March 21, 2023.
77 Jeszenszky 2020, 335–336. See also Steed 1924, 2: 12.

ential members of the Armenian elite were imprisoned and killed, and in 1915 the population began to be relocated to the empire's southern outskirts and systematically exterminated at the behest of the Turkish government.[78] The Turkish brutality provoked international outrage, and in Britain it echoed reactions by Gladstone to the "Bulgarian horrors" a generation earlier. Once again Christians were being persecuted by Muslims, and the Foreign Office commissioned James Bryce, a Northern Irish-born British Liberal politician and member of the House of Lords (1838–1922), to conduct a thorough investigation of the events. Bryce, soon to be called "the Byron of Armenia," did not travel alone: he picked as his assistant the young Arnold J. Toynbee, who had become an expert on the region. The result of their labours was the so-called *Blue Book*, a prodigious collection of 700 pages of survivors' and eyewitness accounts of Turkish atrocities, "appalling in uniformity."[79] It highlighted that orders had come from the government, "a gang of unscrupulous ruffians,"[80] not from any religious fanaticism. Bryce quoted Sultan Abdul Hamid: "The way to get rid of the Armenian question is to get rid of the Armenians."[81] The Armenians are described as "the oldest of the civilised races in Western Asia according to Toynbee" as well as "[...] a commercial genius among a rather stupid, conservatively inclined Turkish population."[82] Bryce warned Toynbee that the book should not serve as a "campaign document,"[83] however, garnering the interest of the still-neutral United States was of the utmost significance.

The publication of the *Blue Book* was soon followed by two short pamphlets in which Toynbee defended the number of Armenians exterminated as 600–800,000 Armenians,[84] as opposed to the 300,000 "civil war casualties" reported by the Turkish authorities. Both Bryce and his assistant were therefore accused by the central powers of warmongering, and levelled claims that the two ex-

---

78 Toynbee recalled in 1941: "The orders always came from the central government [...] which was inspired by the ideology of turning Turkey into a uniform national state [...] Local Turkish communities living for centuries as next-door neighbours of the Armenians, were horrified at these orders from above and did what they could to avoid carrying them out." Toynbee to Professor McKenzie, May 12, 1941. Toynbee Papers, BL Oxford MS13967/63/2.
79 Lord Bryce [Arnold Toynbee]: *Armenian Atrocities: The Murder of a Nation*, London: Hodder and Stoughton, 1915, 23.
80 Ibid., 27.
81 Ibid., 6–8, 13.
82 Ibid., 17.
83 David Monger, Networking against Genocide during the First World War: the international network behind the British Parliamentary report on the Armenian Genocide. *Journal of Transatlantic Studies*, 2018, Vol. 16, No. 3, 295–316, https://doi.org/10.1080/14794012.2018.1482714, 300.
84 A Foreign Office Statement titled "Allies' Debt to Armenians" confirmed the 700,000-person loss, which corresponds to Toynbee's findings. Toynbee Papers BL Oxford MS13967/44/1 Armenian Question: Pamphlets 1917–21.

perts exaggerated the suffering of the Armenians to compensate for Russian abuse of the Jews on the Eastern Front. In response to a question about the authenticity of the report, Toynbee stated that the collection was an almost verbatim account of the testimonies of American missionaries in the region and was based on the experience of the German consul in Turkey, who himself was "appalled at what he had seen."[85]

In addition to the *Blue Book*, Toynbee's first solo work, his 1915 "juvenilia," *Nationality and the War* was also published. In a letter to his uncle, he confessed that

> the real object of the book is to give account of the various national problems as they stand at present and thereby to get at what Nationality means. It is probably rash to prepare solutions and I have barred myself to criticism, which I am getting from both sides [...]. I suppose I want to get the best of both worlds—to draw enough of Germany's claws to make her harmless, without embittering her so much that she will use any weapon she retains on the first opportunity [...]. My general scheme is to weaken Germany by breaking-up her allies, and conciliate her (perhaps a hopeless idea) by leaving her the maximum elbow-room in the colonial areas.[86]

Toynbee highlighted that the reconstruction of Europe was "incomparably graver than the military struggle": he advocated an equitable postwar settlement by calling attention to the danger of beating Germany and simultaneously humiliating her. By 1915, not only was his attitude toward Germany different from that of Seton-Watson or Steed but he also paid attention to another factor: the economy. In June the same year, he put forward to Bertrand Russel his liberal internationalist ideas:

> One factor of 'nationality' which in my opinion is most probably the principal and indispensable factor, ie. the common economic interests and the trade relations [...] Common language, religion, ethics, government, historical traditions—neither are capable of building up or characterising a nationality [...] but the combination of one of these with common economic

---

85  Toynbee to Professor McKenzie, May 12, 1941. Toynbee Papers BL Oxford MS13967/63/2.
86  Toynbee to Uncle Paget, April 20, 1915. Toynbee Papers BL Oxford MS13 967/39 General Miscellaneous Correspondence 1911–1956. With a manuscript closed in February 1915, right in the middle of an unforseen world-wide conflict, writing such a book seemed to display utmost bravery: "To walk where diplomatists fear to tread argues either folly or courage; and this book, though not altogether wise, is not a work of a fool." Thus sounded the *Times Literary Supplement*'s verdict. "The Reconstruction of Europe," April 22, 1915.

interests or aims gives a sufficient basis for the formation of nationality [...] if two or more of these elements are combined with common economic interests, the nationality [...] is stronger [...] if all are combined with developed common econ interests, the nationality becomes a very strong one.

No wonder, he argued, that France and England became the strongest "Nationalities"; Germany evolved to become a "Nationality" with the formation of the Zollverein and became a strong one, whereas Austria formed one by a combination of common economic interests and common Government, which Toynbee believed was a weak manifestation of nationality. He also asserted that economic relationships and shared interests were not just the main and necessary factors of the establishment of nationality, but were the very roots of language, ethics, governance, and ultimately historical links: "National free trade makes nationalism; international free trade makes internationalism." On the other hand, protectionism, that is economic isolation, he opined, would lead to the expansion of nationalism and eventually, to war.

At this point, Toynbee, a subject of the British Empire, could not see beyond his own shadow and stated bluntly that an open door policy between two countries could "complete" the possibilities of cooperation, an "equivalent of the annexation of the two countries, one by the other." He clearly oversimplified the process of nation building by generalising the western, more civic model and downplaying the role of language and lineage— the dominant factors in culturally and ethnically determined nations. Additionally, he advanced the somewhat utopian notion that small nations would benefit equally from the expansion of the international free trade system, just as much as large ones, which would no longer seek to subjugate the smaller or even retain portions of their terretory. In this way, the autonomy or independence of smaller ethnic nationalities could be guaranteed in a natural, peaceful manner.[87]

Toynbee also noted that there was a tendency in England to couple the fate of Armenia with that of Belgium, partly to awaken the conscience of the British so that they support the war-torn people. A prime example, *The British Armenia Committee*, was founded among others to provide homes for Armenian children.[88]

---

87 Toynbee to Bertrand Russel, June 15, 1915. Toynbee Papers BL Oxford MS13 967/83/1 Correspondence M-.
88 Aunerin Williams acted as chairman, Noel Buxton became the vice-chairman, and Lord Bryce, G.P. Gooch, Samuel Hoare, Oswald Mosley as well as Toynbee also joined. Toynbee's handwritten notes dated November 6, 1917. MS 13967/44/1 Armenian Question: Pamphlets 1917-21.

However, there was another "Belgium of the East"[89] during the Great War: Serbia. Comparing the situation and the role of Serbia with Belgium proved to be effective as it enabled the average British citizen to identify with the situation and the cause of the Serbs. For Britain, the champion of liberalism, it soon became an inescapable duty to help the tormented but tenacious and persistent Serbian people, "whose only hope is God and Britain."[90] The cause of assisting the Serbs became a test not only of generosity but of civilisation.[91]

During the war, Seton-Watson and Steed were particularly involved in pro-Serbian activities. This is all the more noteworthy as only a few years earlier both had been appalled by the country, let alone its leaders: "I am afraid I have quite renounced all sympathy with the corrupt scoundrels who 'run' Serbia,"[92] Seton-Watson asserted in 1909. Five years later, in the autumn of 1914, on the other hand, he chaired the Serbian Relief Fund, which initially helped Serbia with medical supplies. Less than two years later, in July 1916, the Serbian Society of Great Britain also founded, with him as chair[93] and with the primary aim of influencing public opinion "such as cannot be ignored by the authorities when the Serbian question comes up once more."[94] Why the abrupt change? Again, citing simple support for the weak is insufficient. A more plausible argument is instead that since the outbreak of war, debilitating the Central Powers, primarily Germany and Austria-Hungary, had become a British war aim, and embracing nationalist aspirations for freedom served as a remedy against the German threat to essentially British interests. From the outset Seton-Watson rejected the prospect of both an independent Croatia and Greater Serbia, as he always regarded the plan of a common South Slav state as a more advantageous and lasting solution to the South Slav question.

Steed's support for an independent South Slav state was equally unflinching. Upon receiving *Times* owner Lord Northcliffe, a man of unwavering and com-

---

89   Seton-Watson, The Spirit of the Serb. In: Sydney Low, (ed.), *The Spirit of the Allied Nations*, London, 1915, 119.
     In the same year, Seton-Watson applied the popular epithet to yet another country: "A hundred years ago Roumania consisted of two corrupt and backward vassal provinces of Turkey, without influence or consideration in the world. To-day she has been not unjustly described as 'the Belgium of the East,' progressing by leaps and bounds." Seton-Watson, *Roumania and the Great War*, London, Constable and Company Ltd., 1915, 2.
90   *Times*, July 27, 1918.: 3.
91   *Times*, June 16 and 11, 1915. See also *Times*, March 31, 1916, 9.
92   Zimmern Papers, Bodleian Library, Oxford, MSS. Eng. Box 12, fol. 6.
93   From January 1917, after Seton-Watson had been called up for civilian service, Steed became the Chairman of the Serbian Society of Great Britain for two years.,
94   H. & C. Seton-Watson 1981, 174-175.

plete faith, he was essentially given carte blanche to handle the foreign affairs section of the paper. With Seton-Watson's intellectual backing, Steed was able to spread the idea that the creation of a unified Southern Slav state and the dissolution of Austria-Hungary were the main objectives of the British Empire. In an editorial welcoming Serbian Prince Regent Alexander and Prime Minister Nikola Pašić to London, Steed urged the political consolidation of all Southern Slavs. "Serbia re-born will no longer be Serbia," it was asserted, but "a United States of Yugoslavia [...]."[95]

Due to numerous events, articles, and not the least to the Kosovo-Day celebrations[96] in which both friends of the South Slavs were key figures, the British population's support grew not only for the principle of national self-determination but also for the South Slav cause. The "Kosovo Day" edition of the *Times* went even further, pointing to the unification of the southern Slavic peoples as the ideal and desirable solution to the eastern question, which the paper claimed had begun with the Battle of Kosovopolje.[97] All in all, Kosovo Day in the UK was an overwhelming success, with 4,800 daily, weekly, religious and popular newspapers covering the commemoration, which in fact was the culmination of a long struggle to radically change the Serbian image in Britain. By the end of the First World War, Serbia had undoubtedly achieved a level of popularity in Britain unmatched by any other country in Central or Eastern Europe, either previously or since, and Serbs were widely regarded as the "guardians of the gate."[98] The term "Serb" came to be used interchangeably with "Yugoslav" because pro-Slavic propaganda implied that the national interests and objectives of Serbs and other southern Slavs were identical. As a result, the other South Slav peoples acquired the favourable assessment accorded to Serbs, which more or less survived until the establishment of the royal dictatorship in 1929.

---

95 *Times*, March 31, 1916.
96 The published pamphlet did a wonderful job describing and glorifying the famous battle of Kosovopolje, on June 15, 1389, between Serbian Prince Lazar Hrebeljanović's army and an invading army of the Ottoman Empire. A textbook example of falsifying history, the pamphlet put forward the question: "Who are the true Christian people: the Serbs, who struggled without support and suffered terribly for Christianity for five hundred years, or the Germans, who gained glory by allying themselves with Islam to overrun the tiny Serbian people?" *Kosovo Day: Report*, 1916: 13, 16, 20–21; SEW/5/3/1; Patrik Szegő, *A béke bajnokai. A délszlávbarát brit lobbi és Ausztria-Magyarország feldarabolása* [The Champions of Peace: The Dissolution of Austria-Hungary and the Pro-Southslav British Lobby], Budapest, MCC Press Kft., 2024, 147–149.
97 *Times*, June 28, 1916, 9.
98 The name was borrowed from a speech by David Lloyd George on August 8, 1917. See Laffan, R. G. D., *The Guardians of the Gate: Historical Lectures on the Serbs*, Oxford, Clarendon, 1918, 3.

## 1.5. "Efficient propaganda must be the handmaid of policy."[99] 1916–1918

*"Without victory there can be no New Europe."*[100]

During the First World War, the year 1916 seemed a watershed time when not only disillusionment and anti-war criticism gained ground, but also, as a reaction, new tools of propaganda were established to promote the liberation of the subjected nationalities of Austria-Hungary. In October 1916, Seton-Watson and Steed founded the Serbian Society of Great Britain to promote the cause of the unified Yugoslav state. The immensely prestigious former Viceroy of Egypt, Lord Cromer, was elected honorary chairman. That month also witnessed the first issues of a weekly, *The New Europe*, which championed the rights of nationalities and was launched by Seton-Watson, Henry Wickham Steed, Ronald Burrows (a distinguished archaeologist as well as Principal of King's College), and the former secretary of Winston Churchill, Sir Alexander Whyte. As Steed remembered: "When we founded the *New Europe* and the *Serbian Society*, we hardly realized what a hornet's nest we were about to stir up. [...] We had touched pro-Germanism, active and latent, conscious and unconscious, at its most sensitive point; and we were few against many,"[101] Seton-Watson regarded the time and money he devoted to *The New Europe* as a patriotic contribution to Entente triumph.[102] He was even forced to take on a substantial part of the costs of publication and distribution from his family inheritance, despite Masaryk also contributing £2,000 (equivalent to £138,000 in 2024) from donations from Czechs who had emigrated to the United States.[103]

Steed's and Seton-Watson's wartime propaganda and that of their supporters did not of course exhaust itself in anti-German or anti-Austro-Hungarian agitation. Rather, they found it important to act as mediators, or "bridges,"[104] especially in inter-Allied conflicts. The most notable of these was the Italo–South Slav enmity regarding the fate of the officially Austro-Hungarian territories along the eastern coast of the Adriatic Sea. In January 1915, Steed wrote emphatically that "the whole of Dalmatia is Slav and the Italian-speaking portion

---

99 Steed to G. Murray, February 26, 1941. Steed Papers MS 74133.
100 R. W. Seton-Watson: President Wilson and Europe, *The New Europe* Vol. II. No. 16. February 1, 1917. 77–82.
101 Steed 1924, II/ 128. See also Seton-Watson's letter to Ronald Burrows, *Korespondencija* 1976, I/ 235
102 Seton-Watson to Steed, October 8, 1920. Qtd. in Arthur J. May, R. W. Seton-Watson and British Anti-Hapsburg Sentiment, *The American Slavic and East European Review*, February 1961, Vol. 20, No. 1, 40–54, 54.
103 Steed 1924, II/124.
104 Seton-Watson to Steed, April 2, 1918, Rome. Steed Papers, MS 74101.

## 1. Steed, Seton-Watson and Toynbee on National Self-Determination

of the Slav population is less than 3 percent [...] Our true policy is to promote an agreement between the Italians and the South Slavs on the basis of the principle of nationality."[105] However, the exact opposite happened. Less than three months later, in the Secret Treaty of London in April 1915, Britain and France awarded Italy Dalmatia, an overwhelmingly Slavic territory of the future South Slav state. Upon learning of the provisions, both Seton-Watson and Steed were exasperated and set out to bridge the gap between the rival claims. Steed, for example, offered his London home for informal meetings, , with Seton-Watson often being present; or he gave advice to both sides, and indeed had contacts up to the highest circles.[106] "In matters of sufficient importance" he had permission to communicate directly with Italian prime minister Vittorio Orlando himself, urging "continual coordination" between British policy in regard to Italy and Italian policy in regard to Austria-Hungary, and emphasizing that "any policy not aiming at the complete victory of the Allies represents semi-defeatism."[107] At the same time, Steed was convinced that as the British and French were bound by their signatures to the secret treaty, President Wilson alone could settle the Adriatic dispute.[108]

Interestingly, after Austrian Emperor Karl, King of Hungary succeeded Franz Joseph at the end of 1916, the South Slav representatives in the Austrian Parliament formed a party grouping called the Yugoslav Club and issued a manifesto calling for the political unification of the Monarchy's Slovene, Croat, and Serb-inhabited territories. On May 30, 1917, they made a proclamation at the ceremonial opening of the Reichstag, the Austrian Parliament. It was based on the historical Croatian state law and the political equality between nations, and advocated a trialist solution "under the sceptre of the Habsburg-Loraine dynasty," that is, within the Monarchy. Thus, in this phase of the First World War, the South Slav political elite in the Monarchy did not identify with the radical views and proposals of the South Slav political emigration and their British patrons, such as the dismemberment of Austria-Hungary and the unification of the South Slav territories.[109]

---

105 Steed to Noel Buxton, January 31, 1915, McGill Library Archival Collections Catalogue, https://archivalcollections.library.mcgill.ca/index.php/w-Steed Accessed May 15, 2023.
106 See for example his letters to Prime Minister Orlando in Steed Papers MS 74102 and Memoranda upon discussions ca 1918 btw Italians and South Slavs in Lodon in regard to an eventual Adriatic Agreement. Steed papers, MS 74101.
107 Steed to Signor Vittorio Orlando, June 24, 1918. Steed Papers 74101.
108 Sir Edward Grey to Steed, September 16, 1919, asking about information upon his impending travel to USA. Steed Papers, Ms 74 125.
109 Seton-Watson 1981, 211. John W. Mason, *The Dissolution of the Austro–Hungarian Empire, 1867–1918*. London–New York, Longman, 1997, 85.

## 1.5. "Efficient propaganda must be the handmaid of policy." 1916–1918

But this remained largely hidden for the outside world. The decades-long disinterest in the peninsula meant that both the British Foreign Office and the War Office had only a superficial knowledge of the peninsula, and it was therefore inevitable that the new experts should be involved, as they could provide valuable insights into the Dual Monarchy and the Balkans, which had hitherto been largely ignored.[110] In April 1918, Steed worded the Joint Declaration of the Subject Peoples of Austria-Hungary at the Rome Congress which according to Seton-Watson was "a very great success."[111] They had every reason to be satisfied, since Italy, as the first of the Entente countries, had officially embraced the programme of dissolution of the Monarchy. In addition, the joint final declaration seemed to transform the hitherto hostile Italian–South Slavic relations, as the Rome agreement recognised the legitimate national and territorial aspirations of the South Slavs.

Reliance on experts was even stronger when in January 1918 the Department of Enemy Propaganda was set up under Lord Northcliffe, also called Crewe House.[112] Steed outlined the policy: "You have got to make up your mind where and how you can hit the enemy hardest," and the only way to influence Bulgaria, Turkey, Germany by propaganda was to break the cohesion of the Austro-Hungarian Army by demoralizing actions, dropping leaflets, etc.[113] He later asserted that he had been "solely responsible" for the formulation of the policy on which the greater part of the propaganda was based (during the First World War).[114]

Toynbee was moving in the same direction. His *Nationality and the War* which appeared back in 1915 had received few courteous reviews and fairly little attention, mostly due to the escalation of the military conflict. Focus shifted to winning the war, and thus his next writings were obvious war propaganda: in his pamphlet *Subject Nationalities of the German Alliance* he asserted that four nations—"Germans, Magyars, Bulgars, and Turks"—were strategically connected through possession of the national territory of foreign subject-peoples, constituting a "nefarious league of interest to hold and extend their wrongful possessions." The fundamental tenet of Austro-Hungarian policy in this area, Toynbee opined, was to geographically isolate the Southern Slav provinces, hinder their economic development, keep them divided, poor, and uneducated, so they could

---

110 Szeghő 2024, 92–93.
111 Seton-Watson to Steed, March 30, 1918. *Korespondencija*, I/316–317, as well as Seton-Watson to May Seton-Watson, Rome, April 12, 1928, I/319–320.
112 Named after the liberal leader of the House of Lords, Robert Crewe-Milnes, whose home in Curzon Street, Mayfair, became the centre of propaganda during the First World War.
113 Steed, *Fifth Arm*, London, Constable and Company, 1940, 15–16, and Steed Papers MS 74 101, 102.
114 Steed to Frederick Whyte, April 27, 1928. Steed Papers MS 74120.

be exploited by the Germans and Magyars, and "never come into their rights as a nation." To sum up Turkish policy he quoted a Turkish gendarme during the massacres of 1915: "First we kill the Armenians, then the Greeks, and then the Kurds." The power over subject nationalities thus abused, the author was convinced, "made a moral breach" between "the four tyrant nations" and "all the free peoples in the world."[115]

The prolific year 1917 saw the publication of Toynbee's *The Murderous Tyranny of the Turks*, which claimed that the responsibility for Turkish atrocities actually lay with the Allies, Austria-Hungary and Germany. The young Turks went to a "Hungarian school," he argued, that is, they simply copied the Magyarization policy against the Romanians, Slovaks, and South Slavs. Therefore, the war grew to become a struggle against three—Prussian, Hungarian, and Turkish—"tyrants," who should not be allowed to return their territories to their pre-1914 states.[116] His further pamphlets of denunciation—*The Destruction of Poland: A Study in German Efficiency*, *The Belgian Deportations*, *The German Terror in Belgium*,[117] and *The German Terror in France*—all became apparent success. Toynbee, however, was far from pleased, and he confessed many years later: "I can remember the relief of getting out of propaganda into work where one's business once more was to find out and state the truth."[118]—

---

115 Toynbee, *Subject Nationalities of the German Alliance*, London, Cassel & Company Ltd, 1917. MS 13967/43 Diaries and offprints (quotations on pages 1, 4).
116 Toynbee, *Murderous Tyranny of the Turks*, London, Hodder & Stoughton, 13-14, 32-34. Toynbee Papers BL Oxford, MS 13967/45. Armenian Question: off-prints, pamphlets and reports.
117 The German atrocities in Belgium in 1914 he continued to believe had been "though relatively few, but the most significant in our time as they started our moral sliding, as killings were a breach of a convention which, by 1914, had been maintained for more than two centuries in Western countries. [Thus] it rightly shocked us." Toynbee to Mr Isidor Thorner (LA, California), June 3, 1970. Toynbee Papers, MS 13 967/63/1, Correspondence 1931-74. While not intentionally false, *The German Terror in Belgium* exaggerated German cruelty toward women and children and failed to refute the panic-induced assertions made by refugees, such as the claim that German forces cut off children's hands and ears in front of their shocked parents. By the end of 1915, the Bryce Report had been translated into every major European language, and it had a significant influence on public opinion in allied and neutral countries, particularly the United States. After the war, the Report's veracity was seriously questioned, which could have led to a global scepticism of "official accounts," most notably to an underestimation of Nazi atrocities during World War Two. See "Various allegations of German War Crimes in Belgium, (November-December 1914)" FO 371/1913, and Trevor Wilson, Lord Bryce's Investigation into Alleged German Atrocities in Belgium, 1914-15. *Journal of Contemporary History*. 14 (3), July 1979: 369-383.
Toynbee regretted his propaganda activity half a century later: "We were also naively sure that our cause [ ...] was one hundred percent righteous [...] we behaved irresponsibly in shutting our eyes to the possible long-term consequences of our hand-to-mouth acts." Toynbee, *Experiences*, London, Oxford University Press, 1969, 304-305.
118 Toynbee to Geoffrey M. Gathorne Hardy, March 31, 1938. Toynbee Papers MS 13 967/39 General Miscellaneous Correspondence 1911-1956.

Devastated by the violence he had witnessed in May 1917, Toynbee was invited to join the energetic team of the newly created Political Intelligence Department within the Foreign Office. He became an expert on Turkey, reporting week by week to the War Cabinet on that country and working alongside James Headlam-Morley,[119] the historical advisor to the FO, his former professor Alfred Zimmern, Lewis Namier, Rex and Allan Leeper, and in frequent communication with Steed and Seton-Watson, who reported on Austria-Hungary. All these experts upheld the principle of national self-determination and regularly contributed to *The New Europe*. No wonder that Toynbee, too, grew to advocate national self-determination (alongside the working class). In July 1918 he told his mother: "The middle class have had their fling for a century and produced this [war]; now let the working class have their try. I am for nationality at one end and internationalism at the other, as essential parts of reconstruction, and if existing states and their traditions cannot square with them, let them go to the devil, the United Kingdom and the Dual Monarchy and all of them."[120]

As is well-known, by the time Toynbee jotted down these lines, the British decision-makers had already been convinced of the necessity of dismembering Austria-Hungary; but it was not so much the result of the radical articles in the *New Europe* weekly, or Seton-Watson's analyses, or Steed's, or previously Toynbee's propaganda campaign. Rather it was due to Emperor Karl's courageous, but—owing to the formidable German pressure—failed attempt at a separate peace.[121]

---

119 As head of the Political Intelligence Department, he was close to the New Europe Group, too. At Versailles, he was the one to propose the clauses on the protection of minorities.
120 Toynbee to Edith Toynbee, July 1918. Toynbee Papers BL MS 13967/65. Family correspondence 1895-1975.
In 1918, Toynbee and his wife joined the Labour Party, which caused serious resentment in the Foreign Office, as well as in the family: Toynbee's wife lost a significant inheritance.
121 A detailed analysis on Karl's peace attempt is Tibor Frank, "C'est La Paix!"–The Sixtus Letters and The Peace Initiative of Emperor Karl I, *Hungarian Review*, Vol. VI, No. 5, September 2015. https://hungarianreview.com/article/cest-la-paix-the-sixtus-letters-and-the-peace-initiative-of-emperor-karl-i/ Accessed June 26 2023.

### 1.6. Ruins into Patterns? The Peace Conference 1919–1920

> "We toil and treasure up a hoard
> By mind, by cunning, or the sword."
> Seton-Watson[122]

> "Did you ever hear the rhyme?
> S.W. [Seton-Watson] and W.S. [Wickham Steed],
> The two of them made the hell of a mess."
> Edith Durham[123]

Amid the fall of empires and royal dynasties, as well as the birth of new countries or nations, in 1919 the Big Four set out to achieve nothing less than to fix the world, an overly ambitious task: during the 101 days of the Versailles Peace Conference, the Council of Four met 206 times and recorded 674 conclusions. The following chapter aims to provide an overview of Steed's, Seton-Watson's and Toynbee's roles in this vast project.

Early in November 1918, David Lloyd George had requested Lord Northcliffe to transfer the principal members of Crewe House Staff to Paris, where they would have their headquarters in a flat in charge of Conference publicity, while carrying on the special educative propaganda in Germany. On November 3, 1918, the day of the Padua-armistice with Austria-Hungary, Steed set out for Paris. At Lord Northcliffe's request, from January 16 onwards he wrote a leading article every day for the *Paris Daily Mail,* the only English-language morning paper available in Paris during the Peace Conference. Every morning Steed and Northcliffe also made sure that a copy of the current issue was placed on Lloyd George's and Wilson's desks. Junior officer Harold Nicolson was right to claim that the figure of the press tycoon "brooded over the Conference as a miasma."[124] From February 9, Steed became editor of the *Times,* too, keeping an eye on the paper's general policy. In addition, according to his secretary, Vernon Bartlett, the daily average number of people who came to see him during the Peace Con-

---

122 Change (excerpt). In Seton-Watson 1898, 44.
123 A rhyme the Albano-phile Edith Durham shared with historian G. P. Gooch in a letter dated December 13, 1943. Frank Eyck MSS, University of Calgary Special Collections (Calgary), Eyck 333.83.30.2.12.2. Qtd. in David Kaufman, The "One Guilty Nation" Myth: Edith Durham, R.W. Seton-Watson and a Footnote in the History of the Outbreak of the First World War, *Journal of Balkan and Near Eastern Studies,* Volume 25, 2023, Issue 3, 297–321, 298.
124 Harold Nicolson, *Peacemaking 1919,* London, Constable, 1934, 60.

## 1.6. Ruins into Patterns? The Peace Conference 1919-1920

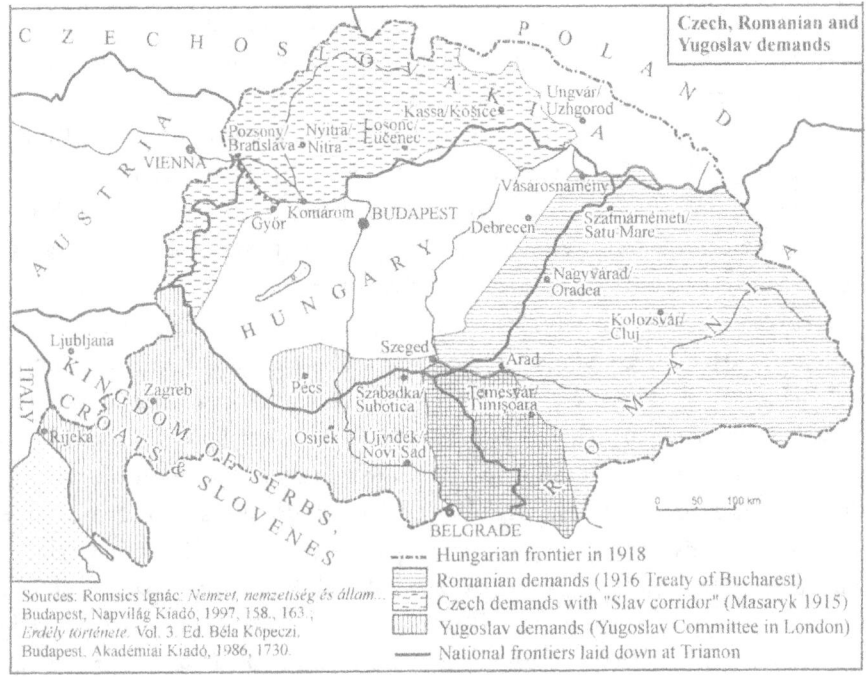

WWI Proposals concerning Hungary's Frontiers. Source: Ignác Romsics, *Hungary in the Twentieth Century*, Budapest, Corvina-Osiris, 1999, 10.

ference was 27.3; Czech, Romanian and South Slav diplomats were lobbying for their grandiose plans.[125]

In his Paris flat, Steed was soon joined by Seton-Watson, whose authority on Central-Europe was unrivalled in Britain. He put forward that "so far as there is any sacrifice it must be made by the losers rather than the winners in this war."[126] But it was far from easy. First, the Italian–South Slav rivalry lingered on well into the opening of the conference and even beyond. It is enough to quote the strongly-Slavophile president of a provisional inter-allied Danube Commission, Ernest Troubridge (1862–1926) in a letter to Steed on March 4, 1919:

For four years I have laboured in pursuit of the fulfilment of our British policy- to create [...] a strong Slav State [...] as a buffer between the Teutonic Group and our Near and Far Eastern Possessions and interests [...] now fulfilment is almost complete, it is extremely disturbing that Italy with vehemence beyond

---

125 Steed to Reginald Coggeshall (undated, an answer to RC's letter dated November 12 1938), Steed MS 74131
126 Seton-Watson, *War and Democracy*, London, MacMillan & Co, 1919, 272.

parallel [...] is endeavouring to bring our efforts to nought [...]. In Czechoslovakia Italian officers of the Slovak army endeavour to seduce the Slovaks from their allegiance to new state, in Hungary and Bulgaria the Italian fraternisation is, open and unashamed [together with] Italian propaganda in Croatia, Dalmatia, Montenegro [...] if Italy succeeds there stands nothing between the Teutonic lands and our possessions. It is dangerous that we make no protest against this.[127]

The second problem craving Seton-Watson's and Steed's cautious mediation was the constant clash between the two rival South Slav nationalism. The two Croatian émigrés, Frano Supilo, who had long been viewed in the Foreign Office as the foremost expert on South Slav affairs, and the Dalmatian Ante Trumbić both envisaged a new state based on legal equality and constitutional foundations. Serbian prime minister Nikola Pašić, on the other hand, regarded the future united state as an extension and continuation of Serbian authority and institutions. He, along with the majority of Serbian delegates, found the name "Yugoslavia" offensive and believed it to be part of the Grand Croatian Catholic-scheme to destroy Serbian identity and statehood. In a joint Croato–Serb declaration, the term "the Kingdom of Serbs, Croats, and Slovenes" was eventually approved by both Pašić and Trumbić: it contained the word "Serb" but also the guarantees that it would not be a Greater Serbia.[128] For Seton-Watson and Steed, the Declaration seemed to be the triumph of reconciliation between the domineering Pašić and the idealist Trumbić. However, it was more like an armistice; neither politician renounced his own concept of a South Slav state. The structural contradiction between the centralist and federalist state-concepts thus lingered on to erupt in the future.

Interestingly, in 1918–1919 Seton-Watson considered both the Croats and the Slovenes unprepared for separate, fully independent statehood, but more suited to lead the united country owing to their more "western" character.[129] As a result, the new state of Yugoslavia, or first, the Kingdom of the Serbs, Croats and Slovenes, was reminiscent of the former multi-ethnic Dual Monarchy that had vanished at the end of the First World War. The varied traditions, religious beliefs, and historical experience of its people soon became another source of escalating conflict and strife.[130]

---

127 Ernest Troubridge to Steed, March 4, 1919. Steed Papers, MS 74125
128 Zdenko Zlatar, The Yugoslav Idea and the First Common State of the South Slavs, *Nationalities Papers* 25/2, 1997, 387–406, 396.
129 Stephen Clissold (ed.), *A Short History of Yugoslavia*, Cambridge, 1966, 167.
130 Giuseppe Motta, The Birth of Yugoslavia: A Vision from Italy, 1918-20. In: Srđan Rudić, Antonello Biagini (eds.), *Serbian–Italian Relations: History and Modern Times*, Požega, The Institute of History Belgrade and Sapienza University of Rome, 2015, 142.

As regards Czechoslovakia and Romania, the two British experts most closely working on their new frontiers were junior diplomats Harold Nicolson and Allen Leeper. In room 108 of the Paris Astoria Hotel, they were busy processing and organising the vast amount of material on the Danube and Balkan border disputes, working as the most valuable and tireless assistants to Sir Eyre Crowe (1864–1925), then Assistant Under-Secretary of State. On February 4, 1919, Leeper was appointed to the Romanian territorial claims commission, which coincided with his main area of expertise, and Nicolson was assigned to the Czechoslovak commission, despite the fact that he considered himself inexperienced and totally unprepared.[131]

Both former Balliol College students were closely linked to Seton-Watson and the New Europe circle. Leeper, who had a rare talent for languages[132] and was unflinchingly pro-Romanian,[133] described his first encounter with the "master" as follows:

> The conversation was tremendously interesting. Seton-Watson knows everyone worth knowing in Hungarian, Serbo-Croatian, Rumanian and Čech political circles. He is a charming man and most friendly. I was able to keep the conversation going from my fairly thorough knowledge of events in 1915, but I was of course just a child with him. And most of the little knowledge I have is based on his books [...].[134]

---

[131] Nicolson 1934, 33. For a comparative analysis of Leeper's and Nicolson's roles in the peace process, with particular reference to the later assessment of their activities, see: Ágnes Beretzky, In Close Tandem? The Parallel Biographies of Harold Nicolson (1886–1968) and Allen Leeper (1887–1935), *Orpheus Noster* 15: 3, 2023, 25–35.

[132] In addition to Western languages, he also read Hebrew, Russian, Czech, Serbian, Romanian, Bulgarian and Hungarian: fifteen languages in all. Nicolson, Allen Leeper, *The Nineteenth Century and After, Annual Bulletin of Historical Literature*, October 1935, 477.

[133] The London-born actress Bessie Richard was Ionescu's first spouse. His parents were adamantly against the relationship since they wanted their son to marry a girl from an affluent family, but they were powerless to stop the marriage. As a result, they disinherited him and broke off contact for a long time. https://dosaresecrete.ro/iubirile-lui-take-ionescu-bessie-richards-si-adina-olmazu/ Accessed April 28, 2023.
Leeper was close to the unwaveringly anglophile Romanian Conservative politician Take Ionescu, the founder of the Council of Romanian National Unity, one of the select few to receive first-name billing in Leeper's diary, and the Romanian ambassador in London, Nicolae Mişu. Leeper to his father, Alexander Leeper, January 26, 1919. Allen Leeper Papers, University of Cambridge, Churchill Archives Centre, [further on: Leeper Papers] 3/9. For Leeper's pro-Romanian stance see his *Justice of Rumania's Cause*, London, Hodder and Stoughton, 1917.

[134] Leeper to his father, Alexander Leeper, February 3, 1916. Hugh Seton-Watson, Cornelia Bodea (eds.), *R.W. Seton-Watson and the Romanians 1906-1920*, Bucharest, 1988, Vol. I/558.

# 1. Steed, Seton-Watson and Toynbee on National Self-Determination

The official border proposal of the British peace delegation regarding Hungary, presented in Paris in February 1919, was duly based on the Seton-Watson Memorandum of December 1918, but its most positive feature, the concept of the ethnically disputable territories, the so-called "gray zones," was abolished, except for the Austro-Hungarian border, since no on-the-spot investigations had taken place until then, and there was no prospect for them to be carried out in the future. By comparison, to settle the Italo-Yugoslav dispute, in a Memorandum written around the same time, most probably by Seton-Watson, it is suggested that the "gray" zones be applied between the two lines, and that an expert commission be instructed to draw the final frontier after advice by men with knowledge of the local topography.[135]

Thus, although the border line proposed by the British left the island southeast of Pozsony (Pressburg, Prešporok) called Grosse Schütt (Csallóköz, Veľký Žitný ostrov) with Hungary, it followed the Danube and River Ipoly from Komárom (Komárno): the deviation from the ethnic boundary was justified for economic reasons in the west (free access to the Danube) and in the east by the need for uninterrupted rail links between Romania and Czechoslovakia. The Romanian border also ran within the "gray zone," separating from Hungary Szatmárnémeti (Satu Mare), Arad and the north-western part of Banat, again the importance of rail links was cited. In comparison, the Yugoslav-Hungarian border along the Zombor (Sombor)-Danube-Drave line was considered ethnically relatively fair.[136] One of the signatories of the document was Harold Nicolson, who confessed in his memoirs:

> My feelings toward Hungary were less detached. I confess that I regarded and still regard that Turanian tribe with acute distaste. Like their cousins the Turks, they had destroyed much and created nothing. Budapest was a false city devoid of any autochthonous reality. For centuries the Magyars had oppressed their subject nationalities. The hour of liberation and retribution was at hand.

As for the roots of his convictions about the reconstruction of Europe, he was in agreement with Leeper and acknowledged that he had been "overwhelmingly imbued" with the doctrines put forward by *The New Europe*, to which he had devoted diligent study.[137]

---

135 Seton-Watson's Memorandum, February 5, 1919, Paris. *Korespondencija*, II/30–31.
136 Seton-Watson, Hungary: Frontier Delineation between Hungary and Her Neighbours, Public Records Office, Political Intelligence Department, No. P.O. 52, f. 301-311.
137 Nicolson 1934, 34 and 33.

As is well known, it was not only the historical borders of Bohemia and Moravia that were seen as justified but the Danube frontier, too, including the overwhelmingly German Pressburg as the new Slovak capital, renamed as Bratislava, together with, among others, the Hungarian-inhabited Grosse Schütt. The latter went against Nicolson's convictions: "It is heart-breaking to have to support a claim with which I disagree. I am anxious about the future political complexion of the Czech State if they have to digest solid enemy electorates [...],"[138] he wrote in his diary. In fact, gaining the loyalty of the roughly 15 million people who made up the population proved to be a difficult undertaking: along with the Czechs and Slovaks, some three million Germans, 890,000 Hungarians, around 500,000 Ruthenians, and some 75,000 Poles were also included inside the borders of Czechoslovakia.

Unlike Nicolson, Leeper had no second thoughts about the future frontiers of Romania, which, in Nicolson's words, finally obtained "all and more than all."[139] Due to its 55 percent Romanian majority, Transylvania was annexed by Romania along with Bessarabia (being two thirds Romanian). The British and French placed a strong emphasis on economic viability in the region to the west of Transylvania, called the Partium, giving Romania a sizable strip that included the Magyar towns of Arad, Nagyvárad (Oradea), and Szatmárnémeti (Satu Mare). The hard-working diplomat attended every meeting of the respective Boundary Commissions set up to finalise the borders, and he usually managed to convince the other delegates who proposed a more favourable settlement for Hungary or—to a lesser extent—for Yugoslavia. In Paris, Leeper was by no means an intellectual hermit. His unflinching support for Romanian interests was a reflection of his affiliation with Robert Seton-Watson's and Steed's *New Europe*.

In 1919, the then-thirty-year-old Toynbee was sent to Paris as a pro-Greek member of the Turkey section of the British Delegation to the Peace Conference, where his presence was considered "really vital" for Greek and Armenian minorities.[140] He rented an apartment with his wife in November 1918 in the hope that he would help bring about peace as a specialist in the Foreign Office. His

---

138 Nicolson 1934, 279.
    By May 1919, Seton-Watson, on the other hand, did not oppose the annexation of Hungarian Grosse Schütt to Czechoslovakia. Seton-Watson to Headlam-Morley, May 26, 1919. Géza Jeszenszky, "The British Role in Assigning Csallóköz (Žitný ostrov, Grosse Schütt) to Czechoslovakia." In Péter László, Martyn Rady (eds.), 2004, 123–138, 133.
139 Nicolson 1934, 137.
140 Ronald Burrows to Toynbee, April 20, 1919, MS 13 967/39 General Miscellaneous Correspondence 1911–1956.

initial excitement soon faded, and in March 1919, he bitterly admitted that he was "gloomy" about the Conference: "A sort of paralysis has come over it: the top gets more and more out of touch with the bottom (at any rate in our delegation and the American)—and the different Powers with one an-other. [...] The outlook for relations between Europe and the East is very bleak."[141] The main reason for his pessimism was that almost all of his expert suggestions were turned down by the plenipotentiaries, most notably the one arguing that Smyrna (Izmir) and the surrounding district ought not to be separated from Turkey. He had been given the job of suggesting the boundaries of a possible Greek enclave around Smyrna. The plan was a geographical absurdity, he recalled, and it was not until he visited the then Greek-occupied area in 1921 that he realised how small the Greek minority was, even within the area that he had delimited. He remembered getting letters from consular, naval and military authorities at Smyrna "all pleading unanimously; much best to send no troops to Smyrna," but if necessary, "send troops of any nationality other than the Greeks." These telegrams, Toynbee recalled bitterly, had been ignored by the men who took the final decision.[142]

Owing to his inability to influence conference outcomes, Toynbee departed Paris permanently in April 1919, while simultaneously suffering a nervous breakdown and depression. This was partially caused by his frustration with Versailles and the futility of his work, but the reasons were more deeply rooted. After the First World War began, as we have seen, twenty-five-year-old Toynbee requested an exemption from military service on the grounds that he had consumed tainted water in Crete in 1912, which led to dysentery. The fact that he escaped the war still haunted him. "Just at my back in the study, [there is] a row of photographs of schoolfellows of mine, killed in the 1914-1918 war. This is for me [...] a constant reminder, and it grows more poignant with each year that is added to my already long life."[143] According to his biographer, William H. McNeill, Toynbee's frenetic pace of work was the only way he felt he could repay his debt of survival to those who had died in the trenches.[144]

---

141 Toynbee to Edith Toynbee, March 24, 1919. Toynbee Papers BL MS 13967/65. Family correspondence 1895-1975. See also McNeill 1989, 81.
142 Toynbee to Mr Walworth, Massachusetts, August 23, 1968. Toynbee Papers BL Oxford MS13967/86 Correspondence.
143 Toynbee to Professor George Panichas, October 23, 1969. Toynbee Papers, BL MS 13 967/128/1 Reviews and Correspondence 1915-1970.
144 Toynbee himself drew the attention of the authorities to his previous illness, so his biographer regards it as evidence that he did not really want to enlist. Dysentery recurred neither in 1914 nor later. McNeill 1989, 67-71.

## 1.6. Ruins into Patterns? The Peace Conference 1919-1920

On the fifth anniversary of the June 28, 1914 assassination of Archduke Franz Ferdinand and his wife in Sarajevo, the Treaty of Versailles was signed, followed by subsequent treaties with the former enemy states. The territory of East-Central Europe and beyond was completely recast: two new states were born, Czechoslovakia and the Kingdom of the Serbs, Croats and Slovenes (the future Yugoslavia) , with an enlarged Romania, an independent Poland and an independent Austria, as well as a somewhat smaller Bulgaria together with a much-diminished Hungary, and a, for a while similarly truncated, Turkey. (Interestingly, Montenegro became the only victorious First World War "little allied" state to lose its statehood.) A glance at the map in 2024, nevertheless reveals that none of these once allied states exists in the form in which they were created in 1919-20. So, rather than drawing borders in Middle Europe or elsewhere, Versailles' most long-lasting legacy may be the founding of a significant organization, the British, subsequently Royal Institute of International Affairs (RIIA), or Chatham House.[145]

In May 1919, twenty-eight members of the British and American Delegations who were not permanent officials, including Colonel House, Henry White, General Tasker H Bliss, Lord Cecil, Headlam-Morley and Lionel Curtis as well as Arnold Toynbee and others met at the Hotel Majestic.[146] Their aim was to engage continuously in informed debate, whether in peacetime or in war, by creating an informed public opinion on international affairs. To meet this aim—as Philip Kerr, David Lloyd George's secretary (1916-1923) argued—one needed "representative and authoritative" membership, a "political" but "not partisan"[147] executive committee, and last but not least, a stable budget.[148] On July 20, 1920, within three

---

A few months into his job as Director of RIIA, H. Crichton Miller, a Scottish physician and psychiatrist, the founder of the Tavistock Clinic informed James W. Headlam-Morley that Toynbee looked so overworked that rest was imperative, adding: "I doubt whether he can last out to the end of his job without a break down, a week rest." H. Crichton Miller to Headlam-Morley, February 19, 1925. RIIA Archives 4/TOYN/1.

145 British Institute of International Affairs (1919-1925) and subsequently as Royal Institute of International Affairs (1926-). G.M. Gathorne-Hardy and Lionel Curtis became the joint secretaries of the Institute. The US sister institute was called the Council of Foreign Relations.
146 Michael L. Dockrill, The Foreign Office and the 'Proposed Institute of Intenational Affairs 1919'. In: Andrea Bosco, Cornelia Navari 1994, *Chatham House and British Foreign Policy 1919-1945: The Royal Institute of International Affairs During the Inter-war Period*, London, Lothian Foundation Press, 1994, 74.
147 As late as 1970, Toynbee could state confidently that Chatham House's role was to act as a venue for the presentation and debate of other people's perspectives and that it had "no version of its own." Toynbee, "Was Britain's Abdication Folly?" The Round Table, 1970. 60:238, 219-228, DOI: 10.1080/00358537008452875221."221.
148 Archives of the Royal Institute of International Affairs, Chatham House, London [hereafter: RIIA Archives]. 4/Loth, Kerr to Lord Cecil, March 20, 1920. Kerr continued to play an active role in the affairs of the Institute. On this see Andrew Crozier, Chatham House and Appeasement. In: Bosco-Navari 1994, 208-221.

months of the inaugural meeting, the British Institute of International Affairs was established with 756 members, an annual survey and a quarterly journal.[149]

## 1919: Macartney in Hungary

While Steed, Seton-Watson and Toynbee were busy making peace in the French capital, Macartney arrived in Budapest. As a child, in the corner of school library, he had spent long hours reading a wonderfully illustrated geography of the Hungarian Kingdom, a vast and fascinating land he had been adamant to visit. One thing is certain: the young man could not have found a more inopportune time to fulfil his long-cherished dream than the autumn of 1919: economically exhausted by a lost war, on the verge of disintegration, with its neighbours trying to carve out an ever-larger part of it and Romanian soldiers marching through its capital,[150] the country could hardly have been anything but disappointing. "The little patch in the centre, the rainswept desolation on which the gypsies had camped, seemed to be Hungary still," he recollected.[151]

Maxwell, his only older brother by fifteen years, was at the time a well-known Vienna correspondent for the *Times* and an expert on Eastern Europe and the Balkans.[152] He invited Macartney to Vienna and helped launch his diplomatic career as the British vice-consul there between 1921 and 1925. In Vienna the young historian fell in love with and married Nedella Mamarchev (1899–1989), the daughter of Bulgarian Colonel Dimitri Mamarchev. She became an interwar expert on Bulgaria and due, among other things, to her knowledge of Slavic languages a support in her husband's academic career.[153]

---

149 Soon arose a conflict of interest with the Foreign Office, Sir Eyre Cowe as well as Lord Curzon doubted Foreign Office participation in the Institute "whose main object is the free interchange of opinions and propagation of opinion upon Foreign Policy matters," arguing that excepting the prime minister, the secretary of state ought to be "the sole mouthpiece of the Government in matters of Foreign Policy." Curzon to Balfour, July 28, 1919, FO 608/162. Qtd. in Bosco-Navari 1994, 80.
150 Romania occupied a greater part of Hungary, including its capital from August 1, 1919. Despite ultimata by the Council of the Four, the systematic confiscation of goods, grain crops, livestock, transport and rail vehicles was not terminated and the full withdrawal of the army from Hungarian territory occurred only in April 1920. Edward Woodward, -Rohan Butler, *Documents on British Foreign Policy, 1919-1939*, London, First Series, Vol. II, 1948, 289–293.
151 Macartney, Hungaria Aeterna, *The Hungarian Quarterly (HQ)*, 1936/1, 50.
152 Between 1932–38 there was a sporadic correspondence between Maxwell Macartney and József Balogh, the editor of *Hungarian Quarterly*. See OSZK KT Fond 1/2065-2067.
153 See her Chatham House Lecture titled "The Situation in Bulgaria" on January 30, 1933. The Russian-born, Oxford-educated scholar Isaiah Berlin called her "noxious." Berlin to Sheila Grant Duff, October 18, 1937. Henry Hardy (ed), *Isaiah Berlin: Letters*, Vol. 1, 1928-1946, Cambridge University Press, 2004, 60.

During his years as vice-consul in Vienna, Macartney met some prominent right-wing members of the opposition who had found refuge from the Hungarian Soviet Republic. They included Gyula Szekfű, who was doing research in the Austrian capital in the early twenties and soon introduced Mcartney to Hungarian sources and became a lifelong friend.[154]

---

[154] An exchange of letters between the two friends can be found in OSZK KT Fond 7/1271 and Eötvös Loránd Tudományegyetem, Egyetemi Könyvtár és Levéltár KT [Eötvös Loránd University Library and Archives Manuscript Archives], Budapest. G628/3.

# 2. "This new order has come to stay": From Versailles to Paris (1920–1947)

## 2.1. "Peace as a Conquest": The League of Nations Union

After the Congress of Vienna (1815), which ended the Napoleonic Wars, the so-called "European Concert," a consensus, was established at the initiative of William Pitt Jr, the British prime minister, which provided for regular consultation of the great powers on any event that might disturb the status quo. By staying away from the Vienna congresses, Britain tried to play the European powers off against each other and maintain the balance. In 1920, the United States was essentially repeating what Britain had done a century earlier, and the United Nations, President Wilson's dream that had been created to preserve world peace and promote international cooperation, suffered a serious loss of prestige because of his country's absence. Thus, in the words of William Medlicott, Britain and France were left to fend for themselves "as the embarrassed nursemaids of a rather endearing spastic infant, the product of some injudicious international lovemaking."[1]

Besides the USA refused to join the League of Nations, the organisation was left without an effective armed force, which put the stability of the organization in jeopardy and raised questions about the usefulness of the guarantees it provided. France and the Little Entente states were primarily interested in maintaining the status quo, and they were fully convinced that even the slightest change to the balance of the system could endanger it. As a result, they were adamantly opposed to any concession or compromise that would not only result in their loss of prestige but would also weaken their power position.

---

[1] William Norton Medlicott, *Contemporary England 1914-1964*, London, Longmans, 1967, 109.

## 2. From Versailles to Paris (1920-1947)

Despite such shortcomings, many Britons had great faith in the League, as well as in its sister-organisation, the League of Nations Union (LNU), especially in their ability to maintain global peace. The LNU was established in Great Britain in October 1918 with the goal of advancing the objectives of the League of Nations, including international justice, collective security, and a lasting peace between nations through education and raising awareness. By the middle of the 1920s, the organisation had over a quarter of a million registered subscribers, making it the largest and most powerful organization in the British peace movement.[2] Toynbee claimed that there had never been a time in human history "when people tried so hard, so persistently to establish a world-order."[3] In the first two *Surveys*, 1920-23 and 1924, his commitment to the League of Nations and what may loosely be called a liberal policy is clearly evident: he became a prominent public proponent of the League of Nations from the early 1920s, more because of the principle of collective security that it advocated than because he held any enthusiasm for its institutions. Originally, Steed, too, was a zealous supporter, describing himself as "a militant sort of peace-monger" when he, together with Gilbert Murray, Toynbee's father-in-law, had joined the LNU group, which he was convinced was "the best means of preventing war in the future."[4]

In 1918, as member of the LNU Executive, Steed was also instrumental in collating an optimistic booklet arguing that following the "dream of intensified nationality," the world awoke to a new system of realities: permanent peace should and could be organised based on a general agreement, the alternative of which was "the preparation for war [...], which must [...] destroy civilization." The authors concluded that it was not nationality that the League of Nations threatened but "power obsession," the product of the competitive European courts of the eighteenth century, which had used national feeling in an entirely Machiavellian spirit.[5] However, by the time the booklet was pub-

---

[2] A detailed analysis of the birth and role of the LNU can be found in Donald S. Birn, *The League of Nations Union*, Oxford, Clarendon Press, 1981.

[3] Toynbee, "World Order or Downfall?" Six Broadcast Talks BBC, November 10-December 15, 1930, 4th talk: The Abolition of War, December 1, 1930. Toynbee Papers BL Oxford MS13 967/6 Broadcasts 1929-1955.

[4] Steed, however, added that when some pacifists joined forces and attempted to make the agenda "pacifically sanctimonious and muddleheaded," he quit out of disbelief in the promotion of peace "by pious resolutions and inter-national goody-goodiness." In: "Steed and League of Nations Union." Carbon copy of material supplied to the BBC used by Stephen Watson as a background for questions. April 1953. Steed Papers MS 74186.

[5] H.G. Wells, in collaboration with Viscount Grey, Lionel Curtis, William Archer, A Zimmern, J.A. Spender, Viscount Bryce, G Murray and, H.W. Steed, *The Idea of the League of Nations*, Boston, Atlantic Monthly Press, 1919, 8, 39. https://babel.hathitrust.org/cgi/pt?id=hvd.32044098467368&view=1up&seq=40&skin=2021 Accessed April 4, 2023.

lished, simultaneously with his appointment as editor of the *Times*, Steed had dropped out of LNU Executive and never rejoined it, despite LNU Chairman Gilbert Murray's firm request.⁶

Although Steed recalled later that the "crusade" for lasting peace had been "the most wonderful and the most worthwhile" act,⁷ since the mid-1920s, he turned against what he termed "the intolerable goody-goodiness of its [LNU] partisans [insular philistines] who play upon deep dislike of British people for any thought of war, something in between a prayer-meeting and international pacifist picnic [...], which has made normally constituted people vomit."; if peace is worth having it is worth taking risks for, working for and fighting for.⁸ Fundamental to Steed's arguments stood two firm beliefs: the need for British–US close cooperation to preserve international peace together with reliance on the rule of law in countering the transgressors of peace by applying sanctions. Steed grew to be critical of the belief that collective security and arms reduction were possible simultaneously by pinning all hopes on the League. Instead, he supported a view of defence that was as strong and as unified as possible through consultations with the dominions as well as by applying a sensible level of arms spending. He was soon joined by naval expert Sir Herbert Richmond, Downing-Street-secretary Sir Edward Grigg, and Esme Howard, the former consul general to Budapest, with whom, however, he did not see eye to eye on Hungary.⁹

After 1933 the role of the League of Nations diminished, and after 1933 Steed was among the first to grow disillusioned. Instead of backing the institution, he tended to engage himself in private matters, for example, he joined the protest against the political persecution of former *Schutzbund* leaders on charges of high treason, this time with Toynbee's father-in-law, Professor Murray, Macartney, and Noel-Buxton.¹⁰

Unlike Steed, or Toynbee, Macartney was employed by the British League of Nations Union and the Intelligence Department of the League of Nations, and he published extensively between 1928 and 1934 in addition to promoting the activities of the League of Nations. The studies contain many optimistic statements about the role, importance and future of the League of Nations and the LNU, such as, it was " the first time in history the art of peace is taught on an

---

6 G. Murray to Steed, February 8, 1928. Steed Papers, MS 74 127, and Steed to Murray, February 9, 1928. Steed Papers MS 74 127.
7 Steed to James Garvin, Editor of *Observer*, December 30, 1926. Steed Papers MS 74126.
8 HWS to Colonel House, April 18, 1925. Steed Papers MS 74126.
9 Steed, Howard and Richmond to the Editor of the *Times*, December 19, 1933, and March 28, 1934, and B.J.C. McKercher, *Esme Howard: A Diplomatic Biography*, Cambridge University Press, 1989, 364.
10 "Austrian Treason Charges," *Daily Telegraph*, April 1, 1935, 7, and *Manchester Guardian*, April 1, 1935, 18.

organised basis," or "the indirect work and influence [of LNU...] increases every year,"[11] or the League's scheme of reforms contributed to "the phenomenal progress of Austria,"[12] etc. However, Macartney, a man of remarkable social sensitivity, could not fail to notice the fundamentally unresolved situation of the major losers as a result of the post-Versailles order, the minorities, their legitimate grievances and their possible redress by revision.[13] The most enduring part of his work in the LNU was concerned with exploring these issues, but that is the subject of a later chapter.

## 2.2. Politics, Propaganda and the University: I

October 9, 1915, was the day Masaryk, the exiled academic from the University of Prague, delivered a public lecture at King's College titled "The Problem of Small Nations in the European Crisis," and it has long been acknowledged as the founding date of the School of Slavonic and East European Studies (SSEES).[14] In less than a year, Ronald Burrows, co-founder of *The New Europe* as well as principal of King's College (1913–1920), could boast that his institution became "the chief centre in London for lectures of this political kind," and owing to the "scandalous" lack of teaching of Romanian in England, he raised the question of a Romanian lectureship to Nicolae Mişu, the Romanian minister to London, to be financed either by the Romanian government or private individuals.[15] During the war, the School unapologetically endorsed the principle of national self-de-

---

11   Macartney et al., *The International Federation of League of Nations Societies*, League of Nations Union, April 1933, 5. In: C.A. Macartney, League of Nations Union [Macartney LNU]: Miscellaneous Pamphlets, Vols. 1–10, British Library, 3685–3805.
12   Macartney et al., *What the League has done for Austria*, May 1934, 12. Macartney LNU: Miscellaneous Pamphlets Vols 1–10 British Library 3685–3805.
13   As in Macartney, *Minorities*, A LNU Pamphlet, London, January1929. Macartney LNU: Miscellaneous Pamphlets Vol. 4. British Library 3685–3805; Macartney et al. *A Memorandum on the Protection of Minorities*. (A Recommendation to HM's Government), London, 1934. Macartney LNU: Miscellaneous Pamphlets Vol. 6. British Library 3685–3805; Macartney et al. *Treaty Revision and the Covenant of League of Nations*, 1933. Macartney LNU: Miscellaneous Pamphlets Vol. 6. British Library 3685–3805.
14   Andrea Orzoff, *Battle for the Castle The Myth of Czechoslovakia in Europe, 1914–1948*, Oxford, Oxford University Press, 2009, 44.
15   "It would have political consequences of considerable importance if we could at this juncture found such a chair." Burrows to Nicolae Mişu, September 8, 1916. Mişu politely responded on September 15: "I shall take the first opportunity to go further with you into this matter." As a result, the teaching of Romanian language and history had already begun in 1919, and by 1925 the Romanian government had provided funding for three posts at the institute. H. Bodea, Seton-Watson (eds.), 1988, I/ 418 and 557; and Peter Sherwood, Magyar stúdiumok Londonban [Hungarian studies in London], *Hungarológia 1*, 1993, 111–121, 112.

termination. After Romania's entry into war and Seton-Watson's public lecture at King's on the country and Transylvania in October 1916, Burrows sent the following message to the University of Bucharest:

> Great gathering of University of London assembled at King's College to hear address on Rumania [...] sends warmest greetings to University of Bucharest, and enthusiastic good wishes for victory of gallant Rumanian army and liberation of Transylvania from intolerable foreign yoke. Linked inseparably to heroic France, and firm allies of Italy and Portugal, we rejoice that yet another of the Latin nations has drawn the sword in the cause of freedom. We pledge ourselves to loyal comradeship in arms, and we look forward to ever-growing intimacy between Great Britain and Rumania.[16]

In fact, its two most notable founders, former Liverpool Professor of Russian History, Bernard Pares and especially Seton-Watson, assisted in urging His Majesty's Government to support the liberation of small nations.

As a result of the victory in the war, those like Masaryk and Beneš became convinced that their cosmopolitan, enlightened view of Czech history and nationalism had always been correct. The "Czechoslovak modern national narrative" became the focal point of Czechoslovak cultural diplomacy: in 1918 Czechoslovakia was saved from the Austro-Hungarian oppressors, making itself a safe haven for "democratic values, rationalism, and fair-mindedness" in the much-troubled region of East Central Europe. Masaryk, Beneš, and those close to them understood the immeasurable worth of Western public support and made a conscious effort to develop lasting connections with Western elites. For instance, twenty-six French newspapers, press outlets, and radio stations were supervised by the Czechoslovak Foreign Ministry,[17] which, alongside Romania, and Yugoslavia, contributed a portion of the income of the School of Slavonic and East European Studies up until the end of World War II. In the autumn of 1922, the Masaryk Chair in Central European History was at last established at University College London, and was first held, not surprisingly, by Seton-Watson.

During the same month, the new proprietor of the *Times*, John Jacob Astor, intended to keep in his own hands the direct and absolute political control of the paper, which was incompatible with the presence of so strong a personal-

---

16  "Events Leading to Rumania's Entry into War." *The Christian Science Monitor,* Boston, Massachusetts, November 11, 1916. Qtd. in H. Seton-Watson-Bodea, Vol. II, 722.
17  Orzoff 2009, 145–147.

## 2. From Versailles to Paris (1920–1947)

ity as Steed in the editorial chair.[18] In need of a fresh start, thanks to a recommendation from Seton-Watson Steed was finally offered a position as the Romanian department chair at SSEES, originally Burrows's idea back in 1916 but never realised. In 1925 Steed became "only" "a Lecturer in Central European History with Special Reference to Romania and the Near East," which lasted until 1938. He quickly endorsed what Seton-Watson stated in his Inauguration Lecture "The Historian as a Political Force in Central Europe":

> Finally, the Great War brought home to the general consciousness the need for mutual interpretation November 1922 London University between nation and nation, and at the same time the crying need for a basis of sound historical knowledge in the statesmen who settle the world's affairs. [...] The commonplace according to which the past is a key to the present is true to every country and period, its opposite, namely the present as key to the past is peculiarly true of Central- and Central-East Europe.[19]

From 1920 onwards, as holders of major academic positions, Seton-Watson and Steed both worked very hard to serve "the present," that is the new post-1920 European order, by (re)interpreting "the past" in two ways: first, by debunking several widely held beliefs about the Treaty of Versailles in order to justify the righteousness of the peace settlement. They referred to "the myth of uninformed specialists" as the first and primary of these beliefs, vehemently asserting that "there never was a more unjust and foolish mare's nest put forward than the allegation as to ignorant experts. For months Allen Leeper, Nicolson and a number of others, and the bevy of brilliant Americans were bombarded with material of all kinds from the most opposite and conflicting sources, and steered a steady and unflinching course through them all."[20] If experts were not ignorant, statesmen did seem so, at least according to Steed's own account: "[...] informants at the sittings of the Grand Committee: proceedings are often very comical. They are like classes in the primary school. Wilson, L.G. and Pi-

---

18 Steed Papers MS 74120.
19 Seton-Watson, The Historian as a Political Force in Central-Europe, An Inaugural Lecture Delivered before the University of London, November 22, 1922, 5 and 16.
20 Seton-Watson, Allen Leeper, *Slavonic and East European Review*, April 1935, 684–685. He added that those were ignorant, in Seton-Watson's term, "very well-meaning but inadequately informed" people who envisaged the conclusion of peace on terms which would not give the oppressed races of the Danubian area their full freedom, but would ensure some kind of federalisation of Austria-Hungary." Seton-Watson, "Austria and Her Neighbours," *Slavonic and East European Review*, April 1935, 554.

chon constantly take lessons in geography and appear greatly to admire people [...] who can pronounce outlandish names without stuttering, and actually know off-hand what places the names refer to.[21]

The second "myth" that Seton-Watson and Steed sought to dispel was the idea that Austria-Hungary had been overthrown "from the outside," with the idea being that new states had emerged prior to the Peace Conference and even before the armistice without the help of Allied forces as a result of spontaneous national movements that had swept the previous system. Hence, in their opinion, the role of the Allies had been limited to ratifying accomplished facts.

Seton-Watson's and Steed's second interwar academic activity did not limit itself only to defending the 1919–1920 treaties but also included the creation of such subsequent historical analyses that were to further justify the necessity of creating Czechoslovakia, Yugoslavia and enlarged Romania. As Steed put forward to Seton-Watson:

> It is far too commonly assumed that the unific of Yugoslav race, like the creation of the new order in Central and South-Eastern Europe, was an unhappy accident arising from the unfortunate dismemberment of the venerable Habsburg Monarchy. People need to learn that it was no accident but the outcome of historical forces which were too powerful even for the statesmen at the Paris Peace Conference to resist. This new European order has come to stay. [...] I personally, should welcome close associations between Yugoslav Society and kindred bodies in this country for the purpose of enabling our people to understand that the unification of Yugoslavia, Czechoslovakia, Roumania and Poland were among the beneficent results of the war."[22]

Thus, the former supporters of national self-determination sought to refute the historical arguments put forward by the 1920 Hungarian Delegation, which that relied on the historical right of Hungarian presence in the Danube basin coupled with moral superiority, which, as Steed opined, "consists not only in claiming it, but in practising it so that it may be spontaneously recognised by others."[23]

Yet perhaps what East-Central Europe lacked back then was spontaneity itself. Instead, it appeared that the Successor States' every move was the result of highly premeditated decisions. As Zsolt Nagy so aptly put it:

---

21  Steed Memorandum, February 4, 1919, *Korespondencija*, II/29.
22  Steed to Seton-Watson, March 12, 1928. Steed Papers, MS 74 127.
23  Steed to Ferenc Hampel, May 22, 1921. OSZK KT Fond VIII 2346.

Intellectuals and politicians mobilized their respective countries' cultural capital in order to gain essential Western support for their foreign policy goals. The borders between scholarship and politics evaporated as scholars became members of parliaments and politicians found themselves in lecture halls. In this mobilization, academic institutions became fortresses, scholarly publications turned into weapons, and scholars left their ivory towers to become warriors.[24]

Hungary was relatively slow to wake up after the trauma caused by Trianon. Alongside Czechoslovakia and Romania, but some six years later, the leading politicians and public personae also approached London University with the idea to establish a Hungarian chair as well as to ask Macartney to take it. He felt very much honoured, noting,"I imagine that *in my case* the holder of the position of which you speak about would not be wanted to [...] mix in controversial political problems of today—and do not indeed think that London University would admit such a conception of a chair."[25]

All this coincided with a letter written by Seton-Watson to Oszkár Jászi six years earlier, in which he expressed his wish ("we at University") to introduce the teaching of Hungarian language and literature, but to do so without having anything to do with the Horthy-Bethlen system.[26]

## 2.3. Politics, Propaganda and The University II: Toynbee and Graeco-Turkey 1919–1924

In line with the establishment of the School of Slavonic and East European Studies, the connection between King's College principal Ronald Burrows and the Greek prime minister, Eleftherios Venizelos (1917-20), led to the establishment of the Koraes Chair of Modern Greek and Byzantine History, Language, and Literature at King's College, London. Its first holder, Toynbee, was appointed in 1919 for a five-year tenure. With the fields of academic and political activity inextricably linked, however, conflict was soon under way.

---

24 Zsolt Nagy, *Grand Delusions: Interwar Hungarian Cultural Diplomacy, 1918-1941*, A dissertation submitted to the faculty of the University of North Carolina at Chapel Hill, Department of History. Chapel Hill, 2012, 174.
25 Macartney to conservative philosopher-political scientist László Ottlik, OSZK K Fond 7/1210, undated.
26 Seton-Watson to Oszkár Jászi, February 5, 1923. Seton-Watson Papers SEW 17/11.

In October 1920 Toynbee received two periods of paid leave from the Senate in order to visit Greece and forge academic ties that would improve the relationship between that country and the Department of Modern Greek at King's College. The fact that he would serve as a special correspondent at the invitation of the editor of the *Manchester Guardian*, C. P. Scott, was not mentioned. Neither was the fact that Toynbee had not been particularly inspired by teaching. Instead, and accompanied by his wife, he was eager to report first-hand to the British public on the war between Greek troops, which, backed up by the British, were trying to enforce the draconian Treaty of Sevres, and the Turkish nationalists defending the integrity of Anatolia.

In his reports Toynbee initially took the side of the Greeks, which met the expectations of the Greek diaspora that funded his university professorship. He was, however, eager to see the Turkish side of the conflict, too, and joined Red Crescent expeditions to the eastern shores of the Sea of Marmara. After witnessing massacres by the Greeks in the north-eastern Pontus region, he soon changed his mind and began to express pro-Turkish views, much to the surprise of British liberals who had traditionally been anti-Turkish since Gladstone. He was convinced that the *Manchester Guardian* "stood for publishing the truth, as it saw it, without fear or favour,"[27] and he even assisted in the evacuation of some of the remaining terrified Turkish refugees.

A year later in 1922, Toynbee set out to discuss his findings in more detail in his *Western Question in Greece and Turkey: A Study in the Contact of Civilisations*. In western Anatolia, he claimed, Turks and Greeks had been living peacefully side by side for half a century until seized by "fits of homicidal national hatred," which broke out among Turks in 1914 and 1916 and among local Greeks (and Armenians) after May 1919, resulting in wholesale destruction and terror.[28] The massacres, Toynbee argued, were the "extreme form of national struggle between mutually indispensable neighbours," instigated by the "fatal Western idea" of nationalism. He went on to say that the historian may ponder whether "the inoculation of the East with nationalism has not from the beginning brought in diminishing returns of happiness and prosperity."[29] One of the most important conclusions he drew from his stay was

---

27  Toynbee Papers BL Oxford MS 13 967/128/1 Reviews and Correspondence 1915-1970.
28  Twenty years later Toynbee confessed: "Atrocities are...sensational occurrences...reported in an atmosphere of strong feeling [where] the credible evidence is generally accompanied by a certain amount of exaggeration and legend...as a result of a good deal of work...I should say that it it not very difficult to sift out the credible evidence from the tall stories." Toynbee to Prof McKenzie. May 12, 1941. Toynbee Papers BL Oxford MS 13967/63/2
29  Toynbee 1922, 34-35.

## 2. From Versailles to Paris (1920–1947)

that "no nation will treat its minorities well if it believes that they menace its vital interests [...] general law [is] that the protection of minorities is incompatible with the instability of frontiers."[30]

The book was received like "a treatise on nationalist volcanoes by a cool-headed seismologist," praised for its "painstaking fairness,"[31] with evidence strongly damaging to both sides often offered on the same page.[32] A second edition was soon to follow. "It has played no small part in shaping public opinion in this country,"[33] the *Times* wrote, but the conclusion drawn by *The Nation* seemed most disturbing for the supporters of the Versailles Settlement: "If we accept [Toynbee's] conclusion, it is a melancholy one for those among us who have fought so long in the cause of 'subject nationalities', and the other doctrines summed up in President Wilson's general principles at the so-called Peace."[34]

Boastful about being the only Englishman "both in the confidence of the Turks and in touch with the FO [Foreign Office],"[35] Toynbee was determined to help stop the massacre by any possible means. In the spring of 1923, at the request of the editor of the *Manchester Guardian*, he visited Ankara again to mediate between the by then victorious Atatürk and the British government in order to promote a new, enforceable settlement. He was willing to dismiss and overlook all the wrongdoings carried out by Turkish soldiers during the First World War, which he had then been so eager to report, all the more so as by 1923 he saw them as the result of the breakdown of civilization rather than as simply the fault of the offenders.

Much in line with Toynbee, the 1923 Lausanne Conference allowed the Turks annul Sèvres, and negotiate a completely different peace. Moreover, the compulsory exchange of the Greek Orthodox population of Anatolia, Turkey, with the Muslim population of Greece was expected to prevent the recurrence of further hostilities, let alone massacres in both directions. However, Toynbee had to acknowledge, too, that the publication of the *Blue Book* and the uproar caused by the global network of activists during the First World War could not

---

30  Ibid., 586.
31  W.H. Buckler, A Study in the Contact of Civilizations, *New Republic*, December 6, 1922, 48.
32  Francis Haffkine Snow, "Assaying the Guilt of the Greek and Turk," *New York Times Book Review*, February 4, 1923, 6.
33  *Times*, October 13, 1922.
34  When Greek meets Turk, *The Nation*, August 26, 1922, 713–714.
35  Though his assessment in the Foreign Office was rather overshadowed by his regular attacks on Prime Minister Lloyd George's vigorous pro-Greek attitude, which turned out to be just, however, as one of his confidants explained "politicians don't like successful prophets." Toynbee Papers, Eric Forbes Adams to Toynbee, I I September 1923. Toynbee Papers, MS 13967/51? McNeill 1989, 118.

lead to Ottoman Armenians obtaining a new homeland; Armenia's aspirations were defeated by the post-war Republic of Turkey and Soviet Russia, with its former champions, Britain and the USA turning a blind eye.

Having witnessed Toynbee's about-turn on Turkey and Greece, six of the King's College professors were about to take action, and the principal antagonist and fellow Czechoslovak-government-funded chair-holder, Seton-Watson, also issued a warning in the interest of the Greek financiers: "In my opinion you are simply asking for trouble,"[36] he wrote, but Toynbee seemed unrelenting. On Toynbee's behalf Ernest Barker (King's College), with the support of Gilbert Murray and the Professoriate Committee sent a letter to the Subscribers' Committee stating that in the view of the University "the Koraes Professor must be free to form his own opinions and to state his own views, alike in matters of history, and in matters of politics."[37] But the donors in the Subscribers' Committee were far from convinced:

> Professor Toynbee, having accepted a Greek Chair, founded by Greeks, with a Greek endorsement, and graced by the illustrious name of Koraes, has used most of his energies, resources, and spare time to conduct a virulent and sustained attack on the Greek nation in its hour of utmost peril. He has also gone to Angora [Ankara], and engaged in close and friendly understandings with our enemies, to the propagation of whose interests he has devoted his enthusiastic endeavours... This is a view taken not only by Committee, but by a large and influential body of Englishmen, [...] who would consider it impossible for a Prof of English, occupying a Chair endowed with English funds, to become a notorious and emblazoned enemy of England engaged in open propaganda against her. Prof Toynbee has not withdrawn, nor apologised for his violent and bitter accusations against the Greeks...his visits to and his acceptance of the hospitality of Mustafa Kemal [...] are quoted as evidence.[38]

---

36 Seton-Watson to Toynbee, January 7, 1923. Toynbee Papers BL Oxford MS13967/46/1. Uni of LDN, Institute of Historical Research 1914-1924.
Eventually, Seton-Watson was instrumental in not letting the chair fall with its holder. Seton-Watson to historian and journalist William Miller, February 17, 1925, *Korespondencija*, II/126.
37 Ernest Baker (King's College) to Toynbee, June 26, 1923. Toynbee Papers BL Oxford MS13967/46/1. Uni of LDN, Institute of Historical Research 1914-1924.
38 Eumorfopoulos, Hon Secretary (Koraes Chair- Subscribers's Committee) to The Principal, University of London, October 25, 1923. Toynbee Papers BL Oxford MS13967/46/1. University of London, Institute of Historical Research 1914-1924.

On January 3, Toynbee's letter to the *Times* on his resignation[39] added fuel to the fire, as it provoked continued newspaper controversy and a now-angry private letter from Seton-Watson: "I am horrified," he wrote to his colleague, "at your sudden plunge into public controversy, and am bound to warn you that I am not alone in regarding your action as an open declaration of war [...]. You have shown an utter disregard for the interests of the University and the College and your own Chair in the future [...]."[40]

Toynbee did foresee such conflict of interest between the right to freedom of expression and the contributors' aim to influence professorial activity, thus it is worthwhile quoting a relevant section from the introduction to his 1922 book:

> It may, I fear, be painful to Greeks and 'Philhellenes' that information and reflections unfavourable to Greece should have been published by the first occupant of the Koraes Chair. I naturally regret this, but from the academic point of view it is less unfortunate than if my conclusions on the Anatolian Question had been favourable to Greece and unfavourable to Turkey. The actual circumstances, whatever personal unpleasantness they may entail for me and my Greek friends and acquaintances, at least preclude the suspicion that an endowment of learning in a British University has been used for propaganda on behalf of the country with which it is concerned. Such a contention, if it could be urged, would be serious; for academic study should have no political purpose [...].[41]

### 2.4. Toynbee and The Chatham House: The New Director and the Surveys 1925–

Less than two weeks after his letter of resignation from the Koraes Chair at the University of London appeared in the *Times*, Toynbee received an invitation to lunch from the historical adviser to the Foreign Office, James W. Headlam

---

39 "[...] I have taken every opportunity to study Greco-Turkish relations from both sides and have given free public expression to my opinions as the situation has developed. This freedom I believe to be my right as a Professor in a British University; and personally, I should not be willing to hold an academic Chair under other conditions." "The Liberty of Professors. Modern Greek Chair at London. Mr Toynbee's Resignation," to the Editor of the *Times*, January 3, 1924.
40 Seton-Watson to Toynbee, January 4, 1924. Toynbee Papers BL Oxford MS 13967/46/1. University of London: Koraes Chair. Qtd. in McNeill 1989, 119.
41 Toynbee, *Western Question in Greece and Turkey*, London, Constable and Company Ltd, 1922, xi. Half a century later, in 1974, Toynbee recalled the whole controversy as "ancient history;" however, the relevant papers still held a permanent interest "because of their bearing on the perennial question of academic freedom." Toynbee to Richard Clogg, July 27, 1974, Richard Clogg *Politics and the Academy: Toynbee and the Koreas Chair*, London, Routledge, 2013, vii.

Morley, once his immediate superior in the Political Intelligence Department. Headlam-Morley was also one of the founders and leading spirits of the British (later Royal) Institute of International Affairs. "It was to him that I owed my post at Chatham-House," Toynbee remembered. "It was he who taught me how to write our 'Survey of International Affairs', and now that I am again working temporarily for HMG in the same kind of work though in a more responsible position than in the last war, I again find myself constantly profiting by things that I learnt from him long ago."[42]

Toynbee always believed his "first duty"[43] as Director of Studies was to write the *Annual Survey of International Affairs*. However, he received funding for a chair at the University of London from Glasgow industrialist and coal magnate Sir Daniel Stevenson on the condition that he split his time between teaching international relations and creating annual surveys for the institute. There was no mention of how the dual position holder would split his time between the two organizations. Toynbee duly delivered an opening address at the University of London in the early months of 1926, arguing that developing an international perspective could help one escape from national bias. He also claimed that his dual affiliation with the university and the institute would keep him up to date on both academic and global affairs—a combination that was "ideal for historical work and rare in our times."[44] Yet teaching at any university failed to interest him, and through a renegotiation of his contract, he hoped to abandon it for good.

Education, however, did remain in Toynbee's life, albeit in a different form: between 1924 and 1939 he published thirty-four volumes of the annual *Surveys* with the aim to create an enlightened public opinion. War "is the wickedest of all living human institutions," he opined; "[...] in persisting with the *Survey*, I was not merely helping to expose the major evil of our time [...], I have also always felt that I was helping to try to suppress this wicked institution before it annihilates us, its makers."[45]

The best indicator of the prevailing policy regarding the surveys was the following clause printed on the inside cover of each issue of the journal since its foundation in January 1922: "The Institute is precluded by its rules from ex-

---

42  Toynbee to Reverend Lord Bishop of Glouchester [Headlam-Morley's brother], July 8, 1943. Toynbee Papers, MS 13967/82/1 Correspondence.
43  The Stevenson Research Chair: Notes on the Chair and the work involved by Dr. A.J.Toynbee, Princeton, New Jersey, June 23, 1953. Toynbee Papers, MS 13967/40 General Miscellaneous Correspondence 1931-64.
44  McNeill 1989, 130.
45  Toynbee *Experiences*, 82-83.

pressing an opinion on any aspect of international affairs. Any opinions expressed in the Journal are, therefore, purely individual."[46] Prior to publication, the director would send a draft of the *Survey* to the Foreign Office for comment and proofreading, which after years had received a "quasi-official status."[47] The reviewers gave the surveys their undivided regard and Toynbee, too, was surrounded by growing respect at the Foreign Office: William Tyrell, the permanent under-secretary of state for foreign affairs (1925-1928) regularly consulted the director of Chatham House on foreign affairs and assured him that he had "a great admiration for [his] knowledge and flair in that sphere."[48]

The degree to which Toynbee's own viewpoint was apparent in subsequent volumes varied greatly. In the 1925 *Survey* for example he treated "The Islamic World since the Peace Settlement" at such length that it required its own separate volume. Everything else for 1925 was entrusted to a large extent to a new member of the RIIA, Carlile Aylmer Macartney.[49] The *Times* claimed that Macartney's authorship resulted in "no diminution of the value of the work, very well-informed account of a large number of subjects, very clearly and skilfully written."[50] The *Manchester Guardian* was likewise full of praise: "Toynbee has succeeded in imparting to his successor, Carlile A Macartney [...] his own passion of accurate and impartial of presentment of fact [...]. The *Survey* has established itself as a necessary part of any reference library."[51]

The next year saw the publication of Toynbee's *Turkey*, in Toynbee's narrative "written under terrible pressure." This probably accounts for the fact that Toynbee believed to have protected himself over the Armenian massacres by devoting a page to saying that the book did not deal with that subject. However, topics like the Armenian Genocide cannot be dismissed in that manner, so co-founder of RIIA Lionel Curtis, Valentine Chirol and possibly others made him understand how damaging it must be to the rest of his work if people started

---

46  "Policy in Regard to International Affairs," RIIA Archives, 4/TOYN/9
47  McNeill 1989, 133.
48  William Tyrell to Toynbee, May 6, 1925. Toynbee Papers, MS 13 967/39 General Miscellaneous Correspondence 1911-1956.
49  McNeill 1989, 134, 309 (fn)
50  "International Affairs," *Times*, April 12, 1928.
51  *Manchester Guardian*, July 25, 1928. The *Survey* for 1926 stands out further due to the addition for the first time of distinct pieces on economic and legal issues as an addition to Toynbee's political narratives. Given his lack of interest in such issues, Toynbee willingly delegated such chapters to others. He then adopted this as standard procedure: he compiled most of the text but was increasingly reliant on, among others, his indispensable secretary Veronica Boulter, as the title page for the *Survey* from 1929 on suggests: the text "Assisted by V. M. Boulter" would appear under Toynbee's name.

to believe that he had a strong prejudice on one particular issue. It is worth citing Lionel Curtis on the matter:

> I asked him to examine in his own mind and to ask himself whether he had not got a bias on this Turkish question. He is a humble person [...] and not all opinionated, and quite frankly admitted the possibility of bias, instead of flying into rage, as so many people would have done, and complaining that his intellectual honesty was being attacked [...] I have never before had to deal with a man who was so dispassionate and detached in listening to criticisms of himself.

Toynbee's *Turkey* (1926) did subject the author to vicious criticism from both Armenians and some similarly fervent pro-Greeks. "Hardly anyone seems able to deal with the Balkan situation without being somewhat Balkanised themselves"—sounded Curtis's verdict.[52] Former *Times'* foreign editor Valentine Chirol was also critical, and harshly so: he was positive that Toynbee had used his sympathy for the underdog, "a very undeserving one," to cloud his judgment, which had extremely regrettable consequences. "I have a very strong bias against the Turk," he added, [...] "from a very much longer acquaintance with him than Toynbee's. [...] Gladstone was right and Dizzy wrong when we were at a new parting of the ways."[53]

## 2.5. Four Britons and the Successor States of the Austro-Hungarian Monarchy 1920–29

Seton-Watson agreed with Louis Eisenmann that the historian who was out of touch with contemporary events "was not likely to attain to sound estimates of remoter periods."[54] Although to a varying extent, all four Britons were eager

---

52 Lionel Curtis to Valentine Chirol, July 15, 1926. RIIA Archives Correspondence with Sir V Chirol 1926-7: 4/TOYN/24
53 Chirol to Curtis, July 18, 1926. RIIA Archives Correspondence with Sir V Chirol 1926-7: 4/TOYN/24
  Interestingly, in his book published the same year, Toynbee's later colleague and mentoree, Macartney shared Chirol's opinion: "What the Turks touched, they destroyed. They wiped out the culture of the Balkans, annihilated hardly less completely that of Hungary, threatened all the Mediterranean. Twice they pressed up to the walls of Vienna." Macartney, *The Social Revolution in Austria*, Cambridge, Cambridge University Press, 1926, 251.
54 Seton-Watson, Obituary: Louis Eisenmann, *International Affairs* (Royal Institute of International Affairs 1931-1939), Vol. 16, No. 4 (July 1937), 601-602.

## 2. From Versailles to Paris (1920–1947)

to establish and maintain contacts with the newfound states in East and Central Europe and beyond.

### 2.5.1. Macartney on Austria

*The Social Revolution in Austria*, Macartney's debut book, was released in 1926, with the author's aim to provide an "impartial" analysis of Austrian socialism and Austria's position in Central-Europe.[55] But before doing that he offered the readers a summary of its Habsburg past, stating that Franz Joseph's autocratic, as well as feudal Monarchy rested on three pillars, the Catholic Church, the army and bureaucracy. After the 1867 *Ausgleich*, in Macartney's analysis a "thoroughly unfortunate" agreement, both Austrians and the Magyars in the Dual-Monarchy were occupied with inter-racial warfare, often fought on linguistic trivialities; nevertheless, while the "sublimely selfish and unscrupulous" Magyars pursued a policy of "frankest oppression," cunning as well as ruthless, Austria was playing its nationalities off against each other relatively successfully until the Great War, and it fell at last over the Southern Slav question.[56] After Emperor Karl issued his proclamation and left the country on October 11, 1918, the Provisional Government proclaimed to be part of the new German Republic in accordance with the wishes of the majority of the population. However, as Macartney highlighted, due to Entente veto this never happened, and the new state was to change its name from "German-Austria" to "Austria," to the "universal distaste" of its people.[57]

Before discussing contemporary Austria, "one of the smallest, weakest, poorest States in Europe," and especially its far-reaching social legislation,[58] Macartney devoted another chapter to the Social Democratic Party, which he argued had been responsible for the changes in the country, whether "for good or bad."[59] Established in 1889, with the main focus on social legislation, the party had opposed the war and became the most powerful among Austrian workmen, with Vienna as its stronghold. By late 1917, its leading figure Otto Bauer's interpreta-

---

55 Macartney 1926, ix.
56 Ibid., 12, 16 and 20.
57 Ibid., 92.
58 On page 153 and 154 Macartney provided a list of "model" welfare legislations, adding that the measures passed under the auspices of the minister of social welfare, Ferdinand Hanusch, during a few months "did more to better the condition of the masses than had previous decades of legislation from above." At the same time, the author also added that, unlike in other Successor States, expropriation of privately-owned land hardly ever happened. (149).
59 Ibid., 36.

tion of socialism stood in support of Nationalist leaders' claims. Thus, increasingly in line with the Czechs and Poles, Austrian socialists demanded the abolition of Dynasty, the transformation of Monarchy and the termination of war.[60] The Habsburgs on the other hand, argued Macartney, could never come to terms with the idea of allowing their fellow nationalities "elbow room," at least until October 1918, but were adamant to preserve unity more as a façade and much less the reality.[61]

In chapter ten, Macartney elaborated on contemporary Austria's position in Central-Europe, claiming once again that it "was forced to exist" quite against the will of its citizens and political leaders. Regarding the self-determination of nations, which in Versailles had been the "popular cry," Macartney opined that the country came off entirely empty-handed: no unification with Germany was allowed and several German-inhabited regions were cut off from the new state: South Tirol and most importantly three million Germans, many of whom living directly along the new frontier, were assigned to Czechoslovakia—quite against the will of the people. The result, according to the author, was

> a most unexpected [country] and certainly a misshapen creature whom nobody really wanted. She is no natural birth, gradually and inevitably formed, as a State ought to be; rather the product partly of [...] the rivalry between France and Germany, natural sympathy between Professor Wilson and Professor Masaryk; partly of conditions in the past which were themselves artificial.[62]

Macartney's first major work received overall positive reviews: a "clever little book" with "well-balanced judgement,"[63] was Austrian economist-sociologist Alois Schumpeter's verdict. Seton-Watson, too, was supportive regarding the book, "much the best critical summary of the problems which confront post-war Austria," albeit he noted at the end of his review that what Macartney wrote about the other peoples of the Monarchy was "not quite accurate."[64]

---

60 Ibid., 73.
61 Ibid., 254.
62 Macartney 1926, 249-251.
63 Joseph A. Schumpeter, The Social Revolution in Austria by C.A.Macartney, *The Economic Journal*, Vol. 37, No. 146 (June 1927), 290-292, 290.
64 *Social Revolution in Austria* by C.A. Macartney, reviewed by Seton-Watson, *Slavonic Review*, March 1927, 694.

In *Social Revolution in Austria*, Hungary was referred to as "the most *difficile* of all nations,"⁶⁵ but during his long stay in Vienna, Macartney developed a love for Hungary's history and its people that lasted the rest of his life.

### 2.5.2. Merry Wilsonian Establishments? Seton-Watson, Steed and the Little Entente States: Czechoslovakia, Romania and Yugoslavia

The establishment of the Little Entente, the common anti-Habsburg-restoration and anti-Hungarian defence alliance formed by Czechoslovakia, the South Slav state and Romania in 1920–21, was greeted by Seton-Watson in *The New Europe* as the prelude to "the process of consolidation on the Middle and Lower Danube."⁶⁶ On tours of the region, he paid several visits to these countries, and was welcomed as befitted a national hero.

In the Czechoslovak Republic, the Parliament was democratically elected by the citizens according to the Act of 1920. Its leader, T. G. Masaryk, the intimate friend of both Steed and Seton-Watson was acclaimed as an idol who "set us all that measured ideal of optimism without illusions."⁶⁷ Besides democratic liberties the state provided its citizens with relative well-being. These factors were given emphasis in Seton-Watson's book *The New Slovakia* together with the balanced budget and well-checked corruption— therefore "universal credit is accorded to statesmen of Prague because of their sober and pacific policy."⁶⁸

In truth, the majority of Slovaks did not see themselves as belonging to the "Czechoslovak nation" even in 1918. With the Czechs only making up a relative majority, the new state was, according to Jan Rychlík, "just a smaller copy of the deceased Austria-Hungary," having inherited all the problems of the former empire, plus some more.⁶⁹ Accordingly, between 1918 and 1938 Seton-Watson became involved in the ongoing conflict between the Czechs and Slovaks as a result of the latter's desire for administrative decentralization and autonomy. In the Žilina Memorandum of the Slovak People's Party of August 1922, it was stated, with no small exaggeration, that "the Slovaks were bamboozled out of the freedom promised to them" which resulted in their "deadly struggle [...]

---

65 Macartney 1926, 265.
66 *The New Europe*, October 14, 1921.
67 Seton-Watson 1922, 33.
68 Seton-Watson, *The New Slovakia*, Prague, F. Borový, 1924, 78–79.
69 Jan Rychlík, The Situation of the Hungarian Minority in Czechoslovakia 1918–1938, 27–38. In: Ferenc Eiler, Dagmar Hájková et al., *Czech and Hungarian Minority Policy in Central Europe 1918–1938*, Prague-Budapest, 2009, 29.

to escape extinction."[70] Although Seton-Watson had been a firm supporter of Slovak self-determination rights since 1907, he not only rejected the document as "evidence of political immaturity," but also urged Andrej Hlinka, the head of the Slovak People's Party to act likewise. Once the hero of the 1907 Černova tragedy, Hlinka, however, published a series of articles in his party paper claiming that Seton-Watson had been misled by Prague and inviting the historian to visit Slovakia to judge their grievances in person.[71]

Seton-Watson worked quite tirelessly to mediate between the two parties, "busy engaged in the onerous process of national reconstruction."[72] He complained to his wife, "I find that everybody, on all sides here, expects me to act as a kind of magician to solve the problem!"[73] By 1924 at the latest, the originally at least emotionally pro-Slovak historian had turned visibly pro-Czech: although he, quite anachronistically, claimed that the "Slovakia of today is already as different from Slovakia of 1910 as it is from Slovakia of Middle Ages,"[74] he described the people of the Highlands as being "in the position of a pampered child who has received so many Christmas presents as to be incapable of appreciating any of them."[75] The Czechs, on the other hand, "wrested [freedom] from the hand of destiny."[76] In other words, he was by then convinced that the Slovaks were not mature enough for freedom, therefore they ought to be grateful that fate had rendered them reliant on a people "so efficient, so well educated and disciplined"[77] as the Czechs. In the meantime, he habitually attributed the Slovaks' difficulties to the pre-1919 administrative machine which was "not merely Magyar, but chauvinistically Magyar."[78] Slovak dissatisfaction with the overly centralized government in Prague could finally subside in 1927 when the Slovak People's Party joined the coalition government in Prague and an administrative reform was enacted.

---

70 "A Country Doomed to Death, A Nation in Her Last Agonies Implores the Civilized World For Help." The Žilina Memorandum of the Slovak Peoples's Party, August 3, 1922. Rychlík, Marzik, Bielik (eds.) 1995, I/319.
71 Andrej Hlinka, Scotus Viator. In: Rychlík, Marzik, Bielik (eds.) 1995, I/ 345–353.
72 Seton-Watson 1924, 11.
73 Seton-Watson to May Seton-Watson, May 27, 1923. Rychlík, Marzik, Bielik (eds.) 1995, I/374. In the same letter he acknowledged, too, that the misunderstanding between the two nations was "deeper and wider" than what he had believed, but it did not rest on such serious foundations as in Yugoslavia or Romania, and "and it ought not therefore to be impossible to smooth it over [with tact]."
74 Seton-Watson 1924, 2.
75 Ibid., 51.
76 Ibid., 4–5.
77 Ibid., 8.
78 Ibid., 19.

## 2. From Versailles to Paris (1920–1947)

Seton-Watson's attitude toward interwar Czechoslovakia rested on two pillars: the unrelenting criticism of Hungarian politics before and after 1920, "stifled by red and white terror,"[79] and the staunch support for the integrity of Czechoslovakia by, among others, rejecting Slovak autonomy from the outset, as a prelude to possible independence, which he believed would weaken the Central European cordon sanitaire against a possible aggressor as well as strengthen Hungarian revisionist propaganda.

Steed's support for Czechoslovakia was also considerable. The journalist, who in 1922 had been relieved of his duties as editor-in-chief of the *Times*, undertook among other things to translate *The Making of a State* by Masaryk, complaining to a friend that "if you had seen the material, [...] you would have condoled with me."[80] In fact, the work took him two years to finish; his foreword, on the other hand, revealed nothing of his toils, but rather offered a mythical portrait of Masaryk, "the lonely Slovak in Prague," "a mixture of Tolstoy and Walt Whitman" for many, who championed democratic freedom and moral uprightness with a nationalism unbefouled by any racial intolerance while leading his people "from Hapsburg servitude to the green pastures of freedom."[81] No hired bard could have performed more effectively.

The creation of a "compact Roumanian State"[82] had been one of the two most important radical political changes brought about by the Great War, argued Seton-Watson in a series of articles published two years after the Trianon Treaty. During the interwar period, he paid several visits to that country as part of his East-Central European journey, and in 1922–23 he took some time to meet with his Romanian acquaintances, particularly his old Transylvanian friend Iuliu Maniu, who criticized the centralizing practices of the Bucharest government: "Those states neighbouring us, which have perished in recent years, have perished due to their lack of legal sense and public morality and a disregard for popular rights, which form the basis of a state. We are disturbed to see that the public life of our state is suffering from the same abuses."[83]

In order to downplay such malfunctions or abuses carried out by the Romanian state of the time, Seton-Watson generally applied two methods: he either traced the post-war problems back to the pre-war Hungarian heritage, arguing

---

79 Seton-Watson 1924, 79.
80 Masaryk, *The Making of a State*, London, George Allen and Unwin Ltd, 1927. Steed to Sir Arthur Evans, January 28, 1928. Steed Papers, MS 74 127.
81 Masaryk 1927, (Introduction by Steed), 18–20.
82 Seton-Watson. Transylvania. (I), *The Slavonic Review*, Vol. 1, No. 2 (December 1922), 306.
83 Seton-Watson Papers, SEW11/2/2.

for instance that the result of the 1848–49 war of independence was "a legacy of hatred, still actively at work,"[84] or he came to view the Romanian atrocities via a comparative lens, i.e., by comparing them to the—frequently exaggerated—crimes of pre-1918 Hungarian rule, which deprived [the Hungarians] "of the right to criticise." A prime example of the latter was the parallel he drew between the Carpathian summits and strategic points, some 1250 square miles, annexed and "plundered very systematically" by the Hungarians after the Treaty of Bucharest (February 1918) and the Romanian occupation and looting of a large portion of Trianon Hungary, about twenty-five thousand square miles, a year and a half later. Seton-Watson acknowledged in his 1925 study that he had personally witnessed trucks full of machinery taken from factories in Hungary remaining unpackaged and idle on the railway sidings of Cluj (Kolozsvár) more than a year later, yet his support for Bucharest seemed unwavering:

> [...] slower than expected development did not mean that Roumanian Unity was itself a blunder, or that it rests upon unsound conditions, but merely that it came before the masses of the nation were ripe for it, and under conditions of crisis and suffering that exhausted all reserves and strained the very foundations of the State. Situation can only be aggravated rather than solved by the exaggerated centralist tendencies of the present regime.[85]

However, within the same year, a dynastic crisis set in owing to Crown Prince Carol's abdication of the throne as a result of an affair, which put Seton-Watson's goodwill towards Romania to the test. In a letter to his friend Viorel Tilea, he sounded rather disillusioned: "The plain fact is that I've been so utterly disgusted by the course of events in Roumania that I didn't know what to write."[86]

Seton-Watson's and Steed's other grand wartime project, the unification of the Southern Slavs, produced considerably more disillusionment than that of the Czechs and Slovaks. In emigration, the Yugoslav Committee had been a political organisation in which Croatian predominance prevailed and the Slovenians had not been treated as equal partners, which indirectly contributed to the Slovenian–Serbian axis at the Peace Conference and later on. The result was a disparity in leadership: the only non-Serbian head of government of interwar Yugoslavia was Anton Korošec of Slovenia, which the Croats duly resented. No

---

84 Seton-Watson, Transylvania in the 19th Century, *The Slavonic Review*, Vol. 3, No. 8 (December 1924), 313–314.
85 R. W. Seton-Watson, Transylvania since 1867, *The Slavonic Review*, Vol. 4, No. 10 (June 1925), 122.
86 Seton-Watson to Tilea, October 11, 1926. Seton-Watson Papers, SEW17/28/7.

wonder that in the 1920s the Serbo-Croat conflicts absorbed almost all of Seton-Watson's attention. His visit to the country in 1923 made him fully disillusioned. In a letter to his wife, he acknowledged that the Serbo-Croat conflict created the "most perplexing" situation he had come across in his entire life, and that "literally no one seems to see the way out."[87]

In 1925, Seton-Watson addressed a separate memorandum to King Alexander, summarizing his own and his fellow South Slav correspondents' experience and their objections to the untenable domestic political situation, for which they blamed the centralising policies of the Serbian parties. He stated bitterly, "What alarms me above all in the present situation in Jugoslavia is to observe [...] that at the head of the Government there is no real respect for law and order, that only those clauses of the constitution are observed which happen to suit the party interests of those in power."[88]

### 2.5.3. Edith Durham's "First-Class Tomahawk"[89] against the South Slav State: Three Britons and the Question of Responsibility for WW1

According to the South Slav narrative, Serbia, the main unifying force of the country, was an innocent victim of the unjustified aggression of the Central Powers in 1914, with her land invaded and her sovereignty infringed, very much like Belgium. The Yugoslav state as an innocent party and the victim of Austria–Hungary's unjustified assault in 1914 served as a foundation for much of its overall legitimacy. However, Ljuba Jovanović, the first history professor at the University of Belgrade and the minister of education between 1911 and 1914, suggested in a commemorative volume titled *Krv Slovenstva [Blood of Slavs]* published in 1924 that the Serb government, with at least three weeks' notice of the plot, could—and even ought—to have prevented Franz Ferdinand's assassination. Thus, it seemed that the narrative of innocent Serbia got into serious trouble.

On the evening of December 3, 1924, the British Institute of International Affairs' Near East Group convened at Chatham House to discuss "Serbian Responsibility for the War." The historians G.P. Gooch and Seton-Watson, Sir Maurice de Bunsen, former British ambassador to Vienna between 1913 and 1914, Sir James Headlam-Morley, Henry Wickham Steed, Lionel Curtis, and Arnold Toynbee as chair were among the prominent British figures who attended. The

---

87 Seton-Watson to May Seton-Watson, April 22, 1923. *Korespondencija*, II/103.
88 Seton-Watson, Memorandum [1925]. *Korespondencija*, II/146.
89 Seton-Watson, in reference to Ljuba Jovanović's article. Seton-Watson to poet-essayist Milan Ćurčin, February 28, 1925. *Korespondencija*, II/129.

notoriously pro-Albanian Serbophobe Edith Durham rose to speak armed with a copy of Jovanović's memoir. She claimed victoriously to "have bamboozled poor Watson and Co. [Wickham Steed]" into silence, scolding the "pro-Jugger and anti-Hun" [pro-Yugoslav, anti-German] group at the table so harshly that Arnold Toynbee was called to silence her.[90]

The revelation about the possible Serb complicity in the Sarajevo murders quickly found its way to the press through Durham and her confidant, Emil Torday, the London correspondent of the German-language Budapest daily, *Pester Lloyd* and other Hungarian papers.[91] For the Foreign Office, the situation was a major headache. "The indirect results of the recent disclosures are very likely to be serious," argued James Headlam-Morley. [... People] will say that our government entered the war, as they were told, in the defence of the liberties of small nations, Belgium and Serbia; they now find that Serbia was merely a den of robbers and assassins."[92] Miles Lampson, head of the Central Department, powerfully advocated that the whole issue "should be left to the historian of the future."[93]

After having arrived home from a US lecture tour as well as the Annual Conference of the American Historical Association in Richmond, Virginia, Seton-Watson undertook several months of research to equip himself powerfully for the attack on Durham's newly found evidence. Having chaired the meeting in December, Toynbee was horrified by Durham's tirades and confrontational style, and offered Seton-Watson his full support: "[You] heaped coals of fire on Miss Durham's head. I hope she will feel them and have the grace to say that she does."[94] The result of Seton-Watson's labours, *Sarajevo: A Study in the Origins*

---

90  Qtd. in David Kaufman, The "One Guilty Nation" Myth: Edith Durham: R. W. Seton-Watson and a Footnote in the History of the Outbreak of the First World War, *Journal of Balkan and Near Eastern Studies*, Vol. 25, 2023/3, 302.
    In a letter to Serb diplomat, publicist Jovan Jovanović on December 4, 1924, Seton-Watson himself acknowledged that the "poisonous woman" forced him "completely into the defensive." *Korespondencija*, II/ 122.
91  "Londoner Momentaufnahmen," *Pester Lloyd*, December 11, 1924, 2; and „A hivatalos Szerbia a szarajevoi gyilkosságról" [Official Serbia on the Sarajevo murder], *Budapesti Hirlap*, December 12, 1924, 5.
92  Headlam-Morley minute, January 16, 1925, FO 371/10794/C 530/530/92. Qtd. in Kaufman, 2022, 304.
93  Lampson minute, January 19, 1925, FO 371/10794/C 530/530/92. After the original text of the Memoir was translated into English, it was clear that Durham had indeed distorted Jovanović's meaning for her own anti-Serb purposes. Nevertheless Seton-Watson warned the Serbs that "mere silence" was the wrong strategy and if Durham's campaign remained unanswered, Serbia's reputation in Britain "will be irreparably damaged." Seton-Watson to poet-essayist Milan Ćurčin, February 28, 1925. *Korespondencija*, II/130.
94  Toynbee to Seton-Watson, February 16, 1925, Seton-Watson Papers SEW 17/29/1.

*of the Great War*, concluded: "Vienna and Berlin had by 23 July created a diplomatic situation from which nothing short of a miracle could have saved Europe, and that the main responsibility for the outbreak of war must therefore rest upon their shoulders."[95] On Hungarian participation he remarked that although "PM István Tisza showed sanity and foresight" his hesitation was due to the "uncertainty of German support." Therefore Seton-Watson clearly rejected any "disingenuous tactics" that aimed at disclaiming any responsibility by describing the Hungarian prime minister as "one of the staunchest advocates of drastic action" when German support was unreservedly guaranteed. Thus Seton-Watson failed to take into account in his book that Tisza rejected Bosnia's annexation, since upon entering the war Hungary—as opposed to Germany—did not aim at territorial growth. Tisza was convinced to choose the lesser evil, that is, proclaiming war instead of losing the German al In Seton-Watson's interpretation, the ostensibly anti-Slav Hungarians and the Hungarian prime minister, István Tisza, the most decisive and influential political figure in the Monarchy, became the prime warmongers.

The responsibility for the Sarajevo murder had been "most ably discussed"[96] by Seton-Watson, Steed commented a few years later, agreeing that the main burden unquestionably rested upon Germany and Austria-Hungary for not having accepted Prime Minister Grey's proposal for mediation.[97] However, he also added that Tisza warned Franz Ferdinand not to travel to Sarajevo, let alone on Kosovo Day, a day of mourning for 524 years,[98] which due to the Serbian victories in the first and second Balkan wars was to be celebrated in 1914 for the first time as a festival of Serb redemption. Thus, the heir's visit was resented by all, and Steed put part of the blame on Franz Ferdinand's "avaricious disposition" and intense devotion to his wife and children, as the visit had been intended to secure recognition for them despite the morganatic marriage. This somewhat explained why no special precautions had been made, even after a bomb was thrown at his carriage and "a regular avenue of bomb throwers" was lying in wait for him.[99]

Interestingly, by the end of the 1920s, Seton-Watson's and his friends' voices were more dissenting, arguing that direct responsibility for the outbreak of war rested in one way or another with the Central Powers, which view came

---

95 Seton-Watson, Sarajevo, 1926, 289
96 Steed, The Great War, 1914–1918. In: *Great Events in History*, ed. Stirling Taylor, London, Cassell and Company, Ltd., 1934, 819.
97 Ibid., 824.
98 Owing to the overthrow of the Serbian Empire by the Turks on the field of Kosovo.
99 Steed, The Great War, 1914–1918. In: *Great Events in History*, ed. Stirling Taylor, London, Cassell and Company, Ltd., 1934, 816–817.

to be overshadowed by the prevailing idea of shared responsibility for the First World War, coupled with the belief that some boundary adjustments were eventually necessary.[100]

In the meantime, Serb-Croatian relations hit a low point in 1928 with the murder of Stepan Radić, the leader of the Croatian peasant movement and a proponent of decentralization. Seton-Watson's letterbox was flooded complaints from Croatian intellectuals expressing "great hatred for Serbia'"[101] and claiming to feel like "slaves and servants of Serbian hegemony."[102] The Monarch made an attempt to control the chaos and quell national differences by dissolving Parliament in 1929 and imposing a royal dictatorship, which Seton-Watson considered "a disastrous step." In order to mediate between the opposing camps, he visited the country in January, but to no avail. "[I] came away far more depressed than I ever was in the darkest days of the war," he explained to Oszkár Jászi. "Turkey and Austria-Hungary were incapable of solving the South Slav Question. The Serbs seem bent on proving themselves equally bankrupt."[103]

Thus in 1929, as in 1913, Seton-Watson once again re-evaluated Serbia, the former "Piedmont of the Southern Slavs." This, however, did not imply calling Yugoslavia's existence or sustainability into question. On the contrary, as the Serb–Croat conflict deepened, the need to preserve the status quo dictated to Seton-Watson that he repeatedly assert that "Yugoslav unification was the consequence of a process as spontaneous and inevitable as those which joined Italy and Germany last century." Fault, therefore, should be found not in the events of 1918, but in the excessive centralisation after 1920.[104]

In line with Serbo-Croat relations, the late 1920s saw a widening of the gulf between Edith Durham and Seton-Watson: she even accused him of getting funds from the Yugoslavs, which rendered objective analysis difficult. This brought back painful memories of Hungarian allegations about him having been a paid agent of Vienna. In 1929 the well-intentioned but naive Toynbee made an attempt to reconcile the two Balkan experts, but Seton-Watson's contempt for Durham proved to be enduring. "I am not disposed to admit her title as a seri-

---

100 Catherine Ann Cline, British Historians and the Treaty of Versailles, *Albion: A Quarterly Journal Concerned with British Studies*, Vol. 20, No. 1 (Spring, 1988), 43-58, 52-53.
101 Jovan Jovanović to Seton-Watson, September 30, 1928. *Korespondencija*, II/175. Also Seton-Watson Papers, SEW17/12/1.
102 Ivo Lupis Vukić to Seton-Watson, October 11, 1928. *Korespondencija*, II/183. Croatian emigrant Vukić (1876–1967) was the first US reporter to cover Balkan issues since the end of the nineteenth century.
103 Seton-Watson to Oszkár Jászi, February 9, 1929. Seton-Watson Papers, SEW17/11/2.
104 Seton-Watson, Yugoslavia and Croatia (a lecture in the Royal Institute of International Affairs. January 29, 1929), *Journal of International Affairs [IA]*, 1929/3, 118.

ous student of history," he explained to his colleague. "Her methods of controversy, her reckless and infamously untrue charges against all and sundry, make it difficult for any friend of Yugoslavia to find any common ground on which to meet." On the same day, he wrote to Durham, too: "I resent most intensely your whole treatment & interpretation of the question." Durham replied, sharply criticising Seton-Watson's attitude towards the fate of smaller European nations.:

> You seem to regard these populations as mere pawns to be shifted on the board according to political needs. To me they are all suffering human beings with whom I have been under fire—for whose sake I have risked enteric, smallpox and have wrestled with poisoned wounds. And with whom I have hungered and been half frozen. I feel it a duty to show the means by which they have been annexed and trampled on. And to call for a consideration of their cause.[105]

Seton-Watson then cut off communication with her, anticipating the trajectory of his relationship with Macartney some nine years later.

### 2.5.4. Three Britons and Hungary 1920–27

From 1919/20 until the end of his life. Seton-Watson was consistent in his attitude towards Hungary. He would cite the short-lived Károlyi government (October 31, 1918–January 1919) as the liberal example for the country to follow, conveniently overlooking the fact that the Great Powers declined to grant it direly-needed diplomatic recognition. From the fall of the Communist Béla Kun in August 1919, he envisioned Hungary as "a mainly peasant community [...] reduced to complete and permanent impotence."[106] Two months later, in an article titled "Hungary in the Grip of Reaction," he commented with rather mixed feelings on the entry of Miklós Horthy into Budapest; he believed that the dangerous Bolshevik regime had been replaced by the old political establishment, which was expected to strengthen chauvinism and reaction. "Hungary is the last State to be invited or included [in the Little Entente]. Those who are at present at power have learnt nothing from the war,"[107] he opined. His mistrust remained, therefore:"So long as the Hungary of Admiral Horthy survives, it is use-

---

105 Seton-Watson to Toynbee, February 12, 1929, Seton-Watson to Durham, February 12, 1929, and Durham to Seton-Watson, February 14, 1929. Seton-Watson Papers SEW, 17/6/9.
106 Seton-Watson, The Fall of Béla Kun, *The New Europe* 12, No. 148, August 14, 1919, 100.
107 Seton-Watson, Hungary in the Grip of Reaction, *The New Europe*, October 14, 1921.

less to expect really consolidated and normal conditions among the Succession States of the former Dual Monarchy."[108] This resignation is reflected in the fact that the former Wandering Scot never visited Hungary after the war, so there was no opportunity to study the Horthy regime more closely.

Steed remained equally denunciatory and detached regarding interwar Hungary while staying busy with his new project, *The Review of the Reviews*.[109] When, due to his personal sympathies "from boyhood with the best of the Magyar-race,"[110] *Observer* editor James Garvin would not publish his highly critical paper on Hungary, Steed retorted:

> I shared your sympathies for the Magyars until I had to deal with them at first hand, and was compelled to learn their language enough to enable me to look behind the elaborate façade [...] which they are apt to believe in themselves. If I have a grudge against them, it is because they are [...] blind to everything that runs counter to their desires, and because this blindness caused them to throw away one of the most magnificent opportunities ever offered to a Central-European people and to wreck the Hapsburg Monarchy and their own country in the process.[111]

The only direct contact Steed and Seton-Watson had with interwar Hungary was through their meetings and correspondence with prominent members of the October emigration, "the very cream of Magyar intellectuals,"[112] especially Oszkár Jászi,[113] who the Scottish historian expected would counteract the "poisonous rubbish" spread by Hungarian revisionist propaganda in his articles,

---

108 Seton-Watson in: Oszkár Jászi, *Revolution and Counterrevolution*, London, P. S. King and Son, 1924, XXII-XXIII.
    Toynbee reviewed Jászi's work in the Chatham House journal. While praising the Károlyi Government for "gallantly attempting to carry out profound social and political reforms at the eleventh hour," he added quite erroneously that such reforms "might have averted the war, and so saved Hungary from partition." *Journal of the British Institute of International Affairs*, Volume 3, Issue 5, September 1924, 269.
109 The monthly journal was labelled as "The Busy Man's Magazine," with the aim to inform its readers on "What the World is doing and thinking." The *Review of Reviews* was initially a real success story under Steed: in the first four years, 1923-27, the number of copies sold increased ninefold, from 1000 to 9000. Liebich 2018, 224.
110 James Garvin to Steed, June 27, 1928, MS MS 74 127.
111 Steed to Garvin, June 28, 1928. Steed Papers MS 74 127.
112 Seton-Watson, Weekly Reports on Hungary, June 9, 1917. Seton-Watson Papers, SEW/4/1.
113 Socialist Jászi believed that "the road to internationalism leads through the national." He worked to keep the Hungarian emigration united in Vienna after May 1919 while he engaged in negotiations with the rulers of the Successor States and wrote about the significance of a democratic Hungary for the stability of East Central Europe. Oszkár Jászi, "Two Mighty Forces 1905," cited in György Litván, "Oscar Jászi (1875-1957), A Biographical Essay" (Manuscript, Budapest, 1984), 6.

books and other manifestations.[114] The other Hungarian émigré with whom the two former champions of national-self-determination maintained relatively regular correspondence was former Hungarian prime minister Mihály Károlyi, whom Jászi introduced to Seton-Watson in 1923 in Yugoslavia.[115] Despite the reservations of the Hungarian Legation in London, the historian soon succeeded in obtaining a residence permit for Károlyi, who remained in the British capital until May 1925. While in London, he was urged by Seton-Watson to use his memoirs, articles and contacts with prominent figures in British public life to persuade them that his "Hungary will be a sounder, more stable member of European Commonwealth than the Hungary of Horthy and Bethlen."[116]

Despite Steed's and Seton-Watson's distrust of and even antipathy towards Hungary, between 1921 and 1927 the Foreign Office supported the country in a number of conflicts in order to balance the expanding French economic and political dominance in Central and Eastern Europe, and also to prevent the spread of extremism, Bolshevism and Fascism. Therefore, Seton-Watson and Steed, too, frequently found themselves at variance with their own government. Notwithstanding feudal remnants such as the open ballot save in the municipal cities, Regent Horthy was widely regarded as a "person of capacities,"[117] and the formation of the Bethlen government in 1921 was also welcomed in London. The Foreign Office credited the Hungarian premier with a sound home- and foreign policy in the early 1920s, and the Count was seen in London as a "straightforward, honest, intensely patriotic man without fanatical excesses."[118]

### 2.5.4.1. Habsburg Restoration

The pro-Hungarian tone of British policy first became apparent in October 1921, during Karl's second Habsburg restoration attempt in Hungary.[119] The mobiliza-

---

114 Seton-Watson to Oszkár Jászi, October 23, 1923. Seton-Watson Papers, SEW17/11.
115 Seton-Watson to May Seton-Watson, April 22, 1923, Korespondencija, II/105. This also contains Seton-Watson's impressions of Károlyi. On this also see Seton-Watson's letter to Alfred Zimmern (July 27, 1923). Zimmern Papers, MSS. Eng. Box 18, fol. 28.
There, during a series of top-secret encounters, the British historian and the two Hungarian exiles, joined by former defence minister Béla Linder, devised an alternative system to Horthy's Hungary which also received the backing of the Serbs as well as Beneš.
116 Seton-Watson to Mihály Károlyi, June 27, 1923. Seton-Watson Papers, SEW17/12/4.
117 Gábor Bátonyi, *Britain and Central Europe, 1918-1933*, Oxford, Clarendon Press, 1999, 113.
118 Hugh Seton-Watson, Robert W. Seton-Watson and the Trianon Settlement. In: *War and Society in East-Central Europe. Essays on World War*, in *Total War and Peacemaking, A Case Study on Trianon*, Béla K. Király, Peter Pastor and Ivan Sanders (eds.), New York, 1982, 11.
119 The former monarch of Austria-Hungary renounced his ability to participate in Hungarian and Austrian state affairs in a proclamation he made on November 13, 1918, freeing the authorities

tion of four Little Entente divisions and Beneš's uncompromising attitude questioned the pivotal role assigned to Prague as an element of stability in Central Europe. As Gábor Bátonyi explains, overwhelmed by fears that Karl regarded the Hungarian throne as a stepping stone to the restoration of the Habsburg Empire, the Little Entente demanded serious reprisals: not only Habsburg dethronement but also full disarmament of Hungary, reimbursement of mobilization costs and even the restoration of the Sopron area to Austria.[120] Great Britain, backed by Italy, however, took energetic steps to solve the crisis, threatening to break off diplomatic relations with Czechoslovakia and vetoing every excessive demand of the Little Entente and France and calling for Habsburg dethronement only.[121]

Reacting to the event in a speech on November 9 in the House of Lords, Hungarophile Lord Newton declared the imposition of the dethronement to be irreconcilable with the much-trumpeted principle of self-determination, therefore "a gross and most intolerable interference in the internal government of a free nation." Furthermore, the speakers in the House went on to call the principle of equal treatment to account asking: How can states with their own monarchs object to Hungary having a king if it so chooses? Newton added: "We seem [...] to have worked ourselves into a frame of mind in which we consider that an ex-Ally cannot possibly do any wrong, and that an ex-enemy cannot possibly be in the right. [...] if we do not insist upon justice between one nation and another being properly adhered to, then we are only preparing for fresh trouble in Europe."[122] In a letter to Oszkár Jászi, Seton-Watson expressed his dissatisfaction with the failure of the Little Entente endeavour and assured his Hungarian friend that Lord Newton had expressed a private opinion as an "isolated" member of the House of Lords.[123]

---

in the empire from their oath of allegiance to him. Even though it has been described as such, he purposefully avoided using the word "abdication" in this statement lest the people of either nation recall him.

120 On December 14–16, 1921, the approximately 100 square-mile Western-Hungarian Sopron-region held a plebiscite on whether to join Austria or remain in Hungary resulting in a 65 percent majority in favour of Hungary. That was the sole plebiscite on disputed borders on territory belonging to the former Kingdom of Hungary that the Entente permitted following the First World War.
121 Magda Ádám, *The Little Entente and Europe (1920–1929)*, Budapest, Akadémai, 157–167.
122 The pro-Hungarian speakers besides Lord Newton were Lord Sydenham, Lord Phillimore, Lord Oranmore and Browne, Lord Weardale and the Earl of Crawford. "The Hapsburg Dynasty," House of Lords Debate, November 9, 1921. Vol. 47, cc 229–245. https://api.parliament.uk/historic-hansard/lords/1921/nov/09/the-hapsburg-dynasty Accessed April 1, 2023.
See also *Times*, November 10, 1921, 14.
123 György Litván (ed.), *Jászi Oszkár naplója* [Oszkár Jászi's Diary], Budapest, MTA Történettudományi Intézet, 2001, 235.

After 1920, vehement opposition to the Habsburg Restoration was one of the cornerstones of Steed's East Central European policy. He tried his utmost to refute "inopportune" arguments in- and outside Britain. When, for example, Sir Frederick Ponsonby, the lieutenant governor of Windsor Castle, informed him that, quite in line with the 1921 House of Lords speakers, he found it "intolerable" that Britain forbade Hungary to restore the monarchy, which is permitted for "Yogo Slavia" [sic] and Romania, Steed reacted emphatically: "You hold one of the highest positions, [...] anything you write [is] supposed to reflect the views of the king. [...] the French would be offended, and the Americans would look upon it as British effort to start royalist propaganda.[124]

The Habsburg dynasty was deposed by the Hungarian Parliament in November 1921, and Karl was eventually exiled to Madeira, where he passed away in April 1922. It was certain that Otto, his 10-year-old son and successor, would not engage in active politics for many years, and the Hungarian royalist movement would never regain its former prominence.

*2.5.4.2. The Hungarian Economic Reconstruction*

In order to stabilize the bankrupt Hungarian state, a foreign loan in a large amount was indispensable. The condition of obtaining the loan and a securing a guarantee for its repayment was, however, the release of some public revenues that had been blocked as a security for reparations in the Treaty of Trianon. The pivotal visit to London by Prime Minister István Bethlen and Finance Minister Tibor Kállay of Hungary from May 7-10, 1923, was the turning point. They met with the most prominent British politicians, including Foreign Secretary Lord Curzon, Prime Minister Bonar Law (1922-23), and above all Montagu Norman, the governor of the Bank of England (1920-44), who would play a crucial role in the League of Nations loan that would ultimately put Hungary's finances on a stable footing.[125]

But ideologically driven motives intervened. With French backing, representatives of the Little Entente states, particularly Beneš and Romanian Foreign Minister Nicolae Titulescu, renewed their efforts to prevent Hungary from re-

---

124 He was assistant private secretary to Queen Victoria 1897-1901, too. Ponsonby to Steed, July 7, 1930, and Steed's reply, July 8, 1930, MS 74 128.
125 Miklós Lojkó, *Meddling in Middle Europe. Britain and the 'Lands Between' 1919-1925*, Central European University Press, 2005, 64-65.

ceiving a loan, while trying to obtain huge loans for themselves.[126] Nevertheless, the treasury took a tough line and brought home to Beneš and Titulescu that "the City is not keen to advance money to countries pursuing the suicidal policy of making one of their neighbours go bankrupt."[127]

Unsurprisingly, Seton-Watson sided with the Franco–Little Entente position on the Hungarian loan. In a letter to his old friend Allen Leeper, he went so far as to state that it was a „disastrous step" that the premier had found his way to the king with the sole aim to "'rush' everyone into the Hungarian loan policy," which he believed was neither in the true interest of Hungary nor of pacification in the Danube Basin.[128] The once pro-Romanian British expert in Versailles, however, called for moderation: "I hardly think that the King could or ought to have refused to see Bethlen. [...] I dislike their present Government, but I disagree with you in this, and I strongly disapprove of any British interference in internal affairs of other countries."[129]

Interestingly, not only Little Entente nationalism and Seton-Watson were the ones to get in the way of cordial British–Hungarian relations. A Hungarian Labour Delegation (Social Democrat Ernő Garami, Gyula Peidl and Rusztem Vámbéry) travelled to London to lobby against the loan being given to Bethlen, but they had considerable difficulty in getting a hearing in the Foreign Office. In desperation, they also reached out to Steed to try to convince Beneš to state publicly that Czechoslovakia would rather the loan be given to a democratic regime in Hungary. Steed was, on the other hand, rather realistic, and he wrote to Beneš: "I thought your policy much too prudent to permit of a hostile declaration against Bethlen [...] [you are] unlikely to come out in public opposition to an arrangement which had the support of the British Government."[130] The former *Times* correspondent was active behind the scenes, and in July 1924, while in Geneva, he got acquainted with Jeremias Smith, the new commissioner gen-

---

126 Unsurprisingly, Steed, a lifelong critic of Hungary, supported the Romanian loan throughout the 1920s: "I fancy Roumania will have got her loan through the Bank of France, our fools having headed her off from the London market." Steed to Brumwell, April 16, 1928. Steed Papers, MS 74 127
127 Lampson to Sargent, FO, June 26, 1923. Edward Woodward, Rohan Butler, *Documents on British Foreign Policy, 1919-1939*, London 1949-1955, Vol. XXII, 737. See also Zoltán Peterecz, Hungary and the League of Nations: A Forced Marriage. In: Peter Becker and Natasha Wheatley (eds.), *Remaking Central Europe. The League of Nations and the Former Habsburg Lands*, Oxford, Oxford University Press, 2020, 145-165, 153.
128 Seton-Watson to Allen Leeper, January 23, 1924. SEW Papers, box 17.
129 Allen Leeper to Seton-Watson, January 29, 1924. SEW Papers, 17/14/5.
130 Steed to Beneš, February 11, 1924. Steed Papers MS 74103.

eral for the financial control of Hungary, whom he hoped the Magyars were "unlikely to insulate or to short-circuit."[131]

In contrast to Seton-Watson or Steed, Toynbee assessed the Hungarian reconstruction in a different light. After offering a balanced outline of the economic background in his 1924–*Survey*, he came to the following conclusion: "considering the political turmoil through which Hungary passed during the three years immediately following the Armistice [...] the tenacity of her will to live was remarkable."[132]

### 2.5.4.3. The Francs Forgery Affair

The goodwill of the Foreign Office and of Toynbee toward Hungary was soon going to be put to another test. In a bid to harm the French economy and finance revisionist propaganda, counterfeit franc notes were produced by the Hungarian far-right and a few legitimist politicians with the support of Hungarian government officials. In mid-December 1925, Arisztid Jankovich arrived at The Hague with a diplomatic courier's passport issued by the Hungarian Ministry of Foreign Affairs containing a package of ten million counterfeit French francs. When he tried to cash the first 1,000-franc notes, he was caught immediately. The so-called francs-forgery scandal ignited an immediate international crisis.

The situation was degrading and extremely awkward. The head of the Foreign Office Central Department, the pro-Hungarian Miles Lampson, noted with shock and resignation that "it was quite incredible that anyone outside the lunatic asylum should take up such a scheme."[133] Despite such scathing opinions, British diplomacy sought to apply the least harmful strategy to Hungarian interests: claiming ignorance, hoping that international reaction would soon abate. A few weeks later, however, it became painfully evident that some Hungarian government officials had also been involved in the forgery, which contributed to the escalation of the conflict and the formation of an international anti-Bethlen pressure group. This group included members of the Hungarian emigration, mainly Oszkár Jászi and Mihály Károlyi as informers, the governments of France and the Little Entente states, and a few British academics and journalists shepherded by Seton-Watson and Steed. Understandably, they were

---

131 Steed to Mrs Balch, July 12, 1924. Steed Papers MS 74 139.
132 Toynbee, The Reconstruction of Hungary, *Survey of International Affairs 1924*, Oxford University Press, 1926, 424.
133 Lampson to Phipps, January 8, 1926. Bátonyi 1999, 147.

greatly disturbed by the *Times* leader on February 4 describing the forgeries as a trifling affair that the French and Czechs exaggerated.[134]

Alarmed, Steed sent a letter to William Tyrell, then Permanent Under-Secretary of State for Foreign Affairs, in a high-handed style eerily similar to that of Count Apponyi at their first meeting back in 1902, which he had found so hurtful. Steed was confident enough to explain that neither Jeoffrey Dawson nor any of his assistants truly understood the Magyars and that extensive first-hand experience with them, as well as some familiarity with their language were required "before even the beginnings of sound judgement could be formed." He also called to attention that the Magyar irredentists started to forge francs to obtain funds for "a monarchist restoration" of some kind: "Horthy was in it, his brother-in-law was in it, opposed to Bethlen who, however, knew of it, did nothing to suppress it, although he asked for its postponement." Given the close proximity and strong relationships amongst members of the Magyar nobility, he continued, he had never heard of a significant political secret being held in Budapest "for more than a fortnight," thus the plan must have been "well known." Steed once again emphasized that "the treaty of Trianon and the other Peace Treaties stand and fall together." Possibility of revision would thus greatly affect the Germans "for whom, in reality, the Magyars are acting as peace-makers."[135]

Seton-Watson prioritized the scandal for months, expecting it would not only cost Bethlen his head but would also bring down the Horthy regime. He moved to Paris and thus could easily synchronise action with professor of Slavic Studies at the Sorbonne Louis Eisenmann as well as with Mihály Károlyi, who both resided in the French capital. The former prime minister provided the British academic with newspapers and other sources which Seton-Watson intended to publish in a denouncement pamphlet perfectly timed to appear just a few weeks before the League of Nations would put the issue on the agenda. Fallen prey to his own wishful thinking, he assured Károlyi that "the Foreign Office is really negative, if Bethlen is compromised at the trial [...] nothing will be done here to save him,"[136] In fact, the opposite was true. Although privately upset and disappointed in the Hungarians, "the incredible donkeys," [137] as Lampson called

---

134 *Times*, February 4, 1926.
135 Steed to Tyrell, February 4, 1926. Steed Papers MS 74 126
136 Seton-Watson to Károlyi, May 13, 1926. In: Tibor Hajdú, György Litván, *Károlyi Mihály levelezése*, Vol. 3, Budapest, 1991, 226. For the role of Bethlen in the affair see Ignác Romsics, *Bethlen István. Politikai életrajz* [István Bethlen. Political Biography], Budapest, Magyarságkutató Intézet,1991, 169–172.
137 Lampson to Barclay FO, January 11, 1926. Qtd. in Bátonyi 1999, 148.

them, the Foreign Office publicly supported the Bethlen Government since it was thought in London that his resignation would be detrimental to British interests.

By the summer of 1926, the hopelessness of the anti-Bethlen campaign had become glaringly obvious, and, refusing to confront the Foreign Office, Seton-Watson abandoned the plan for the denouncement pamphlet. "It would not do very much good," he explained to Károlyi, "but would confirm people in the conviction that I was hopelessly prejudiced."[138] Later he experimented with the relaunch of his once successful journal, *The New Europe*, in order to provide the members of the October emigration with a platform, much as he had done in 1916–19.

Louis Eisenmann, Seton-Watson's aide de camp in the forgery affair, had long been respected by Toynbee as "a chief authority on Central-Eastern Europe."[139] The two could finally meet in May 1926, which in no way affected Toynbee's low-key description of the forgery affair in his *Survey*. He claimed that the danger lay "in the peculiar quality of Magyar patriotism," but also added that the crisis exposed the inability of the Little Entente to take coordinated action, as owing to the improved Yugoslav–Hungarian relations, Yugoslavia remained effectively "passive."[140]

The period after 1927 brought about significant change, that is, the apparent cooling in British-Hungarian relations. Yet, it was not the anti-Hungarian British intellectuals like Seton-Watson or Steed or the Hungarian émigrés who initiated the change, let alone French or Little Entente diplomatic successes. The end of the British–Hungarian "special relationship"[141] was brought about by the

---

138 Seton-Watson to Mihály Károlyi, December 11, 1926. In: Tibor Hajdu (ed.), *Károlyi Mihály levelezése*, Budapest, 1991, III/255.
139 Toynbee to Zimmern, May 3, 1926. RIIA Archives 4/TOYN/40 1926-.
140 Toynbee, *Survey of International Affairs 1926*, London, Oxford University Press, Humphrey Milford, 1928) 148-149 fn.
In a similarly neutral tone Toynbee described the incident that followed the discovery of a shipment of machine gun parts on January 1, 1928, at Szentgotthárd on the Austrian-Hungarian border, with, according to Hungarian officials, Warsaw as final destination. The Little Entente states requested investigation by the League of Nations Council, as the Treaty of Trianon had placed restrictions on the amount of machine guns Hungary could own. It was the first time the Council had been requested to use its power of supervision over armaments of four countries disarmed by Peace Treaties. The investigations revealed "illegal presence of military material," but they also found "no evidence that the war material was intended to remain in Hu territory." As a result, the Hungarian government was found neither guilty nor innocent; the report's lack of resolution led to widespread displeasure. Toynbee quoted Prime Minister Austen Chamberlain declaring that "we should have to seek ways more efficacious" in response to a new event. Toynbee, *Survey of International Affairs 1928*, 1930?, 161–166.
141 Though in 1939 Toybee called it a "half-hearted" one. Toynbee, After Munich: The World Outlook. *International Affairs* (Royal Institute of International Affairs 1931-1939), Vol. 18, No. 1 (January–February, 1939), 1-28, 11.

new Italian orientation in Budapest together with the appearance of the issue of revision at the forefront of Hungarian foreign policy.

## 2,6. Four Britons and the Question of Hungarian Frontier Readjustment (1926–1929)

As we have seen, throughout the early 1920s, Britain continually committed its support to the Hungarian government, frequently to Steed's and Seton-Watson's vehement objection. This relatively pro-Hungarian attitude, however, did not extend to the revision of the Treaty of Trianon, on which the official British position at the time, as well as the statements of Seton-Watson and Steed, were in agreement.[142]

Even so, despite the status quo-friendly stance of British foreign policy makers, British public opinion, particularly in higher social circles, had a perception of the legitimacy of Hungarian revisionist aspirations, based primarily on personal connections.[143] One such protest against the injustice done to Hungary was made in a letter written by L.W. Lyde, a professor of geography at the University of London, which was published in the *Times* on March 18, 1926. The author provided a brief history of Hungary highlighting (though not devoid of errors) the geographic and hydrographic unity of the Carpathian Basin. Finally, appealing to the conscience of the British public, he declared that for the sins of their leaders during the dualist period, this "proud and ancient nation" had been punished: "We reduced Hungary from the size of the British Isles to that of Ireland," leaving around two million Hungarians at the wrong side. Lyde also included a map estimating the number of Hungarians living along the Trianon borders at two million, whom he alleged could be returned to the motherland with "relatively minor border adjustments."[144]

The New Europe circle, working to preserve the status-quo, would react immediately, this time to the geography professor's letter. In an article already in the next day's *Times*, Steed offered a quick lecture on the real nationality ratios and Hungary's "oligarchic, semi-feudal" system. The only thing worthy of Brit-

---

142 Up until the early 1930s, responsible British government officials frequently advocated for maintaining the status quo, advancing interstate cooperation, and opposing any revisionist initiatives. "The British Cabinet hold strongly the view that there is no question of revision of the treaty of Versailles," the *Times* reported in 1924. July 8, 1924, 14.
143 See *The Hungarian Question in the British Parliament. Speeches and Answers thereto in the House of Lords and the House of Commons from 1919 to 1930*, London, Grant Richards, 1933.
144 L.W. Lyde, "The Frontiers of Hungary," *Times*, March 18, 1926, 17.

ish sympathy, he insisted, was the October-emigration, such as Jászi or Károlyi who, by extending freedoms, would enable Hungary to cooperate with its neighbours and thus bring peace to the Danube basin.[145]

The Hungarian government formally put the issue of revision on hold in order to placate the Western powers and obtain crucial loans after the Versailles Treaties. The year of 1927, however, provided an unexpected boost to Hungarian revisionism. First, Hungary's isolation in international affairs was greatly reduced by the Hungarian–Italian Treaty of Friendship, which was signed in April 1927. Prime Minister István Bethlen, who had hitherto been quite circumspect in his remarks on foreign policy matters, emerged as a vocal opponent of Trianon at the end of May, claiming that "the world is beginning to realize" its injustice and that "public opinion is beginning to swing towards the country." The Hungarian country had "paid its debts in the peace treaty," the prime minister added, but it still had legitimate claims which he anticipated would be resolved by, among other things, "the course of world history."[146] Second, during the summer of 1927, the British press tycoon, Harold Sydney Harmsworth, or Viscount Rothermere, the late Lord Northcliffe's brother, published an editorial in his *Daily Mail* titled "Hungary's Place in the Sun." It argued that

> Eastern Europe is strewn with Alsace-Lorraines. By severing from France, the twin provinces of that name the Treaty of Frankfurt in 1871 made another European war inevitable. The same blunder has been committed on a larger scale in the peace treaties which divided up the old Austro-Hungarian Empire. They have been created dissatisfied minorities in half a dozen parts of Central Europe, any one of which may be the starting point of another conflagration.

In his article the Viscount concluded that the Trianon frontiers were arbitrary, economic nonsense and unjust; their peaceful revision would prevent the outbreak of a new European war. Alongside Professor Lyde, he also favoured the return of one million Hungarians from Czechoslovakia, 600,000 from Romania and a further 400,000 from Yugoslavia.[147] Though the distribution of the minorities was quite inaccurate on Rothermere's map, his taking up the Hungarian cause was excellent news for Budapest and equally worrisome for the-

---

145 Steed, "The Frontiers of Hungary," *Times*, March 19, 1926, 15.
146 Magyarország hivatása a Dunamedencében [Hungary's Vocation in the Danube Basin]. In: *Bethlen István gróf beszédei és írásai* [Count István Bethlen: Speeches and Writings], Budapest, Genius, 1933, Vol. II, 185.
147 Viscount Rothermere, *My Campaign for Hungary*, London, Eyre and Spottiswoode, 1939, 81–89.

## 2,6. Four Britons and the Question of Hungarian Frontier Readjustment

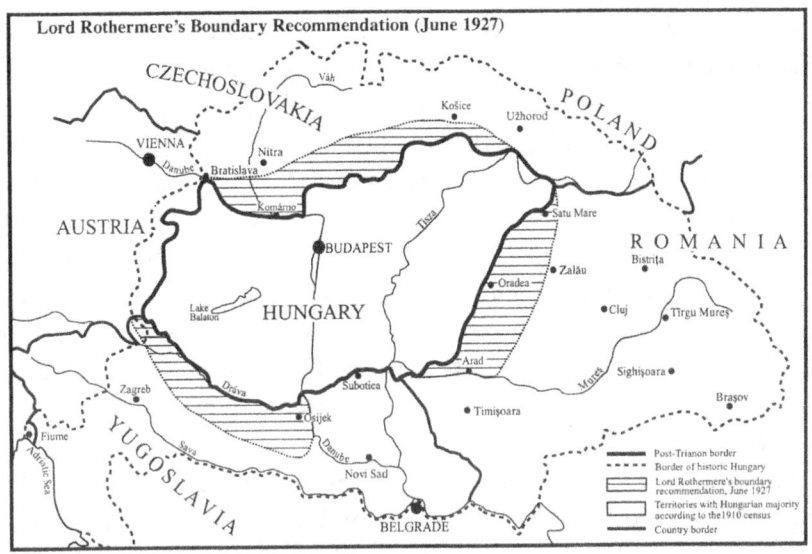

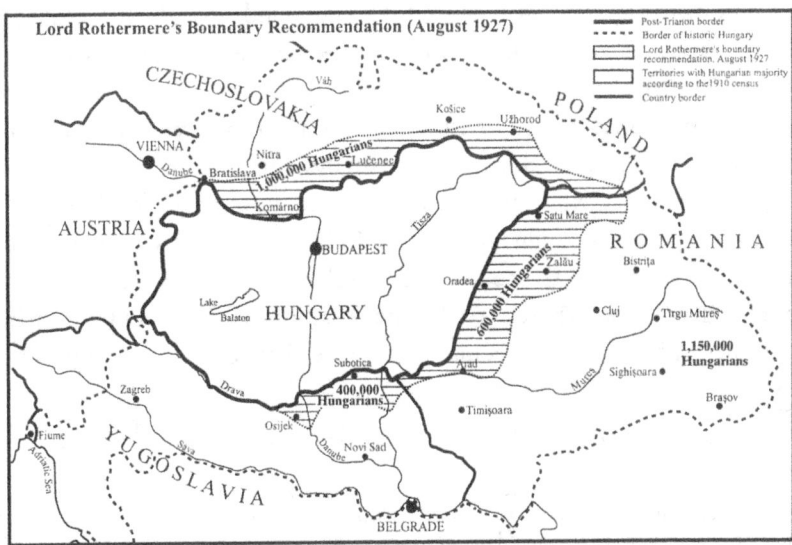

Rothermere's Boundary Recommendations June 27 and August 27.
Maps drawn by Edit Völgyesi, courtesy of Miklós Zeidler

Little Entente. In Britain, many were taken aback by the unusually fervent support for the Hungarian cause of a man who not long before had not been able to tell Budapest and Bucharest apart.

As Britain's first secretary of state for air during the First World War, the Viscount was instrumental in creating the Royal Air Force, earning Lloyd George's praise for his "inestimable service." Yet the war brought him not only esteem but irreparable loss, too: the death of two of his three sons on the Western Front, and estrangement from his wife. In 1922 his brother, Lord Northcliffe, owner of the *Times* (1908-21) died, and thus Lord Rothermere inherited the Amalgamated Press empire, becoming the third richest man in Britain, however still, in the eyes of many, a jumped-up vulgarian. For three months out of the year the owner of the *Daily Mail* and *Daily Mirror*, as well as a number of magazines gambled in Monte Carlo, which is where he was introduced to his "mysterious woman," who was equally as charming and sophisticated as Steed's Madame Rose.

Having married into the family of Franz Joseph, Princess Stephanie von Hohenlohe Waldenburg-Schillingfürst had a high-sounding name that was a fig leaf over her lowly origins as the illegitimate daughter of Czech Jewess Ludmilla Kuranda and a Jewish money lender. The princess carefully guarded this secret for the rest of her life.[148] Stephanie and her husband divorced in 1920, but she continued to represent herself as a princess and developed friendships, sometimes intimate ones, with powerful men, including influential Nazi Party members such as Joachim von Ribbentrop. Harold Sidney Harmsworth, the later Lord Rothermere was also charmed by the Princess's beauty and quick wit, and her justifications and awareness of Hungarian grievances impressed him.[149]

According to Miklós Zeidler's superb analysis in *Ideas on Territorial Revision in Hungary, 1920-1945*, whereas the Little Entente states made an attempt to kill Rothermere's press campaign with silence, in Hungary the viscount was looked upon as the "saviour" of the country: one million signatures were collected in support of his action. These were bound in albums and presented to him in the summer of 1927 in a spectacular London celebration. Soon newspapers out-

---

148 Jim Wilson, *Nazi Princess: Hitler, Lord Rothermere and Princess Stephanie von Hohenlohe*, The History Press, 2011, 23.
149 Rothermere wrote the following letter to the Princess on April 30, 1928: "[...] it was largely through my conversation with you that my interest in Hungary was aroused. I had no conception that a recital of Hungary's sufferings and wrongs would arouse such world-wide sympathy. Now from all parts of the world I am in receipt of such a flood of telegrams, letters and postcards that the work entailed in connection with the propaganda is rapidly absorbing all my energies and my most valuable time. I have to make the decision whether I shall neglect my work and interests and be preoccupied with the cause of Hungary only, or whether I should neglect the cause of Hungary and remain preoccupied with my worldwide interests. [...] Will you reply and let me know, without undue delay, your views. You may say I am necessary in this matter. A woman's intuition—I mean yours—is usually much better than a man's reasoning, and anything you say will, as you know, receive my most careful consideration [...]." Papers of Prinzessin Stephanie von Hohenlohe. Hoover Institute Archives, Box 1, File: 1928. Qtd. in Katalin Kadar Lynn, Strange Partnership: Lord Rothermere, Stephanie Von Hohenlohe and the Hungarian Revisionist Movement, *Independent Scholar* [Quarterly] 25.4 (November 2012), 1-13. Reprinted in *Independent Scholar*, Vol. 5 (August 2019), 74-82, 78-79.

did each other to write articles in praise of the Viscount,[150] whose London castle had to establish a special room for the thousands of gifts, "ornate albums, elaborately carved shepherd's crooks, allegorical statues, [...] folk embroideries, crowns fashioned from pumpkin seeds, and other wonders [...] sent from the rural nests of Hungary to him from patriotic enthusiasm."[151] The fervour of the Hungarian public, however, was in sharp contrast to Prime Minister Bethlen's quiet demeanour. He soberly stated that

> [...] the point of view of the Hungarian Government in this matter is well known: we have no intention of at present demanding the revision of the Peace Treaty because in our opinion the situation is not yet ripe for this purpose. The public opinion of the world must demand consideration of this matter and we are only endeavouring to encourage this method of approach by constant but honest information and propaganda to be carried on by Hungarian society in general and the world press.[152]

The Rothermere press campaign thus highlighted the dichotomy between cautious official diplomacy and ambitious propaganda. A forum for the latter, The Hungarian Fronter Readjustment League was founded in the summer of 1927 to support the Viscount's campaign,[153] and its excitement and unprofessional activities frequently impeded the more circumspect diplomatic efforts of the Hungarian government. This conflict of interests and methods was best demonstrated by the visit to Hungary in May 1928 by Esmond Harmsworth, a British MP and the Viscount's only living son. The visit was initiated by the League despite stern warnings from the Hungarian Legation in London and the British government. In addition to cheering audiences, and notable League leaders, Harmsworth was welcomed by the prime minister, the governor, and the mayor of Budapest, which could suggest that an official decision had been made to arrange the visit. The response to the tour in English government cir-

---

[150] Miklós Zeidler, *Ideas on Territorial Revision in Hungary, 1920–1945*, Columbia University Press, New York, 2007, 109.
[151] Ferenc Herczeg, *Hűvösvölgy*, Budapest, Szépirodalmi, 1993, 148.
[152] *Magyarország*, August 6, 1927.
[153] Ferenc Herceg, a writer of ethnic German origin, was elected president, and at the very first meeting made it clear that "the so called Rothermere-proposal is not representative of Hungary's aims and has not been advanced by Hungarians, as the Hungarian nation will not resign her right to restore its territorial integrity." Qtd. in Romsics, *Hungary's Place in the Sun*, László Péter and Martyn Rady (eds.), 2004, 200. By 1929 the organisation had more than 500 member organisations and a board of directors counting up to 900 members. See Zeidler 2007, 117–118.

cles was very negative as a result; thus the attempt to advance the cause of border revision backfired.[154]

Rather than on the MP's visit, the New Europe circle concentrated much more on opposing the Rothermere effort, since it created a considerably bigger stir than any former action that had questioned the status quo. Seton-Watson was in charge of assuaging Little Entente public, and in numerous letters to his Czech, Slovak, Romanian, or Croatian acquaintances, he attempted to expose the wealthy but frugal Viscount, who was not only hated in his own party but was also regarded with deep mistrust by Liberals and Labour. "The Magyars could not have chosen a worse person to push their propagandist cause,"[155] he argued, adding rightly that the Foreign Office was "furious" at Rothermere and had "nothing whatever to do with him."[156]

In order to effectively counter the Viscount's campaign, Seton-Watson also suggested taking positive steps: he advised "constructive educational work"[157] to his Slovak friend Milan Hodža on his visit to London in November, and in a letter to his Romanian confidante, Viorel Tilea, he urged the Bucharest government to reaffirm their public commitment to the unity of Romania and condemn the Rothermere campaign.[158]

In 1928, another constructive step taken to counteract "damaging" Hungarian propaganda was Seton-Watson's plan to compile a collection of articles by prominent Slovak intellectuals on the occasion of the tenth anniversary of the creation of Czechoslovakia. The work, *Slovakia Then and Now*, was published in English, German and French, to demonstrate the loyalty of Slovaks to the state.[159] It was no coincidence but rather very deliberate timing that simultaneously with the young Harmsworth's somewhat infamous visit to Hungary in May 1928, Seton-Watson travelled to Czechoslovakia. "When we arrived at

---

154 Baron Iván Rubido-Zichy, the minister in London complained that "there is no influential Britisher who is willing to come forward in any matter related to Hungary, because Hungary is at present viewed here as a 'Rothermere stunt'[...]." Qtd. in Zeidler 2007, 124.
155 Seton-Watson to Alois Kolísek, October 4, 1927. Rychlík, Marzik, Bielik (eds.) 1995, I/394.
156 Seton-Watson to Ivo Lupis Vukić, November 10, 1927. *Korespondencija*, II/157.
157 Konstruktive Aufklärungsarbeit [German original]. Seton-Watson to Alois Kolísek, November 15, 1927. Rychlík, Marzik, Bielik (eds.) 1995, I/397.
158 Seton-Watson to Viorel Tilea, October 26, 1927. Seton-Watson Papers, SEW17/28/6. Tilea, the future Romanian Legate to London in 1939, named his son "Scotus" out of respect for Seton-Watson. For more, see Ileana Tilea (ed), *Envoy Extraordinary: Memoirs of a Roumanian Diplomat*, London, 1998.
159 Although the book was published in 1931, that is three years later than planned, it proved nevertheless to be effective. According to the *Times Literary Supplement*, it "leaves no room for doubt that the Treaty of Trianon, at least as far as Slovakia is concerned, provided the necessary corrections of past injustices." *The Slavonic Review*, April 1932, back cover.

the station, they came in thousands," reads his wife's account of the experience [...]., "they took the horses out of the carriage we were in, and dragged us all through the streets, cheering and singing their national songs, and shouting out [...] Long live Scotus Viator, long live the friend of the Slovaks, welcome to our dear English friends."[160]

Like Seton-Watson, Steed worked hard to counter the Rothermere campaign by disseminating information to both the victors and the vanquished. While trying to reassure his Little Entente friends, in a long letter to Miklós Lázár, the editor of the Hungarian political weekly *A Reggel*,[161] he explained that the articles on "dismembered Hungary" that had appeared in various papers, as well as official Hungarian propaganda were both extremely harmful to the country. Instead, he opined, it would be necessary to reveal the true causes of its downfall and dismemberment: instead of admitting the non-Magyar nationalities to equal and effective citizenship, the blindness of the Hungarian coalition had dominated and the annexation of Bosnia-Herzegovina had made the great war "inevitable." "Hungary smashed herself to pieces and has no right to complain of mutilation," he argued coldly, somewhat prophetically concluding that in case Hungary kept going in the same direction, she would sooner or later cause further unrest in Central Europe, "in which her governing class may disappear entirely."[162]

Two months later, in February 1928 Steed received a letter from Richard von Coudenhove-Kalergi.[163] The pioneer of the idea of a federal Europe asked Steed to mediate for Baron Hatvany, a writer and patron of literature as well as a former member of the Hungarian National Council. Alongside Mihály Károlyi, Hatvany had been a key figure during the Aster Revolution of October 1918, who after returning to Hungary was sentenced to seven years imprisonment.[164] Steed opted not to assist Hatvany: "If anything can be done it is certain that I

---

160 Rychlík, Marzik, Bielik (eds,) 1995, I/37.
161 The political weekly appeared from 1922; the morning the last issue appeared, August 30, 1948, the editor left Hungary.
162 Steed to Nicholas Lázár, the editor of *A Reggel*, Deceember 28, 1927. Steed Papers MS 74 127.
163 Steed was acquainted with Coudenhove's mother and other family members, and after the publication of his *Pan-Europe* in 1924, Coudenhove sent Steed a copy. Henry Wickham Steed was one of the few British who were interested in the pan-Europe-movement at that time. https://www.zum.de/whkmla/sp/1112/sunghyun/sunghyun4.html
Steed remained in touch with the Austrian-Japanese political philosopher; in 1938 he prefaced Kalergi's book and found it important to state about the author's parents' mixed marriage that "the difference of race" was not "an insuperable obstacle to their union" and referred to Richard Kalergi as the holder "in one person [of] several ethnic qualities." R. Coudenhove-Kalergi, *The Totalitarian State against Man*, Glarus, Paneuropa, citations on 5 and 4.
164 Kalergi to Steed, February 13, 1928. Steed Papers MS 74 127.

must take no public part in any initiative, because the present Hungarian Government loves me with the same intensity as the Italian Fascists love me, and their affections are equalled by Lord Rothermere [...] it would probably do him [Hatvany] more harm than good."[165]

Steed was well aware of the inherent dangers in the Viscount's pro-revision campaign[166] and was therefore more active than ever to advise public opinion in general, as well as fellow Britons who, having been inspired by Rothermere, were calling for treaty revision in favour of Hungary. In a letter to the *Times* editor in March 1928 he claimed that "an order, notwithstanding its inevitably and largely remediable defects [is] incomparably more just than the old order that was characterised by the oppression of a majority of non-Magyars in pre-war Hungary by a minority of Magyars."[167] When a few months later, the editor of the *Observer*, James Lewis Garvin, also a staunch critic of the Versailles settlement, approached him backing some frontier readjustments, Steed did not apply the usual defence strategy of calling on, sometimes erroneous, statistics or his own unique expertise. Therefore, his somewhat naive reply is worth quoting in some detail:

> I agree with you that the present state of things in Central-Europe is unlikely to be eternal. The sooner it can be modified by mutual understanding and cooperation, the better. [...] it may last as long as Bismarckian Europe [...] if those who think it can be modified by pressure without bringing on catastrophe continue to foster a sense of insecurity. This is one reason why I never use the word "revision" [...] it tends to defeat its processed object by making bristles stand on end when it is to the general interest that they should be permanently smoothed down. The general understanding between Magyar people and neighbouring peoples is not only conceivable but practicable; and it will come when the Magyar people, as distinguished from the oligarchy of magnates, are able to speak for themselves. Until then it will be out of the question, because there is no guarantee that any arrangement with the present system in Hungary would be accepted as final.[168]

---

165 Steed to Count Coudenhove-Kalergi, February 16, 1928. Steed Papers MS 74 127.
166 He warned Geoffrey Dawson, the former editor of the *Times* that "the Rothermere stunt and the Hungarian campaign with Robert Gower [...] will end by starting war in Central-Europe if people are not very careful." Steed to Dawson, March 15, 1928. Steed Papers MS 74127
167 Letter to the Editor, *Times*, March 16, 1928.
168 Steed to J.L. Garvin, June 28, 1928. Steed Papers, MS 74 127

Given his record in Greco-Turkey between 1920–1923, it seems logical that preservation of the status-quo was not a question of life and death for Toynbee. His general line of conduct in the *Surveys* was to be as objective as possible. Thus, his first volumes were largely dry accounts of diplomatic events. In a letter to an acquaintance, he revealed something similar: despite having dealt a good deal with Hungary in two volumes of the *Survey* published so far, his treatment of the related topics was "studiously colourless." "I have attempted to state the facts as far as possible without showing my own feelings," he explained. In the same letter he concurred that prior to the war Hungary was an economic unity, and that the new frontiers had damaged its industries and caused a political injustice as well, in that whenever there was a disputed or mixed area, they gave it to the Successor States. On the other hand, in line with Seton-Watson or Steed, he added that he did not believe the remedy was "restoration of the old frontiers," which could only be brought about by a similar war, and "would certainly bring back old evils or greater ones without getting rid of the ones we now have." Similarly, alongside Steed and Seton-Watson, Toynbee also looked forward to some kind of "economic Entente" in Eastern Europe "when the feelings have begun to die down," which he was convinced would take a long time.[169]

Despite his relatively distanced attitude regarding frontier adjustments or the lack of thereof, the director of the RIIA followed very closely the line taken by Steed and Seton-Watson regarding the Rothermere campaign. He soberly stated that Prime Minister Bethlen poured oil on troubled waters by declaring that neither he nor his cabinet had had any relations with the affair and that in his view the moment had not arrived for any suggestion of treaty revision. In his 1927 *Survey of International Affairs* Toynbee explained that Lord Rothermere's proposed borders resembled Hungary's new borders much more than its old ones had done, and rectification along some of those lines, presuming that upon closer examination it were found to be geographically feasible, might have helped to advance the cause of peace and stability in South-Eastern Europe had it been put forth at a wisely chosen time and in a wisely conceived form.

Toynbee was undoubtedly right to identify the great gulf between the more restrained official position and the "intransigent Hungarian nationalists" who had lulled themselves into believing that Lord Rothermere's efforts had created a real opportunity for the "integral restoration" of the former borders.[170] How-

---

169 Toynbee to Hunter Blair, Esq., Savoy House, Ayr, April 6, 1926. RIIA Archives 4/TOYN/6a.
170 Toynbee, *Survey of International Affairs 1927*, Oxford University Press for the Royal Institute of International Affairs, 1929, 206 fn.

ever, the situation was worse than that. To start with, the Hungarian government's cautious approach was at least as much the result of avoiding renouncing *restitutio in integrum* as it was of statesmanship. Second, in Hungary between the two world wars, all people, whether politicians, other public figures or ordinary citizens, were prisoners of revisionism, which became a national obsession. One should bear it in mind that almost every Hungarian politician had either his origin or at least family ties in the detached territories, a circumstance Seton-Watson or Steed overlooked.

To see the desire to change borders where there was no sign of it led to a distortion of thinking from which Hungarian society has perhaps never recovered. One glaring example is the interpretation of Seton-Watson's late-1928 statement in the *Times*: "As one who freely criticized the Magyars for their handling of the Southern Slav question, I am bound in common fairness to add that on each of these three occasions the Magyars had far better technical excuses for their high-handed action than any which Belgrade can put forward today."[171] In the otherwise eminent classical scholar[172] József Balogh's article "The About-Turn of Scotus Viator" it reads as follows: "The attempt to create historical uniformity here is sinful and hopeless. In particular, Croatia, which has maintained its autonomous status for eight centuries in union with Hungary, is capable of a passive resistance that will test the centralists in Belgrade. It should be emphasised that Belgrade is even more inadequate than Constantinople, Budapest or Vienna to solve the Southern Slav question."[173] The original article does not include these terms, so we are dealing with a case of deliberate misinterpretation. Judging from the title, it is probable that the author aimed to prove—as

---

171 *Times*, December 13, 1928, 10.
172 In the late 1930s Balogh did much to popularize Toynbee's former "boss" James Bryce in Hungary. Bryce had had strong ties with Transylvania and had delivered a speech in the House of Lords in May 1921 against the vindictive Treaty of Trianon and in support of ethnic revision. See: *The Hungarian Problem in the British Parliament: Speeches, Questions and Answers thereto in the House of Lords and the House of Commons from 1919 to 1930*, London, Grant Richards, 1933; and József Balogh, *A magyar revízió angol előharcosa: Lord Bryce születésének századik évfordulójára* [The English Pioneer of Hungarian Revisionism: On the Centenary of the Birth of Lord Bryce], Budapest, Franklin-Társulat, 1939.
173 József Balogh, "Scotus Viator pálfordulása," *Magyar Szemle*, March, 1930, 25. The journal *Magyar Szemle* [Hungarian Review] was launched by the Magyar Szemle Társaság [Hungarian Review Society] and founded with the goal of addressing the difficulty of publishing high-caliber scholarly works in 1927. It had strong official and unofficial ties to the government. The fact that Prime Minister István Bethlen served as its president and that some among Hungary's most well-known political and intellectual elite were among the board members speaks volumes about the importance that was attached to this society's achievement. The Society was terminated after the German occupation of the country, largely due to its anti-Nazi tone. Matthew Caples, "Et in Hungaria Ego: Trianon, Revisionism, and the Journal Magyar Szemle (1927-1944)," *Hungarian Studies* 19, No. 1, 2005, 68.

he himself perhaps believed—that the historian had acknowledged the failure of the Versailles treaty.

\* \* \*

Steed-biographer Andre Liebich argues that between Steed and Seton-Watson, the latter looked at Hungarian frontier readjustment claims "with more understanding."[174] This, given his legacy, is highly doubtful. Despite allowing frontier rectification *in theory*, both former champions of East-Central European national self-determination adamantly opposed any *de facto* revision of the Versailles system. Moreover, Carlile Aylmer Macartney, whose early career as a historian had its way paved by Seton-Watson, also echoed such views. The young historian regarded the prominent Oxford scholar with unshakable respect and, as late as 1932, still believed that criticizing the more experienced and competent historian on Central and Eastern European matters was "the rashest of acts" and "an impertinence."[175]

Owing to Seton-Watson's backing, Macartney's first article on Hungary was published in his mentor's own journal, the *Slavonic and East European Review*, at the onset of 1929. In "Hungary since 1918," the author emerged as a staunch critic of interwar Hungary, which he described as "reaction in the truest sense of the world,"[176] with political power concentrated in the hands of "a rather narrow" Hungarian or Magyarized landowner oligarchy. Tough words, which either Seton-Watson or Steed could have authored.

Macartney could not, of course, ignore the increasingly influential revisionist tendencies, which from 1927 onwards became more and more integrated into official Hungarian propaganda. He noted that the break-up of the dual monarchy had occurred due to the principle of self-determination, which, however, was not applied consistently and especially not with strict impartiality. Few would deny, he argued, that the peace treaty did not "bore harshly on Hungary." But this was a far cry from admitting that the break-up of historic Hungary was a mistake. Those foreigners, he continued, "who do proclaim it, seem to be generally quite under-

---

174 Liebich 2018, 258.
175 Macartney, *Slovakia Then and Now* by R.W. Seton-Watson, review, *International Affairs*, 1931/2, 269.
176 Macartney identified the rural open ballot, the maintenance of virilism and the anti-working-class character of the 1921 Law as, among others, major sins of the political system which in fact reinforced the authoritarian tendencies. However, it was not the political situation that received the most criticism in the article, but the post-war failure to resolve the land question. In line with Seton-Watson and Steed, the author believed the biggest problem of interwar Hungary to be the continuation of the essentially unchanged agrarian structure of pre-1918, the social aspect of which was the hopeless situation of landless servants and agricultural labourers. Macartney, Hungary since 1918, *Slavonic and Eastern European Review (SEER)*, 1929/3, 581.

informed about either the history or the current conditions of the countries they write about." This latter remark could be taken as an implicit criticism of the Rothermere campaign, but the author equally disparaged the tendency to give the realignment of borders a higher priority than the burning social problems. He perceived the growing dominance of revisionist policy as a double threat: not only did the spread of revisionism obstruct long-overdue socio-economic reforms, but it also severely strained relations between Hungary and the Little Entente states, for which, in Macartney's opinion, "the exaggerated nationalism" of the neighbouring states was not the only cause.[177] At the end of his article, the young historian expressed his somewhat naïve hope that the Little Entente would surely make concessions, and that Hungary would not only follow Austria's example and resign itself to its losses but would also embark on the inevitable social reforms that would create better living conditions for Hungarians, rich and poor alike.

Macartney's first detailed analysis of Hungarian politics, society and the question of frontier readjustment thus marked the young historian's place for the time being as more in line with Seton-Watson and Steed than against them. This is duly borne out by the fact that when, in the spring of 1929, Gyula Szekfű, his old acquaintance from the Vienna Archives asked Macartney to head the Hungarian department to be established at the University of London on behalf of the Hungarian government, Macartney, dismissing Hungarian enthusiasm, declared: "I should very much like the job if it was quite clearly understood that I make no propaganda. Also, that I didn't want Old Hungary restored."[178] To reinforce his point, he sent his friend a few copies of his paper "Hungary since 1918," eagerly awaiting the effect. According to a later letter from Macartney, the article may have discouraged Szekfű, and the Hungarian department could not be established for several more years due to the lack of funds caused by the economic crisis.[179]

As we have seen, the views of Macartney and Seton-Watson on Hungary under Horthy–Bethlen and on frontier readjustment largely overlapped, but the two historians approached the minority question, the importance of which they both recognised, differently.

---

177 Macartney, Hungary since 1918, 592–594.
178 Macartney to Seton-Watson, July 12, 1929. Seton-Watson Papers, SEW 17/15/15. This nicely echoed Toynbee's attitude back in the early 1920s when he claimed that "academic study should have no political purpose."
179 The lack of money was indeed a recurring topic in Macartney's letters to József Balogh. On September 23, 1930, for example, he wrote: [For the establishment of a Hungarian department] the School of Slavonic Studies "would be ready, but for the time being no money is available." (German original) József Balogh to Macartney, September 23, 1930. Országos Széchenyi Könyvtár KT, Fond 1/2064, 18454.

## 2.7. Four Britons and the Post-Versailles (Hungarian) Minorities: 1920–early 1930s

If Hungary's post 1927 diplomatic strategy aimed at revising the Versailles system, it is perhaps not an overstatement to argue that the Little Entente states' top priority was to keep it. As a result, obsession countered obsession, which, as much as in Hungary, was indulged by all segments of their respective native populations, except for Communists. One significant difference, however, was that after 1920 the Hungarians' fixation with revisionism was fuelled, among other things, by the fact that the peace treaty annexed 3.5 million of their fellow citizens to the successor states, of whom nearly one and a half million lived in close proximity to the mother country, serving as a permanent reminder of the "unfortunate" borders drawn in 1919–20.

The first major product of the British Institute of International Affairs was *The History of the Peace Conference of Paris* which was published in six volumes until 1925—a comprehensive account of the decision-making process and its results. Toynbee's *The World After the Peace Conference,* an epilogue to the *History of the Peace Conference of Paris* came out a year later in 1926. The author acknowledged that in Central-Europe the growing consciousness of nationality had attached itself "almost exclusively" to mother tongues, which resulted in "revolutionary changes" in the pre-existing political map. "Great Powers no longer dominate the landscape," [180] Toynbee asserted. In line with Seton-Watson and Steed, he explained that the Peace Conference attempted to work on an abstract principle, that is to base the new map upon nationality, which was "successful on the whole," within the limits permitted by the co-ordinate factor of economic geography (e.g., the Magyars in Rumania and Czechoslovakia).

Again in the footsteps of Steed and Seton-Watson, in 1926 Toynbee excused the excesses of minority policy in the successor states of the Monarchy as follows:

> The political atmosphere of Eastern-Europe in particular, could not be purified instantaneously by drawing fresh lines on a map. All parties alike had breathed it for generations, and all would therefore continue to show the pathological effects of the contagion for some time to come. The first impulse of a nation just released from duress is to behave like the Unmerciful Servant towards weaker neighbours and especially towards its former masters. Indeed, a nation suddenly enabled to indulge the instinct of domina-

---

180 Toynbee, *The World After the Peace Conference,* issued under the auspices of the British Institute of International Affairs, Humphrey Milford, Oxford University Press, 1926, 18, 21–22.

tion after long repression will usually take greater advantage of its opportunities than a nation satiated by a long enjoyment of power.[181]

So there was no shortage of indulgent goodwill, but did the successor states of the Monarchy live up to that?

2.7.1. Czechoslovakia

In agreement with His Majesty's government's position, as we have seen, Seton-Watson opposed any treaty revision, which nevertheless was not accompanied by a disregard for the plight of the minorities. On the contrary, the historian-publicist had been devoting increased attention to the cause of minority Hungarians since the early 1920s; for example, he included a whole chapter on the problems of Hungarian minority in his 1924 book, *The New Slovakia*, for which he had gathered information while visiting that country and had spoken with opposition party officials a year earlier. His work is distinguished by a specific logic that compared the circumstances of the Hungarian minority with the rights of Slovaks in pre-1918 Hungary, which usually resulted in downgrading their problems. Equally odd is his explanation that Hungarians in some majority villages were lacking schools because they in fact had originally been Slovaks, the victims of Magyarization: "Seldom has any nation [...] fallen so completely a prey to nationalistic megalomania."[182]

Despite sometimes odd reasoning, the book could be somewhat regarded as a reverse of *Racial Problems*; a fair summary of minority problems, this time the Hungarian grievances (without leaving the status quo once again untouched as in his previous work): the violation of the 1920 language law, inadequate schools or teacher supply. Seton-Watson urged that serious steps be taken to facilitate the higher education of Hungarian youth in their own language, to provide special Hungarian courses and department chairs at Bratislava (Pozsony) University, to found the Hungarian Cultural League, and finally to abolish the anti-Hungarian tone of the censorship. He described the government plan to break up the ethnic Hungarians' border areas by resettling Czechs and Slovaks as a "short-sighted design," and even as "Slavisation."[183] Although he referred to 600,000 in-

---

181 Ibid., 61.
182 Seton-Watson 1924, *The New Slovakia*, 101. See also András D. Bán, Seton-Watson és a csehszlovákiai magyar kisebbség [Seton-Watson and the Hungarian Minority in Czechoslovakia], *Valóság*, 1997/6, 46–47.
183 Seton-Watson 1924, 111.

stead of to the more accurate one million Hungarians throughout the text, at the end of his conversations with opposition politicians in May 1923, the minority Hungarians themselves asserted: "We did not hope that Seton-Watson would wish to deal with the Hungarian case, but we were all the more pleased with the rebuttal at the two hearings, and we only ask him to study and judge the matter fairly and impartially."[184]

Four years later, based on his research on the situation of the Hungarian minority in Slovakia and his conversations with their representatives, Seton-Watson compiled a thirty-page memorandum for President Masaryk. The historian was primarily disturbed by the difficulty of obtaining Czechoslovak citizenship, as the often contradictory decrees resulted in 50–100 thousand former Hungarian citizens living in Czechoslovakia becoming stateless, according to estimates by representatives of the Hungarian minority.[185] Although the latter figure was described by Seton-Watson as an obvious exaggeration, he suggested a "beau geste" to avoid an international scandal by resolving the situation as soon as possible. Further on in the memorandum, the author criticised the imposition of the exclusive use of the Slovak language, condemned the creation of the so-called "longitudinal" north–south districts, which further reduced the proportion of Hungarians, and spoke out against the injustices of the land reform. At the end of the memorandum, and in a covering letter to President Masaryk, the historian proposed setting up an impartial committee to investigate the situation and grievances of the Hungarian minority, whose reports could be used as a basis for making concrete concessions to remedy the problems, possibly on the occasion of the tenth anniversary of the Republic. In a brief reply,

---

184 András D. Bán, Dokumentumok a csehszlovákiai magyar ellenzéki politikusok R.W. Seton-Watsonnal folytatott megbeszéléseiről [Documents on the Discussions of Hungarian Opposition Politicians in Czechoslovakia with R.W. Seton-Watson], 1923. In: *Regio*, 1992/1, 143.

185 Compared to his earlier writing, in his 1931 *Slovakia Then and Now* Seton-Watson's voice turned even more critical: "It is a crying scandal that twelve years after the war Europe should be full of thousands whose citizenship is unregulated." At the end of his chapter, however, Seton-Watson provided Czechoslovakia with some good advice and assured the state in case of removing "certain blemishes [...], it has the opportunity of becoming a model State [...], on a level with Switzerland." *Slovakia Then and Now*, A Political Survey by many Slovak Authors, Arranged by R. W. Seton-Watson, London–Prague, 1931, 56 and 61.
It is worth adding that in a 1931 memorandum, Macartney put the number of stateless persons in (Czech) Slovakia at 20–50 thousand, thus much less than that. Macartney, Memorandum on Statelessness, April 1, 1931. Macartney Papers, MSS. Eng. C. 3284, Box 5, D oc 3/b, (fols 16–42).
In his superb analysis, Zbyněk Zeman claims that in Geneva Beneš skilfully dealt with all kinds of complaints: a Slovak complaint was turned down based on the argument that Slovaks did not constitute a minority but were part of the Czechoslovak nation; Sudeten German grievances were ruled out because of their political motivation and eventually "there was little the League could do." Zbyněk A.B. Zeman, "Edvard Beneš's foreign policy and the minorities," 75–84. In: Eiler-Hájková (eds.), 2009, 79.

Masaryk thanked Seton-Watson for the document and added that it "will have the needed effect I hope I'll see to it."[186] However, he made no mention of it either then or later, despite the generous proposal in his 1927 book that not only should German be taught in Czech and Slovak secondary schools, but in Slovakia the analogous rule "should apply [...] to Slovak and Magyar."[187]

Seton-Watson sent the document to James Headlam-Morley, too, who replied that it was "much too valuable to be lost." In his letter, the advisor to the RIIA also noted that the memorandum seemed to confirm his previous view that "beyond a certain point it is practically impossible to do any real good by international action."[188] This was a sad recognition of reality, all the more so because Trianon actually gave new impetus to the assimilationist aims of many politicians, and also reignited nationality problems in the new multi-ethnic states.

2.7.2. Romania

Seton-Watson was interested in the Hungarian minority in Romania to the same extent as in Czechoslovakia. A 1924 letter to his friend Viorel Tilea, the Romanian minister to London, revealed considerable optimism: "It seems to me that autonomy could go further in Roumania than in Czechoslovakia, as geographic conditions are so much more favourable."[189] In a 1925 article, however, he turned more critical, acknowledging that whereas post-1867 Romanian intellectuals in Transylvania selected for their children names that did not lend themselves to Magyarization, the trend had been inverted against the Magyars as a "childish mania for Romanising place names, rechristening streets and removing monuments."[190]

In addition to the Romanianising tendencies, the other source of the longstanding conflicts in the country was the Optants Question that dominated Hungarian–Romanian relations throughout the 1920s. As is well known, the lands that the Romanian state annexed in 1919–1920 had never been administered by a single government before, and the disparate socioeconomic dynamics of regions with various rates of development resulted in a relatively heterogeneous country. The creation of a homogenous nation-state, however, remained

---

186 Seton-Watson to Masaryk, August 5, 1928. Seton-Watson Papers SEW 17/16/6. Masaryk to Seton-Watson, November 6, 1928; Rychlík, Marzik, Bielik (eds.) 1995, I/426.
187 Masaryk, *The Making of a State*, London, George Allen and Unwin Ltd, 1927, the English version arranged, prepared with an introduction by Steed, 388.
188 Headlam-Morley to Seton-Watson, May 4, 1929. Seton-Watson Papers, SEW17/9/3.
189 Seton-Watson to Tilea, December 6, 1924. Seton-Watson Papers, SEW17/28/7.
190 Seton-Watson, IV, Transylvania since 1867, *The Slavonic Review*, Vol. 4, No. 10 (June 1925), 110.

the overarching objective, and shortly after the Peace Treaty came into force, the Bucharest government introduced a scheme of agrarian reform expropriating the whole of absentees rural estates.[191]

According to Articles 61 & 63 of the Treaty of Trianon, Hungarian people over the age of eighteen who were relocated by a peace treaty automatically acquired the nationality of the state that gained sovereignty over their land, although they were offered the option to choose Hungarian citizenship within a year. If they did so, they had to relocate to Hungary, while being allowed to keep their real estate. Despite this, the Hungarians living in the detached territories but opting for Hungarian citizenship were deprived of their land without any compensation. In Transylvania alone there were 367 people of Hungarian origin who declined Romanian citizenship and demanded that they should not be subject to expropriation; these "optants" owning almost 80 percent of agricultural and forest land. In 1923 alone, 250 agrarian lawsuits worth a hundred and thirty million gold francs had been brought before the Romanian-Hungarian Mixed Court in Paris. At the core of the controversy lay a significant legal dilemma: whether or not international law or institutions supersede the domestic law of a state, as anything more than observation would mean infringement on national sovereignty.[192] British Minister to Budapest Sir Colville Barclay reported that "there was a widespread feeling [...] that it would be futile for Hungary to remain a member of the League if the League did nothing to safeguard Hungarian minorities beyond the frontiers."[193]

The second wave of optant lawsuits in 1927–28 led to heated press polemics in Britain and the suits were covered at great length in the *Times*. A few Members of the House of Lords and Lord Phillimore, the eminent international lawyer, together with a pro-Hungarian group of nobles, Lord Newton, Sir Frederick Pollock, Lord Buckmaster and others criticized the League Council's indecision in a letter to the editor, and Seton-Watson considered it crucial to respond and enumerate the three main refutations regarding the Optant case. Interestingly, first, much like the First World War-grand plan, he based his arguments on Brit-

---

191 Zoltán József Fazakas, The Romanian Agrarian Reform Following World War I - a tool for building the nation-state, *Journal of Agricultural and Environmental Law*, ISSN 1788-6171, 2022, Vol. XVII No. 33, 32–502.
192 Cameron J. Watson, Ethnic Conflict and the League of Nations: The Case of Transylvania, 1918–1940, *Hungarian Studies* 9/1-2, Budapest, Akadémiai Kiadó, 1994, 175. See also Francis Deák, *The Hungarian-Rumanian Land Dispute*, Columbia University Press, 1928, and Elek Nagy, *Magyarország és a Népszövetség*, Franklin Társulat, 1930.
193 Sir C. Barclay to Mr. Austen Chamberlain, Budapest, November 6, 1923. Qtd. in C. Seton-Watson, ed., *Confidential Print*, Series F, Vol. 2, 171.

## 2. From Versailles to Paris (1920–1947)

ish strategic interests, this time to prevent the spread of Bolshevism rather than that of the German *Drang nach Osten*. According to Seton-Watson, the post-war Agrarian Laws in Eastern Europe distributed land to the peasantry, essentially blocking the growth of a Marxist-collectivist utopia.

Second, Seton-Watson viewed the Optant case as an opportunity to expose Hungary again, this time not as an oppressor of minorities but as the region's most backward, semi-feudal country. He was right to observe that whereas the governments of Romania, Czechoslovakia, Yugoslavia and finally, of Poland had introduced whole-scale land reforms between 1919 and 1925, more for political rather than economic reasons, in Hungary approximately two thirds of the land was still held by great landowners (less than one-half of one percent of the population), together with the Roman Catholic and to a lesser extent the Calvinist Churches.

Last, Seton-Watson made the case that Romanian agricultural reform applied to the entire landed elite of the country and did not specifically target Hungarian landlords. He concluded by suggesting that a fair compromise between the viewpoints of Romania and Hungary would be required in place of "Shylock-like reliance on legal niceties."[194]

Once the main lines of argument had been laid down, the "old student of Hungarian affairs," Steed, had nothing else to do but talk the politicians and the public into accepting them. In several letters to the *Times*, he came up with the old mantra of Trianon having been a consequence of the "oppression of a majority of non-Magyars in pre-war Hungary by a minority of Magyars," which was quite out of context in 1928. In line with his friend, Steed also urged agreement, either complying with the needs of "a convalescent Europe,"[195] or based on "common sense and equity."[196] The latter he believed to be jeopardised by the fact that whereas thousands of Rumanian landowners accepted compensation at a lower post-1920 rate, the 300 optants required compensation in gold (at the 1917 rate).[197]

In private, however, Steed was rather alarmed, describing the optant affair as "an offensive, shrewdly conceived" against the Romanian land reforms, which "may become very dangerous." He also believed it possible that in the background

---

[194] Seton-Watson, "Hungary and Rumania: The Land Dispute," *Times*, March 12, 1928, 10. In his 1928 memorandum Seton-Watson even noted that the official Hungarian propaganda would achieve much greater results if it based its cause not on the Transylvanian Optant question but on the stateless Hungarians in Slovakia.
[195] Steed, "Hungary and Rumania: A Settlement by Equity," *Times*, March 16, 1928, 10.
[196] Steed, "Hungary and Rumania," to the Editor of the *Times*, March 24, 1928, 10.
[197] Steed, "Hungarian Land Dispute, Rumanian Motives," *Times*, April 11, 1928, 8.

the Germans had been secretly encouraging the Hungarian "petty-foggers" to make the peace treaties "unworkable."[198] However, compared to Seton-Watson or Steed, as early as 1923 Eric Drummond, the secretary-general of the League of Nations between 1920 and 1933, issued a communication to the Foreign Office in a somewhat different tone:

> The conclusions which our people who have been in Brussels have come to are that the Hungarians have really a weak legal case [...] it seems pretty clear that a clever lawyer, such as the Romanian Government possess in M. Titulesco [sic], could make out a fairly strong case. At the same time the fact remains that the Hungarians are discriminated against unfairly by the agrarian law, inasmuch as the law is applied in a much severer form in Transylvania than in Old Romania [...] While recognising the above, and desirous of doing our part as regards holding Romania to her treaty obligations, we do not wish to appear as protagonists on behalf of big Magyar landlords.[199]

In June 1928, the still unsettled Optant Question unleashed a debate in the House of Lords, too, with eighteen members present. "Nearly everybody is sick of the whole thing," asserted the pro-Hungarian Lord Newton, once again criticizing the League for having been unable to stifle the debate as an impartial authority, and as a result, it not only lost credibility and power but also rendered itself utterly laughable:

> Here are these Ministers, the Foreign Ministers of the great Powers of Europe, who proceed periodically to Geneva in all the pomp and circumstances of peace, [...] and they make long and eloquent speeches to each other, [...] in which they tell the world in so many words that the new era is at hand and that everything is for the best in the best of worlds. And yet, when these illustrious people are called upon to decide what ought to be a mere trumpery dispute between two small nations, they openly admit that they cannot do it and say that the parties must settle it somehow between themselves.

---

198 Steed to Murray Brumwell, *Times* Office, April 10, 1928. Steed Papers MS 74 127.
199 Note for the British Representatives at the Council of the League of Nations on the Question of the Expropriation by the Romanian Government of the Property of the Hungarian Optants, Foreign Office, June 27, 1923. Qtd. in: C. Seton-Watson ( ed.), *Confidential Print*, Series F, Vol. 2 (1923-June 1930), 45.

## 2. From Versailles to Paris (1920–1947)

Others, like the Earl of Birkenhead or Lord Thomson defended the League and Romania arguing that the whole Optant Question seemed "an indirect action" towards treaty revision and expressing their conviction that any attempt at revision "will certainly lead to failure and dispute, and not improbably to ever more serious consequences."[200]

In his 1928 *Survey* Toynbee remained balanced in his discussion of the controversy expounding on both standpoints, the Hungarian (the optant remained the rightful owner of his land and international treaty-obligations cannot be overridden by the rules of domestic law) and the Romanian (the impartial nature of the Romanian agrarian legislation as well as the consideration that the optants' property was subject to laws of a sovereign state).[201] Toynbee was convinced that there was more at stake than a few hundred people in a local disagreement between two governments, and he argued that the optant incident had shown the tension between treaty duties and domestic law as well as the tension between the legal and political approaches to resolving international conflicts. In his opinion the debate also posed the questions of whether unanimous consent was required when asking the Permanent Court for advice during protracted discussions about the Council's powers and responsibilities, whether the Council could put a question on its agenda against the wishes of one of the parties involved in the dispute, and finally, to what extent it was authorized or permitted to interpret treaties.[202]

The long optant debate ended with a compromise between Hungary and Romania as late as in 1930, when as a result of the Paris arbitration court's decision the Romanian state paid compensation to Hungary of over a hundred tonnes of pure gold (equivalent to twenty-four carats) through the Agrarian Fund opened in a Swiss bank. Despite the compensation, however, as a result of the Romanian agrarian law of 1921 centuries-old property relations broke down for good: 539,694 persons received land in Transylvania, of which 369,000 were Romanians and 87,426 were of Hungarian nationality. Another key fact was that the Land Reform Act in the Old Kingdom only expropriated the property of those

---

200 Hungarian Claims Against Rumania, House of Lords Debate, June 25, 1928. Vol. 71 cc 634–682. https://api.parliament.uk/historic-hansard/lords/1928/jun/25/hungarian-claims-against-rumania Accessed April 1, 2023. Newton turned out to be quite prophetic. "Already it is fairly easy for anybody to prophesy on what side nations will be found in connection with questions of this kind. The result will be that you will split the Council and the League into two or three camps like the blocs or alliances which existed before the War and we shall return to the position which existed before 1914." Ibid.
201 Toynbee, *Survey of International Affairs 1928*, Oxford University Press, 1930, 171
202 Ibid., 182.

owing more than 100 hectares of real estate. In contrast, no limit whatsoever was applied to the former Hungarian territories. Moreover, despite their amiable connections with the Romanian state, the German minority was unable to prevent the legal dissolution of the Saxon Universitas that had served the Saxon community since the Middle Ages, together with the confiscation of three quarters of its remaining assets that were unaffected by the land reform. Finally, the system of tax legislation that discriminated against minorities, particularly the property tax, exacerbated the detrimental components of the agrarian reform, turning the minorities into second-class citizens.[203] Hence, apart from advancing social justice, as had been the purported intent, the reform's underlying purpose was to limit the property rights of national and religious minorities, a crucial step of Romanianization towards a uniform nation-state.[204] Finally, as Cameron Watson cogently states, the handling the Optant Question in Transylvania was both symptomatic and emblematic of the failure of the League of Nations to develop a cogent strategy for protecting minorities, which directly contributed to its own demise.[205]

In the meantime, at the peak of the Romanian–Hungarian Optant Debate in 1928, the National Peasants led by Steed's and Seton-Watson's old friend from Transylvania Iuliu Maniu, came to power. While meeting Maniu in Cluj (Kolozsvár) a year later, Seton-Watson brought up the situation of the Hungarian minority, which the progressive prime minister took "fully seriously" and was "full of enlightened ideas."[206] Nevertheless, he had no time to realize them, since the Romania of 1930s was characterised by the rule of King Carol and the premiership of "Fascist degenerate"[207] Octavian Goga. In a reminiscence, Seton-Watson

---

203 Zoltán József Fazakas, The Romanian Agrarian Reform Following World War I— a Tool for Building the Nation-State, *Journal of Agricultural and of Environmental Law* 33/2022, 46. http://real.mtak.hu/156055/1/jaelno33_FINALfinal-032-050.pdf. Accessed April 4, 2023.
204 According to Romanian official statistics, in Transylvania 73.6 percent of the beneficiaries from land reform were Romaniana, 6.2 percent Germans and 16.54 percent Hungarians, whereas the overall proportion of national minorities in Transylvania amounted to 42.7 percent. In Czechoslovakia: according to statistics of thr League Secretariat, Germans were almost entirely excluded by the Czechoslovakian Land Office and the Hungarians were clearly underrepresented. In Yugoslavia, people of German and Hungarian origin could not get land as they were not considered to be confirmed nationals of Yugoslavia. Thus, it can be safely argued that discrimination was a common element of land reforms in the Little Entente states. Berkes, Antal, "The League of Nations and the Optants' Dispute of the Hungarian Borderlands: Romania, Yugoslavia, and Czechoslovakia," in: Peter Becker and Natasha Wheatley (eds.), *Remaking Central Europe. The League of Nations and the Former Habsburg Lands*, Oxford, Oxford University Press, 2020, 283–314, 291–292.
205 Cameron J. Watson, Ethnic Conflict and The League of Nations: The Case of Transylvania, 1918–1940, *Hungarian Studies* 9/1-2 (1994), Akadémiai Kiadó, Budapest, 177–178.
206 Seton-Watson, *Transylvania: A Key Problem*, Oxford, 1943, 9.
207 Ibid., 8.

summarised this period as having been dominated by "rabid chauvinism stimulated from above," "exaggerated centralisation," and "bribery and corruption," all resting on a "xenophobe sentiment."[208]

### 2.7.3. The South Slav State

As to strengthen the ties between the Kingdom of Serbs, Croats and Slovenes and Britain, Seton-Watson founded the *New Yugoslav Society* in 1928, which Steed also joined, but he was sceptical enough to also accept membership in the Committee, as by the late 1920s he believed the usefulness of such individual societies to be "questionable," unless their activity could be coordinated with "that of a general Central-European Society."[209] The following year British pro-Slavism grew even more uncomfortable when Alexander I introduced a royal dictatorship to prevent the domestic political situation from deteriorating further. By suspending the constitution and banning "national" parties, the king sought to eliminate divisive forces while attempting to create a "Yugoslav" national identity by, among other things, officially renaming the country the Kingdom of Yugoslavia instead of the Kingdom of Serbs, Croats and Slovenes. In line with Czechoslovakia, in 1930 Seton-Watson penned a South-Slav memorandum, too, but he found much more to frown upon: the abolition of mother-tongue education for Albanians, the curtailment of the rights of Muslims as well as those of the Hungarians and Romanians, all signalled in his opinion, "a steady evolution towards a Police State."[210]

In October in the same year, upon realising that his friendly warning had failed, Seton-Watson adopted a harsher tone and condemned the Yugoslav regime in public in a series of articles in the Czech *Lidové Noviny*.[211] Simultaneously, Steed sent an open letter to King Alexander in his own journal, *The Review of Reviews*, putting forward his main reason for not joining Seton-Watson's campaign: foreign individuals ought not "to butt in at every stage of a nation's difficulties," he argued, adding that "it might be well to leave King Alexander in no doubt what his former helpers were thinking of his present conduct."[212] Alexander's policies to create a unified "Yugoslav" identity soon backfired, further

---

208 Ibid., 10.
209 Steed to Sir Arthur Evans, January 28, 1928. Steed Papers, MS 74 127.
210 Seton-Watson, Memorandum [1930], *Korespondencija* 1976 II/198.
211 Seton-Watson to Ćurčin, October 21, 1930, *Korespondencija* 1976 II/207.
212 Steed to Philip Graves, *Times* Office, November 10, 1931. Steed Papers MS 74 130.
  Macartney was similarly negative in his Chatham House address in February 1931: "I cannot see the necessary goodwill among the present Yugoslav Government." Macartney, "Political Relations in the Balkans," address given on February 2, 1931, in RIIA. RIAA Archives, 8/120, 22.

strengthening separatist aspirations. (He himself fell victim to these when, during a visit to Marseilles in 1934, he was assassinated by a member of the Macedonian national liberation movement.[213])

As discussed above, Seton-Watson and to a lesser extent, Steed, used the tried and true policy of exerting personal pressure on their friends, in private or in public; however, after 1920—except in a few cases—it generally failed. Macartney, on the other hand, worked for eight years from 1928 as an expert on Central and Eastern Europe in the *League of Nations Union*, the British organisation which was the flagship of minority protection. In one of his early studies, the young historian highlighted two reasons for the failure of the League of Nations to protect minorities: on the one hand, any activity of an external authority on behalf of a minority could easily be interpreted as "unjustifiable interference"[214] in the internal affairs of the state, which—in the absence of coercive means—could easily avert accusations. On the other hand, due to the practice of favouring governments over minorities, the vast majority of complaints of violations of rights could not even reach the Council, let alone the Permanent Court of Justice, and thus could not be redressed. As Macartney bitterly observed: "The more crying a grievance, as a rule, the less chance it has, under the present procedure of being heard [...] the greatest sufferings are endured by minorities which are either wholly unacquainted with the existence of the Treaties, or afraid to appeal on account of the reprisals which they know will follow."[215]

The imperfection of the protection of minorities between the two world wars and its dependence on international power relations, as Macartney also revealed, is well illustrated by the fact that whereas Hungary bombarded the League of Nations with petitions about violations of minority Hungarians' rights in the multi-ethnic Successor States, only one of petition reached the Council until 1930. Therefore, it is no accident that Macartney's conclusion was largely pessimistic: the League of Nations's defence of minorities "is inoperative to such a degree as to cause profound dissatisfaction;" but he moderated his claim by pointing out that since the minority question was "one of the most burning topics"

---

213 *Korespondencija* 1976 II, 194.
214 Macartney, *Minorities. The History of Racial, Religious and Linguistic Minorities in Europe*, League of Nations Union, London, 1929, 7. Carlile Aylmer Macartney LNU Miscellaneous Pamphlets Vol. 4. British Library 3685-3805.
215 Ibid., 36.

of the time, the League of Nations would be forced to approach the matter "in a courageous fashion."[216]

\* \* \*

Although the decade following Versailles was a period of relative stability in the international political arena, the isolationist-nationalist aspirations of the Central and Eastern European countries were not conducive to the development of a fair minority policy. However, despite the obvious flaws in the protection of minorities, neither Seton-Watson nor Steed, nor Macartney went so far as to challenge the status quo. The marked differences in their thinking became increasingly apparent from 1930 onwards, as the impact of the global economic crisis on the Versailles order led them to draw opposite conclusions.

## 2.8. A Period of Reflection on Central and Eastern European Economic Cooperation (1929–1932)

As a result of Western financial infusions, East-Central Europe saw a relative economic boom in the second half of the 1920s, but none of the seven states of the Danube basin, which had previously formed an economic unit, could match the prosperity of the pre-war years. Yet, the 1929 world economic crisis not only upended the area's already precarious equilibrium but also altered global economic and political agendas: the United States was forced by the crisis to return to its isolationist policies of the early 1920s, and Britain pursued a tight profitability strategy, persistently refusing to grant any more loans to Central and Eastern European countries.

However, the British withdrawal from a more effective financial support plan for the region was not accompanied by a lack of interest in its economic consolidation. In a speech at Chatham House in February 1930, former foreign secretary Austen Chamberlain considered it essential for Britain to take a "watchful interest" in European events, since, in his view, post-1914 history had shown "how disparately the affairs of another country today affect our own existence."[217] In order to promote economic consolidation in Central and Eastern Europe, Britain supported the economic integration plans in the Danube Basin which had been popping up from time to time since 1929. These included Czechoslovak Foreign Minister Eduard Beneš's 1931-plan for a customs

---

216 Ibid., 37–40.
217 Austen Chamberlain, Great Britain As a European Power, *IA*, March 1930, 185.

## 2.8. A Period of Reflection on Central and Eastern European Economic Cooperation

union between his country, Hungary and Austria, the Foreign Office's proposal for a customs union with Romania, Yugoslavia and Bulgaria, in addition to the above countries, and French prime minister André Tardieu's 1932 customs union plan.[218]

When the Hungarian prime minister arrived in London in May 1930 for the second time to negotiate a sizeable new loan with British political and economic leaders, the Ramsay Macdonald government explicitly stated that Britain could not provide the proposed amount of money but urged the improvement of relations between Hungary and the Little Entente. The news that his government backed initiatives to foster economic cooperation in Central and Eastern Europe naturally thrilled the supporters of the status quo. Through the mediation of Ferenc Rajniss, a journalist of the extreme right-wing newspaper *Magyarság*, in June 1930 Seton-Watson encountered PM Bethlen, who did not make an unfavourable impression: "reserved, slow of speech, suddenly smiles, seemingly frank, obviously so," reads the historian's diary. Seton-Watson appreciated the prime minister's intention to improve Hungarian–Romanian relations, which was all the more possible owing to the resolution of the prolonged Optant Question and the appointment of the moderate Transylvanian politician Iuliu Maniu as prime minister at the end of 1928. However, any further reconciliation with the other two Little Entente states was far less likely: Bethlen saw "the chief obstacle" to reconciliation with Czechoslovakia in the very person of Seton-Watson's friend Edvard Beneš, and both of them regarded Yugoslav–Hungarian relations as quite hopeless because of Belgrade's blind nationalism.[219]

In June 1930, at the same time as the meeting with Betheln, an article by Seton-Watson appeared in *Magyarság*, in which the author portrayed Bethlen's visit to London in a much more favourable light compared to the Hungarian prime minister's loan negotiations in 1923. Seton-Watson avoided his previous tried-and-true tactics: missing were the pamphlet-like simplifications to justify the Little Entente states' attempts at centralization and the exclusion of the Hungarian minority, comparisons between the nationality laws of the successor states and the Monar-

---

218 For details of economic unification plans conceived during the economic crisis, see László Diószegi, Gazdasági egyesítési tervek a Duna-medencében az 1929-1933-as világgazdasági válság időszakában, [Economic unification plans in the Danube basin during the world economic crisis of 1929–1933]. In: Ignác Romsics (szerk.), *Integrációs törekvések Közép- és Kelet-Európában a 19. és 20. században* [Integration Efforts in Central and Eastern Europe in the 19th and 20th Centuries], Budapest, 1997, 63–103.
219 Seton-Watson Papers, SEW11/1/2.
It is an interesting fact that in the ten years following Versailles, Beneš travelled abroad fifty times, but only once to Berlin and Warsaw, never to Budapest.

chy, an overemphasis on Hungary's role in the war, and the "reactionary" character of the Horthy regime. However, this positive turn of events and the surprising objectivity of the article was not due to Bethlen's personal charm but rather to the fact that from 1930 onwards, cooperation among the states of East-Central Europe, paralysed by the economic crisis, was given much greater emphasis, which for a time overshadowed the—often justified—criticism of the Horthy regime.

In his article, Seton-Watson distinguished between three basic conditions for the improvement of the relationship between Hungary and the Little Entente. First, he argued, it must be acknowledged that it is impossible to establish perfect (ethnic) borders in the region; second, what drives Hungarians must be discovered (in his view, it is not so much the pursuit of integral revision as the fear of assimilation of minority Hungarians); and finally, reduction of the divisive nature of political, economic and cultural borders, which is a pan-European task independent of revisionism. Seton-Watson believed that the first step towards rapprochement should be taken by the victors, first because he had found in his negotiations with Hungarians both in Upper Hungary and Transylvania in 1928–29 that 90 percent of their legitimate grievances could be fully redressed, and second because he considered both the Romanian and Czechoslovak governments to be capable of pursuing a policy of concessions. The author concluded his article in an advisory role: "To insist upon either the renunciation of revisionist aims by Hungary or upon the acceptance of the revisionist principle by the succession states as a preliminary basis of discussion, is simply another way of declining all discussion. But there can be a great deal of amicable, and I believe fruitful, discussion without either side renouncing its principles."[220]

In the following months and in several forums, Seton-Watson urged the promotion of economic cooperation between the countries of Central and Eastern Europe, in particular the rapprochement of Hungary and Czechoslovakia. The great powers, he argued in a letter to the *Times*, should exert "constant friendly pressure" on Prague and Budapest, because "there is not a moment to be lost if [some of them] are to be saved from actual collapse."[221] Another indication of how significant the historian-publicist considered cooperation among the governments of the Danube Basin is the fact that, according to a private letter, he was already planning to go to Hungary in the summer of 1931 to foster dialogue despite his dislike of the Horthy regime. The visit was intended to occur

---

220 Seton-Watson's article in Hungarian. In *Magyarság* 1930/6. Original English, typed, corrected version: Seton-Watson Papers, SEW17/22/5."
221 Seton-Watson, "Danubian States, Steps to Economic Agreement," *Times*, March 16, 1932, 10.

## 2.8. A Period of Reflection on Central and Eastern European Economic Cooperation

concurrently with Bethlen's resignation and the installation of the new pro-French prime minister, Gyula Károlyi, but it never materialized.

In contrast, Macartney, who was becoming increasingly immersed in the history of Hungary and the region, arrived in Budapest in June 1931 and found the resigned Bethlen to be more trusted and the elections less rigged than had been thought; however, regarding the prospects for the Hungarian economy, his predictions were gloomier than ever: high unemployment–800,000 according to the speaker–coupled with the budget deficit cried out for a loan of five million, partly obtained from France. France, Macartney observed, was still the second most unpopular country in Hungary (after the Beneš-led Czechoslovakia).[222] While in Budapest, Macartney met several prominent members of Hungarian public life, such as former Prime Minister Pál Teleki, historian and university professor Bálint Hóman, industrialist and patron of the arts, Móric Kornfeld, who was an MP, as well as the former mayor of Budapest, István Bárczy. "I was deeply touched by the kindness I encountered, and I really feel that I have learned to appreciate Hungary and its cause."[223]

Another example of Macartney's enthusiasm for Hungary was his letter to his friend József Balogh at the beginning of 1931: "Perhaps this incredible crisis will end one day, and then we will really do the Hungarian [Department]," which he characterized as "actually much closer to my heart" than the post in the Department of International Relations at the University of London, which he had applied for at the time, relying on, among others, Seton-Watson's recommendation.[224] Unfortunately, the world economic crisis (1929–32) not only

---

222 "All Eastern European countries are in the same boat. [...] Unless debts are washed out, these Eastern European countries were sinking down and down, and this affected Great-Britain," concluded the speaker. Macartney, "The Situation in Hungary," Address Delivered at RIIA, October 12, 1931. RIIA Archives 8/161, 4–7, 9 and 25.
223 Macartney to József Balogh, August 24, 1931. OSZK KT, Fond 1/2064, 18457. In 1930, before Macartney's visit to Budapest, his first book on the subject of Hungarians, *Magyars in the Ninth Century*, was published, in which the author attempted to shed light on the rather unexplored period of the migration of the Hungarians from the Byzantine and Persian Arabic sources to the conquest of Hungary. In its review, Gyula Moravcsik, a Greek philologist and professor at the University of Budapest, welcomed the work, despite its "cynical" tone in discussing certain figures and events in Hungarian history. The book, he said, had enriched research on the early history of the Hungarians with "novel results." (German original) Gyula Moravcsik, Review: Macartney, *The Magyars in the Ninth Century, Review*, Leipzig, 1933, 383–386.
224 József Balogh to Macartney, September 23, 1930. OSZ KT, Fond 1/2064, 18454.
Eventually the London University Hungarian Department was established, but without Macartney: from October 1937, Hungary offered £350 a year for four years to create a post of lecturer of Hungarian language and literature, which was taken by Miklós Szenczi (1904–1977). It is noteworthy that the Hungarian government covered the costs of the post until February 1945: Szenczi was paid through the Swedish Embassy in London after Hungary's entry into the war on the side of the Axis. Sherwood 1993, 112.

halted the realization of the young scholar's academic plans but soon cast a dark shadow over Europe.

### 2.9. "The dragon of sovereignty is doomed to perish."[225] Toynbee on Nationalism during the World Economic Crisis 1929–1931/2

From the 1930s onwards, Toynbee started to abandon the formerly typical neutral narrative in the *Surveys*: the year 1931, which he labelled *annus horribilis*, was for example a time when "men and women all over the world were seriously contemplating and frankly discussing the possibility that the Western system of Society might break down."[226] What kind of remedy could he offer? First of all, he opined, one must denounce nationalism as an ideology and its product, the national states, which "have been placed on pedestals as idols [...] and the worship of these idols is the most widespread form of genuine religion in the Western world today [...]. We do not like to admit this idolatry and we feel inclined to protest that we are Protestants or Catholics, Jews or Agnostics, but not worshippers of the Sovereign National States.[227]

In an address given in Copenhagen on June 8, 1931, Toynbee went even further. First, he called attention to the "dangerous discrepancy" between the "new-fangled" international life in the economic sphere and the "antiqued parochial life" on the political and cultural planes. He was certain that the post-war era would be characterized by a comprehensive internationalization of political and economic life: in substituting internationalism for nationalism. Looking at, among others, the Covenant of the League, the Statute of the Permanent Court of International Justice, he boastfully asserted that the progress having made between 1919 and 1931 by the post-war generation in this field exceeded that of their predecessors during the previous four centuries.[228] The main target of action for his generation, he asserted, should be "the fetish of local national sovereignty" indulged by some fifty-sixty sovereign national states which had inherited the prestige and prerogatives of the medieval Western Church:

---

225 Toynbee, "Trends of International Affairs Since the War," Fourth Conference of Institutions for the Scientific Study of International Relations, Copenhagen, June 8-10, 1931. In: *Pacific Affairs*, Vol. 4, No. 9 (September 1931), 753-778, 760.
226 Toynbee, *Survey of International Affairs 1931*, 1.
227 Toynbee, "World Order Or Downfall?" Six Broadcast Talks BBC, November 10–December 15, 1930, 3rd talk: November 24. Toynbee Papers BL Oxford MS13 967/6 Broadcasts 1929-1955.
228 Though he also mentioned the US and Soviet rebuffs to the League as failures. Toynbee, "Trends of International Affairs Since the War," Fourth Conference of Institutions for the Scientific Study of International Relations, Copenhagen, June 8-10, 1931. In: *Pacific Affairs*, Vol. 4, No 9 (September 1931), 753-778. 753-757.

## 2.9. "The dragon of sovereignty is doomed to perish."

The local national state, invested with the attributes of sovereignty [...] is an abomination of desolation standing in the place where it ought not [...]. Our political task in our generation is to cast the abomination out, to cleanse the temple and to restore the worship of divinity to whom the temple rightfully belongs; we have to retransfer the prestige and the prerogatives of sovereignty from the fifty or sixty fragments of contemporary society to the whole of contemporary society [...] an institution embodying our society as a whole [...] something like the League of Nations.

These local states, however, were not, in Toynbee's interpretation, all doomed to perish; once having reconciled themselves to the surrender of their supremacy, they could look forward to the preservation of familiar characteristics, "harmless trappings" like language and folklore, the regional markers of the past. Worshippers, he added, would be likely to feel almost as much fulfilment in continuing their cult through non-bloody sacrifices as they had done previously when "their idol [had] demanded from them the sacrifice of their children's lives in the ritual of war." [229]

"Shall we cure international anarchy by voluntary organisation, or shall we leave it to cure itself by the blind operation of force?" was Toynbee's somewhat platonic question. Although Europe had been dwarfed in the post-war era, the idea that the non-European world could safely leave Europe to handle its own problems was a misconception: if Europe were to erupt in flames once more, there would be no country in the world so far away, so isolated, or so well protected that it would survive unharmed.[230] Thus, before the World Disarmament Conference, the most important gathering of its kind since Versailles according to Toynbee, one should organise an exchange of speakers to offer "an accurate, impartial and authoritative exposition of what public opinion in their own country is thinking and feeling about Disarmament and why." He believed it was essential to engage the public in each country to understand their neighbours' point of view: "People who really understand each other can disagree without rancour; people who disagree without rancour can discuss their differences with frankness; and frank discussion of differences is a sovereign means of arriving at an agreement in the end." Quite uniquely, he set out to praise Ger-

---

229 Ibid., 758–760.
230 Ibid., 761–769.

many, too, as one of the top nations in the modern world, with a public system of education and other social services "still second to none."²³¹

Toynbee's optimism was largely unfounded. When the World Disarmament Conference did finally convene in Geneva in February 1932, the commission's preparatory work was disregarded and the issue of German equality took precedence over everything else. France had no faith in Germany at all and vice versa. In July 1932, the German delegation withdrew and did not reappear until December, when it was assured that it would have the same rights in the eventual treaty as the other signatories. However, a month earlier, the last free *all-German* elections until 1990 had turned most of its federal states brown, predicting a dark future for the country and Europe alike.

## 2.10. The Four Britons on the Four Power Pact and the Question of Frontier Rectification in Central-Eastern Europe: (1932–34/35)

By the end of the world economic crisis, despite the support of France and Britain, plans for a customs union among the countries of Central and Eastern Europe had come to a standstill, mainly because of interstate tensions and the vetoes of Italy and Germany, which showed increasing interest in the region. Seeing the irresolvable political differences and the mounting economic problems of the small states created at Versailles, British diplomacy broke with its rigid anti-frontier-readjustment stance by the early 1930s, and several British politicians became advocates of peaceful border changes. On November 23, 1932, in the British House of Commons, Winston Churchill expressed his view, to loud cheers, that questions like the Danzig corridor and Transylvania should be reopened "in cold blood and in a calm atmosphere, and while the victor nations had still ample superiority [...]."²³² A few months later, Mussolini's proposal—later dubbed the Four Power Pact—was presented to the British prime minister during his visit to Rome,: Article Second stated the principle of the possibility of the revision of treaties "as provided for in the Pact of the League of Nations 18 and in a spirit of mutual comprehension and solidarity of interests involved." In more concrete terms, it meant the Polish corridor and the frontiers of Hungary.²³³

---

231 Ibid., 778.
232 "Mr. Churchill's World Review," *Times*, November 24, 1932, 7.
233 Foreign Relations of The United States, Diplomatic Papers, 1933, General, Volume I, 740.0011 Four Power Pact/17. https://history.state.gov/historicaldocuments/frus1933v01/d292 Accessed April 19, 2023.

During debate in the House of Commons a week later, Ramsay MacDonald expressed his support for the Pact: "Every treaty is holy, but no treaty is eternal," he quoted Mussolini, referring to the fact that while the Covenant of the League of Nations enforced all respect for treaty obligations, it also contemplated the possibility of a revision of treaties when conditions arise which may lead to conflict or war. During the same debate Under-Secretary of State Anthony Eden also endorsed the Pact, claiming that the entire plan would be carried out within the framework of the League, which could secure better than anything else that all nations will have "their points of view safeguarded."[234]

In parallel with the pro-revisionist turn in British politics, Arnold Toynbee also grew increasingly critical towards the Versailles settlement. In a 1932 roundtable discussion, he recalled the "paradox of the peace conference," where the victors, while denouncing Communism, seized German property. He did not forget to mention that the treaty had contradicted economic considerations, too, by creating numerous frontiers: "The conflict between economics and politics resulted in great tension, which is one of the causes of present critical situation."[235]

As director of studies at Chatham House, Toynbee was convinced that the time was ripe for action. He first established a group that he thought would be a good starting point to deal with the "plague-stricken" areas of Europe, primarily the German–Polish zone, followed by the ex-Hungarian territories. In a private letter he was nevertheless concerned that the problem was "too delicate" to be handled even by a non-official scientific organisation like Chatham House.[236] Therefore, in addition to meetings and study groups and the publication of the *History of the Peace Conference* as well as the annual *Survey of International Affairs*, he put forward providing the support of long-range monographs by individual scholars. Such works, he wrote in notes for the project, could deal with the

---

234 MP Churchill was also supportive: "[...] my argument has always been that the removal of the grievances of the vanquished should precede the disarmament of the victors." British Parliament, House of Commons Debate, March 23, 1933. https://hansard.parliament.uk/Commons/1933-03-23/debates/98cfde64-ad84-4467-a146-cdb41eb747c7/HouseOfCommons. Accessed April 23, 2023. See also G.P. Gooch, *Studies in Diplomacy and Statecraft*, London, Longmans, 1942, 192–193.
Interestingly, the British did not appear to have been impacted by Hitler's accession to power in January. Nobody was surprised when Germany asserted in Geneva and London that the new chancellor would not mean any change to foreign policy. The French lamented what had occurred, but they had done it so often that their constant alarms were not taken seriously. Aage Trommer, MacDonald in Geneva in March 1933, *Scandinavian Journal of History*, 1(1–4), 1976, 293–312, 312. doi:10.1080/03468757608578907

235 Toynbee, The Disintegration of the Modern World Order—The Growth of Modern World Order, Roundtable, 1st and 4th meetings July 29 and August 5, 1932, Institute of Politics, 12th Series. Toynbee Papers, MS 13967/3.

236 Toynbee to Zimmern, June 8, 1932. Toynbee Papers BL Oxford MS13967/ 85 Correspondence.

## 2. From Versailles to Paris (1920–1947)

given subject "so thoroughly and authoritatively" as to become permanent "classics" like Seton-Watson's *Racial Problems* or *South Slav Question*, both of which, he continued, "affected the course of European history." He suggested that English scholars do "first hand local studies" of the social, cultural, economic and political circumstances in some European regions where there had been a sustained call for treaty revision since the Peace Settlement: the German–Polish, the Polish–white Russian/Ukrainian, the Hungarian–Czechoslovak and the Hungarian–Romanian borders. Treaty revision, he concluded, "crops up again and again. It has made the United States fight shy of European [...] entanglements and Great-Britain fight shy of an 'Eastern Locarno'; and it has made the problem of security so far insoluble." There had not been much objective research conducted on the ground, Toynbee claimed, despite the fact that the question of treaty revision in these areas would probably become a "crucial question," like the Austro-Hungarian problem during WW1.[237]

Seton-Watson also noticed the change in British foreign policy, but until the summer of 1933 he still saw hope for the establishment of cooperation between the countries of Central and Eastern Europe through Britain's "active intervention." By the latter, according to a letter to the *Times*, he meant, among other things, that Hungary must be made clearly aware that "territorial revision is impracticable save by war," and "to sweeten this bitter pill," the Little Entente had to be put under pressure to adopt a truly effective minority law which could redress existing grievances.[238]

The MacDonald government's pro-revisionist stance compelled Hungarophile British public figures to advocate for rectification even more vehemently than before. The parliamentary committee that had previously been established to advance revisionism quickly attracted around one quarter of the MPs. Under the leadership of Sir Robert Gower, they wrote to the *Times'* editor challenging Seton-Watson's claim about the impossibility of territorial revision. The letter also advocated amending the treaty of Trianon "so that Hungary may have restored to it those parts of its former territory which are essentially Hungarian."[239]

The activities of the pro-revision group galvanised the defenders of the status quo as well, leading to a press polemics similar to the one during the Rothermere campaign. In response to the letter from the Gower group, Seton-Watson once again took up the pen, and in a letter which is part of his legacy but was

---

237 Toynbee, Chatham House Research Project: Research at Chatham House –Long-Range Monographs by Individual Scholars, (handwritten notes), undated, 1932? Toynbee Papers, MS 13 967/39
238 Seton-Watson, "The Middle Way in Europe, Tasks for British Statesmanship", *Times,* June 30, 1933, 10.
239 Robert Gower et al, "Middle Europe, Treaties by Agreement," *Times,* July 5, 1933, 10.

## 2.10. The Four Britons on the Four Power Pact and the Question of Frontier Rectification

not published in the *Times*, he reiterated that it was impossible to draw borders in Central and Eastern Europe along strict ethnic lines, as is shown by the fact that substantial minorities—about 800,000 people—had remained in Hungary after 1920. In order to enlighten public opinion as planned, he also noted that the new Hungarian borders were drawn by "experts of very high ability and knowledge" who had made use of Hungarian maps and statistics. It was high time, he argued, that the proponents of the revision, and especially the Hungarian government finally explained in detail which territories they really wanted to see returned. He believed it was typical that whereas the revisionist organisations endorsed the policy of *restitutio in integrum*, the government could not limit its demands to the Hungarian-inhabited areas along the border, which would then be considered by public opinion as a "rank betrayal."[240]

In the above-mentioned article, the publicist-historian brilliantly highlighted one of the weakest points of Hungarian revisionist propaganda. In fact, official government departments in Hungary took utmost care not to take the question of revision into "the perilous zone of concreteness," which would have had adverse effects. A 1929 circular sent to embassies and consulates revealed that in case the Hungarian government exercised restraint and, in effect, was "forced to bargain over the belonging of small bands of territory and then villages," it would renounce integrity, which would turn public opinion against it. However, if integral revision was declared openly, Hungary would appear to be trying to subjugate foreign nations anew.[241] It was not surprising then that Seton-Watson advised his Little Entente friends, all alarmed by the news of the proposed Four-Power Pact, to make an attempt to exploit the contradiction between the official Hungarian foreign policy and unofficial propaganda: "I have no doubt that if they get into the specifics, their cause will fail. As a result, we must make them comply! [...] The Magy[ars] will undoubtedly make excessive demands. Then, up to a point, even their friends will reject them; they will disagree and fight among themselves."[242]

In the debate between those arguing for and against frontier revision, Wickham Steed, too, made his voice heard. In a letter published in the *Times* in July 1933, he pointed out that the peace treaties were obviously imperfect, but the Versailles settlement was "undoubtedly far less imperfect than the territorial re-

---

240 Seton-Watson Papers, SEW17/22.
241 Qtd. in Pál Pritz, *Magyar diplomácia a két háború között* [Interwar Hungarian Diplomacy], Budapest, 1995, 236–237.
242 Seton-Watson to Milan Hodža, (German original), August 31, 1933. Rychlík-Marzik-Bielik (eds.) 1995, I/450.

lations of pre-war Europe." Those who advocated the need for revision, he advised, rather than making vague claims, should study Seton-Watson's article(s) on the problem of treaty revision, which appeared in the *Slavonic and East European Review*[243] and *International Affairs* at the same time.[244]

The articles were based on a lecture delivered on May 17, 1933, at the RIIA, which can be considered the most coherent formulation of the pro-status-quo position of the time. In his talk, Seton-Watson analysed the problem on a Europe-wide scale, and he saw the possibility of a relatively easy ethnic reorganisation in only two of the six areas concerned, the Austrian–German and the Italian–Austrian borders. The main part of the lecture, however, was devoted to the complex issue of Hungarian revision, and the author went on to analyse the situation of the Hungarian minority from border section to border section: on ethnic grounds, he supported the annexation of Burgenland to Austria, and he explicitly opposed the 1921 reunification of the Sopron (Ödenburg) area with Hungary, "a sharp and quite unnatural salient."[245]

Regarding the Hungarian–Czechoslovak border, however, Seton-Watson refrained from the ethnic principle, but instead justified the Danube border by stating boldly that in Paris "economics were held to outweigh ethnography." However, concerning Grosse Schütt, the island lying south-east of the Slovak capital, he noted that although economically it gravitated to the market of Bratislava, it was essentially Hungarian in nature, thus revision might be possible. The same applied to the areas twenty miles north of the Danube, he opined, the eventual return of which would allow 250.000 Hungarians to reunite with their homeland without "sacrificing" more than about 15.000 Slovaks. However, the speaker added that due to economic realities as well as the artificial Magyarization of the past, especially in the city of Košice-Kassa, any further ceding of territories should be flatly rejected.

Regarding Transcarpathia, Seton-Watson took a similar view: he considered it theoretically possible to move the border twenty miles northeast, quickly adding that this would deprive the area not only of its farmlands but also of its railways. Another argument against revision would, he opined, be Hunga-

---

243 In the article that appeared in his own journal, Seton-Watson issued a warning to the Little Entente states: "It would be a grave blunder [...] to adopt the tactics of the ostrich [...], they must be ready to defend their cause by a full array of argument and fact and will be well advised to insist upon their opponents, without further delay." Seton-Watson, The Problem of Revision and the Slav World, *Slavonic and East European Review*, Vol. 12, No. 34 (July 1933), 24–35, 24.
244 Steed, "The Map of Europe," *Times*, July 18, 1933, 10.
245 Seton-Watson, The Problem of Revision and the Slav World, *Slavonic and East European Review*, Vol. 12, No. 34 (July 1933), 24–35, 28–29.

ry's "utter denial of [Ruthenian] education, culture, land and progress." Here he mentioned Czechoslovakia, his model Central European state as a counterexample, which, nevertheless, is quite problematic. In 1918 the country was founded as a national state of the Czechs and Slovaks; the most important laws as well as the 1920 constitution and language laws were all passed by the Revolutionary National Assembly, the new state's legislative body comprised exclusively of Czechs and Slovaks. Hence, decisions about the fundamental legal framework of Czechoslovakia were passed without the participation of minorities.[246] Until the dissolution of the Czechoslovak Republic in 1939, despite the guarantees of Article 10 of the Treaty of Saint-Germain of 1919, Transcarpathian territorial autonomy had not been realized.

When discussing the Romanian–Hungarian or the Yugoslav–Hungarian borders, Seton-Watson stated that he only saw the possibility of a revision of the territories adjacent to the frontier, however, the return of Hungarian-speaking Oradea and its environs would cut off the road and rail network. He questioned the return of Arad on economic grounds, and as in the case of Košice-Kassa, he rejected outright the readjustment of Cluj-Napoca (Kolozsvár), too, on the grounds of past Magyarization, as well as, regarding Yugoslavia, he expressed doubts about the "100,000-strong, predominantly South Slav" Subotica (Szabadka).

Looking at his proposals on each of the frontier sections, it is clear that, in theory, Seton-Watson did not reject revision per se, but he had more doubts about its practical implementation. He rightly saw purely ethnic borders as more often than not impossible in the region and argued effectively that the re-annexation of the border areas would not cure the ills of the Hungarian economy, but rather would strengthen the agrarian character of the country. In addition, he reiterated his quite exaggerated old claim that "there never was in modern history a more fanatical and unnatural concentration of effort upon a policy of assimilation than in Hungary from say, 1840 to 1918." Moreover, since the same anti-democratic, pre-war oligarchy continued to rule after 1920, he found Horthy-Hungary unworthy of any concessions. Therefore, instead of a revision, which in his opinion would have returned only one fifth of the minority Hungarians to the mother country, he suggested the strict observance of minority laws[247] and eco-

---

246 Elizabeth Wiskemann, *Czechs and Germans: A Study of the Struggles in the Historic Provinces of Bohemia and Moravia*, Oxford, Oxford University Press, 1938, 94.
247 In a 1935-article he acknowledged that some of the most important provisions of certain of these minority treaties had "remained on paper"; and he added that what he believed indispensable was the public recognition that "nationality" is not identical with his "citizenship" but is "something compounded of race, language, tradition and innermost feeling-something physiological

nomic cooperation between the states of Central and Eastern Europe, first of all by reducing the separating character of the borders.[248]

After the talk, there was a discussion in which numerous specialists from the RIIA rose to speak. Despite largely concurring with Seton-Watson, Macartney disagreed with him on three areas that already clearly demonstrated the stark disparities in their views. One of the young scholar's objections concerned the assessment of pre-war Magyarisation: Macartney considered it a manifest exaggeration to always portray it as "forcible," "artificial" or "bogus," and believed rather that there were segments of every nation that were ready to assimilate into the majority nation, a point he tried to make precisely with Seton-Watson's reference to the Jews as the "willing instruments" of Magyarization. Steed, however, quickly came to Seton-Watson's aid: while acknowledging that it was accurate to say that the Magyarization process depicted in the statistics was not entirely artificial, it was only because the nationalities had accepted Hungarian-dominated education, knowing that doing otherwise would prevent them from pursuing a career.

Macartney's second comment in the debate related to the question of frontier adjustment and was closely linked to his assessment of the 1920 Peace Treaty. In contrast to Seton-Watson and Steed, who had been stressing the amount of expertise involved, Macartney shared the view that the peace concluded at Versailles was a punitive one with a particularly negative impact on vanquished Hungary. For this reason, he believed that "the minor alterations mentioned by the speaker should be made" and could only rightly be rejected if the victors of First World War who had been unduly favoured in the peace treaties were willing to comply with the law of minorities.

Finally, Macartney also disagreed with Seton-Watson's analysis of Beneš's "statesmanlike" attitude and especially with the Czech politician's three preconditions for any revision: lack of outside pressure, correction preceded by years of peaceful cooperation, and equal compensation. Macartney soberly stated that the Successor States had not even hinted at revision, despite the lack of any pressure for more than a decade; a prelude to cooperation should be the implementation of the Minority Treaties; and finally, regarding compensation he retorted: "How could the shorn lamb compensate the lion?"[249]

---

and sacred, which should be as inviolate as his religion." Seton-Watson, The Question of Minorities, *Slavonic and East European Review*, Vol. 14, No. 40 (July 1935), 34.
248 Seton-Watson, The Problem of Treaty Revision and the Hungarian Frontiers, *IA*, July 1933, 481-499.
249 Ibid., 500-501.

## 2.10. The Four Britons on the Four Power Pact and the Question of Frontier Rectification

The next encounter of the three experts on Hungary took place soon after. In November 1933, former Hungarian prime minister István Bethlen gave four lectures in England which constituted the first clear-cut statement of the Hungarian position on the revision. The third lecture, on the future of Transylvania, delivered at the RIIA, was based on the traditional and somewhat pretentious arguments of Hungarian historic right and cultural superiority against the quantitative majority of a largely uneducated people, the Romanians, originally "shepherds and herdsmen": "Our ancestors never imagined," Bethlen claimed highhandedly, "that those Romanian fugitives whom they permitted out of pity to settle in the country were in time to expel from their ancestral property their own offspring, the reward for the magnanimity of our forebears is the Peace Treaty of Trianon."[250] The former prime minister described Transylvania with its mixed population as a separate geographical entity with a rich historical tradition. As for the solution of the interethnic conflicts, he rejected both population transfer and Seton-Watson's and Steed's "magic formula," the spiritualisation of frontiers. The latter, in his view, would not bring genuine reconciliation, but coupled with the painful experience of the worthlessness of the guarantee of the League of Nations, it would be the equal of the continuation of Romanian atrocities amidst utter disregard for minority rights: "This plan has been invented merely in order to distract public attention from the topic of a territorial revision,"[251] he opined. Instead, Bethlen put forward the view that, as in the seventeenth century, Transylvania should become an independent state with a structure similar to Switzerland, and he issued a prophetic warning:

> If the revision of the peace treaties and the subsequent reconciliation of the small nations of the Danube basin would not be successful, [both peoples] have to look forward to a dark and stormy future, since all of the small peoples of Central Europe will be engulfed either by the Slav ogre or by the German "Drang nach Osten," if not perhaps—in mutual understanding—by both."[252]

As usual, the prime minister's talk was followed by a discussion. The angry Steed, himself an advocate of Daco-Romanian continuity, described Bethlen's interpretation of Hungarian history as "little more than a beautiful fairy story."

---

250 Stephen Bethlen, The Transylvanian Problem, *IA*, May–June 1934, 362–367.
251 Ibid., 368.
252 Ibid., 371.

In order to counter Hungarian cultural superiority, he then called the speaker's attention to two of the most glorious Hungarian rulers, the ethnically Romanian János Hunyady and Matthias Corvinus.[253]

Seton-Watson commented on Bethlen's presentation in a similar vein. With an excellent tactical sense, quoting from the former prime minister's wartime parliamentary speeches, reprimanded him for his 1917 imperialist demands for the annexation of Serbia as well as some territories (about 1250 square miles) along the Romanian–Hungarian border, and he also severely criticised the abolition of the secret ballot in rural areas (in 1922). The publicist-historian regarded Transylvanian independence as impractical and the future of the region able to be secured only by border spiritualization, which was in turn rejected by Bethlen, and the chances of which, however, Seton-Watson believed were further damaged not only by interwar Hungarian propaganda but also by the former Hungarian prime minister's 1933 lecture tour to England.[254]

After the grand old scholars, Macartney once again represented a more restrained tone: he considered it important to stress that there was no existing evidence on historical right or precedence, which, in his opinion, should be preceded by the wishes of the current population. This was not good news for Bethlen. Summing up his personal experience, Macartney concluded that minorities had been better off in historical Hungary than in Yugoslavia or Romania, both economically and in terms of administrative organisation, but that the cultural life of minorities had to be ranked in the opposite order. Thus, he argued, if Hungary were to adopt a liberal cultural policy similar to that of Romania, the vast majority of Germans and perhaps even some Romanians would wish to return to Hungary.[255]

Despite the chairman having alluded to the confidential nature of the meeting and the subsequent debate, the information was leaked to the Hungarian, and consequently the Romanian press; thus, Steed received telegrams of exuberant gratitude from Romanian associations and universities. Complaining about the "gross breach of rules," he confessed:

> Had I been aware that any account of my remarks would be published in the Hungarian press I should not have let Count Bethlen off as lightly as I did. I should have reminded him that he owed his premiership to the

---

253 Ibid., 372.
254 Ibid., 275–377.
255 Ibid., 373.

## 2.10. The Four Britons on the Four Power Pact and the Question of Frontier Rectification

White Terror which was set up after the Romanians had overthrown Béla Kun and had occupied Budapest in 1919, that this White Terror had slain its thousands where the Red Terror had slain its hundreds.[256]

Less than year later, *Treaty Revision and Hungarian Frontiers* by Seton-Watson was published containing the publicist-historian's anti-revisionist statements from 1933. The timing was excellent: the short book came out just before the English edition of Bethlen's lectures. Seton-Watson could not help but evoke the dark past, which this time became even darker: Magyarization, which "the whole apparatus of Hungarian Government was placed at the service of,"[257] takes up ten pages with the starting point of 1830 instead of the usual 1867. In addition, the former Hungarian prime minister, "the foremost Magyar feudalist," also got his due: according to Seton-Watson, the Bethlen administration between 1921 and 1931 had been conducted "in intelligent anticipation of Nazi methods."[258] Hungary in general failed to learn its lesson from the past but rather went on pursuing the pre-war aim of the "thirty-million Magyar realm," which Seton-Watson saw as best justified by the fact that the number of Slovaks in Hungary had fallen from four hundred eight thousand to one hundred four thousand within ten years.[259]

As we have seen, from early on in his career, Seton-Watson treated the Hungarian statistical data with reservations: in contrast to the 1900 election statistics he harshly criticized the 1910 data as grossly unreliable. Regarding post-war figures, however, the reverse was the case: his figure regarding the number of Slovaks in Trianon Hungary in 1920 (four hundred eight thousand)[260] was almost three times the official Hungarian one (141.915 thousand Slovaks), but,

---

256 Steed to R.C. Arnold. RIIA, December 5, 1933, MS 74 129.
257 Seton-Watson, *Treaty Revision and Hungarian Frontiers*, London, Eyre and Spottiswoode, 1934, 24.
258 Ibid., 59. Today the moderate right-wing, anti-Nazi, pro-British politician István Bethlen is among the least controversial twentieth-century Hungarian figures, having a more positive balance sheet.
259 Ibid., 42. According to the Slovak demographer Ján Svetoň, who thoroughly researched the official Hungarian statistical records from 1880 to 1941, the loss of Slovak nationals that emerged from the sixty-year trend was more the result of official misrepresentation. Thus, unlike Seton-Watson, he was sceptical about the -official 1930 figures, putting forward that the idea of a Slovak population of about two hundred eighty five thousand in 1940, at least claimed what it should be. Unfortunately, during the 1946–48 population transfers, Svetoň's estimate was used to define the number of Slovaks in Hungary who were to be evacuated. It proved impossible, and despite wholesale agitation by prominent politicians from Prague, only one fourth of the original record number left for Czechoslovakia. Ján Svetoň, *Slováci v Maďarsku* [Slovaks in Hungary], Bratislava, Vydala Spoločnosť pre zahraničných Slovákov, 1942, 162–165. See also István Tóth, *Szlovákok a megmaradás és a beolvadás válaszútján* [Slovaks at a Crossroads between Survival and Assimilation], Szeged, 2013, 16.
260 Here Seton-Watson's estimate roughly coincides with that of Beneš's January 29 territorial claims speech in Versailles.

as shown above, he was willing to accept Hungarian statistical data from ten years later (104.918 thousand in 1930), probably in order to further justify the continuity and effectiveness of Magyarization. However, despite his sometimes-outlying numbers, official data did support his critical stance. After the Treaty of Trianon had made Hungary bereft of most of its former nationalities, the percentage of which sank from 45.5 to 7.9 percent, Law XXXIII of 1921 was to provide protection of the rights of the remaining national minorities; in any commune with at least forty children belonging to an ethnic minority, instruction in the mother tongue had to be introduced upon request. However, during the late 1920s, out of the seventy-eight, so-called A-type primary schools where Hungarian was taught only as a subject, with instruction otherwise carried out in the mother tongue, fifty were German and twenty-eight Serb, but not a single one was Slovak. Slovaks had only one B-type elementary school, with instruction both in Slovak and Magyar, and fifty C-type, essentially Hungarian schools with Slovak as one of the many subjects. In comparison, there were 756 purely Hungarian primary schools in Czechoslovakia in 1928[261] (though only seven Hungarian secondary schools in contrast with ten Slovak secondary schools in Hungary).[262]

Regarding the population of the Hungarian islands along the Trianon border, which Seton-Watson put at three quarters of a million, a significant underestimation, he was not, in principle, opposed to their return to Hungary.[263] On the other hand, after a thorough discussion of the various Hungarian claims for redress, he rejected the practical border readjustment, claiming that he had never met a Czech or a Romanian who would not gladly hand over "a few towns and villages" if that could end the conflict, "but it'd be followed by fresh demands and a fresh offensive."[264]

In June 1934, forty-one members of the House of Commons, led by Robert Gower, again bombarded the editor of the *Times* with open letters insisting that plans for economic cooperation between Central and Eastern Europe were doomed to failure unless they started from the adjustment of "artificial and un-

---

261 For 691,923 Hungarians according to 1930 Czechoslovak statistics.
262 G.C. Paikert, Hungary's National Minority Policies, 1920-1945, *American Slavic and East European Review*, Vol. 12, No. 2 (April 1953), 201-218, 218.
263 Seton-Watson, *Treaty Revision and the Hungarian Frontiers*, 1934, 7.
264 Ibid., 45. A year later Seton-Watson called himself "the open opponent" of revision, and referring to Count Bethlen's proposed Transylvanian independence he added: "From the point of European peace it does not really very much matter whether they only demand the break-up of Czechoslovakia, Romania and Yugoslavia into separate States which they know could not possibly stand alone, or whether they demand their reincorporation in Hungary." Seton-Watson, Austria and Her Neighbours, *Slavonic and East-European Review*, April 1935, 549-570, 561-562.

natural" borders.²⁶⁵ Very much in line with this pro-Hungarian wave of sympathy, and in order to counterbalance anti-Hungarian or pro-Versailles propaganda, István Bethlen proposed to launch a periodical in English under the name *The Hungarian Quarterly (HQ)*, very much in line with *La Nouvelle Revue de Hongrie*: "The entire periodical, constructed in this fashion, would be in the service not of vulgarising and of cheap sensation hunting or propaganda, but would speak exclusively to the most educated in the Anglo-Saxon countries: to Parliaments, to universities, to the leading figures in economic and social life."²⁶⁶ The first volume appeared in 1934 as a joint, semi-official publication of the Bethlen-circle and the Department of Foreign Affairs, with the aim of producing high-quality Hungarian propaganda. József Balogh, the co-editor and later editor of the journal, as well as the founding secretary general of the *HQ Society*, took great pains to request articles from reputable British authors.

Soon both *Nouvelle Revue de Hongrie* and the *Hungarian Quarterly* became crowning achievements of the Hungarian government's efforts to present the Hungarian past and present to a foreign audience in a positive light, with the active support of Bethlen and the Hungarian Foreign Ministry. In his pioneering study, Tibor Frank also points out that about 60 percent of the necessary funds came from the leaders of Hungarian industry, commerce and banking. Individuals such as Baroness Rothschild in England, also contributed to the annual budget.²⁶⁷

*The Hungarian Quarterly* employed an editor in London, too. When Owen Rutter sent a letter to Steed on the question of frontier readjustment, the former *Times* editor retorted with Seton-Watson's anti-revisionist arguments: the Hungarian governing classes' intrigues with Italy, Germany and Poland as well as their revisionist obsession and their *"nem, nem, soha"* [no, no, never] agitation were to distract attention from the urgency of domestic change, that is social reconstruction and a thorough-going agrarian reform. Steed put forward somewhat naively that

---

265 Robert Gower et al., "The Treaty of Trianon, Frontier Rectification," *Times*, June 27, 1934, 12. See also Gower, "The Treaty of Trianon," *Times*, June 9, 1934, 10.
266 Memorandum, July 3,1934, OSZ KT. József Balogh Papers: Litteræ Originales (Litt. Orig.), Fond 1/1525. Qtd. in Tibor Frank, "To Comply with English Taste: The Making of *The Hungarian Quarterly*, 1934–1944." See also Tibor Frank, (2009), Patronage and Networking: The Society of the *Hungarian Quarterly* 1935–1944, *New Hungarian Quarterly* 50, 3–12.
267 Tibor Frank, Editing as Politics: József Balogh and *The Hungarian Quarterly*, in *Ethnicity, Propaganda. Myth-Making: Studies on Hungarian Connections to Britain and America, 1848–1945*, Budapest, Akadémiai Kiadó, 1999, 267.

if the neighbours of Hungary could be convinced that all she desires is such readjustment of frontiers as may be ethnographically desirable and economically feasible the whole problem would appear in a new light it might then be not too much to hope that, after a period of neighbourliness, frontiers themselves would tend to become invisible and an era of co-operation would replace the era of strife in the whole Danubian region.[268]

\* \* \*

The year 1934 saw another new arrival on the subject of revision: *National States, National Minorities*. In it Macartney summarised his experience as a minority expert in the Intelligence Department of the British League of Nations Union and argued with academic rigour for the need for territorial adjustment. The book has long been regarded as one of Macartney's most original and valuable works; it incorporated Toynbee's suggestions for alteration,[269] and Seton-Watson, who at the time was already more a rival than a mentor, also paid tribute, calling it "an authoritative handbook on the whole theory and practice of the subject, full of learning and sanity."[270]

Both experts on Central-Eastern Europe agreed that the 1919-20 boundaries were not "sacrosanct," but as regards practical revision they held contrasting opinions. Quite against Seton-Watson's (and Steed's) anti-revisionist stance, Macartney argued that, unlike previous settlements, the Treaty of Versailles had been concluded *expressis verbis* on the basis of the principle of national self-determination. In the meantime, however, it became apparent that the settlement had "either wilfully or in ignorance and prejudice" violated these principles in more than one instance, so "there is stronger reason than ever for invoking them once again to modify it."[271] As the most glaring example of injustice, the author of *National States, National Minorities* specifically addressed the situation of minorities living in a block in the annexed border areas, and he came to a very pessimistic conclusion. He argued that their very existence constituted a "permanent menace" to the dominant nation, which would do everything in its power to further weaken them in order to avoid a legitimate ethnic revision. It seems, he opined, that a nation state and national minorities are "incompatibles."[272]

---

268 Steed to Owen Rutter, October 5, 1935. Steed Papers MS 74130. See also OSZK KT Fond 1/2923.
269 A Chatham House employee to Toynbee, August 16, 1933. RIIA Archives 4/TOYN/2. The letter reports that Macartney was "most grateful" for Toynbee's suggestions for revisions and the publication.
270 Seton-Watson, The Question of Minorities, *SEER*, July 1935, 68. fn.
271 Macartney, *National States and National Minorities*, London, 1934, 427-428.
272 Ibid., 416.

## 2.10. The Four Britons on the Four Power Pact and the Question of Frontier Rectification

According to Macartney, the ethnic principle was generally violated when border demarcation was subjected to two criteria, the strategic and the economic. The strategic claim had been particularly unjust, he opined, precisely because, as the war had waned, there was no justification for the argument that the victor needed security more than the vanquished state. The more so, as the disarmament obligations had also been imposed on the latter. The other aspect most often used in Versailles to counter the ethnic principle was the economic one, illustrated in Macartney's book by the example of Hungary (the loss of the farmlands of Burgenland and Bácska). "The split of Hungary [...] put an end to one intolerable situation only by creating another," argued Macartney, that is, the empowerment of the oppressed nationalities of the Austro-Hungarian Monarchy created a system of small states, which were at loggerheads with each other, unable to cooperate economically. As long as nationality was considered to be the almost sole organising principle of the state, the author claimed, a revision along the Rothermere line would be an "act of mere justice," but would tend to exacerbate economic problems.[273]

It is clear from the above that Macartney's revision of the Treaty of Versailles on the basis of the ethnic principle was not inspired by a belief in the lofty concept of self-determination: "It is very arguable, whether the ills from which Central and Eastern-Europe are suffering today do not arise more out of the excessive deference paid to [that criterion in 1918] than out of occasional disregard of it."[274] Macartney regarded the absolutisation of the ethnic principle as a harmful phenomenon, since it implied the creation of the nation-state, which could only be carried out by assimilating minorities, i.e., by eliminating them. He saw the ideal solution to the problems of Hungary and the Danube Basin in the economic and political cooperation of the states concerned, perhaps on the model of Great Britain, that is, within the framework of a supranational state that would guarantee equality and democratic freedoms for its members. Thus, Macartney agreed with Seton-Watson and Steed on the necessity of border spiritualization. However, while the two friends believed that political-economic cooperation was the first step in reducing the significance of borders, their younger colleague was convinced that no genuine regional collaboration could be facilitated until after a fair ethnic-based frontier readjustment.

---

273 Ibid., 477–478.
274 Ibid., 429.

During 1934, although he would acclaim the Versailles Treaty for effectively reducing the number of minorities by millions and creating a more favourable situation overall in Europe, Toynbee continued to voice criticism, very much along the lines of Macartney's arguments: more territories had been taken from Germany, Austria, Hungary and Bulgaria for the benefit of the continental victors and the new successor states than a strict application of the principle of nationality would have allowed. [275] In fact, Toynbee referred to the most dissatisfied minorities along both the Polish corridor and the Hungarian borders and denounced the Council of the League of Nations for having been largely powerless to address their grievances. The Chatham House director managed to establish a research-fund to finance "first-hand local" investigations into the social, cultural, economic and political circumstances of the relevant regions. As an example, he cited Seton-Watson's 1908 *Racial Problems in Hungary*, which had "made history."[276]

Under the auspices of RIIA and Arnold Toynbee himself and financed by the Rockefeller Research Fund, Macartney soon set out for a two-year-long trip to the Carpathian Basin to study the post-war successor states of Austria-Hungary on the spot, with special regards to the situation of their minorities. "I'm glad that Macartney's piece of research has gone through [...] he will do it exceedingly well [...] it will be a good thing for the League Nations Union," Toynbee enthused in a private letter.[277]

Interestingly, despite the growing distance between Macartney and Seton-Watson in their perceptions of national conflicts in Central and Eastern Europe after the world economic crisis, there were still a few occasions for joint action. In April 1935, for example, together with Noel Buxton and G.P. Gooch they joined the Anglo-Ukrainian Committee which had been formed in London. The new organisation issued the following statement: "[...] ethnographically Ukrainian peoples occupy a more or less contiguous block of territory (greater than that of France and Great-Britain) now divided btw USSR, Poland, Czechoslovakia and Rumania. [...] Very few attempts have been made to give justice to

---

[275] "The Treaty of Versailles and After: Territorial Arrangements," BBC talk, May 7, 1934, Toynbee Papers, BL MS 13 967/6. BBC Broadcasts 1929-1955.

[276] Chatham House Research Project (Toynbee's partly handwritten notes.), 1934 [?]. Toynbee Papers, BL, MS 13 967/39.

[277] Toynbee to Gilbert Murray, March 8, 1934, Toynbee Papers BL Oxford MS13967/117, Miscellaneous Correspondence 1934-35.
In his *1934 Survey*, Toynbee used Macartney's 1934 book *National State and National Minorities*, quoting its statistical data regarding the number of Magyars (539 ftn): In Romania 1.87 thousand (official figure) and 1.9 M (Hungarian figure). Toynbee, *Survey of International Affairs* 1934, Oxford University Press, London: Humphrey Milford, 1935, 488.

Ukrainians and the continued neglect of this complicated question may ultimately involve all Europe."[278]

The collaboration is worthy of our attention: Seton-Watson, self-labelled as the "open opponent" of revision, shared the same platform as the Germanophile revisionist historian[279] G.P. Gooch and the Bulgarophile Noel Buxton,[280] both friends and admirers of Prime Minister Ramsay Macdonald and both staunch appeasers. It is quite obvious, therefore, that between the two world wars, Seton-Watson considered the preservation of the status quo above all else and only sided with minority-ethnic issues when they did not affect it.

## 2.11. Histories, Historians and Propaganda: Seton-Watson's *History of the Romanians*, and Macartney's *Hungary* (1934)

During the early 1930s, the economic crisis did not spare Seton-Watson's private funds, and the publicist-historian's severe financial losses prevented him from traveling for five years, which appeared to benefit his scholarly endeavours. To counterbalance the increasingly vociferous Hungarian revisionist movements and Bethlen's tour of England, Seton-Watson set out to expand on the lectures he had given at the University of London a year earlier. He soon published a book on the history of the Romanians that was the first work of its kind in English, based on Allen Leeper's works and the Romanian writer-politician Nicolae Iorga's magnum opus.[281]

Former Romanian prime minister Iorga was a historian and rector of the University of Bucharest, and he naturally regarded history a useful weapon in the country's cultural diplomatic arsenal. His formidable intellect was instrumental in presenting Romania, in the words of Seton-Watson, as the "Latin sentinel upon the Danube."[282] Once again, as academics entered parliaments and

---

278 "Anglo-Ukrainian Committee Formed," *Herald and Express*, April 30, 1935, 8.
279 Gooch had been educated in Germany and had a German wife. He published excessively on shared responsibility in the First World War, the real cause of which had been in his opinion the division of Europe into two rival armed camps. J. P. Gooch, Recent Revelations of European Diplomacy, *Journal of the British Institute of International Affairs*, Vol. 2, No. 1 (January 1923), 1-29, 9.
280 https://fontanus.library.mcgill.ca/article/view/37/38, Accessed May 10, 2023.
281 Nicolae Iorga, *A History of Roumania. Land, People, Civilisation*, London, 1925.
282 Seton-Watson in his preface to Nicolae Iorga, *A History of Anglo-Romanian Relations*, Bucharest: Societate Anglo-Română, 1931, 4. Very much in line with this statement, Iorga claimed that owing to the synthesis of Byzantine high culture and traditional Romanian culture as well as the supposed continuity of its ancient past Bucharest became "the true intellectual capital of South Eastern Europe." Nicolae Iorga, *My American Lectures*, Bucharest, State Printing Office, 1932, 192.

## 2. From Versailles to Paris (1920–1947)

politicians found themselves in lecture halls, the lines between politics and research began to blur.

The first few chapters of Iorga's six hundred-page heavy hitter were predicated on the idea of Daco-Romanian continuity, which had been a major theme in all of Seton-Watson's publications on the Balkan nation. In 1915, Seton-Watson claimed for example that the Romanians had "unquestionably" descended from the Roman colonists of Dacia, continuing that "their Latin origin is obvious to anyone who walks through the streets of Bucharest; still more to anyone who visits the remoter villages of Transylvania and sees the pure Roman types among the peasantry."[283] Seven to eight years later, in 1922, he argued that "sober research" had already endorsed the main thesis[284] that Romanians had been present in Transylvania (three centuries) before Magyars.[285] Again in 1934 he stressed, already on page twelve, that Romanians were in fact "Romanised Dacians infiltrated with Slav and Tatar blood."[286] Instead of regarding the *prior tempore, potior iure* argument as irrelevant, as it would be for a civic nationalist, Seton-Watson consistently took sides—with Romania.

"The surest test of a historian lies in his attitude to the capital problem of omission and selection that is a judgment itself,"[287] Seton-Watson acknowledged back in his 1922 inaugural lecture, which the *History of Romanians* seemed more closely to comply with, corresponding to the Romanian master narrative: János Hunyadi, the hero of Nándorfehérvár (Belgrade) who halted Turkish advance for seventy years in 1456, appeared to have lost his identity upon entering Hungarian nobility.[288] And both the liberal statesmen Ferenc Deák, the author of the 1867 Compromise, and Lajos Kossuth, labelled the Hungarian Washington, became in Seton-Watson's interpretation "dictators"—although "less truly" ones.[289] The evaluation of Prime Minister István Tisza also took a turn for the worse: the prime minister formerly "showing statesmanship and foresight"[290] in the 1934 book was depicted as a man "combining the arrogance of a gentry, fatalism of a strict Calvinist with an ardent belief in Magyar predominance."[291] Moreover, whereas in 1919 Seton-Watson would have left the eastern strip of

---

283 Seton-Watson, *Roumania and the Great War*, 1915, 8.
284 Seton-Watson 1922, 29.
285 Seton-Watson, Transylvania (II), *Slavonic Review*, Vol. 1, No. 3 (March 1923), 546.
286 Seton-Watson, *A History of the Roumanians*,1934, 12.
287 Seton-Watson 1922, 34.
288 Ibid., 37.
289 Dualist prime minister Kálmán Tisza (1875–1890) became "far more a truly dictator than Kossuth and Deák have ever been." Ibid., 401.
290 Seton-Watson 1926, 168.
291 Seton-Watson, *A History of the Roumanians*, 1934, 417.

the Hungarian Plain in Hungary, let alone his recommended autonomy for the Székelys, sixteen years later he strenuously defended the 1920-settlement: in his book, the number of Hungarians living in Transylvania decreased to eight hundred thousand (the data in the second appendix are more acceptable: 1.3 million), the compact bloc of Székelys appeared as an "uncomfortable fact," while the majority of the rest of the Magyars he claimed to have been "a result of two generations of intensive Magyarization."[292]

The book ended with the author's hope that "two generations of peace and clean government might make of Roumania an earthly paradise." The optimism of this statement is all the more surprising because, as we have seen, the post-1920 period was defined not by the friends of the freedom-loving historian but also by the centralising, particularly anti-minority policies of his opponents.[293]

Nevertheless, regardless of who was in a position of power in Romania, the country kept its foreign friends in high regard. Under the direction of the talented diplomat Nicolae Titulescu, especially after 1932, the country's foreign policy, described by one British Foreign officer as "very much a one-man show," sought to promote the idea that Romania's territorial integrity was the key to future peace and stability not only in the region but in Europe as a whole. The foreign secretary maintained personal relationships with Western political and public figures, as well as journalists (both at home and abroad) and scholars whom he subsidized from a "secret fund" of the Foreign Ministry. It was no surprise that Seton-Watson was among those who received regular payments from the Romanian government.[294]

"It is important not to read [Seton-Watson's] book in the light of post war [...] unrestrained nationalism," opined the *Cambridge Review*, "with all its defects the Monarchy was a bind of union of many nationalities. Its destruction has left chaos of jarring fragments."[295] However, such a rather nostalgic reception of the *History of the Romanians* was far from typical in Britain: the *Times*, for example, found it "able, scholarly and very readable," emphasising the balanced argument and the impartiality of the ground-breaking work.[296]

---

292 Ibid., 553.
293 Ibid., 554.
294 Dov. B. Lungu, *Romania and the Great Powers*, Durham and London, Duke University Press, 1989, 1–15, and 15–16. See Also Zsolt Nagy, *Grand Delusions: Interwar Hungarian Cultural Diplomacy, 1918–1941*, A dissertation submitted to the faculty of the University of North Carolina at Chapel Hill, Department of History, Chapel Hill, 2012, 153.
295 *Cambridge Review*, February 15, 1935. Qtd. in: Seton-Watson Papers, SEW 8/3.
296 *Times*, August 10, 1934, 6.

## 2. From Versailles to Paris (1920–1947)

It was no surprise that in Hungarian circles—Jászi, Károlyi and their close allies excepted—Seton-Watson's book was interpreted as a work of propaganda "unworthy of a great historian."[297] The following conclusion of the Transylvanian lawyer and politician, Zsombor Szász, also a frequent contributor to the Hungarian journal *Magyar Szemle*, however, also reflected the Hungarian political elite's misjudgement of the situation: "The decisive reason for the annexation of Transylvania to Romania was the theory of the 'Daco-Roman continuity', the autochthonous nature of the Romanian people in Transylvania."[298] Macartney—as we shall see—tried on several occasions to prove the untenability of this view, apparently without much success.

Based on his experience during his lecture tour in England, which Seton-Watson's recent publications only reinforced, former Hungarian prime minister István Bethlen came to the "painful conclusion" that Hungarian national history was not available in any (major) Western language.[299] In the summer of 1934, when Bethlen had put his thoughts on paper, he could not have known that Macartney's book on Hungary would soon be published in London. Its foreword was written by H.A.L. Fisher, who had been the young Seton-Watson's history tutor at New College, Oxford, thirty years earlier.

In two-fifths of the book, Macartney summarised the history of the Hungarian people, "Asiatic, but not inferior."[300] On most of the controversial points, he tended to present the contrasting arguments but, unlike Seton-Watson, often without taking sides. On the question of historical primacy, for example, in the debate between the Daco-Romanian continuity and the Hungarian counter arguments, he endorsed neither claim but calmly stated: "Neither side can produce any indisputable proof of its case, and each finds it much easier to demolish the arguments of its adversary than to support its own." The author was reticent about the origin of the Szeklers, too: he considered the Turkish-Tatar, Avar or Hungarian versions equally viable, but—in contrast to Seton-Watson's close friend, the Romanian expert in Versailles, Allen Leeper—he insisted that the ethnic group should be considered Hungarian both in language and in sentiment.[301]

Macartney considered the 1867 Settlement a reasonable compromise, but added that the "tacit alliance" of the Crown and the Hungarians against the na-

---

297 Zsombor Szász, "M. Seton-Watson et l'histoire des Roumains," *Nouvelle Revue de Hongrie*, November 1934, 352.
298 *Magyar Szemle*, 1935/1.
299 Qtd. in Tibor Frank, Luring the English-Speaking World: Hungarian History Diverted, *Slavonic and East European Review*, 1991/1, 60.
300 Macartney, *Hungary*, London, Ernest Benn Ltd., 1934, 7.
301 Ibid., 48–51.

tionalities could not solve the nationality question;[302] the progressive Nationality Law of 1868 remained a "dead letter," and in both the administration and the judiciary, the anti-democratic tendencies dominated: rotten boroughs, electoral fraud and an unusually low franchise: around 6 percent of eligible voters.[303]

The World War ended an era of "astonishing progress" and "spectacular failures," the assessment of which, as we have seen, was rather mixed. But Macartney's view of post-war Hungary was much gloomier, and in 1934 he reiterated even more strongly his criticism of five years earlier: the Horthy-regime in his opinion was "a reaction in the most exact sense of the word" and added that "it would be ludicrous to pretend that Hungary bears any resemblance to what we understand by a democracy."[304] Moreover, the Hungarian ruling classes, Macartney argued, had indeed not learned from the experience of war and collapse, since they still believed that the superficial Magyarisation of their nationalities would turn them into Hungarians in sentiment. The treatment of minorities, sounded the author's warning, far exceeded the importance given to them in Hungary: on the one hand, only an "exemplary" minority policy could ensure the success of the protection of the interests of fellow Hungarians beyond the borders, and on the other hand, if the economic problems of the Danube Basin were to be addressed through revision, Hungary would definitely regain some of its minorities.[305]

Macartney's strictures on Hungary were further relaxed in the chapter on the Treaty of Trianon, which "ruthlessly dismembered" that country; like Seton-Watson he attributed the "draconic terms" neither to the alleged incompetence of experts nor to inaccurate sources. Rather, in his opinion, the injustice was due to two facts: Hungary's exclusion from the negotiations and the preceding political instability and turmoil in the country (Soviet Republic, Red and then White Terror), which only made impartiality even less likely to prevail.

In this work, Macartney refuted Seton-Watson's (and Steed's) oft-repeated premise that advocating revision was equal to inciting war. Quite prophetically, he advised the proponents of the theory to remember "how often, within the last century or century and a half, the failure to resolve national injustices peacefully has led to war." Further on, he claimed that a peace based on the principle of self-determination should have meant referendum, adding that if polled, a significant proportion of the population usually decided against ethnicity in

---

302 Ibid., 97–99.
303 Ibid., 103.
304 Ibid,. 122.
305 Ibid., 286–288.

favour of the state to which they had historically belonged. However, he did not consider this argument to be applicable retrospectively, since in 1934 he did not share the view of the Hungarian political leadership, which he believed was completely out of touch with reality, that in the event of a referendum, the Slovaks and especially the Romanians would have returned to Hungary.[306]

Regarding its historical analysis and the attitude to frontier readjustment, Macartney's *Hungary* could in fact serve as a powerful counterpoint to Seton-Watson's, both works published in 1934 (*History of Romanians* as well as *Treaty Revision and Hungarian Frontiers*), nevertheless, its Hungarian reception was mixed, to say the least. "I have not found it easy, as I cannot pretend that I think the nationality policy just, and that I like the present social system," Macartney confessed in a letter to József Balogh, "but I am very anxious not to be unjust in any way."[307] Balogh asked Zoltán Trócsányi, assistant editor of *Magyar Szemle*, to write a review. It acknowledged the "objectivity of Macartney's work, free of any sentimental approach," but criticised the negative assessment of the post-1920 political and social system in the book, which, as Trócsányi claimed, could easily play into the hands of Hungary's adversaries.[308]

The mixed reception of the book in Hungary is also perfectly illustrated by the circumstances of its Hungarian translation. The idea probably originated with the author's left-wing detractors, but it soon led to serious complications, as the translation had to be revised several times because of the author's understandable unwillingness to agree to abridgements and omissions. The whole project had been opposed from the beginning by the semi-official circles of the *Magyar Szemle* and the *Nouvelle Revue*, who believed that "no other motivation could have driven the publisher and translator but to use a foreign man's voice to preach left-wing facts."[309] However, as time went on, the Hungarian version could be abandoned only at the risk of Macartney's goodwill, and so the decision was finally taken to publish the whole work with a polemical preface.

"If there is an international institute of propaganda, it ought to present a diploma to the Hungarian entrusted with the task of placing Hungary's grievances before the world," British writer Bernard Newman claimed in 1939.[310] However, the situation surrounding the translation of Macartney's book and the eerily similar Hungarian reactions to Rothermere's campaign a few years earlier

---

306 Ibid., 309–333.
307 Macartney to József Balogh, February 22, 1934. OSZK KT, Fond 1/2064, 18477.
308 Georges Trócsányi, La Hongrie inconnue, *Nouvelle Revue de Hongrie*, February 1935, 133.
309 OSZK KT, Fond 1/2064, 18498.
310 Bernard Newman, *Danger Spots of Europe*, London, The Right Book Club, 1939, 286.

cast a serious challenge to this claim: official and semi-official Hungarian circles tried to keep alive the sympathy of those whose pro-revisionist statements sought to awaken the conscience of international public opinion, while at the same time being scrupulously careful to distance themselves from the ethnic revisionism they advocated or from criticism of the political and social order of the Horthy-era.

Moreover, after the First World War, very much unlike Steed or Seton-Watson, as we have seen, and despite his pro-Hungarian leanings, Macartney was much unwilling to bend to propaganda. His letter to József Balogh is worth quoting in detail:

> [...] The trouble has been all along that the only people who enjoyed any reputation of having anything whatever about the county were uniformly hostile to it, and although a certain number of MPs and similar people from time to time made speeches about it the immediate reply has been that they knew nothing about it, that they were only repeating what they were told from one side, and that the real facts are quite different, will be found in the works of authorities referred to (hostile to Hungary). I believe my book [*Hungary*, 1934] has changed this a good deal. I have no doubt that you will find in it things that you don't like and I am sorry for this, but there are one or two points I should like to mention. Firstly, if the whole book is not entirely agreeable to all Magyars, it certainly is not agreeable to her neighbours. I have had my head politely but thoroughly washed by the Czech Legation here. Secondly if I had written the ordinary "Justice for Hungary" book, it would have been instantly dismissed here as the "usual propaganda stuff." [...] Thirdly I must of course admit that you know (and I have never pretended anything else) that I do not agree with all the [...] [c]ontentions and ambitions of the Revision League [Hungarian Frontier Readjustment League] and cannot write what I do not believe.[311]

József Balogh was perhaps somewhat offended by Macartney's seemingly neutral position and asked him to find a competent English publicist-scholar to make the case for integral revision. The historian's reply was in the negative: "I regret to have to tell you that I know of no English publicist who supports the totalitarian view [i.e. integral revision] [...] none at least who would carry weight [...] and be accepted by them as both competent and impartial." The next

---

311 Macartney to József Balogh, November 13, 1934. OSZK KT Fond 1/2067, 18590.

section of the letter, however, went further, revealing the conclusion of Seton-Watson's 1934 book on frontier revision:

> One of the great complaints made over here against the Hungarians is their extreme intransigence [...] Thus it is said that Hungary cannot be given a small revision, because it would not satisfy her—and so, because she wants everything, she gets nothing at all. If your readers find my book, which has been criticized over here as too pro-Hungarian, attacked by you, I cannot help believing, that this complaint will be repeated [...] that you must be a people impossible to please [...] I believe that I have gone a considerable way towards awakening more sympathy for and interest in your country.[312]

Toynbee was equally bent on having nothing to do with (Hungarian) propaganda. In November 1938 he wrote a letter to Hungarian prime minister Béla Imrédy, whom he had met at British minister Geoffrey Knox's house at lunch, in order to introduce Professor Allan G.B. Fisher, the Price Chair of International Economics who had been on his journey through East-Central Europe to study the economic situation and hoped to meet the Hungarian prime minister. However, Toynbee was also quick to point out in his letter that Chatham House was a scientific body bent on "an objective study of facts of international relations," which was forbidden by its statutes to have any policy on carrying on any propaganda.[313]

## 2.12. Appease or Oppose? Steed, Seton-Watson and Toynbee in the Shadow of Nazism (1933-1936)

The Japanese aggression in 1931 against Manchuria was a foreshadowing of post 1933 events: neither the USA nor Britain was prepared to defend collective security in the Far East, and no sanctions were imposed against the aggressor. Toynbee described the Tory policy of "peace at any price" as "a complete breech with the traditions of English imperialism," actually "finis Britanniae." [314] However, when his father-in-law, Gilbert Murray, urged him to join the League of Nations Union executive to take action and at least organise a boycott of Japanese goods,

---

312 Macartney to József Balogh, December 14, 1934. OSZK KT Fond 1/2067.
313 Toynbee to Béla Imrédy, November 6, 1838. RIIA Archives 4/TOYN/ 6D.
314 Toynbee to Gilbert Murray, February 18, 1932. Toynbee Papers MS 13967/72/1 Family correspondence 1914-1957.

Toynbee declined, claiming he wished to devote all of his time to his beloved project, the multi-volume *Study of History*.[315] "I think I have never sat on a committee without wishing all the time that I was otherwise employed," he retorted, sharing Steed's similar doubts about the efficacy of such moves. Thus, Toynbee biographer McNeill rightly claims that his behaviour reflected that of His Majesty's Government,[316] which, further alarmed by the news from Germany, in the summer of 1933 agreed to amend the draft treaty of the Four Power Pact. Signed on June 7, the treaty ultimately made no major changes to Section 19 of the League of Nations Charter as regards revision.

Hitler's seizure of power in 1933 gave rise to two conflicting interpretations of German history as well as two different attitudes towards Germany in British historiography. The revisionists, e.g. G.P. Gooch,[317] William H. Dawson or Charles Beazley,[318] who had been opposing German war guilt and had been looking at German grievances with moralistic concern and the need for redress, tended to view Nazism as an aberration, a dead end. Nevertheless, in order to secure peace, they continued to advocate frontier readjustments. The latter intention was joined by enthusiasts,[319] often from the British high-society: in 1933 and 1935 both the Anglo-German Study Group and the Anglo-German Fellowship were established to further good Anglo-German relations.

Several prominent members of the Institute of International Affairs also joined the Anglo-German Study Group to bolster ties between the two countries, or at least to avoid drifting into a new war. A founding member, Lord Lothian or formerly Philip Kerr, actively campaigned for peace: on March 5, 1935 Lothian's paper *The Basis for a Permanent Settlement in Europe* declared that the ma-

---

315 Toynbee gave Austria-Hungary or the Successor States in East-Central Europe only passing attention in *A Study of History* (10 vols., London, 1934-1954). His thesis was that national history, even British history, had never been and never would be an objective, "intelligible" field of historical study. "The 'intelligible fields of historical study [...] are societies which have a greater extension, in both Space and Time, than national states or city-states, or any other political communities. [...] Societies, not states, are 'the social atoms' with which students of history have to deal." Toynbee, *A Study of History*, Vol. I, Oxford, Oxford University Press, 45.
316 Toynbee to Gilbert Murray, July 7, 1932. Toynbee Papers MS 13967/72/1 Family correspondence 1914-1957. McNeill 1989, 152–153.
317 With Harold Temperley, he co-edited *British Documents on the Origins of the War, 1898-1914*, which elevated his status among British historians.
318 J. P. Gooch, *Recent Revelations of European Diplomacy*, Longmans, 1928; Charles Beazley, *The Road to Ruin in Europe 1890-1914*, J. M. Dent & Sons Ltd, 1932; W. H. Dawson, *The Urgency of Treaty Revision*, Contemporary Review 144 (July 1933), 15–23.
319 Richard Griffiths, *Fellow Travellers of the Right: British Enthusiasts for Nazi Germany, 1933–1939*, London, Faber and Faber, 2011. Griffiths differentiated between two groups of people with pro-German views in the 1930s: active politicians, that is, appeasers, and pro-Germans, often prominent members of the public who held no political position (enthusiasts).

## 2. From Versailles to Paris (1920-1947)

jor problem in Europe was the artificial military dominance of the Entente over the former Central Powers. Thus, German rearmament, though illegal, was real and understandable, coupled with peaceable German intentions: national unity and the end of a defeatist attitude. He advised discussion with Germany and the relaxation of economic sanctions through the League of Nations. Macartney joined the ensuing debate and agreed that through Article XIX of the League Covenant adjustments of the international order could be made.[320]

On the other hand, especially when Hitler's radicalism and threats to the Versailles system became increasingly apparent, the thesis of shared war guilt began to lose its hold within the British historical community, and many began to develop a more favourable view of the Versailles settlement.[321] In contrast to the anti-revisionist spectrum, as we have seen earlier, stood Seton-Watson and Steed, who had long been the lone voices to advocate the Central Powers' sole responsibility for the First World War.[322] As early as 1926, after his visit to Germany on a speaking tour, Steed drew the conclusion that the British attitude had to be "conciliatory, but very firm" and should never allow any sector of German opinion to imagine that they were being "hoodwinked."[323] In his private letters he called the last months of 1932 "extraordinarily critical,"[324] when—in accordance with David Lloyd George—he found the optimistic attitude to Germany "entirely unjustified."[325] Steed, and Seton-Watson likewise viewed Nazism not as an aberration but as the flowering of the evil genius in German history

---

[320] "The Basis of a Permanent Settlement in Europe," Address by Lord Lothian, Chatham House, March 5, 1935. RIIA Archives 8/371.
See Lothian's letters to the *Times* (on January 31 and February 1, 1935) and Steed's efforts to neutralize him, for example his "corrective" letter to the *Times* (February 2). The Foreign Office often did not see eye to eye with Lothian regarding Nazi Germany, which however did not prevent him from being appointed British Ambassador to the USA. Watching European politics from a distance, greatly due to the Nazi occupation of Prague in March 1939, he became disenchanted with Hitler and his Reich.

[321] Catherine Ann Cline, British Historians and the Treaty of Versailles, *Albion: A Quarterly Journal Concerned with British Studies*, Vol. 20, No. 1 (Spring 1988), 43-58, 55-56.

[322] From the late 1930s, historian and broadcaster A.J.P. Taylor (1906-1990) would join this anti-revisionist tradition. In his *Course of German History*, for example, he put forward that "it was no more a mistake for the German people to end up with Hitler than it is an accident that a river flows into the sea.[...]." A.J.P. Taylor, *The Course of German History*, New York, Capricorn Books, 1962, 7.

[323] Steed to James Garvin, editor of the *Observer*, December 23, 1926, Steed Papers, MS 74 126.

[324] Steed to G.P. Gooch, October 26, 1932. Steed Papers, MS 74 129

[325] David Lloyd George to Steed, October 2, 1932. Steed Papers, MS 74 129. Sporadic, but amicable correspondence between the two later about Lord Northcliffe took place, and the former prime minister sought Steed's advice about the newer volumes of his war memoirs. See Steed to David Lloyd George, September 28, 1934, and David Lloyd George's answer dated October 1, 1934. Steed Papers, MS 74 130.

since the time of Frederick the Great.³²⁶ Their conclusion matched the one they had reached in connection with Hungarian revisionism long before: any revision of the treaty of Versailles in favour of Germany should be flatly rejected as the insatiable aggressor could never be placated.³²⁷

Unlike many of his British contemporaries, Steed could gain first-hand information on Germany early on: with the help of refugees from Germany, Holland, Switzerland etc., he maintained a special intelligence service between 1928 and 1939, which he later called his "little research group." He gave work to around dozen informants, (among them Count Károlyi³²⁸), even by moving their families from Germany at his own expense if necessary. He occasionally consulted Macartney's "expert knowledge," too.³²⁹ Steed was thus able to supply the War Office, as well as the Air Ministry, the Foreign Office, and even the Admiralty with regular information. He alleged, too, that the intelligence he provided often served as a basis for Churchill's campaign of speeches in 1938.³³⁰ He regularly made often far from inaccurate predictions: the German war would break out against Poland, not against Russia, with the West remaining passive, and he urged "a real show of [British–French] power."³³¹

As a result of his network of loyal informants, Steed was fully aware of the all-encompassing dominance of Nazi power in Germany.³³² As early as April 1935, he provided the following, astonishingly accurate analysis of Hitler as someone constantly breaking his word and "always running true to the original conception [...] of Mein Kampf," the aims of whom were alliance with England, the need to smash France, the „inveterate foe," getting hold of Austria, and finally expansion towards the East at the expense of Poland and the Soviet Union.³³³

---

326 Steed did not believe in the concept of "two Germanies" later either. "[...] gaining the mastery of Europe [...] remains the fundamental aim of German nationalism. [...] I do not like the Russians or trust them. Still less do I like the Germans whom sixty years of experience has taught me to distrust even more thoroughly. [...] I dislike making dangerous concessions to "good Germans" as ostensible representatives of a good Germany that does not exist [...]." Steed to Sir W. Hayley (Director General of the BBC from 1944 to 1952 and editor of the *Times* from 1952 to 1966), September 3, 1954. Steed Papers MS 74134.
327 Steed, "Revision of the Peace Treaties," *Times*, March 27, 1933.
328 Count Károlyi had information, e.g. on German submarines: "Merely personal view of the situ and is therefore of less interest," Steed recalled in a letter. Steed to C.A. Norton, May 14, 1935. Steed Papers MS 74130.
329 For example regarding Dr Rossmann's book *Germania Militans* on whether there was any justification for the irredentist propaganda. Steed to Otto Kyllmann, May 14, 1935. Steed Papers MS 74130.
330 Steed to Miss Lambert, December 1, 1942. Steed Papers MS 74103
331 Steed to the Frankophile British archaeologist Sir Robert Ludwig Mond, December 2, 1936. Steed Papers MS 74131.
332 Steed to Gooch, October 30, 1934, MS 74 130.
333 Steed to W.W. Hadley, April 3, 1935. Steed Papers 74130.

## 2. From Versailles to Paris (1920–1947)

Steed looked at Fascism, Nazism and Communism as three equally totalitarian states, despite the interpretation of the former two as „reactions against Russian Communism." In his interpretation, all three suppressed freedom, brought all property under the control of their "total" States, in complete opposition to the British tradition of ordered freedom and individual responsibility.[334] During the years prior to World War II, despite his vast network and expert knowledge, Steed was almost excluded from the public press and from the BBC for "seeking to tell the truth about Germany." He urged an increase in British air strength without delay to arrive at an approximate equality with Germany and the immediate formation of a common front with the other countries against war.[335] Steed was in regular contact with the War Office, and owing to the services of his informants he claimed that it seemed more important and more urgent for the Germans to cripple England than France, thus "careful training of pilots" was necessary.[336] The neglect of Steed in the public press is understandable, if only because he had a scathing opinion of the conduct of His Majesty's government, which he expressed at every opportunity. In a letter to Henri Brenier, the French economist, for example, he burst out angrily:

> Your Laval [French Prime Minister], our John Simon and, possibly, Hoare [both Foreign Secretaries], together with other fools or knaves among your and our permanent officials can think nothing better than curry favour with Hitler who has always swindled everybody who put their trust in him. [...] The only way would be that Mussolini and Fascism to be smashed asap. Nazism then will be scared [...] especially if it happened under the auspices of the League, I have been writing and predicting these things for years.[337]

It is important to stress, however, that Hitler's rise to power constituted a clear turning point only for posterity. His ideas, which he presented to the world with brutal frankness in *Mein Kampf*, were simply not read or believed (especially since, as a responsible politician, he had constantly talked about peace

---

334 Steed to F.D. Fowler, September 16, 1936. Steed Papers, MS 74 131.
335 Steed to Major Corbett-Smith, April 26, 1935. Steed Papers MS 74130.
336 Secret Report to Herbert Creedy, War Office, February 21, 1939. Steed Papers MS 74132. A few months later he was able to inform the Foreign Office about the concentration of sixty-five German divisions against Poland. Steed to Mallet, FO, July 24, 1939. Steed Papers MS 74132.
337 Steed to H. Brenier, January 9, 1936. Steed Papers, MS 74131. Letter to the *Times*, January 7, 1936. In 1936, Steed came to participate in an anti-appeasement organisation, called Focus in Defence of Freedom and Peace. Its aim was to call British public attention to the Nazi danger. Liebich 2018, 307–313.

until 1938 and there could be no doubt about the legitimacy of the revision of the anti-ethnic clauses of the Versailles Peace Treaty that he had advocated). In the mid-1930s, more than one of his British (and French) contemporaries saw the dictator as the creator of a domestically stable Germany which would be able to effectively fulfil its mission as a barrier against Bolshevism. In the period between 1934 and 1937, the alternatives of opposition to Nazi Germany and reconciliation with Hitler were almost equally present in British political thought.[338]

Fully in line with Steed in rejecting even the slightest rectification of the Versailles settlement in favour of Hungary or Germany, Seton-Watson, continued to pay increasing attention to the "vital" minority problem of—in his estimation—twenty-five million Europeans. "It is unhappily true," he acknowledged in a 1935 study, that most post-war states had failed to enforce those "solemnly guaranteed" rights to the minorities for two main reasons: the exaggerated insistence on absolute State sovereignty, which aimed to pose multi-national States as purely national, and the resentment resulting from the inequality of obligation between the greater and lesser States, which had blocked the efficacy of the League.[339] Interestingly, fully aware of the fifteen years of East-Central European anti-minority tendencies, let alone the revisionist agendas adopted by Hitler and Mussolini, Seton-Watson was still fairly optimistic, offering the sole remedy of universal recognition that "nationality" and "citizenship" were not identical but rather were comprised of race, language, tradition and innermost feeling, "something physiological and sacred, which should be as inviolate as his religion."[340]

Initially, unlike Steed, Seton-Watson took a more cautious attitude regarding British politics towards Nazi Germany. In 1936, right after the German remilitarisation of the Rheinland, for example, he congratulated His Majesty's government and Foreign Secretary Anthony Eden "on having kept their heads, combined firmness with conciliation, rejected the idea of sanctions against Germany [...] and so maintained a certain mediatory position."[341] Nevertheless, the ageing

---

338 In a 1954 BBC talk, Steed was proud to recall his anti-Nazi stance, having called Ribbentrop "an uncouth brute" and having watched with disgust "that all London flock to his parties." At the same time, he was an outsider, too, as neither Neville Chamberlain nor any other people in position made use of his knowledge of Germany: "A fellow who knows too much is apt [...] not to be impartial," he stated proudly. "The Reminiscences of Wickham Steed: Between the Wars, the Advent of the Axis," interview by Steven Watson, January 19, 1954, BBC Home Service. Steed Papers MS 74 186.
339 Seton-Watson, The Question of Minorities, *Slavonic and East European Review*, Vol. 14, No. 40 (July 1935), 68–80, 72–75.
340 Ibid., 68–80, 80.
341 Seton-Watson, The German Dilemma, *Fortnightly*, CXXXIX, May 1936, 519–530. In: Judith S. Libby, *Historiography and British Appeasement in 1936*, Butler University, 77.

historian was deeply troubled by Hitler's rise to power in one particular respect: the growth of German nationalism in Czechoslovakia. Thus he frequently met with Konrad Heinlein, the radical head of the Sudeten German Party, in 1936.

In contrast with Steed or Seton-Watson, in the 1930s Toynbee came to increasingly identify himself with the revisionist stance. Although acknowledging that the Versailles Settlement meant a "substantial change for the better," he quickly added that the top-dog of pre-war regime had been turned into the under-dog: the victors "banded together" to dictate peace terms and more territory was taken from the vanquished "than a strict application of the principle of nationality would have allowed." The end results of all this, he opined were the "particular sore spots": the inclusion of three million Germans in Czechoslovakia, and on the German–Polish or all Hungarian frontiers advantage had nearly always been granted to the allied nation, mounting up to a "formidable load of injustice." He put forward for discussion whether it was right and possible to make the frontiers between states in Europe coincide with the ethnic boundaries and whether "backward" peoples could be "helped on to their feet by Civilized Powers" without being exploited and oppressed by them at all. [342]

Interestingly, after the assassination of the primary figures behind the Franco-Yugoslav mutual assistance treaty, King Alexander of Yugoslavia and French Foreign Minister Barthou, in Marseille in October 1934, Toynbee once again came up with the idea of role reversal before and after the war. An investigation by the French police quickly established that the assassins, Croatian Ustashas, had had strong ties with Italy and had been trained and armed in Hungary. Due to the "widely discrepant accounts" provided by the Hungarian and Yugoslav governments, Toynbee opined that "it would be idle to profess to give judgment,"[343]

---

342 Toynbee, "The Treaty of Versailles and After, Territorial Arrangements," BBC, May 7, 1934. Toynbee Papers, MS 13 967/6 Broadcasts 1929-1955.
343 Toynbee, *Survey 1934*, Oxford University Press, 1935, 543. Seton-Watson explained in the *Times* that "it would be the gravest possible blunder to draw [...] the further conclusion that this crime is a repudiation of Yugoslav unity by the Croat nation." (*Times*, October 10, 1934, 19.) And, in contrast to Toynbee, in his Chatham House Address on October 30 he was quick to state that Hungary and Italy had to bear responsibility for the murder, which not only "killed revisionism," but "has made reasonable and necessary conditions infinitely more difficult." In the subsequent debate, the Albanophile Edith Durham called for autonomy within Yugoslavia, as "contented people do not plot across the border," and Macartney predicted a bleak future for Serbo-Croatian relations. King Alexander's Assassination. Its Backgrounds and Effects. *IA*, January/February 1935, 36, 43 and 45-46.
Unlike Seton-Watson, the LNU Pamphlet titled *Refugees and the League*, which was drawn up based on Macartney's book *Refugees* came to a very different conclusion regarding the Marseilles murder: "Much as one deplores such crimes, one can understand them when one realises the physical conditions and the moral despair which make of the refugees tools in the hands of political

calling attention to the parallel between the assassination of King Alexander at Marseilles and the Yugoslav charges about Hungarian responsibility in line with the Austro-Hungarian arrangement of the Serbian government's responsibility in assassination of Franz Ferdinand some two decades before: "The very closeness of this parallel brings out completeness with which in South-Eastern Europe the pre-war roles had been reversed by the Peace Settlement."[344] A few months later Toynbee voiced his conviction that European Peace could only be secured by Franco-German reconciliation, which should be a part of a general reconciliation of all the countries in Europe naming the plebiscite as the "first and decisive step."[345]

Despite opting for revision, Toynbee grew to be dissatisfied with British policy, too, not only in dealing with Japanese aggression in Manchuria, as we have seen, but also with the Italian occupation of Abyssinia. In September 1935, he wrote to his colleague Ivison Macadam: "[...] if we don't take the risk of a lesser war [...] I feel perfectly certain that we shall soon be fighting for our lives—just to save our skins."[346] Due to "lack of courage and sincerity"[347] the government abandoned collective security, he explained in the Introduction of the 1935 *Survey*, which dealt with the Italo-Ethiopian war. For instance, Toynbee believed Mussolini's project would have failed had the British government closed the Suez Canal. The voice adopted was so critical that the author of the *Survey* needed to insert a disclaimer to clarify that it was not Chatham House's point of view. The incident led to an apparent cooling between Toynbee and the Foreign Office.[348] The Institute never came close to advocating a definite alternative policy for His Majesty's government before or after the 1935 *Survey*. After his fervent criticism of British policy toward Italy and the Ethiopian war, the surveys returned to meticulously detailing events without much, if any, overt criticism of acts of policy.[349]

As Toynbee had long believed that the Versailles Treaty unfairly punished Germany, and he could never completely abandon the idea that peace might yet

---

intrigue and crime. The time has come for a great international effort to end a state of things which is a menace to law and order, and a threat to world peace." Macartney et al., *Refugees and the League*, London, 1935, 60. Macartney LNU Miscellaneous Pamphlets Vol. 8, British Library 3685-3805.

344 He also added that the revenge the Yugoslav government took on the Hungarian minority, that they deported some three thousand Hungarians from their soil, was "cruel and barbarous," sheer "wanton provocation." Toynbee, *Survey* 1934, Oxford University Press, 1935, 574.

345 Toynbee, "The Situation Abroad," BBC Talks, January 22, 1935. Toynbee Papers BL Oxford MS13 967/6 Broadcasts 1929-1955.

346 Toynbee to Ivison Macadam, September 15, 1935. RIIA Archives, 4/TOYN/1. Also McNeill 1989, 169-170.

347 Toynbee, *Survey of International Affairs*, 1935, Vol. II, London, 1936, viii.

348 Arnold Toynbee, "Was Britain's abdication folly?" The Round Table, 1970. 60:238, 219-228, 227.

349 Cornelia Navari, Chatham House and the Broad Church View, In: Bosco-Navari 1994, 359.

be kept, he made an attempt to suggest some kind of settlement between the Third Reich and the victors in the First World War. Therefore, in February 1936, after accepting Ribbentrop's friend Fritz Berber's invitation, he travelled to Germany to deliver a speech titled "Peaceful Change." There were numerous foreign diplomats present, including the Italian ambassador, a representative of the ambassadors of Hungary and Czechoslovakia, five Reich ministers, and a crowded house at the Academy of Law. Toynbee began his talk explaining that international relations had largely been governed by force and violence, and not by law, which would be optimal. "Repressive" law in Toynbee's interpretation prevents or halts any violent change of the status quo, a phenomenon he identified with "collective security," whereas "constructive law" provides for peaceful changes in the status quo. It would be essential, he argued, that both these sides should be put into operation. The dissatisfied Great Powers, Germany, Italy and Japan, he continued, had already voiced their material and psychological or spiritual demands, which if addressed by peaceful means, the demands of smaller dissatisfied countries, e.g., Hungary and Bulgaria, would find satisfaction, too.[350] "If we fail to achieve [the] peaceful change" he envisioned, which had been "extremely rare," "another war between the Great Powers [...] will arise [...] that will destroy our civilization." Among the material demands, Toynbee enumerated the liberation of certain "terre irredente": Austria, Sudetenland, Südtirol, Memelland, Eupen and Malmedy, "all German in language and political feeling," as well as the "German need for markets and raw materials" (which in his opinion could be met in the non-self-governing, colonial areas of tropical Africa and Indonesia[351]). Regarding the psychological demands, Toynbee focused on "the question

---

350 Interestingly, Toynbee's 1936 "Peaceful Change" talk greatly overlaps with his paper from a few months earlier, written in December 1935, titled "Peaceful change or war?" which was also discussing the possibility of the secession of certain territories in order to avert "a catastrophic conflict between the 'haves' and the 'have-nots'" and added: "The present German feeling about the Polish Corridor, and Magyar feeling about Slovakia, is not less bitter than the pre-war feeling in France about Alsace-Lorraine, though the French were mourning the forcible separation of a French-feeling population from the French body politic, whereas the Germans and Magyars are resenting the loss of their dominion over alien populations in whose eyes this alien dominion is a hateful tyranny from which they have been providentially liberated." The paper ends with the following question: "Which course is really the less practicable? To embark on some rather adventurous pioneer work in the direction of partially internationalising the administration of the French, Dutch, British, Belgian and Portuguese non-self-governing colonies? Or to let ourselves drift into another world war between the sated and the hungry Powers?" Toynbee, Peaceful Change or War? The Next Stage in the International Crisis, *International Affairs* (Royal Institute of International Affairs 1931–1939), Vol. 15, No. 1, January—February 1936, 26–56, 37 and 48.

351 In 1938 Toynbee advised the integral restoration of German colonies in Africa, coupled with an arrangement on cooperation, and on common standards for all European administrations in Africa, as well as restoration to Germany of her possessions in the Pacific taken from her by Australia, New Zealand and Great-Britain. He suggested giving Germany the whole of New Guinea

of honour," a rather subjective feeling, and "the restoration of German sovereignty over Tanganyka or Cameroons [...] I think most English people would understand it and would also sympathise with it to a large extent" provided that these natives suffer no detriment from this transfer of sovereignty, Toynbee claimed. Further on he advised to draw a joint British–German, French–Belgian common statute of rights for all native African populations, and invited Germany to join "the thorough investigation of the whole question of peaceful change." The investigation would be under the auspices of an international association of scientific institutes for the objective study of international relations, where the RIIA also belonged.[352]

While in Berlin, Toynbee was invited to a meeting by the "headman" himself. During their two-hour conversation, the anti-Bolshevik Hitler, who had cast himself in the role of Europe's defender and Britain's true ally, made a great impression on the historian: he put forward his aim to build up the Reich on an exclusively national basis, disclaiming any ambition to conquer Europe. "In spite of *Mein Kampf*," Toynbee confessed, "[...] I have a very strong conviction that [...] Hitler was quite sincere in what he said [...] I believe that any response from the English side to his overtures for our friendship would produce an enormous counter-response to us."[353]

Toynbee's Berlin visit aroused unexpected interest and to an extent, alarm outside Germany: Chatham House Secretary Ivison S Macadam and a few days later the director himself sent a text of clarification to the editor of the *Times* that he was not speaking as a representative of the RIIA, but expressed "his own personal view."[354] Soon Toynbee sent another letter, too; this time to His Majesty government including the report of his conversation with the Führer. The very day the material landed on Foreign Secretary Anthony Eden's desk, Hitler began remilitarizing the Rhineland. According to Toynbee, the British were willing to tolerate the events in the Rhineland because of "sympathy with German grievances against the peace settlement and with the German struggle to regain equality of status."[355]

---

and part or all of Borneo. Toynbee to Noel Buxton, October 15, 1938. https://archivalcollections.library.mcgill.ca/index.php/arnold-toynbee. Accessed May 15, 2023.
352 Toynbee, "Peaceful Change," A speech delivered to the Academy of German Law, Berlin, February 28, 1936. RIIA Archives, 4/TOYN/2
353 Toynbee's Meeting/Interview with Hitler, February 21, 1936 [Draft written: March 8, 1936]. Toynbee Papers BL Oxford MS 13967/76/2 Germany Correspondence and papers 1933-50.
354 "'Unsatisfied Nations,' Professor Toynbee on Peaceful Revision," *Times*, February 29, 1936, 11; Ivison S. Macadam, "To the Editor of the *Times*," February 29, 1936. Toynbee's clarification appeared in the *Times* on March 1, 1936.
355 Toynbee, *Survey of International Affairs*, 1936, London: Oxford University Press, 1938, 276-277.

## 2. From Versailles to Paris (1920–1947)

According to his biographer, Toynbee was used by Hitler to "confuse" the British government prior to the remilitarisation of the Rhineland,[356] and the Führer also needed Anglo-German understanding to fulfil his long term desire, the invasion against the Soviet Union. However, as Toynbee was still viewed as an outsider, his mediation was not accorded much importance inside the Foreign Office. Much more in line with Steed and Seton-Watson, the British minister to Germany, Sir Eric Phipps, explained to Foreign Secretary Eden that "no amount of economic concessions will satisfy the German maw. Hitler's desiderate [...] are political, in the first line, and it would be pure self-deception to think that markets or colonies alone can put off the evil of the day."[357] Thus, it became increasingly obvious that the Führer was an expert liar making unreliable statements and demands, among others for a free hand in Central and Eastern Europe, which the Foreign Office was understandably reluctant to meet.[358]

On March 7, 1936, the Hitler marched into the Rhineland, Toynbee was among the prominent guests at a famous and much-quoted weekend at Blickling, Lord Lothian's home. Of the people present, several belonged to the influential upper-class, including the "Cliveden Set":[359] the Astors, former ambassadors and ministers, e.g., Deputy Secretary Tom Jones. After listening to the news on the wireless, the guests, followed Jones's suggestion to resolve themselves into a "Shadow Cabinet." They then drew up a set of eight conclusions, which they phoned into the prime minister. Generally, the tone of these recommendations was conciliatory, and the first proposed welcoming Hitler's declaration, claiming that "Versailles is now a corpse and should be buried."[360]

Toynbee's tour in Germany caused a serious reaction in the Successor States of the Habsburg Monarchy, especially in Hungary, which had been keenly watching the statements on revision of British politicians and public figures. The president of *Society of Hungarian Quarterly*,[361] former prime minister István Bethlen, enquired of Foreign Secretary Kálmán Kánya whether he considered Toynbee's invitation to Budapest desirable. He added that through Toynbee's wife empha-

---

356 McNeill 1989, 171–172.
357 Sir E. Phipps to Eden, February 19, 1936, PRO FO 371/19886/C1180/4/18.
358 A.J. Crozier, *Appeasement and Germany's Last Bid for Colonies*, Basingstoke, 1988, 99–206.
359 Cliveden was the Astors' country residence to which they in fact invited a wide range of guests: "The myth of Cliveden being a nest of appeasers, let alone pro-Nazis, is exploded." Andrew Roberts, *The Holy Fox: Biography of Lord Halifax*, London, Weidenfeld & Nicolson, 1991, 52.
360 Tom Jones, *A Diary with Letters*, 179.
361 Its Hungarian equivalent was *Magyar Szemle Társaság*, with *Magyar Szemle*, a nationalist quality review, in its center.

sis should be laid on favouring her father, Professor Gilbert Murray of Oxford University as well as president of the *League of Nations Union Society*, "who has always shown a certain reserve towards Hungarian affairs."[362] Murray had in fact been convinced that no revision should be made until a system of collective security was established. The Ministry of Foreign Affairs regarded the cause of English rapprochement a priority, and *The Society of the Hungarian Quarterly* (SHQ) was ready to provide the framework for Toynbee's visit and made every effort to request articles from reputable British authors.

By the second half of 1930s Toynbee was convinced that Central Europe in general, and Austria in particular, were even more in the centre of attention than usual, therefore, he embarked on a Central-European tour, visiting Austria, Hungary and Czechoslovakia. In Hungary, Toynbee's aim was to meet ministers and political party leaders, and he also delivered a lecture for *The Hungarian Quarterly* on the question of treaty revision.[363] He had also received introductions to Baron Apor and Count Teleki from the Hungarian Legation,[364] and *The Hungarian Quarterly* was responsible for the invitation, formally published under the auspices of the *Society of the Hungarian Quarterly*, just like *La Nouvelle Revue de Hongrie*. Count István Bethlen was elected president of the *Society*, with Prince György Festetich and Professor Gyula Kornis as co-presidents. The vice-presidents were Tibor Eckhardt and György Ottlik, and the secretary general was József Balogh, with whom Toynbee had already had a sporadic exchange of letters. On May 13, the Count and Countess Bethlen hosted a grand reception in Mr. and Mrs. Toynbee's honour at the Ministry of the Interior, which Toynbee considered "rather important."[365] During the next few days the couple was invited to a small dinner party with H.E. Kornis, rector of Budapest University, they visited the Opera and then travelled through Székesfehérvár and the Lake Balaton region to Iregszemcse, to Baron Móric Kornfeld's chateau, where they stayed until May 18. József Balogh, the secretary general of *SHQ*, organized the entire program with considerable care and

---

362 István Bethlen to Foreign Secretary Kálmán Kánya. [undated, 1936 summer?] OSZK KT 1/3115 (28193 doc).
363 Toynbee to the Hungarian Legation (Massirevich Szilárd) April 5, 1937. Toynbee Papers BL Oxford MS 13967/92 Journeys-Correspondence 1928-48.
364 Toynbee to the Minister at Hungarian Legation, April 8, 1937. Toynbee Papers BL Oxford MS 13967/92 Journeys-Correspondence 1928-48.
365 Toynbee to Frau Jakoby (vice-president of Kulturbund, Vienna), [undated, around May 1937]. Toynbee Papers. BL Oxford MS 13967/92 Journeys-Correspondence 1928-48. On the account of the journey see Thomas L. Sakmyster, *Hungary, the Great Powers and the Danubian Crisis*, University of Georgia Press, 1980, 201.

expertise. A month later, he already addressed the British historian as one of the "friends of *The Hungarian Quarterly*."[366]

From Budapest Toynbee travelled to the Czechoslovak capital and met President Masaryk. Even more significant than this was his visit to the Sudeten-German area, "where Britons were dined and wined; trout fishing expeditions to the estates of Bohemian nobles lent an air of respectability to the SdP [the Sudeten German Party], while trips through the depressed Sudeten German industrial areas generated the desired degree of sympathy." The great inspiration behind all these was Austrian nobleman and politician Karl Khuen, who acted as a mediator between Konrad Heinlein and notable representatives of British diplomacy.[367]

On July 10, 1937, Toynbee published a summary of his findings in *The Economist*. In contrast to the Czechs', Steed's or Seton-Watson's continually voiced claim that Czechoslovakia, the only democratic nation in the area, could facilitate the reconciliation of the German minority, Toynbee sneeringly remarked:

> The truth is that even the most genuine and old established democratic way of life is exceedingly difficult to apply when you are dealing with a minority that does not want to live under your rule [...] we ourselves were never able to apply our own brand of British democracy to our attempt to govern the Irish [...]. In their post-war intercourse with the Western peoples whom they so pathetically admire, the British infection which the Czechs have caught is not 'effortless superiority', but 'British hypocrisy', and they have taken it strong!

According to Toynbee, Czechoslovak minority policy was far from democratic but aimed at assimilating the Germans, and British mediation for a peaceful solution was indispensable in order to avoid Germany attempts "to take the law into her hand."[368]

Toynbee's article was equally criticized by both the Czechs and the Sudeten Germans, which he believed to give some credit to its impartiality. Unlike his report on meeting Hitler, his ideas on the Sudeten-German situation did create

---

366 Balogh to Toynbee, June 10, 1938. OSZK K, 1/3115. Later on, Toynbee grew somewhat collegial with the tireless *Hungarian Quarterly* editor, József Balogh, who would refer to Macartney as "our friend." József Balogh to Toynbee, April 27, 1940. OSZK KT 1/3115, doc 28 221.
367 Eagle Glassheim, *Noble Nationalist: The Transformation of The Bohemian Aristocracy*, Cambridge, Massachusetts, Harvard University Press, 2005, 174.
368 *Economist*, July 10, 1937. The Hungarian *Pesti Hírlap* also offered a summary of the article written by "the excellent teacher of English and Director of the Royal Institute of International Affairs." (July 27, 1937.)

sympathy in the Foreign Office. It was noted that "it is useful, in fact to have someone as authoritative as Professor Toynbee to give the sort of advice that we always wanted to give."[369]

By addressing the problem of growing German demands and aggression, Toynbee thus became an adherent of peaceful revision by the mid-1930s: in his Chatham House talks, articles or BBC radio messages, he advocated frontier rectifications in Central and Eastern Europe together with the redistribution of African colonies, the core of which was the demand of equality of status and to a lesser extent the avoidance of war. Throughout this period, he would flatly refuse the "pacifist" label.[370] After World War II Toynbee was duly reproached for having become an easy target for Hitler, however, he had viewed the dictator as well as his system with a remarkable clarity of insight: in his 1933 *Survey* he argued, for example, that the two major pillars of Western civilization, humanism and Christianity had been replaced by "a worship of unregenerate Human Nature" and described Nazism as "a pagan deification and worship of parochial human communities."[371]

It was no surprise that unlike the pragmatic Toynbee, diehard anti-appeaser Steed would by far avoid the Führer, and after 1933 he gave Germany, too, a wide berth. Thus, when Lord Rothermere's once-mistress Princess Stephanie Hohenlohe-Waldenburg approached him, among several prominent Britons, to meet the German dictator, Steed responded that he preferred "not to associate with murderers." When the appalled Princess demurred at the word "murderer," Steed stated plainly that he would withdraw it upon proof that people had not been killed upon Adolf Hitler's orders, while providing a long list of those who had perished. "You are terrible," replied the princess. "No, I am truthful, and you are not accustomed to truth," Steed retorted.[372]

Later, Steed explained not only his attitude to Hitler but to any dictator, in a letter to the philanthropist-politician Noel Buxton, one of the principal promoters of negotiated peace with Germany:

> You and several other British peers were either misled or thoroughly mistaken when [...] you went to pay your respects or to confer with a murderer or a criminal [...] it is one thing for an ambassador or other diplomatic of-

---

369 C. Bracewell's minute, August 9, 1937, PRO FO 371/21129/R 4215/188/12.
370 Toynbee, "To the Editor of the *Times*," May 1, 1936.
371 Toynbee, *Survey of International Affairs 1933*, 111. Qtd. in: Granville Hicks, Arnold J. Toynbee: The Boldest Historian, *Harper's Magazine*, February 1947. Toynbee Papers BL Oxford MS 13 967/39.
372 Steed 1940, 108.

ficial [....] to treat Hitler formally as though he were a decent human being; but it is quite another thing for men of independent public position to countenance, directly or indirectly, a man who has ordered the torture and the murder of hundreds of decent Germans, especially pacifists, in his concentration camps [...]. I met Mussolini in April 1918 [...] and got the distinct impression that he was a criminal. Consequently, I have never set foot in Italy since he came into power nor have I ever given my hand to a Fascist."373

But this was not really the case for Toynbee, who did not fall into the habit of easy acceptance of German assurances, as for example, was Lord Lothian, and was not mesmerized by the dictator either, as was Lord Rothermere. Instead, Toynbee's attitude to Nazi Germany between 1933 and March 1939 had more to do with his theory of civilizations as the basic units of history, as against the by the mid-1930s "failed" concept of nation-states. He was open to the idea of a united Germany playing the role of Ancient Rome, that is, the emergence of an empire over national self-determination in much-troubled Middle-Europe,374 while remaining highly critical of contemporaries such as Steed who advocated that "all Nazi and Nationalist Germans are the devil [...] and *ex hypothesi*, the devil can't have a case."375

## 2.13. Macartney' *Hungary and Her Successors* (1937)

> "What we need is not a visit from revisionists, but from people who objectively present our real situation to the European public."376

During the 1930s, Chatham House commissioned a number of books on the problem of minorities and the consequences and operation of the peace settlement.377 Before publication, the Chatham House experts would often spend

---

373 Steed to Noel Buxton, April 18, 1941, McGill Library Archival Collections Catalogue, https://archivalcollections.library.mcgill.ca/index.php/w-Steed.
374 Toynbee, *A Study of History, Vol. III*, Oxford, 1934, 212. It was very much in line with what the fellow-historian E H. Carr had in mind in connection with the Soviet Union. E.H. Carr, *The Future of Nations, Independence or Interdependence*, London, 1941, 100.
375 Toynbee to Miss Cleeve, October 26, 1937. RIIA Archives 4/TOYN/2
376 Macartney látogatása Romániában [Macartney's visit to Romania], *Magyar Kisebbség [Hungarian Minority]*, 1934, No. 20, 10.
377 Apart from Macartney's books, the RIIA funded the majority of post-First World War historical studies. For instance, I.F.D. Morrow's *Peace Settlement and the German-Polish Borderlands* (London,

## 2.13. Macartney' Hungary and Her Successors (1937)

"many laborious hours" on proofreading the manuscripts and reducing one-sided interpretation if necessary, as for example in Elizabeth Wiskemann's *Czechs and Germans*, which portrayed the situation and grievances of the Sudeten Germans originally through a distinctly anti-German and sometimes anti-Slovak lens.[378] Thus, when the Cambridge-educated historian and international relations theorist Edward Hallett Carr took up the issue of Chatham House publications and accused them of bias, Toynbee retorted:

> [...] bias is a tricky thing and the greatest difficulty in measuring it is the problem of relativity [...] we have always found ourselves accused to almost exactly the same extent from both sides [...] as long as we are criticised from both sides at once we have the feeling that we are probably somewhere not very far distant from that middle position which an institution like this ought of course to try to attain.[379]

The origin of Macartney's *Hungary and Her Successors*[380] goes back to January 1934 when, while lunching with the younger scholar, Toynbee advised him to undertake a piece of research under the Rockefeller Fund on the working of the peace treaties in the areas taken from Hungary and transferred to the three Little Entente states after war.[381] However, as Macartney had been employed by the League of Nations Union (LNU) Intelligence Section, and in order to obtain a certain amount of leave of absence from his duties, part of the fund was offered to the LNU to provide necessary temporary substitutes on their staff. Despite the extensive travel, Toynbee assured LNU Secretary Maxwell Garnett that there was no need to terminate Macartney's work at LNU. On the contrary, "it would increase his value as a member of your Intelligence Section by

---

1936); R.W. Seton-Watson's *History of the Roumanians* (London, 1934) and his *Treaty Revision and the Hungarian Frontiers* (London, 1934). Toynbee's own *Study of History* came out in two three-volume series in 1934 and 1939, under RIIA auspices, too. RIIA published its own books as well, such as *The Problem of International Investment* (London, 1937) and *Central and South-Eastern Europe. Syllabus for A Study Group* (London, 1938).

378 Toynbee explicitly requested that the last two chapters be rewritten. Toynbee to Ashton-Gwatkin, April 4, 1938. PRO FO 371/22685/4659/41. Qtd. in Crozier, in Bosco-Navari 1994, 249. See also Toynbee to E.H. Carr, November 21, 1938. RIIA Archives 4/TOYN/6D

379 Toynbee to E.H. Carr, November 21, 1938. RIIA Archives 4/TOYN/6D

380 Before the book was published, in the spring of 1937, Macartney's "Memorandum on the Danube Basin - its Problem of Peaceful Change," written for a conference, foreshadowed the conclusion of *Hungary and Her Successors*: "It would be in the interest of peace to revise all cases in which the ethnographical principle was sacrificed against the wishes of peoples concerned to either strategic or historical principles." Macartney Papers, MSS. Eng. c. 3282, Doc 1.

381 Toynbee to C.A. Macartney, January 2, 1934. RIIA Archives 4/TOYN/6H

increasing his already considerable acquaintance with a field which is of capital importance in his work."³⁸²

The first eight chapters of the book are an analysis of Hungarian nationality policy, the central thesis of which is that the 1868 Lex Eötvös, "one of the best of the best nationality laws that have ever been drafted," could have solved the problem, but the Hungarians never applied it. The real nationality policy, Macartney argued, had been therefore not the law but the measures taken between 1868 and 1918, on which he advised his readers to consult the relevant works of Seton-Watson, "much better acquainted with the subject" than he himself."

In the main part of the book, Macartney examined the internal politics of the five states that were part of the territory of historic Hungary in 1920, with special attention to the situation of the Hungarian minority living there. In the case of Austria and Czechoslovakia, he praised their relatively liberal nationality policies, but in the case of the latter state he noted that the Language Law which allowed national minorities representing 20 percent of the population to do business in their mother tongue was "less good that it looks": it did not apply to railway or postal inscriptions, and Hungarian-speaking Jews or Gypsies were registered separately, applying the law on linguistic minorities to ethnic minorities. The proportion of Hungarians or Germans, Macartney argued, was further reduced by the reorganisation of administrative, judicial, etc., districts and the annexation of Slovak villages to Košice (Kassa) and to the capital in order to bring the percentage of minorities below the statutory 20 percent. Bratislava (Pressburg, Pozsony) could achieve the desired result only after 1930! According to Macartney, even more depressing was the fact that according to the Czechoslovak census of 1930, there were about 200,000 stateless persons in Slovakia and Subcarpathia alone, which had hitherto caused "indescribable suffering."³⁸³

Turning to the field of minority education, the author painted a more favourable picture than before, as he found basic education "most satisfactory" for all nationalities. The Czechoslovak government, he stressed, was doing its utmost to ensure that all pupils received education in their mother tongue, with the result that the quality of German and Ruthenian education had improved compared with the pre-war level, and the dissatisfaction of the Hungarians was

---

382 "I have personally no doubt [...] he will produce an important and distinguished piece of work." Toynbee to Maxwell Garnett, February 1, 1934. RIIA Archives 4/TOYN/6H. He repeated his positive expectations in another letter to Garnett dated February 13. Toynbee also suggested that Macartney receive an honorarium "in consideration of the greater strain of work" and for the work during part of his vacations, too. Toynbee to Garnett, February 6, 1934. RIIA Archives 4/TOYN/6H
383 Macartney, *Hungary and Her Successors: The Treaty of Trianon and Its Consequences*, Oxford University Press, 1937, 154–164, 157 and 164.

justified, mainly because of the lack of a university faculty of their own. Regarding the 1930 Czechoslovak census figures, the accuracy of which Hungarians questioned, according to which the population of the Hungarian minority had fallen by nearly 10 percent in nine years to 572,000, Macartney added that the census probably underestimated the number of Hungarian inhabitants, but added that they "assuredly reflect also the continued progress of that natural assimilation of the minority to the majority which goes on in every country," which is a general phenomenon.[384]

The chapter on Romania starts with a historical overview where Macartney was once again balancing between the rival historiographical concepts. Concerning the Daco-Romanian continuity theory and the Hungarian position, he stated:

> We do not know for certain that Romanians were in Transylvania in the year 1000 AD; and we do not know that they were not. [...] But when Transylvania was assigned to Romania in 1919, this was not because any 1,000-year-old historic right was admitted as valid to-day, and if it is ever handed back, I hope it will not be because the statesmen have decided that the Magyar controversialists were right after all.

Together with *prior tempore, potior iure* (historical primacy, a key argument shared by both neighbours), Macartney also disregarded some Romanian historians' assessment of pre-1918 Transylvanian Romanians as "a race of serfs," devoid of any status as a nation. The author instead argued that any ennobled individuals, such as János Hunyadi, of originally Romanian origins had been able to join the unitary Hungarian nation, whereas the remainder had been in the same position as Magyar serfs.[385] He regarded as a blunder not only the Romanian-fostered victimhood culture but also the Hungarian scepticism of the representativeness of the Alba Iulia (Gyulafehérvár) assembly on December 1, 1918, as in his opinion it had fairly reflected the opinion of the Romanian majority in Transylvania, and he remarked that in the case of a referendum, almost 60 percent of the population would have voted for secession.[386]

The chapter on Romania after the First World War was a depressing contrast to the Czechoslovak state's essentially liberal nationality policy. Macartney's analysis made it clear that the Hungarian minority was the "irreconcilable

---

384 Ibid., 165–189.
385 Ibid., 256–257.
386 Ibid., 276–277.

enemy" of the unified Romanian nation-state: the introduction of re-Romanianization (a theory which considered the Hungarians of Transylvania to be Magyarised Romanians and their re-Romanianisation to be legitimate and desirable) he found less harmful than the theory identifying the Szeklers as "the lost sheep from the Romanian fold." The latter was put forward by no less an authority than Nicolae Iorga and thus became an article of faith, which Macartney considered all the more "unfortunate."[387]

Macartney acknowledged that Transylvanian Saxons had been more indulgently treated, however, they had been equally deprived of their local self-government: by 1934, for the first time in their 800-year history, not a single mayor remained, not even in Sibiu (Hermannstadt, Nagyszeben) which had been ruled by them since its foundation.[388] Thus, they joined the disillusioned Hungarians who continuously complained about the intimidation of Hungarian candidates in elections, the curtailment of education in the mother tongue (closing schools, hiring teachers with Romanian mother tongue instead of Hungarian, etc.), the expropriation of Hungarian landowners' land under more stringent conditions than the Regat, and the 1934 law on entrepreneurs, which stipulated that at least 80 percent of the staff of a company must be of Romanian nationality. Given these measures, it was no surprise that the Hungarian minority in Transylvania "present a common front against the Roumanians,"[389] for whom Macartney's conclusion could not be flattering:

> Standards all around have been lowered. The administration and even the justice seem less honest, less hard-working, less efficient. The trains are less punctual, the police regulations more tiresome, the officials more brutal and exorbitant, the streets dirtier, the very bugs in the beds bite more confidently, as though feeling that under the new order people do not mind them so much. Things go to ruin and are not repaired, either because the authorities are accustomed to second-rate, shoddy, patched materials or because someone has pocketed the money voted for repairing the damage. [...] Hitherto, [...] the Roumanians have constructed little in Transylvania. They have simply taken over what the minorities had accumulated in past centuries, and are living on it [...]. All that is beautiful and almost all that is valuable seems to date from long time ago.

---

387 Ibid., 286.
388 Ibid., 293.
389 Ibid., 326.

## 2.13. Macartney' Hungary and Her Successors (1937)

In addition to his scathing assessment of the state of affairs in Romania, Macartney was not silent about the achievements of the period since 1920. The undoubted fact, he stressed, was that Trianon had put an end to the "neither tolerable nor tenable" pre-war situation of the Romanians and had given them the opportunity to develop more self-consciously, one of the stages of which was the establishment of land reform. It is however unfortunate, he continued, that, although they have been joined by a significant minority, the Romanians are "are farther than ever from admitting any of the other nationalities to a partnership within the State, so that their regime continues, more than ever, to be the domination of slightly more than a half the population over slightly less than a half."[390]

Macartney's book revealed that Yugoslav minority policy succeeded in outperforming that of Romania. Belgrade made no attempt to maintain even a semblance of democratic institutions, local elections were not held until 1927, and in 1929 the representative system was replaced by a period of royal dictatorship. "In no other part of Europe with which I have had any personal acquaintance since the War has the atmosphere of terrorization been so unrelieved,"[391] lamented Macartney. Hungarians, who lived predominantly in Voivodina, were particularly adversely affected by the disproportionately high taxes imposed on the province, the expropriation of land they owned with minimal compensation, and the allocation of land to settlers who had earned merit in the war.

The analysis of the minority policy of the Successor States concluded with Trianon Hungary, the only mono-ethnic state in the region besides Austria, where more than 90 percent of the nation was of the same ethnicity. Since after Trianon a large part of the Hungarian political elite and of public opinion came to the conclusion that the modest concessions offered before the war had not only been futile but also harmful, Macartney grew increasingly pessimistic about the minority policy of the Horthy era. He found it particularly damaging that the more than half a million Germans in Hungary had no university, and that the Magyarisation of names was propagated with unchanged fervour. In terms of cultural opportunities for nationalities, he saw the situation as even worse than in Yugoslavia, and found the Hungarian revisionist agitation, which ran parallel to the often-repressive minority policy, particularly incomprehensible, since the desire for frontier readjustments abroad should logically lead to liberal treatment of minorities at home. Macartney also argued that forcing Magyarizaion would do "immeasurable harm" to the country, and it was precisely

---

390 Ibid., 349-351.
391 Ibid., 396.

because of the current practice and the attitude of the public that the promises of autonomy in the event of a revision, made by some responsible politicians such as Bethlen, could not be taken seriously.[392]

Revisiting the views expressed in his *Hungary* in 1934, in the closing chapter of his work, Macartney reiterated that on the one hand, the Treaty of Trianon should be considered an imposed and not a negotiated peace, that is a Diktat, and on the other hand, Hungary, branded with the mark of war-guilt, doubly aggravated by the imputations of Bolshevism and reaction; whereas of her four neighbours and principal prospective beneficiaries, three were "safely ensconced on the side of both victory and moral superiority."

"The truth was that national feeling was not nearly so advanced among the nationalities of Hungary as the Peace Conference was made to believe,"[393] argued Macartney, adding that if Hungary had not been on the losing side in 1918, it would not have been easy to dismiss its historical claims and annex Slovakia, Ruthenia or the Voivodina. Nor would it have become the prevailing idea, as advocated by Seton-Watson and supported by the vast majority of Versailles diplomats, that the new states that replaced the Monarchy would automatically be more democratic and liberal in their nationality policies than were their predecessors. With the right to self-determination equally applied, i.e., with the referendum requested by the Hungarian delegation, Macartney concluded in 1919, Hungary would certainly have lost Transylvania and Croatia-Slavonia, but once autonomy had been guaranteed, the Slovak and Ruthenian regions, and most probably Vojvodina, too, would have decided in favour of Budapest.[394]

Contrary to the arguments often put forward by the leading politicians of the Successor States and Marxist historiography regarding frontier readjustment, Macartney argued that it was approved not only by the landed aristocracy but also by the whole of Hungarian society (just as the majority populations of the successor states were convinced of the legitimacy and rightness of the 1919 territorial acquisitions). However, the author did not spare the main thesis of Hungarian revisionist propaganda either: he claimed nothing less than that in 1937 not only Serbs and Romanians, but also Slovaks and Burgenland Germans would not want to return to Hungary, nor would nearly 30 percent of the Hungarian minority in Czechoslovakia.[395] Therefore, flatly refuting the dream of a "thirty

---

[392] Ibid., 446-458.
[393] He also asserted that "denial of national culture is only oppressive when it is felt to be oppressive... [Magyarization] was in no way resented by the great majority of the Slovaks.." Ibid., 70.
[394] Ibid., 486.
[395] Ibid., 183.

million Magyar Kingdom," i.e., integral revision, he advocated minor border changes in accordance with the ethnic principle and Section 19 of the League of Nations Statute, which he expounded on in detail at the end of each chapter.[396]

In opposition to Beneš's strategic arguments on the Hungarian-Slovak border, Macartney wanted to return to Hungary the "overwhelmingly Magyar" Grosse Schütt and the strip of territory between Komárno-Révkomárom and the mouth of the River Ipel (Ipoly) on the basis of the ethnic principle, as he saw no particular reason "why Czechoslovakia should claim to be a Danubian power." Another interesting feature of the draft was that, while acknowledging Czech efforts towards the political consolidation of Subcarpathia, surpassing all previous British proposals, Macartney suggested the return of the whole of Subcarpathia to Hungary, with autonomy. Here mostly economic considerations dominated, as well as the fact that he considered a Russian or Ukrainian presence within the Carpathians to be unacceptable.[397]

"Transylvania hangs together," claimed Macartney, and regarding the idea of "independent Transylvania" put forward by among others Count Bethlen during his visit to London in 1933, Macartney opined that although historically justifiable, geographically tenable and ethnographically ideal, it was hardly feasible due little to no attraction among the Romanian majority.[398] Therefore, in the east he advised frontier rectification by restoring the whole of Partium together with the predominantly Subcarpathian Maramureș (Máramaros) and the region in the Bácska lying north of Zombor. Based on his two years of extensive travel in the Successor States together with decades of experience as LNU-expert Macartney concluded:

---

[396] Ibid., 489.
[397] Ibid., 198.
A year before his book appeared, based on his findings in the region, Macartney delivered a speech in Chatham House titled "Ruthenia: A Problem of the Future." After describing the pre-war situation of the province as poor, uneducated, with little to no national consciousness, he turned to Subcarpathia under Czechoslovak rule, which "in fact has never received any of the versions of her autonomy," but rather the frequent label as "Czechoslovakia's Siberia"; though it possessed a governor, who was lodged, "appropriately enough" in a local museum. (9.) However, he was convinced that although Prague had obtained the territory "by untruths," it treated its people "probably better" "than they would be by any nation under whom they could expect to be." (13.) According to the speaker, the future of the region was nevertheless completely in doubt: remaining in Czechoslovakia would strengthen the Prague-Moscow axis, while coming under the jurisdiction of Budapest would serve Polish-Hungarian relations. Thus, both economically and ideally the best solution would be *status quo ante* with autonomy, as it is elaborated in the 1937 book, though Macartney added that it was difficult to see how that could be made to work, "the mentality of Hungary being what it was." (16 and discussion 11.) Macartney, "Ruthenia: A Problem of the Future," Address on February 27, 1936, in RIIA. RIIA Archives, 8/399.
[398] Ibid., 352–353.

## 2. From Versailles to Paris (1920-1947)

Hungary's claim to the preponderantly Magyar areas contiguous to her frontiers is even stronger today than it was in 1919, in one important respect. She can no longer fairly be regarded as the sole villain in the nationality drama. [...] Given the form of the national state, which is of its very essence so deeply inimical to national minorities, [...] peace and justice are probably best served by reducing the number at least of such frontier minorities as far as possible.[399]

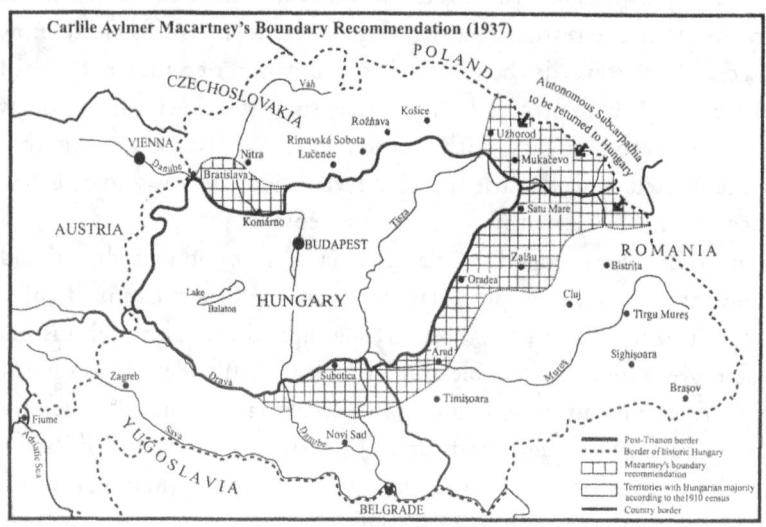

Macartney's map

Compared to the torrent of sympathy that followed Viscount Rothermere's superficial and imprecise 1927 article calling for ethnic revision along the Hungarian frontiers, Macartney's book, written with scholarly rigour, resonated very little in Hungary. Only the opponents of the Horthy-era greeted it with great acclaim. There may have been several reasons for the different reception: the Viscount, was promoting the cause of a small, almost completely isolated country seven years after Trianon and in the atmosphere of *Erfüllungspolitik*, but by the turn of 1937-38, the international situation had fundamentally changed. Not only did Hungary consolidate and see its room for manoeuvre in foreign policy increased, but Germany also kept the overthrow of the status quo on its agenda, and the British government, led by Neville Chamberlain from May 1937, was increasingly willing to compromise. As the issue of border adjustment gradually

---

399 Ibid., 490-491.

came to the fore, a significant part of Hungarian politicians turned away from the ethnic revisionism of the early 1920s, which they had supported mainly for tactical reasons, and more openly stood for *restitutio in integrum*. By comparison, the border adjustments proposed in the Macartney book must have seemed very minor indeed, and this was compounded by the author's—justified—criticism of both the pre-1918 dual system and, in particular, the nationality policy of the Horthy era. Enthusiasm for the book in general thus quickly waned.

Professor Jenő Horváth, the reviewer of Seton-Watson's *History of the Roumanians*, pointed out in *Budapesti Szemle* that Macartney's book was published with the support of the RIIA, which, in his opinion, underlined the timeliness of the Hungarian question. The professor praised the author's "wide-ranging knowledge" and appreciated his efforts to master the "isolated language [of Hungarians]," as well as the "impartial" sections of his book on the minority policy of the successor states, but he was rather critical on the chapter about post-1867 nationality policy. He believed that Macartney drew too much from Seton-Watson's works, and, like him, he did not [?] distinguish between forceful Magyarization and the "natural transformation of the Danube Basin," i.e., voluntary assimilation.[400] If the latter had triumphed, stated Horváth, the Hungarian government would have been "less averse" to granting autonomy, which, in the absence of minorities, one might admit, would hardly have been necessary.[401]

Horváth, an advocate of *restitutio in integrum*, found Macartney's conclusion about the legitimacy of ethnic revisionism (and no more!) unacceptable, as well as the passage from the book saying,

> However wrong the Treaty of Trianon may have been, the developments of the past twenty years have now supplied a post-dated justification of its main principle of dismemberment of Hungary; and so long as the national States in question are able to maintain themselves, no conscientious man could possibly recommend the "integral" restitution of Hungary.[402]

Kálmán Móricz used arguments similar to those of Jenő Horváth in his analysis published in *Külügyi Szemle*, the quarterly journal of the *Magyar Külügyi Társaság* [Hungarian Foreign Affairs Association]. All in all, Móricz's review painted

---

400 In fact Macartney claimed that Seton-Watson "may perhaps under-estimate both the extent and the sincerity of the voluntary assimilation that took place [prior to 1918]. Ibid., 23 fn.
401 Jenő Horváth, Magyarország és utódállamai [Hungary and her successors], *Budapesti Szemle*, April 1938, 79–93.
402 Macartney 1937, 489.

## 2. From Versailles to Paris (1920–1947)

a surprisingly positive picture of Macartney's book, which, in his opinion, "represents a great advance among the English works that have so far dealt with the fate of our country." The reason for this, however, was not some kind of common platform held by author and reviewer on frontier rectification or Hungarian nationality policy, but that Móricz's analysis made Macartney's views appear more favourable than they actually were, Móricz interpreted the chapter on Horthy-era nationality policy as if in Macartney's view the situation of minorities in Hungary had been much better "than in any of the successor states."[403]

Although Hungarian official and semi-official circles were dissatisfied with Macartney's proposals on modest revision, it was exactly these that by the end of 1937 brought him in line with the official British position. The importance of his book is well illustrated by the fact that, in the period of the Munich Conference and the first Vienna Award, it was cited in British government circles as "the most authoritative study of ethnic problems in the Danubian Basin."[404]

*Hungary and Her Successors* did in fact provide an excellent analysis of the situation of nationalities in the Danube-basin, according to Macartney's experience during his travels in the region during 1934–35. However, when he returned to Hungary in the summer of 1937, he noticed a considerable change in the spirit of the country, which he elaborated on in a Chatham House Lecture in December. His analysis, however, fell short in two respects. First, he correctly perceived the visible growth of German propaganda and pro-German sentiment in the country, especially in governmental circles and the army, which was nevertheless quickly offset by the "traditional, deep-rooted and well-justified" fear of German predominance. Another basically accurate perception was related to the rise of anti-Semitism in Hungary, which he countered with the hopeful prediction that "you can talk against the Jews in Hungary; it is traditional. But you could not take action against the Jews [on a German scale]" due to their role in the economy, especially in banking.[405] Unfortunately, it took less half a year for the Hungarian government to launch a series of measures that were a sad refutation of that bona fide British observation.

---

403 Vitéz técsői Móricz Kálmán, Magyarország és az utódállamok [Hungary and her successors], *Külügyi Szemle*, April 1938, 182–191, 191. In fact, as we have seen, Macartney happened to allege the exact opposite: "The separate national-cultural facilities afforded to the minorities in Hungary were probably less than those granted to the nationalities in any Successor State, Yugoslavia not excepted." (449–450.)
404 Public Record Office, Foreign Office Papers (PRO FO), c 12627/2319/12.
405 Macartney, "Some Aspects of Present Day Hungary," December 2, 1937. RIIA,11. RIIA Archives 8/475.

Macartney also discussed the topic of Central European cooperation and reached more valid conclusions overall: in contrast to Steed and Seton-Watson, he argued that the idea of a Central European bloc against Germany was completely hopeless, since the Little Entente states insisted that Hungary completely renounce all revisionist claims, which Hungary could not do. He nevertheless saw a change in Hungarian revisionist sentiment with more stress on the "very considerable belt of Magyars" which were cut off: "I do not think that any Hungarian Government of the present or the future of the younger generation could possibly give up all claims to get back at any rate that belt of Magyars round the frontier. I do not think anybody would do it," the speaker expressed emphatically.

The speech ended with a prediction that Macartney himself did not expect to come true so soon. The only thing to bring about a drastic alteration of the situation in the future, he prophesied, could be if Germany did in fact succeed in bringing about Anschluss and/or eating up the Western half of Czechoslovakia.[406] As is well-known, it took less time than the first Hungarian anti-Jewish law for the first prediction to come true.

## 2.14. From the Anschluss to the Munich Conference (March–September 1938)

Anthony Eden resigned in February 1938 as a public protest against Chamberlain's policy of coming to friendly terms with Fascist Italy. A few weeks later, Chatham House organised a series of meetings titled "Issues in British Foreign Policy." The Director opened the debate calling the audience's attention to the fact that France had a treaty with Czechoslovakia: if Germany invaded Czechoslovakia, France would intervene, and then the same factor that had propelled Britain into war against its choice in 1914 would be at work once more. Thus, isolation or "abdication"; that is, the declaration of British renunciation of great power status was not a possible alternative for the country in and after 1938, "however much, in our weaker moments, we may long to do so. We are the prisoners [...] of our own past greatness," emphasized Toynbee. Moreover, as dominance over Central and Eastern Europe would not, he believed satisfy Germany, Britain would have to fight eventually: "[...] our greatness is likely to demand

---

406 Ibid., 18.

sacrifices from us in the future—which will be heavier than our past experience, even in the War of 1914-1918."[407]

Both Steed and Seton-Watson attended the lecture. After having thanked the speaker for the "brilliant and penetrating" ideas, Steed urged a more transparent government policy, as whole-hearted public support would be necessary in a crisis. He was convinced that up to 90 percent of the population, in his estimation, would support Great Britain's firm stand against totalitarian domination as the heart of the British Commonwealth. Seton-Watson was likewise of the opinion that Eastern and Western Europe were "hopelessly interlocked," so no British neutrality was possible. He also insisted that geopolitical considerations should be taken into account and negotiations with the Soviet Union conducted, leaving aside its "present domestic horrors": in his opinion, an Anglo–Russian alliance could still hold Hitler at bay. [408]

But it was a belated hope. Three days after Toynbee's Chatham House lecture, German troops entered Austria. During the extraordinarily fluid spring–summer of 1938, in a private letter Toynbee expressed his regret that with an eye to a moderate settlement the Sudeten-German question had not been seriously considered many months or years earlier, as he was convinced that it might have been "the key to the European political situation and even the question of war and peace might turn upon it."[409]

However, the Director of Chatham House soon took a step back and tried to assess events in a broader context. Looking at the ever-increasing power and territory of the Third Reich, he was also convinced of the impossibility of "getting by" for Britain. In a letter to the former head of the Cambridge University Fabian Society, Lord Allen, of Hurtwood, also a prominent pacifist and appeaser, he stated that the most terrible issue was not the injustices in the Peace Settlement or "neuroses in certain unhappy countries," but the stagnating level of human conduct in the world; the moral and intellectual error of sustaining the system of national sovereignty, which resulted in modern international anarchy. He was convinced that the time of "Great Powers" ought to be ended by the establishment of law in international relations or alternatively by some *single* Great Power conquering the world. He was convinced that before Britain lay

---

407 Toynbee's lecture and debate took place on March 10, 1938, that is, on the eve of the Anschluss. Toynbee, Viscount Cecil of Chelwood, Marquess of Lothian and R. A. Butler, The Issues in British Foreign Policy, *International Affairs* (Royal Institute of International Affairs 1931-1939), Vol. 17, No. 3 (May-June 1938), 307-407, 332.
408 Ibid., 332-335.
409 Toynbee to Friedrich Fick, March 18, 1938. RIIA Archives 4/TOYN/6c.

the choice of either renouncing its great possessions, thus abdicating its World Power status, or taking up the fight against European dictatorship, hoping that the "prize of World domination will fall not to Germany, but to North America." As he doubted that accepting political impotence and economic poverty was practical politics, only facing up the Third Reich remained, which meant war.[410] A few days later, in another clarifying letter to the same Lord Allen, he added that his stance had not been motivated by any nationalistic desire to stop Germany from overpowering Britain, but to establish "a better system of order in the world." Once becoming unable to promote this, he added, "then for me it becomes the salt that has lost its savour, and I do not much care what happens to it."[411]

Unlike Toynbee, Seton-Watson was horrified by the news of Austria's annexation, and especially by the fact that the survival of Czechoslovakia, which was home to the greatest German minority outside of the Reich, became uncertain. A week after the Anschluss, the ageing professor wrote to Home Secretary Samuel Hoare requesting official recognition of Czechoslovakia's strategic position and a declaration that it was in the common interest of Britain and the Soviet Union to maintain peace and the status quo in Central Europe, but his request was rejected on the instructions of the prime minister.[412]

Sensing a gulf between his opinion and the official British position, in his letters and articles duirng the spring and summer of 1938, the historian-publicist turned over every leaf in an effort to convince more and more of his contemporaries of the need for Czechoslovakian integrity, strongly relying on historical and geographical principles he had previously rejected, with regard to his neighbors.

In his writings, he argued that Prague's minority policy, though it could not solve all problems, was the most liberal by European standards, and that the Czech–German border, one of the best geographical borders in Europe, "has stood for at least 800 years."[413] In a *Foreign Affairs* article he admitted that Czechoslovakia was established based upon two conflicting principles, the "historic State Rights" in the case of the Lands of the Bohemian Crown, and upon nationality and self-determination in the case of the Slovaks, who ever since the

---

410 Toynbee to Lord Allen, of Hurtwood, May 11, 1938. Toynbee Papers BL Oxford MS13967/77 Correspondence.
411 Toynbee to Lord Allen, of Hurtwood, May 16, 1938. Toynbee Papers BL Oxford MS13967/77 Correspondence.
412 Seton-Watson to Samuel Hoare, March 22, 1938. Rychlík, Marzik, Bielik (eds.) 1995, I/ 485.
413 *Times*, March 24, 1938, 16.

ninth century had formed an integral part of the Hungarian Kingdom.[414] Further on, he enumerated various arguments in favour of the status quo; the least bad of several admittedly imperfect solutions, was namely, to leave the old frontiers virtually untouched, as despite the just grievances of the German minority, Czechoslovakia had already carried minority rights farther than any other country, and he believed her government stood committed to concessions so far-reaching that if they had been applied throughout Europe they would have taken the real sting out of the whole vexing minorities problem. Czechoslovakia occupied a strategically key position, he ended, thus her survival was of vital interest to the western democracies, but was "not a matter of complete indifference to America" either. [415] Essentially the same arguments can be found in the "Austrian epilogue" of Seton-Watson's *Britain and the Dictators*: "[Czechoslovakia] is the last democratic state to survive east of Rhine. Once let the Czech fortress fall, and the tide of totalitarian state doctrine will flood across the Danubian and Balkan area."[416]

The annexation of Austria, nevertheless, not only focused attention on the German minority in Czechoslovakia or on territorial integrity but also gave new impetus to the Slovak demands for autonomy led by a former national hero, Andrej Hlinka. In three broadcasts for the BBC in June 1938, Seton-Watson set forth his interpretation of the circumstances leading up to the dilemma that Czechoslovakia was facing. While depicting the Czech–Slovak differences as trivial, Seton-Watson condemned Hlinka, a once-hailed Slovak Catholic priest who had "no clear conception of the European problem as a whole," but who led an "extraordinarily ill-advised" campaign, which Seton-Watson argued played "straight in the hands of those German extremists whose aim is to disrupt Czechoslovakia." As for the situation of the Hungarian minority, he noted that their grievances were "more serious than those of the Germans in Bohemia," and expressed the hope that the generous concessions in the forthcoming "Charter of the Nationalities," that is the extension of autonomy, would satisfy them.[417]

Additionally, interpersonal ties needed to be strengthened, too. On July 2, 1938, Seton-Watson, May, and their son Hugh departed for Prague to attend

---

[414] Though he omitted that the disregard of the same principle of national self-determination led to the formation of the Czechoslovak-Hungarian border. Seton-Watson, The German Minority in Czechoslovakia, *Foreign Affairs*, Vol. 16, No. 4 (July 1938), 651–666, 654.
[415] Ibid., 666.
[416] Seton-Watson, *Britain and the Dictators*, Cambridge University Press, 1938, 442.
[417] Seton-Watson, "The Slovak Question." London BBC broadcast, June 28, 1938. Rychlík, Marzik, Bielik (eds.) 1995, I/ 496–500. (Quotations on 499.)

the Sokols'[418] sixtieth anniversary. While staying at the Hrad as the president's guests, they dined with the Czechoslovak minister to London (1925-1938), Jan Masaryk, along with the Steeds.[419]

Even before his visit to Prague, Steed had been actively campaigning for Czechoslovakia. Based on evidence from his German network of spies, in a letter to Foreign Secretary Lord Halifax in May 1938, he even made the case that "peace of Europe can only be saved by complete firmness on the part of Britain." Hitler's aim, he continued was not to help the Sudeten Germans but to obliterate Czechoslovakia. Amidst continuing German troop movements, the outbreak of hostilities could only be halted "if Hitler and Germany know that England stands firm."[420]

In his battle against Nazi Germany, the former editor of the *Times* once again called on the assistance of historiography. Unlike pro-appeasement historians, who had viewed Hitler's takeover as a dead end in German history, as we have seen, Steed's article in *International Affairs* offered a different analysis of German history by establishing a consistency of German expansionist tendencies from Friedrich the Great up to the concept of Lebensraum from *Mein Kampf*: "From Fichte to Hitler there is a line straight," Steed argued. "It led to the Great War, which Germany waged for the mastery of Europe and, indeed, the world [...] it will again lead to war if the direction in which it runs be not understood, and blocked in time."[421]

During the summer of 1938, Steed renewed his correspondence/contact with "one of the most prominent voluntary devotees of Hitlerism," Viscount Rothermere. The former editor flatly stated that the campaign for the revision of Treaty of Trianon "was a part of a German propagandist campaign for revising the other Peace Treaties out of existence." He also warned the Viscount that the existence of Czechoslovakia with its powerful army impeded German

---

418 The Sokol movement was founded in 1862 in Prague as a voluntary gymnastics organisation and was playing an important part in the development of Czech patriotism.
419 Right after Madame Rose passed away and Steed married Violet Mason, in the summer of 1937, he admitted in a letter to Toynbee, that he had been "extremely fortunate in having received her devotion in earlier years and in having enjoyed for more than a generation the vigorous companionship of one of the ablest minds it has ever been my good fortune to know." Further on he expressed his hope that his wife Violet Mason would keep him in order "as vigorously as Madame Rose did." Steed to Toynbee, September 2, 1937. Toynbee Papers BL Oxford MS 13967/84 Correspondence with individuals.
One sign of Steed's eccentricity could be that Violet Mason (1896-1970) was almost half a century younger than Madame Rose. For details see Liebich 2018, 259-266.
420 Steed to Lord Halifax May 2, 1938. Steed Papers MS 74131.
421 Steed, From Frederick the Great to Hitler: The Consistency of German Aims, *International Affairs*, Vol. XVII, 1938, 672-673.

## 2. From Versailles to Paris (1920–1947)

domination of Central and South-Eastern Europe. Reminding Rothermere of his governmental position as well as his personal loss during the First World War, he urged him to bethink himself, "to learn the truth and proclaim it."[422] The offended Viscount retorted: "You are one of those journalistic Bourbons, you seem to have forgotten nothing and learned nothing," and he condemned Czechoslovakia for oppressing its German, Hungarian or Slovak minorities "without protest," as the League of Nations had entirely been controlled by the French and their allies, the Czechs.[423] "To-day the defensive frontier of Great Britain is no longer on the Rhein as Mr Baldwin once suggested but along the borders of Czechoslovakia,"[424] Steed concluded the debate.

Unlike Seton-Watson or Steed, and more in line with Toynbee, Macartney's attitude toward Czechoslovakia was detached, as is revealed in a private memorandum. He described the country as extremely vulnerable, precisely because of the circumstances of its creation. First, and very much in line with the ageing historian, he argued that the borders of Czechoslovakia had been drawn on the basis of "two dramatically opposite principles," the historical-economic and the ethnic, but also added that only Entente intervention made possible the annexation of the Highlands and Subcarpathia from Hungary. Second, despite its truly democratic constitution, Macartney continued in a more critical manner, the new state of nearly five million minorities failed to become, as Beneš prophesied, a "second Switzerland," as integrity could only be preserved by "extraordinary centralisation." Third, Czechoslovakia was an ally not only of France but also of the Soviet Union, which was tantamount to a breach of the permanent neutrality agreed at Versailles.[425]

Thus, as the crisis deepened, Seton-Watson's and Macartney's positions drifted apart. However, there were occasions to cooperate in the spring of 1938. In May 1938 they were among the eight hundred delegates (from seventy national organisations) to the Twenty-eighth Congress of the National Peace Council in Bristol. In the evening Macartney was the chief speaker and addressed his listeners with his "Minorities and the World Situation," whereas Toynbee's father-in-law, Gilbert Murray, was to chair a later session on the League and its future.[426]

---

422 Steed to Lord Rothermere, July 18, 1938, Steed, 1940, 101.
423 Lord Rothermere to Steed August 3, 1938. Ibid., 104.
424 Steed to Lord Rothermere, August 6, 1938, Ibid.
425 Macartney, Memorandum on the Czechs, June 8, 1938. Macartney Papers MSS. Eng. c. 3280.
426 "National Peace Congress. Bristol Meetings. An Impressive Opening,." *Manchester Guardian*, May 27, 1938, 12.

As we have seen, both Seton-Watson and Steed were desperate to secure British guarantees for Czechoslovakia. It could only be a small consolation that by spring–summer 1938 the British government denied support not only to Czechoslovakia but also to the openly revisionist Hungary against possible German aggression. On May 29, 1938, Sir Orme Sargent of the British Foreign Office stated:

> I am sure there are lots of unhappy Hungarians who would like Great Britain to protect them from being "absorbed" by Germany, and who hope that this may be effected by Great Britain's economic intervention. But all our past experience, and all our present evidence, goes to show that Hungary cannot be rendered independent of Germany by any economic action that we can take. [...] There are other countries where British interests are definitely more important and where moreover we have got the means of reinforcing our position, such as Greece in the first place and possibly also Roumania. Don't therefore let us be tempted to waste our energy or our money in trying to salvage countries like Hungary, where the game is already up.[427]

## 2.15. From Munich to the first Vienna Arbitration: The Break between Seton-Watson and Macartney

On September 10, 1938 Toynbee put forward to his secretary, Miss Cleeve, that Germany would unleash a general war by attacking a small neighbouring country,[428] thus becoming a somewhat false prophet. Four days later, when British prime minister Chamberlain flew to Berchtesgaden to meet the Nazi dictator, he actually avoided war, or so it seemed. By acknowledging Germany as a leading power, Britain became an explicit supporter of the reorganisation of East-Central Europe in 1938–1939.

Fearing the worst, Seton-Watson and Steed set into motion. The Masaryk Professor immediately travelled from his Scotland home to the capital and contacted Jan Masaryk, the Czechoslovak foreign minister. While still on the train to London, he began compiling "The Difficulties of a Plebiscite," a memorandum in which he reiterated his earlier anti-revisionist arguments in seven points and expressed doubts about the fairness of a possible referendum. He argued that, given the mixed Czech–German population, drawing a border in accor-

---

427 Qtd. in Gyula Juhász, *Hungarian Foreign Policy*, Budapest, Akadémai Kiadó, 1979, 138.
428 Toynbee to M Cleeve, September 10, 1938. RIIA Archives 4/TOYN/2

dance with the ethnic principle was not only impossible but also undesirable in order to prevent Hitler's further territorial conquest or avoid creating precedents for similar interference on behalf of other minorities, at the expense of other small countries.[429]

Four days later, Steed delivered a BBC talk titled "Why should the Czechoslovaks not hand over to Germany the Sudeten-German regions?" In it he was, on the one hand, using the same arguments as Seton-Watson: Bohemia depicted as a "historical, economic as well as a strategic unit" as well as being strongly fortified, and the ethnic principle which could not to be implemented due to" the practical impossibility to make a clean-cut." On the other hand, for the first time in his career, Steed recommended the transfer of population, which he believed to have been so successful after the First World War between the Greeks and the Turks that it "might be given to Germans," too.[430]

A week later, in another memorandum on Hitler's demands which was to be circulated in the House of Commons, Seton-Watson described the joint Franco-British note to Czechoslovakia about districts inhabited mainly by Sudeten Germans to be transferred to the Third Reich as an ultimatum with a shorter time limit than that of Austria–Hungary to Serbia in 1914. It was a challenge, he continued, to find a document from the history of British foreign policy "so humiliating and so contrary to the spirit of the country." No one seriously denies that the Germans of Bohemia had just grievances, he acknowledged, and in the name of justice, urged His Majesty's government to at long last publicly acknowledge that compared to other East-Central European states, the German minority in Czechoslovakia had already been "infinitely the best treated." Instead of securing peace, he continued, the "scheme of naked partition," would merely prepare the way for fresh demands such as simultaneous cessions to Hungary and Poland and would finally result in the complete partition of the Czechoslovak state, the last stronghold of democratic government east of the Rhine.[431]

---

429 Seton-Watson, The Difficulties of a Plebiscite. Rychlík, Marzik, Bielik (eds.) 1995, Vol. I/ 510–514. (Quotation on 511) Concerning the Anschluss, Seton-Watson put forward the idea that *"at the very least one-third was hostile"* to Nazi takeover [original italics]; an early interpretation of what was later termed the *Opferthese*, or Austria Victim Theory. This was a fundamental myth in Austrian historiography and society from after World War II until the early 1990s, which quickly became a "double victim theory" of Austria equally suffering from Nazi Germany and the Communist Soviet Union. More on this in Hella Picks, *Guilty Victims: Austria from the Holocaust to Haider*, I.B. Tauris, 2000.
430 BBC Talks 1938–40, September 18, 1938, Steed MS 74 177.
431 Seton-Watson, Memorandum on European Situation. Written and privately circulated by Seton-Watson to all members of the House of Commons and to some select members of the House of Lords on September 26, 1938. Steed Papers MS 74103 and Toynbee Papers, MS 13967/75. Germany: Correspondence and Papers 1938.

As is well-known, neither the memoranda nor the BBC talk succeeded in their objectives. On September 30, 1938, in Munich, the four great powers agreed to the annexation of the Sudeten German territories to Germany. Feeling humiliated by his own government, Steed instantly cabled to Edvard Beneš: "In this hour of supreme betrayal of your country and of unspeakable shame of mine I send you my deepest sympathy. History will surround you with honour and us with dishonour whether or not we escape the destruction which by betraying you we have done our utmost to prepare for ourselves." Shortly afterwards Beneš resigned and relocated to London as an exile, just as to Paris in 1915. Throughout World War II, he remained in touch with Steed, who assisted him wherever he could. [432]

As Steed generally had a better understanding of foreigners than of his fellow countrymen, he quickly came to enjoy the respect of London's other war exiles, too, and used his experience to the fullest to advise and mediate between them, often in a highly condescending manner, as one of his letters to Orme Sargent reveals: "I have been observing or dealing with these people for more than forty years," he stated, adding, "I know well how awkward they can be."[433]

Seton-Watson reacted to the Munich Agreement with yet another memorandum, challenging it on ethnic rather than historical-geographical grounds: in addition to the nearly three million Germans, there had been assigned to Germany more than 700,000 Czechs, he stated, which he regarded as manifestly unjust.[434] Moreover, on the British guarantee to Czechoslovakia, he aptly observed that if Britain could not help Prague while it had a well-equipped army and defence, how could it assert its influence over a country "almost utterly defenceless and robbed of her many economic resources"?[435]

---

432 Steed's cable to Beneš, undated. Steed Papers MS Ms 74 104. On Steed supporting the former president see Emilie Beneš to Steed, March 21, 1939. Thanks for the cheque, 300 Pounds. Steed Papers MS 74103
433 Steed to O. Sargent, July 23, 1943. Steed Papers MS 74 133.
434 The Sudeten German situation mirrored that of prewar Hungarian–Slovak mixed districts, where people with double or undefined nationality challenged officials to define what they meant by "Slovak" or "Hungarian," and likewise "Czech" or "German." An essential component of prewar civil society, the freedom to select one's public nationality, had once again been taken away. As Chad Bryant states, before World War II, three out of every ten people in Bohemia had been Germans, whereas by 1950 this number had sunk to 6 per cent. Chad Bryant, Either German or Czech: Fixing Nationality in Bohemia and Moravia, 1939-1946, *Slavic Review* 61, No. 4 (2002), 683-706, 683.
435 Seton-Watson was, in fact, right. With one of the best armies in Europe at the time, Czechoslovakia was able to mobilize forty-seven divisions, of which thirty-seven were sent to the largely-mountainous German border against Hitler's thirty-nine divisions assigned to conduct operations against the country. Seton-Watson, "Godesberg and Munich." Written and privately

Unlike Steed or Seton-Watson, Toynbee viewed the critical weeks of the autumn of 1938 with the equanimity and neutrality of an outsider. His notes taken on October 3 reveal his main dilemma was whether the Sudeten areas were a real objective for Hitler, or merely an excuse to overrun Czechoslovakia and dominate East-Centra Europe. Unlike Steed or Seton-Watson, however, he seemed quite optimistic about the region: with their claims on Czechoslovakia satisfied, Poland and Hungary might be less eager to join forces with Germany and might even try to halt German expansion eastward, he opined. He even added that after what had happened, it seemed unlikely that the Sudeten regions would ever return to being governed by the Czechs, and keeping them in Czechoslovakia would have left Central Europe with "a permanently disturbing element." Those who argued that the price paid for peace was too high, "really mean that the peace bought is only temporary. But we cannot be certain of this without trying it out. And the experiment can only be condemned if, by waiting, we have seriously weakened our chances of victory in a war fought later on. Of this there would not seem to be on balance any conclusive proof,"[436] concluded Toynbee.

It was precisely this waiting that neither the Hungarian nor the Polish government was willing to do. The latter increasingly pressed for the handover of the part of the old Duchy of Teschen, east of the Olza river (Zaolzie or Trans-Olza) with about a 70 percent Polish majority, which Czechoslovakia had laid hands on based on historic and economic arguments in 1919. Similarly, the Hungarian government soberly demanded the return of only those areas with more than 50 percent Hungarian population, while not breaking with but at least shelving the dream of integral revision.[437] Furthermore, the two countries both aimed at pursuing the rectifications along the borders of Czechoslovakia

---

circulated by Seton-Watson to all members of the House of Commons and to some select members of the House of Lords in October 1938. The memorandum was also sent to the Foreign Office in early November, with the following comment: "[...] in detail it would be hard to refute, and I would not advise that attempts should be made." Rychlík, Marzik, Bielik (eds.) 1995, Vol. I, 526–529. Quotations in Vol. I, 529 and 48.

436 Toynbee: An International Balance Sheet, October 3, 1938. Toynbee Papers BL Oxford MS13967/75. Germany: Correspondence and Papers 1938.

437 They were convinced that the remaining Slovak-inhabited territories would eventually end up with Hungary. This is evidenced by the orders given by the chief of the Hungarian General Staff to the troops involved in the occupation of the reannexed territories: "The troops of the Royal Hungarian Army have halted on the lines designated by the arbitrators in Vienna, but we must trust that the noble enthusiasm and readiness for action which have filled every member of the Army in recent weeks will yet find occasion to perform great deeds." Qtd. in István Janek, Magyar törekvések a felvidék megszerzésére 1938-ban [Hungarian Aspriations to Obtain the Highlands in 1938], Történelmi Szemle, 2010/ 1, 37–66, 64.

without committing their respective countries to Germany. With joint action, they hoped to establish the Hungarian–Polish common frontier and, probably more in Warsaw, the long-term project of "Third Europe" was cherished, too: the establishment of a so-called anti-German and also anti-Soviet bloc of Poland, Hungary, Romania, and possibly Yugoslavia.

While Hitler's demands were fully met by Great Britain, France and Italy, the Polish and Hungarian territorial claims were generally ignored, that is, referred to bilateral negotiations. The ink had barely dried on the document recording the transfer of the Sudetenland, when Poland issued an ultimatum to Prague to hand over Teschen: in the following days, the Polish army, commanded by General Władysław Bortnowski, annexed an area of 801.5 km2 with a population of 227,399 people.[438] However, with nine million inhabitants and no strong army since 1918, Hungary could not follow the Polish example. Thus, in line with the appendix to the Munich Agreement, bilateral Hungarian–Czechoslovak negotiations began in Komárom on October 9. Initially, the two positions were a world apart: in the spirit of Munich, the Hungarian delegation demanded all areas with a Hungarian population of 50 percent or more, and called for a referendum in Slovakia and Subcarpathia, whereas the Slovaks offered autonomy together with the Grosse Schütt.[439]

It was during these stormy weeks that Hungarian prime minister Béla Imrédy's faith in Britain suffered a serious blow. (He admitted during his postwar trial, that Munich brought it home to him that territorial revision would only come if the country sided with Nazi Germany.[440]) There were many more in Hungary who looked "with bitterness towards the West," József Balogh explained in a letter to Toynbee. He also requested the director of Chatham House to write an article to *Hungarian Quarterly* on the fall of Czechoslovakia and other "Central-European questions."[441] Toynbee's response came four days later: "Hungary is certain to regain half a province, but not certain that she herself may not become a province of a larger empire." He also added critically: "If only the Czechs had given a 'parecchio' [that is, quite a lot of territory] to Hungary, and a 'p' to Poland a year ago, they would at last have had only one front to worry

---

438 Erik Goldstein, Igor Lukes (eds.), *The Munich Crisis, 1938: Prelude to World War II*, Routledge, 1999, 57 and 103.
439 Gergely Sallai, *Az első bécsi döntés [The First Vienna Award]*, Budapest, 2002, 82–84.
440 Sakmyster 1980, 208.
441 József Balogh to Toynbee, October 10, 1938. Toynbee Papers BL Oxford MS 13967/75. Germany: correspondence and papers 1938. Also available in OSZK KT 1/3115.

about, but the chief responsibility lies in us in England and France, who since 1918, have made neither peace nor war."442

During the subsequent talks, despite the tense atmosphere, the delegations led by the head of the Autonomous Slovak government, Josef Tiso, and Hungarian foreign minister Kálmán Kánya managed to reach an agreement on 93 percent of the territory to be ceded: the fourth Czechoslovak draft—except for the cities of Bratislava-Pozsony Nitra-Nyitra, Košice-Kassa, Užhorod-Ungvár, Mukačevo-Munkács, and their surroundings—essentially coincided with the Hungarian demands. Negotiations in fact broke down over the status of these cities. In vain did the chairman of the United Hungarian Party in Slovakia, János Esterházy, suggest that the Hungarian government should voluntarily give up some, overwhelmingly Slovak, 380 square miles of territory, which would allow the Hungarians to regain the goodwill of the Slovaks and bring the two peoples closer together.443

Macartney had long been convinced that the control of Minorities by the League of Nations gave way to frontier revision: concerning Czechoslovakia, the only true solution he could endorse was to put all nationalities on an equal footing. Therefore, while in Budapest he wrote a letter to the *Times* on September 19, but it was not published until two weeks later, simultaneously with the bi-lateral Czechoslovak–Hungarian Komárom negotiations:

> Though I have for many years consistently dissented from the chief Magyar [revisionist] claims, I submit that [ignoring Hungarian demands in Munich] is hard on the Magyars because they were incorporated into Czechoslovakia just as much against their own will as the Germans—probably more so, [...] as the historical and economic, as well as national considerations.

As Britain and France seemed to abandon Czechoslovakia, the former "bulwark against Germany" would also become "completely indefensible," therefore Macartney advised creating a realistic basis for regional cooperation by returning the Hungarian-inhabited areas as well as Subcarpathia, which economically gravitated to Budapest: "If Czechoslovakia is to disappear or be emascu-

---

442 Toynbee to József Balogh, October 14, 1938, OSZK KT 1/3115.
443 János Esterházy (1901–1957) a Hungarian MP from the Highlands, later Slovakia, stayed in Slovakia after the Vienna Award and as the president of the Hungarian Party tried to mediate between the two countries. According to Esterházy's recollection, the Hungarian government refused his advice, explaining that "Hungary was deprived of so much territory by Trianon that we cannot now give up a single centimeter of what the Vienna decision gave back." Qtd. in Janek 2010, 64.

lated, then a stronger Hungary linked with a stronger Poland would, I submit, be a much sounder solution than a patchwork with a lot of ragged ends [...especially] if the Roumanians could be persuaded to make a few concessions too."[444]

While undoubtedly overbearing in its treatment of Czechoslovakia, Macartney's letter was not written in the spirit of appeasement. His proposals on frontier readjustment did not aim at appeasing Nazi Germany, but, quite along the lines of the "Third Europe" idea, at creating an anti-German (and anti-Russian) Central European cooperation. What followed Macartney could not have anticipated. It is worth quoting in full Seton-Watson's break of relations with Macartney on October 8 and Macartney's reaction the following day:

Dear Macartney,
I could hardly believe my eyes when I read your letter in yesterday's Times. It is altogether worthy of that paper, more I cannot say.
I never trusted your political judgement, but I did not till now imagine you to be capable of joining the pack of curs who are now yapping round the dying stag. I must ask you to regard our acquaintance as finally closed.
Yours very truly, R.W. Seton-Watson

Dear Seton-Watson,
I received your letter with profound pain. An acquaintance cannot be one-sided, and I can therefore do no more than express the hope that a day will come when you will be able to distinguish between intellectual dissent from yourself and moral obliquity. When that day comes, I hope that we shall meet again.
Yours truly, C.A. Macartney[445]

The relationship between Seton-Watson and Macartney then deteriorated for good, and apart from the most necessary professional matters, they had no further contact. But his older, well-respected colleague and former mentor's somewhat contemptuous grudge did not prevent Macartney from giving a talk at Chatham House two days later titled "Hungary in the Present Crisis." Although both Steed and Seton-Watson duly boycotted the event (and Toynbee was not present either), the speaker recalled the arguments of his former mentor: had there been a referendum in 1919, it would have been highly improbable that the

---

444 Macartney, "Grievances of Minorities. The Case of Hungary," Times, October 7, 1938, 10.
445 Seton-Watson Papers, SEW 17/15/5. Lojkó 1999, 44.

Slovaks would ever have left Hungary, as the number of active nationalists was not more than 750–1000, even according to Seton-Watson's estimate. However, Slovak national feeling had been born since then, unlike the still "extremely vague and undeveloped" Ruthene national identity which, together with the economic gravitation of Subcarpathia towards Hungary would render in his opinion the annexation of the territory by Hungary logical, which Macartney was convinced would serve every party's "real advantage." Regarding borders, Macartney put forward the idea that "One must return on an impartial basis"— and added that neither the 1910-Hungarian nor the 1930-Czechoslovak census was "an absolutely trustworthy" basis.[446]

Further on, in his talk, Macartney was realistic enough to dismiss "the comfortable prophecies" about the spiritualization of the frontiers put forward by Little-Entente leaders. Referring to Seton-Watson's and Steed's often-cited argument about the leaders of Successor States, e.g., Titulescu or Beneš, being fully ready to compromise in the face of harsh and unrelenting Hungarian attitudes, he ironically added: revision under conditions one might translate "as if the moon can be proved to be made of green cheese." Revision could only come through Germany, and Macartney clearly overstated the fear of Germany as "extremely widespread" in Hungary. He put both the percentage of those sympathetic to the Third Reich and those with a deep dislike at 80 percent, arguing that it was "perfectly possible to enthuse for revision and fear Germany."

Some of Macartney's additional comments seemed to be even further detached from reality: he (mis)described the Imrédy-Cabinet as "probably the best government Hungary has enjoyed for a long time," the prime minister and his minister for education and religious affairs, Pál Teleki, were labelled "two of the best men in Hungarian public life today, intelligent, honest, courageous with strong social sense."[447] He gave praise to the government for adopting a "wiser policy of moderation" against the incorporation of large blocks of unwilling alien population as well as for having successfully resisted very strong German pressure. Regarding the Anglo-French Agreement, Macartney expressed his incomprehension:

---

[446] Macartney, "Hungary in the Present Crisis," Chatham House Lecture, October 11, 1938, Royal Institute of International Affairs Library. RIIA Archives 8/161, 3–4.
[447] Ibid., 10. Macartney knew and liked Teleki. (He also noticed his depressing demeanour after Hitler's invasion of Norway in April 1940.) His major two-volume *October Fifteenth*, released in 1956, was unmistakably marked by this affection. On Teleki the most recent and in-depth study is Balázs Ablonczy, *Pál Teleki (1879–1941): The Life of a Controversial Hungarian Politician*, East European Monographs, 2007. Concerning Teleki's attitude to liberalism and nationalism, see pages 148–49.

How on earth could anyone suppose that Hungary, with her natural grievance against Czecho Slovakia [sic], would be willing to abandon that grievance and guarantee Czecho Slovakia? On what ground? That Czecho-Slovakia had been deprived of the advantage she had had from Hungary? It seemed to me as fatuous as it was dishonourable.

Further on in speech, Macartney moved on to more general problems affecting the region, which in his opinion could be either ruled by division, like the French system of cordon sanitaire of certain selected states against a few "incurable antagonists," or by unification: "perhaps the greatest of the difficulties are being removed today by partial liquidation of Czecho Slovakia which had been the most unreasonably favoured at the expense of her various neighbours," Macartney opined.[448] He also expressed his hope that His Magesty's government would take advantage of the "heaven-sent opportunity" to get concessions through "as a gift from us against ill-will from Germany:" the restoration of poor and still rather a-national Ruthenia[449] to Hungary to achieve the Polish-Hungarian common frontier and bring Poland closer to the Danubian countries, which could result in creating "a neutral bloc, neither pro-French nor pro-anything, anti-German, anti-Russian and anti-everybody, except themselves, the best we can hope for."[450] Macartney concluded his speech by adding that whereas the Poles had attacked Teschen and taken it by force, despite "their crime-stained history," the Hungarians had behaved correctly and should get credit for it.[451]

Although Seton-Watson and Macartney terminated their relations, their controversy did linger on. In line with the Munich spirit, the Sargent-Nichols memorandum in the Foreign Office on September 28 had supported the ethnic principle, though with serious limitations, and proposed the transfer of the border towns of Berehove-Beregszász in Sub-Carpathia, with over 80 percent Hungarian population) and the Grosse Schütt based on Macartney's *Hungary and Her Suc-*

---

448 Ibid., 14–15.
449 Macartney likened the region and its poverty to some parts of Ireland and added that an independent Ukrainian national state would mean breaking up Poland and the USSR. Ibid., Discussion 11.
450 Macartney would regularly come back to the topic of the "deep-rooted dislike and fear of Germany and of Russia" in the region, which was more wishful thinking than reality. Ibid., 16. It seemed that Hungary was less responsive to Britain and much more responsive to Germany than Macartney would have liked to believe. See also Becker, 676. Moreover, it might be argued that besides the contrasting statistical data and principles, the failure of the negotiations in Komárom-Komárno was also due to the fact that both delegations had complete faith in German assistance.
451 Ibid., Discussion 12.

*cessors*.[452] After Munich, Macartney himself started submitting requests to the Foreign Office to include the Hungarian–Slovak problem too, arguing that because most Hungarians favoured Britain as against Germany, Hungary could be readily won over by supporting its fair claims.[453] In contrast, during the bilateral Komárom negotiations, the Czechoslovak experts were citing the works of Seton-Watson, trying to prove that the 1910 census, which they considered to have been carried out at the "peak" of Magyarization, could not be the basis for the new state border.[454] In line with the ageing historian, they used the 1930 data, coupled with strategic and economic arguments, as against the Hungarian delegation who relied on ethnic grounds. Due to these two major differences, neither party seemed to demonstrate a strong enough desire to compromise.

At the same time as the start of the Hungarian–Czechoslovak negotiations in Komárom-Komárno, Steed also shared his concerns with BBC listeners, falsely claiming that the Czechs and the Slovaks both "did not wish to take over nearly a million Hungarians," but the frontier line was suggested by Marshall Foch, the Allied commander-in-chief, who wished to obtain as good a strategic frontier as possible. He also added that due to the Czechoslovak land-reforms and political freedoms, for the Hungarians of Slovakia the new border may be "a mixed blessing." If the second-best equipped army in East-Central Europe was weakened, he warned his listeners, it would pave the way to German military expansion of South Eastern Europe towards the Black Sea.[455]

Still amidst the Hungarian–Czechoslovak border dispute, a full-page article appeared in the *Times* titled "Magyar and Slovak. The Rival Claims. An Opportunity for Just Revision." Its author, Macartney, once again made it clear that Slovaks would "stubbornly resist" any attempt to restore historic Hungary, and that to demand a referendum in their ranks was "not particularly tactful." Nevertheless, he noted that Budapest would recognise the result of the referendum as binding on itself, thus settling the question of the territory's iden-

---

[452] Macartney's original proposal was much more than this, though. Interestingly, attached to the first at a later date, a second memorandum by Sargent-Nichols recommended the transfer to Hungary of a far greater territory with 425,000 Magyars. According to Becker, it was unclear which scenario the British favoured, which speaks for the fluidity of their opinions (and, probably, of Macartney's influence). In the meantime, British diplomacy continuously pressed Prague to comply with Hungary's reasonable ethnographic demands. Andras Becker, The Dynamics of British Official Policy towards Hungarian Revisionism, 1938-39, *Slavonic and East European Review*, Vol. 93, No. 4 (October 2015), 655-691, 671-672 and 674.

[453] Macartney, "The Hungarian Question," October 10, 1938. PRO FO 371/21571, C12627/2319/12, Qtd. in Becker, 674.

[454] Sallai 2002, 114-116, 103.

[455] "I have been wondering whether the state of Czechoslovakia ought to have been created." Steed's BBC Talks 1938-40, October 12, 1938. Steed Papers MS 74177.

tity once and for all. As for the Hungarian-speaking areas of the southern part of the Highlands and Subcarpathia, Macartney pointed out that, unlike the Slovaks, almost the entire Hungarian minority in Czechoslovakia remained "irreconcilable," and therefore he endorsed ethnic revision based on a compromise between the results of the Hungarian census of 1910 and the Czechoslovak one of 1930.[456]

The failure to reach an agreement between the rival Czechoslovak–Hungarian claims opened up the prospect of a four-power arbitration in Munich. However, rejecting that as well as the Hungarian referendum initiative, London supported the German–Italian arbitration agreed on by the Prague government. "It would be easier to be silent" as the Hungarians had been making "large, unattainable claims" upon Slovakia, Steed stated in his talk on November second, when the arbitrators met in Vienna.[457] That meeting resulted in the return of 4788 square miles of territory to Hungary with 1.1 million, 84 percent Hungarian inhabitants. According to Czechoslovak figures, however, the Hungarians were much fewer (57 percent) but still constituted a majority.

On the following day, the *Times* commented on the events with the headlines "Ethnic Frontier," "Injustice Removed,"[458] and in the House of Commons, Chamberlain made the following statement: "Agreement was, in fact, reached between the Czechoslovak and Hungarian Governments when they agreed to accept as final the arbitral award of the German and Italian Governments, and in consequence no question of action by His Majesty's Government arises." In response to a question from a member, he also confirmed that regarding the new frontiers there was a moral guarantee "in operation."[459]

Given the yawning gap between the official British opinion and Steed's as well as Seton-Watson's stance, the Munich Agreement and the First Vienna Award culminated in an unprecedented isolation of the aforementioned two experts on East-Central Europe. When Fedor Ruppeldt, a Slovak Lutheran pastor as well as the translator of *The New Slovakia*, appealed to Seton-Watson requesting

---

456 Macartney, "Magyar and Slovak. The Rival Claims. An Opportunity for Just Revision," *Times*, October 26, 1938. 15.
457 "World Affairs." BBC Talks 1938–40, November 2, 1938. Steed Papers MS 74 177.
458 *Times*, November 3, 1938, 14.
459 House of Commons Sitting of November 14, 1938, "Czechoslovakia." https://api.parliament.uk/historic-hansard/commons/1938/nov/14/czechoslovakia (Accessed May 23 2023) Despite the strong advice of the Hungarian minister in London, however, István Csáky, who replaced Kálmán Kánya as head of the Foreign Ministry, did not request British official recognition of the first Vienna Award. (London was definitely relieved that it had not made unnecessary territorial commitments.) See György Barcza, *Diplomataemlékeim* [My memories as a diplomat], Budapest, Európa,1994, I/ 405.

British government intervention,[460] he declined assistance his with the following words: "Practically, as to what is happening in Slovakia [...] Steed & I *can do nothing at all* (I talked to him & we at once agreed). We are both in the sharpest opposition to our [...] treacherous, ill-informed and cowardly Government [...] They have thrown you to the wolves."[461]

Hitler masterfully exploited the fact that the Vienna Award further antagonised the Hungarian and Slovak governments, as well as their rhetoric: in fact, the post 1938-reasoning of the Slovak elite became in many cases literally identical to the Trianon rhetoric prevalent in interwar Hungary, only to serve diametrically opposite interests. On the Hungarian side, they stressed the economic argument that Trianon had deprived Hungary and the Hungarian people of a great deal of economic resources, and that it had also cut off communication channels. In the same spirit, the Vienna Award was presented by the Slovaks as depriving Slovakia of its most fertile agricultural areas and also cutting off communication channels. The Hungarian cultural argument was based on the fact that after Trianon, the Hungarian population was under the rule of people of a lower cultural level was countered by the Slovak discourse of the Vienna Award, arguing that the population was once again placed under the undemocratic, semi-feudal conditions of the Kingdom of Hungary. From the majority-minority point of view, Trianon was perceived as a Hungarian grievance that created Hungarian enclaves in neighbouring states, which the Vienna Award partially remedied. In contrast, in the Slovak community, the view that Trianon liberated the Slovaks became accepted. In both cases, there are also regular references to the great power dimension and to the ignorance of the decision-makers. In this context, criticism of the previous government elites is very frequent: in Budapest, part of the "guilt" was attributed to Count Mihály Károlyi and the October emigration, and in Bratislava to President Beneš.[462]

---

460 "While the former Hungary—and the present Hungary not less—kept its non-Magyar peoples under a most absurd racial and cultural oppression, we in our new Republic have, indeed, given the most liberal rights of race, language and culture to all our minorities, we were even on the best way to make of this State a second Switzerland [...]." So boasted Fedor Ruppeldt in a letter to Seton-Watson, October 15, 1938, Rychlík, Marzik, Bielik (eds.) 1995, Vol. I/531–535.

461 Although he was equally critical of the pro-Hitlerite, "damnable" Tiso Regime. Seton-Watson to Ruppeldt, November 22, 1938. Rychlík, Marzik, Bielik (eds.) 1995, Vol. I/ 536.

462 Discussed in further detail in Miroslav Michela, *Trianon labirintusaiban Történelem, emlékezetpolitika és párhuzamos történetek Szlovákiában és Magyarországon* [The labyrinths of Trianon History, memory politics and parallel histories in Slovakia and Hungary], Magyarországi Szlovákok Kutatóintézete Magyar Tudományos Akadémia Bölcsészettudományi Kutatóközpont Történettudományi Intézet Békéscsaba, Budapest, 2016, 131–134.

While Macartney wrongly described Hungary and East-Central Europe as more restrained, even hostile to Germany, Czechoslovakia's most loyal partisans, Steed and Seton-Watson, were unable even to reconsider their earlier label of Hungary as an "insatiable aggressor." In fact, at the time of the first Vienna Award, and as István Janek claims, especially after the annexation of Subcarpathia, the Hungarian government had already signalled that it would abandon further revision of the Highlands and instead would concentrate on preserving the recaptured territories.[463]

## 2.16. "The Natural Epilogue" to Aggression: Arnold Toynbee on Munich and the First Vienna Arbitration

Toynbee—unlike Macartney, and especially in contrast with Steed and Seton-Watson, who in the autumn of 1938, in the context of the Munich Agreement or the Vienna Arbitration, took a strong stand on one side or the other— initially observed events with a certain detachment from the point of view of international relations as well as their effect on East-Central Europe and the British Empire.

In his paper written in early October, Toynbee captured the essence of the Munich Agreement as a complete reversal of British foreign policy, as Britain had abandoned her traditional balance of power policy of never allowing the dominance of one single power over East-Central Europe. The results of this in his opinion were enormous: Britain would "fall out of the ranks of the great powers," or even had to face "literal annihilation" and together with East-Central Europe would be forced into "a vast confederacy under German leadership."

The paper went on to summarise the pros and cons of the situation, from the German point of view. The country of 80 million inhabitants, an economic and military might in the author's opinion, could benefit from the age-old historic quarrels by "playing off East European neighbours against each other" as well as weakening her stronger neighbours by using the principle of national self-determination. However, as Toynbee believed there existed some obstacles to German domination, owing to the bitter national conflicts it seemed in his view rather difficult to gratify the countries simultaneously, e.g., Hungary and Czechoslovakia or Hungary and Romania; also, having experienced hard struggles against German domination in the past, these countries feared and hated

---

463 Janek 2010, 65.

Germany; and finally their attitude toward the Soviet Union seemed rather uncertain and liable to change.

In Toynbee's absence, two meetings were held in Chatham House to discuss the director's paper. At the first, on October 25, Macartney said he regarded the author's fears about East-Central Europe as exaggerated and his paper "much too pessimistic," as in his opinion it ignored not only the socio-economic development in the region but also the growing anti-Semitism as well as the "widespread dislike of Germany." Macartney asserted that the German domination of East-Central Europe was only seemingly a new occurrence, only because it had been absent from 1918-33, "which caused us to forget three centuries prior to 1914." Two days later, with All Souls' history professor E.L. Woodward as chair, the meeting came to the conclusion that the publication of "so pessimistic a document" ought to be "deplored."[464]

A month later Toynbee greatly modified his earlier tone and summarized the essence of Munich and the first Vienna Arbitration thus:

The principle of self-determination of nations to which the Allied and Associated Powers committed themselves during the war of 1914-18, and which they duly applied, in the peace settlement of Paris for the benefit of nations that then happened to be on the winning side, has now at last been applied equally for the benefit of the nations that happened to be on the losing side in 1918-21.

He went on to argue that although, by about the tenth time Hitler had threatened with force, he had not received any more than what the German people were entitled to on the basis of the idea of national self-determination. Therefore, it was no surprise that Toynbee described the cession of minority populations from Czechoslovakia to Germany, Hungary and Poland as "the first known instance, in the history of the World, of a transfer of populations from one sovereignty to another on the grand scale without war." However, in broad contrast to what had been said so far, he remarked that, provided Mr Chamberlain's peace "for our time" ended the following spring, "we may find ourselves fighting for our lives under circumstances that would be worse for us than if the war had started right now."[465]

---

464 Toynbee, After Munich: The World Outlook, A Report of the Meeting Held at Chatham House on October 25 & 27, 1938. Toynbee Papers BL Oxford MS 13967/75. Germany: Correspondence and Papers 1938.
465 Toynbee, First Thoughts on September 1938 and After, undated (November 1938?). Toynbee Papers BL Oxford MS 13967/75. Germany: Correspondence and Papers 1938.

Toynbee's somewhat rewritten paper was published in *International Affairs* in early 1939 with the title "After Munich. The World Outlook." He was rather convinced that Germany would be successful in uniting the vast territory of Middle Europe between France and the Soviet Union into a system mostly under its control. The new Pan-German state he identified with a great concentration of power and a threat to the liberty of Europe, as he prophesied that Germany would soon be able to transform Romanian oil, Romanian grain, and Hungary's grain into German air power, let alone Czechoslovakia's heavy industries.[466] "Has Hitler, in securing satisfaction for German grievances [...] diminished the willingness of his own people to go to war? [...] Or, on the other hand, has he increased his own prestige and given his people, or any way his own band of followers, greater confidence in the pursuit of an aggressive policy?" He outlined the dilemma and, no surprise, opted for the latter.

As for the policies of the Chamberlain government, Toynbee did not hesitate to express his objections. In his opinion, the survival of the British Empire depended on the climate of the rest of the world. Therefore, he contended that it was a misconception that Britain could safely permit "an aggressive, restless, anti-democratic military Power" to rule in Europe, provided that an attack on the country is made expensive and risky and further concessions were offered, first and foremost, at the expense of other nations:

> To-day we English people wear a medal with "Peace" inscribed on it, but this peace medal has some bars, and, when we look closely, we can see on the top bar engraved "Manchuria," on the next "Abyssinia," on the next "Spain'" and then "China" and "Czechoslovakia." So far, all the bars to our peace-medal have been cast out of other people's coin. But [...] sooner or later we shall have to make concessions at the expense of our own material interests: that is the meaning of the "colonial question."[467]

Simultaneously with his article in *International Affairs,* Toynbee's other paper, "A Turning Point in History," summarized his findings in the post-Munich political situation for the North American audience. After having outlined the pros and cons of a new European situation with an enlarged Germany and its possible domination of East-Central Europe, the author went on to discuss the

---

466 Toynbee, After Munich: The World Outlook, *International Affairs*, Royal Institute of International Affairs 1931-1939, Vol. 18, No. 1 (January - February 1939), 1-28, 8-12.
467 Ibid., 13-15.

history of the application of the ethnic principle and arrived at a very different conclusion.

In Toynbee's summary, the principle of nationality had helped create Belgium, Germany and Italy in the nineteenth century, as well as dismantled four significant multinational empires during and after the First World War. "This wave has had, and still has, such an impetus that any statesman or states that manage to ride it can be almost certain of being carried by it to triumph," acknowledged the author. In 1918, it had called to victory the Allies and Associated Powers; in 1938, Germany. "But how is it that, after twenty years, Herr Hitler has been able to steal President Wilson's thunder?" Despite the fact that the armistice of November 18 was concluded on the basis of the fourteen points, he explained, in the subsequent peace treaty the principle of nationality was applied to the benefit of all Central and Eastern European nations except the three former enemies: the Germans, the Hungarians and the Bulgarians. In order to correct this "one-sided peace settlement" by applying the principle of nationality to their own benefit, the Germans accepted Hitler's leadership or submitted to his tyranny. Nations that had been denied the opportunity to achieve national unification were finally given the chance to do so in Central- and Eastern-Europe: Ten million former German subjects together with a few hundred thousand Magyars who were wrongfully separated from Hungary in 1921 [sic] were being returned to their mother counties. "Are we wholly to regret that a different "Big Four" have applied them belatedly in 1938 at Munich?" Toynbee asked.[468]

Toynbee was harshly critical of the Allies' actions for two reasons: first, for their failure to achieve justice for everyone in Paris in 1919, as well as to atone for the sins of omission between 1920 and 1938, and worst of all, for the belatedness of Allied consent, which in 1938 appeared to be a capitulation to a Nazi dictatorship under immediate threat of war. Germany would have been the most powerful country in Europe much earlier had the idea of nationality been applied honestly. According to Toynbee's diagnosis,

> the tragedy of Europe, and of the whole world, that this now dominant Germany is not the Germany of Weimar but the Germany of Nuremberg [...] when the principle of nationality is applied under a fanatical totalitarian regime, it ceases to be even approximately coincident with the more rational and more humane principle of self-determination.

---

468 Toynbee, A Turning Point in History, *Foreign Affairs*, January 1939, 305-320, 316-317.

In other words, the director of Chatham House had no doubts that the Munich Agreement was off-target, but not because it was ethnically unjust or strategically mistaken, as claimed by Steed, Seton-Watson or the entire (Czecho) Slovak elite, but because it was concluded late. Thus, it could no longer serve the cause of peace, but "encouraged a successful [and totalitarian] Germany to go to war."[469]

In his article, Toynbee also noted that two of the League's principles had remained "virtually dead letters" until 1938: "impartial justice for all" as well as "peaceful change." He added that a population exceeding that of Denmark and Norway had been transferred from Czechoslovakia to German, Hungarian and Polish sovereignty without war: he likened the League to a mother dying in childbirth "because the birth is so long overdue." Besides Germany, Italy and Japan, the French, the British and the United States were equally guilty of the decay of the League: the USA abandoned entry, France misused it for "mischievous and futile anti-German power-politics"; while England failed to both guarantee and restrain it. Towards the end of the article Toynbee returned to his favourite subject: the vision of a future Western civilization within the framework of a provisional secular world order.[470]

---

[469] András Rónai, *Térképezett történelem* [History Mapped], Budapest, Püski, 1993, 103.
Toynbee's aloofness was evident in the four volumes of the 1938 *Survey of International Affairs*, about nine tenths of the first voluminous book of which he wrote himself. Toynbee's discussion of the First Vienna Arbitration was painstakingly balanced: his analysis of the differences between the mother-tongue-centred Hungarian (1910 and 1938) and the 1920 Czechoslovak nationality-based censuses focused on the fact that inter-marriage and bilingualism produced a large number of indeterminate populations; a fact that Seton-Watson had ignored not only in his classic *Racial Problems* but later, too. He also added that economically "probably the worst possible frontier" was drawn separating the minerals of hills from the foodstuffs of the plains, adding that the population's preferences have never once been taken into consideration. Had they been made known, district by district, the issue may have been resolved. R.G.D. Laffan, Arnold and Veronica M. Toynbee et al, *Survey of International Affairs*, 1938, Vol. III, Oxford University Press, 1953, 105-6.
The first volume was celebrated for its "quite amazingly fair" discussion of the triangular negotiations between Britain, France and Italy (The Listener, November 13, 1941, Toynbee Papers BL Oxford MS 13967/16). The second volume was also "excellently done, as we have learned to expect," at least according to the Guardian. ("Europe in 1938," Guardian, September 10, 1943, Toynbee Papers BL Oxford MS 13967/16) The Times was not short of praise either: "a collection as complete as possible" of the relevant German, Austrian, Czechoslovak and Hungarian sources. ("The Year before the War," Times, June 12, 1943.))

[470] Toynbee, A Turning Point in History, *Foreign Affairs* January 1939, 305-320, 318-320. McNeill even claims that German *Mitteleuropa* was created at Munich by British and French application of the principle of self-determination. Further check on Germany was thus impossible. McNeill 1989, 173-4.
Toynbee had in fact been an ardent supporter of the League until the spring of 1936, when Britain and France abandoned Ethiopia to Italian aggression. Then his perspective changed, and he gave up on the notion that there might be a materialistic solution to the problems plaguing Western civilization. Therefore, he was not quite as excited by future political events as he had been by the situation over Ethiopia, and he could therefore declare, as the war threat of 1938 ap-

In early February 1939, Toynbee could still clarify his stance on Munich as well as the failure of interwar collective security. He claimed that there would eventually be an outbreak of force in every society that was unable to bring about just changes by constructive and positive adjustment. However, the outcomes of changes brought about by force were likely to be even more unjust than the outcomes of forcible attempts to oppose change. Therefore, "law and order" and "justice" were not inherently at odds with one another and may even be complementary; Toynbee was convinced that change would undoubtedly occur without law and order, and that it would not be a just change. In the same letter he also criticized the post-1919 French political line:

> One of the main reasons for the present changes [...] which are certainly being made by violence and, in my opinion, not with justice is the French resistance to any kind of change and our British acquiescence in this unhappy French policy during the post-war years [...]. This explains why the League has been breaking down [...] I do not for a moment believe that you can get real justice by abandoning law and order. You have to have the two things together in the right proportion to one another."

In this letter to S.P. Cherrington, Toynbee concluded that he found the temperament of Hitler "one of the most difficult things to gauge."[471] As indeed, it was. But that belongs to another chapter.

## 2.17. Four Britons on March 15 and After: Prague and Subcarpathia

On March 15, 1939, the Führer marched into Prague, and two days later, Chamberlain, who just six months before had done his utmost to secure a German-British settlement, announced the end of the policy of appeasement. Hitler's destruction of what remained of Czechoslovakia in 1939 prompted London to declare the Munich Agreement void. Moreover, for the first time in its history, His Magesty's government offered guarantee to Poland, Greece and Romania,

---

proached the Munich Conference, "I find that the bitterness is past: one had one's excruciating moments in 1935-1936, and this seems just the natural epilogue to that." Toynbee to Veronica Boulter, September 8, 1938, Toynbee Paper, MS 13967/71/1 Family correspondence 1924-1938. McNeill 1989, 170.
471 Toynbee to S.P. Cherrington, February 6, 1939. RIIA Archives 4/TOYN/6E.

increasing the strategic importance of these states, which led to the devaluation of Hungary together with its revisionist agenda.

Certainly, Seton-Watson welcomed that the Foreign Office had reoriented its priorities regarding Central and Eastern Europe, but he continued to criticise its former role in appeasement as harshly as possible. The correctness of his consistently pro-Little Entente and status-quo position seemed to be vindicated by Hitler's March 1939 aggression, which, he argued, "brought home to the dupes of Munich" that the Führer, guided by the sonorous slogan of *Lebensraum*, would not hesitate to subjugate an entire nation and carry out his pan-German programme.[472]

On the eve of a fresh war, Seton-Watson stressed the importance of educating the public, too. His powerful pen contributed to changing the pacifist public sentiment in Britain, especially through his book *Munich and the Dictators - Munich and Danzig*, which was published for the third time in August 1939. Seton-Watson claimed that after the principle of self-determination had been subordinated to German *Lebensraum*, not only Czechoslovakia and Poland, but Hungary, Romania and the other Balkan states as well would be conquered, and war would be unavoidable for Britain, too.[473] The work was dedicated to Beneš, "who trusted the good faith of an ally and the good will of a friend," "a great democrat, a great patriot and a great internationalist [...] whose record [...] will one day stand out as one of the most consistent and constructive contributions to European statesmanship."[474]

Like Seton-Watson, Macartney did not change his position on revision, as the spring and summer of 1939 proved. In his pamphlet "The Danubian Basin," published after Hitler's invasion of Prague, Macartney once again stressed that the Central European system of nation states created in Versailles had not fulfilled hopes, mainly due to two factors: first, the ambiguous nature of national consciousness in both Czechoslovakia and Yugoslavia and second, due to the economic-geographical strategic approach, which had eclipsed the ethnographic principle in some border areas. The invasion of Czechoslovakia—the author continued—made even more obvious the flaws in the application of the nation-state concept in Central and Eastern Europe and the defencelessness of the re-

---

472 Seton-Watson, "The Problem of Small Nations and European Anarchy," Montague Burton International Relations Lecture, 1939, 17.
473 Seton-Watson, *Munich and the Dictators–Munich and Danzig*, London, Methuen, 1939, 272-273.
474 Seton-Watson, *Munich and the Dictators*, 1939, v and xi-xii. See also G.H. Bolsover, *R. W. Seton-Watson, 1879–1951*, from the Proceedings of the British Academy, Vol. XXXVII, London, 1952, 356. See also Rychlík, Marzik, Bielik (eds.) 1995, I/49.

gion. Therefore, after having remedied the most blatant injustices of the 1919 settlement, a "settled and united Danube-basin not directed against any outside power nor the puppet of any, would be infinitely more satisfactory to all Europe [...] than either the position to-day or of ten years ago."[475]

However, this optimistic Independent Eastern Europe concept, first formulated by Macartney in the above pamphlet—and elaborated in detail in his 1962 book of the same title, co-written with Alan Palmer—was no longer a realistic alternative in 1939. Germany's economic hegemony in the region was already a reality, soon to be followed by an even more complete extension of its political and military influence.

Unlike Seton-Watson or Macartney, however, Toynbee's opinions radicalized after the annexation of Prague, as the notion of Nazi ambition being restricted to German national self-determination was in fact irrevocably discredited. As a result, from then onwards he passionately opposed any deal with Hitler.[476] Moreover, not only his political outlook, that is his anti-appeasement but pro-revisionist stance, but also his personal life were greatly affected; a few days prior to March 15, he had to witness the death agony of his first-born son. A committed anti-Nazi, Tony Toynbee had returned home after pausing his German studies and then committed suicide. He passed away the very day the Führer took the Czechoslovak capital, at his deathbed his father was left with a mystic experience: "the veil pulled aside," as Toynbee recalled later, and "God had revealed himself for an instant to give an unmistakable assurance of his mercy and forgiveness."[477] This revelation remained with him for the rest of his life, greatly influencing his historical scholarship.

March 15, 1939, was significant in still another way. The only portion of Subcarpathia that the Vienna Arbitration ceded to Hungary was the Magyar-populated southern region. As we have seen, for strategic reasons as well as for the

---

475 Macartney, *The Danubian Basin*, Oxford, 1939, 8–9, 32.
476 McNeill 1989, 175–176. The appeasers, particularly Noel-Buxton, approached him several times about the chance of a separate peace, but Toynbee was unrelenting: "Unless the restoration of the non-German nations (Poles, Czechs, Slovaks) conquered by Germany is an absolute condition of peace on our side laid down formally and clearly [...] also publicly, [...] any negotiations [...] would be unacceptable," he argued in December 1939. (Toynbee to Noel-Buxton, December 21, 1939. Toynbee Papers BL Oxford MS 13967/76/1 Germany 1926–68.) Eight months later he "decidedly disagreed" with Noel-Buxton's scheme of "compromise peace" with Hitler, as the Allies' first aim should be "to liberate ourselves and the states of Western-Europe from German domination," which implied persisting with war until Hitler collapsed. (Toynbee to Noel-Buxton, August 12 ,1940. Toynbee Papers BL Oxford MS 13967/63/2.)
477 Toynbee, 1969, 176; McNeill 1989, 176–177.

sake of historical friendship, Poland firmly endorsed Hungary's decision to maintain its demand for the entire area and thus establish the common frontier. In February 1939, owing to strategic considerations, that is to counterbalance German hegemony in the region, Hungarian minister to London György Barcza was confidentially informed that Britain would support Hungary's occupation of Subcarpathia and the establishment of a common Hungarian-Polish border.[478] Although Hungary's accession to the Anti-Comintern Pact was frowned upon in London, Prime Minister Chamberlain did not object to the Hungarian occupation of Subcarpathia that took place between March 15 and 18. Despite the violation of the Munich spirit, or the ethnic principle,[479] permanent under-secretary for foreign affairs Alexander Cadogan even argued that it was better to have Hungarians in Subcarpathia than Germans, "for whom it would have meant only a further territorial and prestige gain."[480]

As we have seen, the Hungarian annexation of Subcarpathia had already been recommended by Macartney on various forums for strategic and geographical reasons. Seton-Watson, on the other hand, attacked the move even more vehemently than he did the first Vienna Arbitration, mainly because of the disregard of the ethnic principle. In his Montague Burton International Relations Lecture, "The Problem of Small Nations and European Anarchy," he set out to explain that thanks to Czechoslovak foresight, Subcarpathia, one of the most interesting of the social and political experiments, had been in a "special autonomous situation" between 1919 and 1939, whereas the Hungarians and the Poles "have a record of infamy and oppression which places them high on the list of those morally unqualified to govern subject races."[481] For the sake of fairness, one should note, however, that contrary to the commitment made in the tenth clause of the Treaty of Saint-Germain, Subcarpathian autonomy did not materialize either in Czechoslovakia until its dissolution or in Hungary after 1939 despite Prime Minister Teleki's assurances and support.

It was no surprise that Steed, too, would regularly advance the argument that Slovakia and Subcarpathia had been better off after 1920 than under the

---

478 British foreign policy had been benevolent towards Hungary: Pál Teleki's appointment as prime minister on February 16, 1939–like Imrédy's almost a year earlier–was very well received. Moreover, early in 1939, at the request of György Barcza, the Hungarian minister to London, the unfriendly and unsupportive Geoffrey Knox was replaced by pro-Hungarian Owen O'Malley as British minister to Hungary. Becker 2015, 682.
479 In Subcarpathia, the Hungarians amounted to between 17 and 21 percent, according to the 1910 and the 1930 censuses.
480 Barcza 1994, 407.
481 Seton-Watson, "The Problem of Small Nations and European Anarchy," Montague Burton International Relations Lecture, 1939, 13, 15.

rule of the "Magyar oligarchy," many whom were worried and perplexed, and "beginning to regret the part they played [...] in helping Hitler to break up Czechoslovakia."[482] In his August 1939-talk, that is five months after Hitler's march into Prague, however, Steed disregarded the fact that Slovak nationalists, particularly the Slovak People's Party, which had assisted the Slovaks in 1918 in breaking away from Hungary with the aid of the Czechoslovak army, had played a significant role in the Slovaks' secession from Czechoslovakia in 1939, alongside the occupying Wehrmacht. The centuries-long Slovak national awakening finally culminated in the triumphant achievement of Slovak independence, as interpreted in his speech to the country by President Josef Tiso on March 14. 1939. In reality, the new state was more a mixture of fervent religiosity and narrow nationalism, along with unwavering support for, and dependence on, Nazi Germany.[483]

## 2.18. Three Britons in the Foreign Research and Press Service, Macartney in Hungary 1940

In August 1939, preferred against the rival Foreign Publicity Division at London University under Edward Hallet Carr,[484] the Toynbee-led Chatham House was put at the disposal of His Magesty's government. Under Toynbee's auspices, a special research group, the Foreign Research and Press Service (FRPS) began its work at Balliol College, Oxford. Thus, full time Government work crowded out the usual lecturing or journalism, which was a considerable financial sacrifice for a number of the people whose task constituted monitoring the press in sixty-five countries, and compiling analyses and memoranda. In September 1939 Carlile Aylmer Macartney joined the organisation and Robert William Seton-Watson was appointed his immediate chief, leading the South-Eastern Department.[485] Instead of focusing on a specific area, as he had done with the Mid-

---

482 "World Affairs" BBC Talks 1938–40, August 16, 1939. Steed Papers MS 74 177
483 Thomas Lorman, *The Making of the Slovak People's Party. Religion, Nationalism and Culture War in Early 20th-Century Europe*, London, Bloomsbury Academic, 2019, 1–3.
484 Between 1937 and 1939, Carr led a Chatham House research group on nationalism and later worked in the Ministry of Information. Like Toynbee, he did not hold the interwar European system of autonomous nations or the long-term viability of the British Empire in high regard. The choice largely rested on Rex Leeper, former official in PID together with Toynbee, Lionel Curtis and Philip Kerr. See more in Cornelia Navari, Chatham House and the Broad Church View, In Bosco-Navari 1994, 362–363.
485 The FRPS staff were mainly focused on the tone of the press regarding Britain and its allies in the countries concerned. The four deputy directors were G.N. Clark, H.J. Paton, C.K. Webster,

dle East during the First World War, Toynbee edited the other experts' analyses, kept an eye on administrative issues, and, most importantly, cultivated his relationships with important persons in Whitehall, such as the foreign secretary.

The establishment of the new organisation was not devoid of conflicts: in a letter to his former rival, Carr, Toynbee described the "rather persistent and unpleasant" feeling, that the PID Foreign Publicity Division "got its knife into" the FRPS, criticising their work and salaries. He explained that he had brought the regular permanent staff into the war work, and as for the specialist staff, he referred to the South-Eastern European Section, and its head, "being as he is" Seton-Watson, whose Ł1000 annual salary he found quite reasonable.[486]

However, soon other difficulties arose. "I expected to be fighting Germans and restraining my younger colleagues from hating the Germans too much," confided Toynbee to one of his old schoolmates, David Davies, "but I have had, so far, to spend three quarters of my energies in resisting aggression from other Englishmen and trying to damp down departmental hate, which is much more enormous than any feeling against the Germans."[487] However, the fact remained that Toynbee had never been good at collaborating with others, partly owing to the often too high standards he set for both himself and those around him. Besides, he tended to withdraw when disagreements over thought or policy emerged, or when someone's performance fell short of his standards, assuming that problems would be resolved on their own. He was very sensitive to feedback on his own performance and often took challenges from strangers as rude comments.[488] Despite interpersonal disputes or tension, nevertheless, the FRPS's expertise quickly garnered widespread acclaim, while several of its employees and senior Foreign Office officials believed that the organization's non-official status and its location outside of London had severe drawbacks, such as restricted access to intelligence reports and other official information.

---

and Sir Alfred Zimmern. D. Mitrany was responsible for Romania. Interestingly, Hungary was considered a neutral country until early summer 1943, "among European Neutrals and the Near East." The Government paid 80 percent of the costs and the rest was shared among universities and Chatham House itself. András D. Bán, *Illúziók és csalódások, Nagy-Britannia és Magyarország 1938–1941* [Illusions and disappointments, Great-Britain and Hungary 1938-1941], Budapest, 1998, 159.

486 Toynbee to E.H. Carr, Ministry of Information, Senate House, December 13, 1939. Toynbee Papers BL Oxford MS 13967/81/1 Correspondence. Despite cuts in 1940, Toynbee could employ a large staff of 131. Eleven professors' salaries were paid by the University of Oxford Colleges, and there were twenty-four volunteer researchers, too.

487 Toynbee to David Davies, December 15, 1940. Toynbee Papers BL Oxford, MS 13967/80 Individuals: D 1919-1973. David Davies was legal witness to both of his marriages.

488 McNeill 1989, 181–182.

Already as a member of FRPS, Macartney travelled to Hungary at the beginning of 1940,[489] and paid a visit to Subcarpathia to report his experiences to the Foreign Office. He explained, among other things, that he had been a little surprised to find that the Hungarian authorities were "conscientiously" keeping their promises of equal status for Ruthenian[490] and Hungarian: street signs and the texts of laws and regulations were bilingual, and Ruthenian was being taught "properly" in schools. Macartney had reservations only about the methods of Hungarian officials and police that he found "much less democratic than their Czechoslovak predecessors." Overall, he concluded that he had seen no serious reason to criticise the Hungarian government, as Subcarpathia was "pretty stable politically, and prosperous economically." Hungary had to prove beyond all doubt, it was argued in the Foreign Office, that it was granting to its nationalities the same rights as it claimed for the Hungarian minorities beyond its frontiers. However, more significant than this generally shared view was the commentary of a junior diplomat from the Central Department, Frank K. Roberts, who fundamentally questioned the objectivity of the account: "Macartney has always maintained that the best solution of the Ruthenian problem was union with Hungary, so he can hardly be accepted as an entirely [un]prejudiced observer."[491]

While in Hungary, Macartney also held several lectures and met some of the most prominent members of the Hungarian political elite.[492] His first-hand experience was summarized in a long memorandum which was forwarded by the British minister in Hungary, Owen O'Malley, to the Foreign Office. It is striking that a fairly optimistic and slightly idealised view of the Hungarian internal situation was expounded in the document: according to Macartney, Prime Minis-

---

489 William Strang, then deputy under-secretary of state favoured Macartney's visit as an "outstanding British authority on Hungary," though he added that as he "has not always seen eye to eye with His Majesty's Government," he should not be shown all official documents. PRO FO 371/23 116. 20871.
490 Rusyns, Uhro-Rusyns, Carpatho-Russians, Carpatho-Ukrainians and other names have all been used historically to refer to the Ruthenians. Ruthenian is used here as the English equivalent of the locals' and their cultural leaders' preferred term, Rusyn. Today Rusyns are considered either to be a fourth eastern Slavic people or a branch of the Ukrainian nation.
491 Report by Macartney on a Recent Visit to Ruthenia, 1940/2/17. PRO FO 371/24429 c 2841.
492 During the meeting with Teleki on February 29, the prime minister maintained the view that Hungary was unwilling to accept any settlement in Transylvania without altering the status quo. In: Macartney Papers MSS. Eng. c. 3287, doc. 1. During this meeting Teleki showed Macartney the memorandum compiled by himself and his colleagues on the maximal and minimal territorial claims of the Hungarian government concerning Transylvania. Half a year later the Second Vienna Award was chiefly based on this document, which was according to Macartney "rather indifferent to Romania's future." Therefore Prime Minister Teleki pledged to rewrite it. PRO FO 371/24 985/ 7406.

ter Teleki and Admiral Horthy were clearly pro-western, managing to preserve a considerable measure of political liberty, which was acknowledged even by the Hungarian Jews and Socialists, who themselves were unable to offer a better alternative. The only considerable criticism levelled at Hungarian internal affairs was the failure to implement a wide-ranging land reform which alone would, according to Macartney, be capable of placing the social system of Hungary "on a sound basis."[493] On the other hand, Hitler's potential to offer more gains of territory in the East and South, at the expense of Romania and Yugoslavia, put any Hungarian government in a difficult position to resist German pressure.

The marked tendency to provide a fairly idealised description of Hungarian home politics was revealed in the second section of the memorandum where Macartney emphasized not only Teleki's and Horthy's anti-German leanings, but—owing to the German–Soviet Non-Aggression Pact and the attack on Poland—even that of the "Hungarian Nation." "If sympathy could alone count," he argued, "it is fairly certain that 85 percent of the country prefers the Western Powers." Another clearly unrealistic statement was that if Hitler were to attack Hungary, he would meet with national resistance led by the governor and the prime minister.[494]

The next section of the memorandum was focusing on the Hungarian revisionist claims. As in Macartney's opinion the first Vienna Arbitration restored all territories to Hungary on the ethnic basis, moreover, not only Burgenland but also the Bácska-Banat question seemed rather inopportune, the only possible gains Budapest could hope for in 1940 could come at the expense of Romania. In his memorandum the author once again listed and assessed the six possible solutions for the Transylvanian question, already elaborated on in his 1937 *Hungary and Her Successors*,[495] and clearly pointed out that as a consequence of interwar repressive Romanian nationality policy, Budapest—quite logically—lost its faith in minority protection, and even the more moderate Hungarian poli-

---

493 Macartney, Report on Hungary, FRPS 1940 March. Macartney Papers MSS. Eng. c. 3287, Doc 2. (fols 3-125), 4-5, 12. See also PRO FO 371/24 429.

494 Under the 15 percent he meant the Germanophile general staff and the junior state officials. Macartney, Report on Hungary, 14-17.
In the spring of 1940, Macartney reported on his visit to Hungary in a letter to the Hungarian Quarterly, in which he gave an even more biased description of the Horthy regime: "I have known Hungary now for twenty years [...] I remember the rejoicing in the streets when His Serene Highness, the present Regent brought back to Hungary the institutions to which Hungary had so long been used to ...."). Macartney, Hungary in February 1940, *HQ*, Spring *1940*, 168.

495 The six schemes were as follows: status quo ante 1918, return of the Western strip to Hungary with or without autonomy, independent Transylvania, or the return of the Szekler inhabited territories with a narrow corridor, or with a corridor widened to the south. Ibid., 28-31.

ticians would no longer accept the return of the narrow western strip of land and Szekler-autonomy.[496] The debate over Transylvania's status thus intensified in 1940, but the British guarantee to Romania led the Hungarian government to be more restrained in propagating its revisionist claims.

### 2.19. From the Second Vienna Arbitration to the Tripartite Pact (1940)

But in the spring of 1940, few could have foreseen how short-lived the British guarantee would prove to be. In June, Romania was forced by the Soviet ultimatum to surrender Bessarabia, and in a sudden change of course, Bucharest, denouncing the British and French guarantees, placed itself under Berlin's protection. As Hitler was interested in the normalisation of Hungarian–Romanian relations, he called on the parties concerned to find a peaceful, negotiated solution to the border dispute as early as July 11. However, the discussions, which began in Turnu-Severin in mid-August, were soon interrupted, as the Hungarian demands included under all circumstances the territory inhabited by the Szeklers, while the Romanians were only thinking of ceding a narrow western strip of land.

Thus, on August 30, another German–Italian arbitration took place in Vienna, orchestrated once again by German foreign secretary Joachim von Ribbentrop and the Italian foreign minister Galeazzo Ciano, who recorded in his diary: "Ceremony of the signature at the Belvedere. The Hungarians can't contain their joy when they see the map. Then we hear a loud thud. It was [the Romanian foreign minister, Mihail] Manoilescu, who fainted on the table. Doctors, massage, camphorated oil. Finally, he comes to, but shows the shock very much."[497] As if it had been a reverse Trianon treaty, the Romanian government was in fact counting on a small-scale border adjustment and had hoped that the delegation would be able to expound its position in detail before the decision.

However, according to the plan drawn up by Teleki in early 1940, the arbitration returned 16,792 square miles of territory, i.e., Northern Transylvania, to Hungary.[498] In spite of the de-facto acknowledgement of the First Vienna Arbi-

---

[496] Macartney's document was minuted in the Foreign Office as "a very useful guide," though his observations on Romania's intolerant minority policy were based presumably on Hungarian sources, thus they "should be treated by caution." PRO FO 371/24 429 4663.
[497] Hugh Gibson (ed.), *The Ciano Diaries, 1939–1943: The Complete, Unabridged Diaries of Count Galeazzo Ciano, Italian Minister of Foreign Affairs, 1936–1943*, Simon Publications, 1945, 289.
[498] According to the Hungarian census of 1941, 51 percent of the 2.5 million people inhabiting the area was Hungarian and 42 percent Romanian. On the other hand, according to the 1930 Ro-

tration and the Foreign Office's tacit approval of the acquisition of Subcarpathia in March 1939, the restoration of Northern Transylvania to Hungary was severely criticized in London. In accordance with the Romanian term, "dictatul de la Viena," it was officially announced that the Arbitration detached "one of the most precious parts of the Rumanian Motherland," and the British Government "were unable [...] to accept the settlement, [...] since that was the result of dictation by the Axis Powers and had been imposed on Romania under duress."[499]

Further on, considering the new boundary as a transitory one, both Budapest and Bucharest took an all or-nothing stance regarding the fate of Transylvania. The Romanian administration saw the restoration of Northern Transylvania as its primary objective in terms of foreign policy, while the political leadership in Hungary wanted to complete the Transylvanian revision later. Therefore, no effort was made by either party to stabilize the situation in the fall of 1940 and to permanently mend the relations between the two nations. In their political and diplomatic battles to seize control of Transylvania, the Hungarian and Romanian governments employed the Northern Transylvanian Romanian minority and the Southern Transylvanian Hungarian minority, respectively, as "hostages" until 1944. Both minorities were depicted in official state propaganda as the "rear-guard" of the motherland, defending the country's interests behind enemy lines.[500] A sign of escalating tension was the fact that no fewer than 74 significant border incidents occurred in the three years following the Award, resulting in 25 fatalities (17 Romanians and 8 Hungarians), as well as 24 injuries (17 Romanians and 7 Hungarians).[501]

---

manian census a 49 percent Romanian majority opposed a 38 percent Hungarian minority. In: Romsics, *Hungary in the Twentieth Century*, Budapest, Corvina-Osiris, 1999, 201.
499 *Times*, June 6, 1940, 2.
500 János Kristóf Murádin, Minority Politics of Hungary and Romania between 1940 and 1944. The System of Reciprocity and Its Consequences, *Acta Univ. Sapientiae, European and Regional Studies*, 16 (2019), 59-74, 61 and 65.
501 Balázs Ablonczy, *A visszatért Erdély 1940-1944* [Transylvania regained, 1940-1944], Budapest, Jaffa, 2011, 206.
Serious anti-Romanian atrocities followed the advent of the Hungarian army in northern Transylvania, in part because the military authority in existence until November 26, 1940, was inherently unable to handle the nationality question in a more sensitive manner. One glaring example was when in Ördögkút-Treznea, Szilágy County, on September 9, 1940, the Hungarian soldiers were fired upon while marching into the village, after which nearly eighty Romanian villagers were shot and twenty-seven houses were set on fire. Further balanced analysis of the topic can be found in Béni L. Balogh, *Küzdelem Erdélyért - A magyar-román viszony és a kisebbségi kérdés 1940-1944 között* [Struggle for Transylvania-Hungarian-Romanian relations and the Minority Question between 1940-1944], Budapest, Akadémiai, 2013; and Ottmar Traşcă, *Relațiile româno-ungare și problema Transilvaniei, 1940-1944* (I) [Romanian-Hungarian relations and the Transylvanian Question, 1940-1944], Anuarul Institutului de Istorie, D. A. Xenopol, 2004.

The August 30 decision was followed by a landslide in Romanian politics: King Charles II resigned, and military dictatorship was introduced by Marshal Ion Antonescu, with his "heart and mind" occupied by the problem of Transylvania. "Never—never!—will our territory belong to anyone else besides our people or those born of our seed!"[502] he declared in one of his rousing speeches. It was even one of the main drives behind his decision to join the Nazi war effort against the Soviet Union and get so deeply involved in the East the following year. This Romanian contribution to the Nazi triumph was to urge the Reich to decide in Romania's favour regarding Transylvania."[503]

In Hungary, nothing was more indicative of the post Vienna Arbitration-euphoria than the internationally unprecedented drop in the suicide rate within a single year.[504] However, contrary to unanimous public opinion, many politicians feared that the German orientation and the revision might come at too high a price. Prime Minister Pál Teleki for example expressed his fears to a confidential circle of friends. "If Transylvania comes back, we have committed ourselves forever to the Germans, who will then demand the price. And that price will be to go to war with them, the country itself will be the price of revision.[505] Indeed, German participation in the second Vienna Arbitration came at a heavy price for both countries: Having abandoned the principle of non-alignment, on November 22 and 24, 1940, Hungary and Romania joined the German-Italian-Japanese Tripartite Pact, the members of which pledged to support each other politically, economically and militarily if attacked by any power that had not yet participated in the European war.

The fact that November 20, 1940, had actually become a point of reference in Britain was well illustrated by the report of the Hungarian minister in London, György Barcza, who saw two main lines emerging in the British perception of Hungary at the beginning of 1940. The "radicals" felt sympathy for Hungary as long as it did not offer itself to any belligerent party. But by joining the Tripartite Pact of its own free will, they argued, it had "gambled away all its rights to be treated differently from Britain's open adversaries in the event of an An-

---

Finally, An interesting parallel can be drawn with the concluding idea of Toynbee's 1922 book on the Greco-Turkish atrocities: "No nation will treat minorities well if it believes that they menace its vital interests." Toynbee 1922, 586.
502 Mihai Antonescu, *Warum wir kämpfen*, Bucharest, 1942, 40.
503 Ion Gheorghe, *Rumäniens Weg zu Satellitenstaat*, Heidelberg, Kurt Vorwinckel Verlag, 1952, 227.
504 The number dropped from 29.3 per 100,000 citizens in 1938, to 23.6 in 1939 and remained so until the end of World War II. Romsics, *Hungary in the Twentieth Century*, Budapest, Corvina-Osiris, 1999, 201.
505 Barcza 1994, I/446.

glo-American victory." The group of "moderates," on the other hand, appreciated Hungary's geopolitical position as well as the German pressure, and argued that it "cannot [...] be regarded as a completely hostile state." [506] In this grouping, Seton-Watson's place was clearly among the "radicals" least sympathetic to Hungary, while Macartney belonged at the opposite pole among the most accommodating "moderates."

Naturally, both experts reacted to the Arbitration within days of the decision being announced. Although belonging to two opposite camps, after quite a long time, they essentially stood behind His Majesty's government. The Arbitration was discussed by Macartney in a memorandum for the Foreign Office dated September 4, 1940, with the title "Attitude to Hungary and Roumania." The author argued that the dividing line was "economically and geographically bad," though it would be a grave mistake to nullify any regulation based on the sole fact that it was dictated by Hitler. Macartney reiterated his earlier, quite erroneous conviction that Hungary was Germanophile owing to the revision question only, as the overwhelming majority of the nation "hate and fear Germany." He recommended that the Foreign Office should remain uncommitted to either the Romanian or the Hungarian case, which would not force Budapest to become irrevocably committed to the Third Reich, and "circumstances might yet arise in which we might get more out of her than of Romania."[507]

For Seton-Watson, broadcasting served as the primary tool for propaganda throughout World War II.[508] Under the auspices of the BBC, the historian was involved in the creation of the first clandestine radio broadcasts that sought to create the impression that they were originating from enemy countries under German control. In 1940–41 he was instrumental in setting up secret "Freedom Radios," and the first target country was Romania after the abdication of King Charles and the rise to power of the fascist Ion Antonescu.[509] As we have seen, the trigger for the pro-German turn was the Romanian national tragedy of the

---

506 Ignác Romsics, A brit külpolitika és a "magyar kérdés." 1914-1946 [British foreign policy and the "Hungarian question"1914-1946], *Századok*, (130) 1996/2, 313.
507 Macartney, Attitude Towards Hungary and Romania, September 4, 1940. PRO FO 371/24 985/7406. As well as in his March memorandum, Macartney again overestimated the anti-German leanings of Hungarian public opinion. In accordance with Macartney, Philip Nichols also argued in favour of remaining uncommitted regarding the Second Vienna Arbitration, though he added that "the chances of our getting more out of Hungary than out of Romania are remote in the extreme [...]"). Ibid.
508 During 1940, Steed delivered the "Britain Speaks" Saturday evenings talks and received letters of thanks from all over the Commonwealth and USA. Steed Papers MS 74 116, Correspondence with the BBC 1928-1953.
509 Rychlík, Marzik, Bielik (eds.) 1995, Vol. I/ 51-52.

Vienna Arbitration, which had occurred a few days earlier and on which Seton-Watson himself had expressed his views in one of the first broadcasts, on September 3, 1940. In his speech, the ageing historian sought to reassure the Romanian public, stressing that the British viewed with "anger and disgust" the decision which was not only contrary to justice but also to common sense, and which, like the first Arbitration, should be seen as a unilateral dictate. The assignment of Northern Transylvania to Hungary was, he continued, part of the Nazi programme of "enslavement of Europe" and thus would fall "together with Hitler."[510]

Steed and Macartney were also involved in radio propaganda, but more on that in later chapters.

### 2.20. The Political Intelligence Department during World War II: Post-War Plans or Propaganda?

Besides the semi-official Foreign Research and Press Service led by Toynbee, in 1939 two other organisations were set up in Britain in order to spread energetic propaganda: located in Senate House at the University of London, the Ministry of Information was a central government department primarily responsible for domestic publicity and national propaganda. At the same time, with the main function to produce weekly intelligence summaries, the Political Intelligence Department (PID) was also re-established; a section within the Foreign Office, to which the FRPS was directly responsible as a semi-official advisory and information organisation. The newly launched PID was headed by Rex Leeper, Seton-Watson's and Toynbee's former colleague in the Intelligence Bureau during the last years of the First World War.

When the PID began to build up its own intelligence and propaganda staff, a few "distinguished" people were to render valuable national service by assisting the PID more directly.[511] As a result, in October 1940, the PID lured among others Seton-Watson from the FRPS. His primary responsibility was to write reports on the South-Eastern European region, which included Greece, Hungary, Romania, Yugoslavia and Turkey, with the majority of the FO's confidential documents at his disposal.

---

510 Seton-Watson, "Message to Rumania," 1940/9/3. Seton-Watson Papers, SEW14/1/2.
511 H.W. Hodson to Steed, September 19, 1939. Steed Papers MS 74132.

## 2.20. The Political Intelligence Department during World War II

The establishment of the PID resulted in a potentially harmful overlap together with the already visible demoralization of the FRPS staff.[512] All this was noticed by Alfred Zimmern, the former Oxford tutor, who reproached Toynbee for weak leadership: Chatham House had been unable to prepare the British public for World War II, he argued, "Still less to avert it." Zimmern suggested that the director might bear some of the blame for the British public's response to the reoccupation of the Rhineland and Munich.[513] Steed also joined the chorus of critics when confiding the following in a letter to the head of the Press and Censorship Bureau, Walter Monckton:

> What terrified me was the prospect of our being without any definite policy [...] for the treatment of Germany in case of our victory and Germany's collapse. [...] my definite impression is that the immediate practical value of work hitherto done by Chatham House-people is almost nil as a basis for policy and that the best of Chatham House experts are in a state of mind bordering on revolt."[514]

---

[512] In a letter written in the summer of 1940 to the head of the PID, Rex Leeper, his former colleague (Intelligence Bureau: 1917-18), Seton-Watson complained that as a member of the FRPS he had no access to important official documents and doubted whether he had been performing "any useful purpose" by remaining there." Seton-Watson to Rex Leeper, July 26, 1940. Seton-Watson Papers, SEW12/1/1. See also Keyserlingk, Arnold Toynbee's Foreign Research and Press Service, 1939-1943 and its Post-war Plans for South-east Europe, *Journal of Contemporary History*, London, Vol. 21, 1986, 539-558, 546; and Rychlík, Marzik, Bielik (eds.) 1995, Vol. I, 51.
Unlike the FRPS, in the PID the elderly historian had full access to the necessary official documents. During the war, the countries included in the PID for South-Eastern Europe were Hungary, Romania, Yugoslavia, Greece and Turkey. From July 1941, Seton-Watson also wrote the weekly reports on Czechoslovakia, with Beneš as the main source of information on Czechoslovakian affairs, whom the ageing historian visited at his Hertfordshire home three or four times a month. Initially Seton-Watson played a mediating role in the Czech–Slovak dispute between Milan Hodža, who represented the Slovak interests, and the Czechoslovakist Beneš, but his consistent pro-Czech stance soon forced him to break with Hodža, the former prime minister who had been one of his oldest and most important Slovak friends. Rychlík, Marzik, Bielik (eds.) 1995, I/579-586.

[513] Zimmern to Toynbee, Undated [1940?]. Toynbee Papers MS13967/85. Correspondence.

[514] Steed to Sir Walter Monckton, June 10, 1940. Steed Papers MS 74132.
There is no record of Toynbee's answer; however, in 1941 he was proud to share with his secretary, Veronica Boulter, that FRPS had "definitely turned the corner: Eden has been convinced we are some use." Besides weekly reviews of the foreign press, from then on, they were to produce a new series of short weekly papers on current topics. By the onset of 1942, FRPS was producing handbooks on the historical and political background of any problem area for ministers and officials as well as providing information on "special points desired." As a consequence, Toynbee himself was invited to attend meetings of the War Cabinet (Greenwood's Cabinet Committee) on war aims, thus gaining access to the formulation of questions his team was then required to answer. The weekly average of government enquiries skyrocketed; in the first quarter of 1942 it mounted up to 105 (as opposed to 11.5 a year before). Toynbee to Veronica Boulter, June 5, 1941. Toynbee Papers, MS 13967/71/2 Family correspondence 1939-1945; and Christopher Brewin, Arnold-Toynbee and Chatham House, in: Bosco-Navari 1994, 146-147.

## 2. From Versailles to Paris (1920–1947)

Unlike Seton-Watson, Macartney or Toynbee, Steed had never been employed by the FRPS, but he was invited to the Ministry of Information, which he was ready to assist on the understanding that whatever he wrote or said would be "in support of our primary war aim to beat the enemy, and of our secondary [...] war aim to create a new Europe, federal if possible, in the service of peace."[515] Similarly to his work at Crewe House during the First World War, devising a settlement after the war interested him "little,"[516] but he was rather inclined to work out a basis for propaganda, which the majority of FRPS, including Toynbee, was unwilling to do.

When in May–June 1940, Luxembourg, the Netherlands, Belgium as well as France were captured by Nazi Germany, Steed urged more than ever for effective action. Two days after the French capitulation, he wrote to the editor of the *Times* explaining that Hitler had used the "Versailles complex" in Germany and abroad to mask the truth that his designs were pan-German, which careful readers of *Mein Kampf* (like himself) had long known, but such readers were "few." Steed suggested that Britain should, "once and for all," get rid of this "complex" and "understand that we are faced with pan-Germanism in its crudest form, and lose no further time in taking the offensive against it with determined propaganda based upon sound and comprehensive policy."[517] Two days later he approached the prime minister, too, reminding him of the success of the Ministry of Enemy Propaganda in 1918 and arguing that there should be set up "a small council, committee or board" to coordinate propaganda policy in the light of information received from the Foreign Office, the War Office and Admiralty to the prime minister and war cabinet. "If we succeed in defeating the enemy," Great-Britain with the Dominions would become "'the hub of the universe' towards which the United States would tend to gravitate." He put this forward with no small pride and misjudgment of the international situation.[518] However, Churchill declined to see him, and Steed's idea of finding some competent man for the job was rebuffed, too. Interestingly, Toynbee had not been on his list as a possible head of the board, since he considered the Director excessively bureaucratic-minded.[519]

---

515 Steed to Hodson, Ministry of Information, September 21, 1939. Steed Papers MS 74132.
516 In a letter to the head of PID, Rex Leeper, Steed clarified that what he wanted was "a policy for war that may serve as a basis for all [British] propaganda, closely linked to political and military situation." Steed to R. Leeper, June 22, 1940. Steed Papers MS 74132.
517 Steed to the editor of the *Times*, June 24, 1940.
518 Steed to Churchill, June 26, 1940. Steed Papers MS 74132.
519 Steed to Gooch, October 14, 1954. Steed Papers MS 74134.

Despite not having been offered any part in Churchill's wartime intelligence apparatus, Steed was keen on finding allies for his plan to launch a wholesale anti-German propaganda campaign. His once powerful benefactor, Germanophobe and chief diplomatic adviser to His Majesty's government Robert Vansittart,[520] seemed to be just such an excellent candidate, so he gave him a copy of his book on Nazi propaganda, *Fifth Arm*. In this work, Steed identified World War II as "war of faiths,"[521] with the semi-religious Marxist Socialism and Nazism competing, and he urged the Allied occupation of Berlin as well as of large German cities as a condition of armistice. Further on, he also dismissed arguments about "indefensible or unjust" frontiers drawn in Versailles, and as a solution to interethnic problems he once again advised population exchange, especially between Germany and Poland, as Danzig should definitely return to Poland.[522]

Unlike Steed, Toynbee and many other members of the FRPS took the lead in British discussions on potential terms of peace. As early as 1939, the director established a Peace Aims division of the FRPS to influence official British policy with regard to the peace settlement after the war. By 1941 there was already a shift of focus from press surveys and historical studies to post-war planning with the principal aim of winning the peace rather than winning the war. In a memorandum titled "Second Thoughts on a Peace Settlement," written in October 1939, Toynbee stated that due to its central position in Europe, Germany could easily insulate the small nations lying to its east. Thanks to the Germans' penchant for "despotic and aggressive" rule, in a politically divided Europe not only the liberated Poles, Czechs and Slovaks, but all the other remaining small nations would once again be at the mercy of Germany, and France and Britain would be marginalised. Thus, winning the war was not enough, he argued, but it was crucial to organise Europe "politically on lines which would promise to rule out, permanently, the prospect of Germany being able to establish her domination over Europe at some future time." Toynbee believed that there were two ways to avoid German domination: the dismemberment of Germany with a Europe "parcelled out" to sovereign states or the creation of a European federation. Toynbee was rather sceptical about the first "solution," which he

---

520 Vansittart served as permanent undersecretary of state from 1930-1938. In line with Steed, in his *Black Record: Germans Past and Present* (1941) Vansittart depicted Nazism not as an aberration, but merely as the most recent example of Germany's history of aggression dating back to the Roman Empire. In *Lessons of My Life* (New York, A. Knopf, 1943) he advocated that "the international pestilence that emanates from Germany will have to die out, or rather to be stamped out, slowly." (74). See also, Liebich 2018, 299.
521 Steed 1940, 5.
522 Ibid., 154-156.

believed would be unjust as it would not allow the Germans the right to national unity, "which we French and British claim for ourselves." Federation, on the other hand, would in Toynbee's opinion not only allow German national unity but it would also counter-balance German might by calling into existence a permanent economic and military Anglo–French "act of union." Such federation could preserve the common Christian tradition, too, especially if Germany also joined the organisation.[523] The document was not only circulated among Chatham House members but Toynbee also sent it to the foreign secretary. The idea of a close Anglo–French co-operation grew into a memorandum titled "Act of Perpetual Association between Britain and France," co-authored by Zimmern and Toynbee, which proposed a common Anglo–French government and representative body leaving each state "in control of its own domestic social and economic life."[524]

Certainly, the FRPS experts were also keen to provide material regarding the future peace in East-Central Europe. In a paper on the "Processes of Political Integration" written in April 1941, Toynbee discussed the federation of Central and Eastern European states. He declared that "the old-fashioned conception of sovereignty [...] needs to be recast or even abandoned," as nation-states had been incapable of coping with either war or unemployment.[525] Half a year later, in a thirty-two-page-long FRPS report, the authors explained that the "enthusiastic application of Western ideas," that is, the idea of the nation-state, "torn from their Western context" had been the root of the region's tragedy—a striking resemblance to Toynbee's thesis in his *Western Question in Greece and Turkey* some twenty years prior. The largely history-focused report criticised the 1919 settlement together with the League of Nations, which had offered the regional economic co-operation no real encouragement. Moreover, it stated that prior to the First World War "a more practical alternative appeared to be the maintenance of the unities of Austria and Hungary," with national and cultural autonomy added, thus the best solution could be a Danubian federation with economic and diplomatic support by the West.[526]

---

523 Lionel Curtis Papers, Bodleian Library, Oxford, 100. Qtd. in Bosco, Chatham House and Federalism, in: Bosco-Navari 1994, 327-329.
524 Ibid., 343.
525 Toynbee, "Processes of Political Integration," PRO CAB 117/78. Qtd. in Brewin, 152.
526 Memo written by Mr Laffan, October 2, 1941, PRO FO 371/26538. In: Keyserlingk, 550-551. Interestingly, the text did not discuss a possible Soviet threat or its expansion to the west.

The German–Italian military successes in the autumn of 1940 set the stage for an attack on the Soviet Union, which also foreshadowed the Nazi invasion of Central and Eastern Europe. Therefore, in early 1941, the plan to set up a Bethlen-led Hungarian government-in-exile in London was mooted. The idea was greeted with moderate enthusiasm in the British capital, although it was also reported that the Hungarians were behaving considerably better than the Romanians, which on the other hand did not change the assessment of the Vienna Arbitration of August 1940 as a dictate in London. It was during the preparations for the establishment of the government-in-exile that in February 1941 Count István Bethlen delivered his inaugural speech at the Kisfaludy Society's General Assembly in Budapest, which proved to be his last public appearance. The talk was translated into English by British minister O'Malley and sent to the Foreign Office, hoping that it might give some impetus to the deadlocked cause of the Hungarian government-in-exile in London. On behalf of the British Foreign Office, Arnold Toynbee and Macartney provided the paper with marginal notes and hailed it as a courageous and important step.[527]

However, as we shall see, neither the plan of the government-in-exile nor Macartney's pro-Hungarian activity had any influence whatsoever on delaying Hungary's entry into the war on the Nazi side.

## 2.21. Macartney's BBC broadcasts (July 1940 to August 1943)

Although the British Broadcasting Corporation set up an Empire Service in English in 1932 and a British External Broadcasting Service in the wake of the Munich Crisis, in 1938, Nazi Germany was the first to recognise the importance of radio in delivering political messages and pioneered the use of the new technology. The impacts of Nazi propaganda both domestically and abroad were causing growing alarm in Britain. As a result, the radio became a major medium for the dissemination of both real and false information.[528]

By 1938, the BBC was broadcasting in thirty-nine languages. Although the Ministry of Information, created in 1939, was responsible for developing war propaganda, it respected the principles of impartiality and editorial freedom enshrined in the BBC's constitution. The Political Warfare Executive, set up in the

---

527 National Archives FO 371/2603, C4271, 5355/123/21. Romsics 1991, 283–285.
528 More on this in Edward Stourton, *Auntie's War: The BBC during the Second World War*, London, Doubleday, 2017.

summer of 1941, was responsible for ensuring that public radio programmes were in line with government policy.

The Hungarian broadcasts commenced on September 5, 1939, and the "founding fathers" were the historian Béla Iványi-Grünwald, actor György Tarján and the writer George Mikes. In January 1940, Elisabeth Barker from BBC overseas section sent a letter to Macartney in which she said that following Arnold Toynbee's assent—except for a brief period—the talks could be heard Sunday evenings once a week. From July 7, 1940 to August 15, 1943, he made 186 broadcasts in fluent Hungarian, though with a marked English accent, and each talk commenced with the memorable sentence "Itt Macartney Elemér beszél." (This is Aylmer Macartney speaking.).[529] His speeches primarily focused on three main topics: analyses of the world situation, descriptions of wartime Britain with special emphasis on the country's heroic struggle against Germany to counterbalance Nazi propaganda, and above all Hungarian politics. In the latter he tried to maintain a fine middle ground: while offering support to Horthy and Teleki, he did not lose a single occasion to criticise the growing tendency on the part of the Hungarian government to offer closer cooperation with Germany.

In his talks on the issue of the Second Vienna Arbitration, Macartney emphasised on the one hand that the British press and public opinion viewed the Hungarian revisionist claims with considerable understanding. On the other hand—and in accordance with the Foreign Office—he maintained the view that the territorial revision was dictated by Germany, incapable of satisfying either Hungary or Romania as "it was designed to oppress and exploit Southeastern Europe."[530] Indeed, the Arbitration was definitely not intended as a mere political gesture, since Hitler soon exacted his price for it.

Adhesion to the Tripartite Pact in November 1940 did not create such an unfavourable impression of Hungary in Britain as many observers would have expected. However, it was later frequently quoted as a political decision which terminated independent Hungarian foreign policy.[531] Macartney also found

---

529 As the gramophone records of the broadcasts were destroyed after the war, the researcher has to rely on the written records in the BBC's Written Archives Centre near Reading, most of which are in Hungarian, sometimes in English. It is highly probable that the corrected Hungarian versions constituted the actual broadcasts. Occasionally, criticism was levelled within the BBC against Macartney's "faulty" Hungarian and his "very miming-piming voice," which played a rather insignificant role in silencing him three years later.
530 Macartney, "Transylvanian Diktat," September 1, 1940. Hungarian Talks Scripts, BBC Written Archives Centre [further on BBC WAC], Caversham Park, Reading.
531 Bán 115, 1998

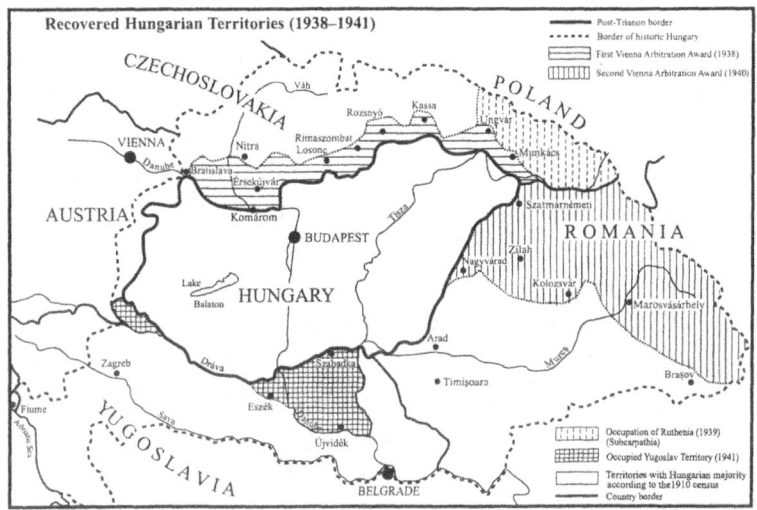

Territorial gains

the event deeply frustrating: "I would rather not have talked today [...]," so commenced his broadcast, "the Fuhrer is not the only person whose patience is exhaustible. I do not know how far, when the time comes, our Government will be willing to make no distinction at all between those Governments who have bravely defended their freedom, and those who have ostentatiously sacrificed it."532

The real friction between Hungary and Britain was precipitated not so much by Hungary's adhesion to the Tripartite Pact, but much more by it joining the German attack on Yugoslavia less than half a year later in exchange for a territory of 4,430.5 square miles and 39 percent—according to the Yugoslav census only 30 percent—of ethnic Hungarians.

In vain did Macartney in his talks praise the "Yugoslav nation" for having clearly demonstrated its commitment to independence, and he warned Budapest that the crisis was going to be a real test of Hungary's "honesty, bravery and loyalty."533 A few days later Prime Minister Teleki, unable either to consent to this policy or to act against it in defiance of the revisionist public opinion, committed suicide. Macartney was shocked by the death of an old friend, and in one of his talks devoted to his memory, he confessed:

---

532 Macartney, "Hungary Joins the Axis," November 21, 1940. BBC WAC.
533 Macartney, "There is a Limit," March 30, 1941. BBC WAC

I think that he believed that truth is universal, and that those who seek it sincerely will never be far apart. So he treated me; and I treasure among the highest praise I received that I was once described as "one of Teleki's young men," and it is the proof of his greatness that I, an Englishman, could feel this and not fear that I had lost my independence of judgement. [...] I learned much from him, argued not a little, I honoured him infinitely, and shall mourn him all my life.[534]

As a consequence of the Hungarian military action against Yugoslavia, Great Britain broke off diplomatic relations with Hungary as early as April 7, 1941, and further on Macartney adopted an openly critical view of the Budapest government. Again, fully in line with the Foreign Office, in his talk on April 13 titled "Loss of Honour" he characterised the Hungarian government's step as "a stab in the back of his friend," and in another speech entitled "Bluffing Bárdossy" he criticised the prime minister who took Hungary into war. On the other hand, he maintained the view that British propaganda to Hungary should not aim at overthrowing his—and later Kállay's—government or even reforming Hungary's social system, as he was convinced that Allies were getting from them "more [resistance to Germany] than we were likely to get from any alternative conceivable regime."[535]

Dazzled by the German military successes in the West, on June 26, 1941, under the pretext of the air raid on Kassa-Košice, Governor Horthy declared a state of war with the Soviet Union under pressure from the military leadership.[536] Soon—quite unexpectedly to most Anglophile Hungarians—Stalin be-

---

534 Macartney, "Count Teleki," April 3, 1941. BBC WAC.
535 Macartney, Aims of British Propaganda to Hungary. February 17, 1942. FO 371/30965; Macartney, British Policy Towards Hungary in the Second World War, Anglo-Hungarian Conference of Historians, 1977, Manuscript, 9. I owe thanks to László Péter for putting Macartney's above manuscript at my disposal.
It is not at all surprising that Seton-Watson even more vehemently condemned the Hungarian government's action in the South as a "crude perfidy" and portrayed Prime Minister Bárdossy as "entirely insincere and unreliable." Seton-Watson, Political Intelligence Department Weekly Summaries 1940/10-1942/8. [PID WS]. Reports dated April 16, 1941 and May 27, 1941. Seton-Watson Papers, SEW 12/2.
536 For more details on the causes and background of the air raid in Kassa-(Košice), which are still unclear, see: N.F. Dreisziger, New Twist to an Old Riddle: The Bombing of Kassa (Košice), June 26, 1941, *Journal of Modern History*, 1972/June, 232-242. Macartney from the outset rejected the official Hungarian position on the provocative Soviet bombing of Kassa, and in his lectures emphasised that the declaration of war was in direct contradiction to the Constitution. Contrary to the loud Hungarian propaganda on the "war against Bolshevism," he stressed that Britain had given its support to the Soviet defenders, and noted that "world public opinion considers Hungarians as accomplices of the Nazis and enemies of freedom." Macartney, "The Bolshevik Myth, July 6, 1941." BBC WAC.

gan to press Great Britain to declare war on Hungary. To placate him and as a clear demonstration of the united war effort, the declaration went out on December 6, and the fundamental principle applied to British–Hungarian relations became "so long as Hungary continues to fight against our allies, and to help the Axis, she can expect neither sympathy nor consideration."[537]

After the British declaration of war Macartney continued his broadcasts, though he took an even stiffer line focusing primarily on the unmasking of Hungarian and German war propaganda. He was instructed to "rub into" Hungarian public opinion "ad nauseam" that "the friends of our enemies were our enemies, and would be treated as such by us."[538] After Stalingrad and especially Voronezh, while indicating the losses and depicting the true nature of the catastrophe, he warned the Hungarian political elite about the futility of sacrificing further lives "as the opponents of Nazism prevail."[539]

The Hungarian audience of Macartney's broadcasts was limited to intellectuals, officials, and wealthy industrialists and merchants in Budapest and bigger cities who had access to the approximately 194,000 radios in Hungary. (In contrast, at around the same time, Britain had nearly nine million sets.)[540] It is likely, however, that Macartney's broadcasts were listened to not only by pro-British circles in Hungary but also by a significant part of the Hungarian political elite, often in disagreement. The implicit support of the broadcasts for the Bethlen–Teleki political line, as well as the speaker's anti-German tone and unshakable faith in the future victory of the Allies were all criticised by the Hungarian far right.[541] The Hungarian emigrants in London lead by Count Károlyi, on the other hand, vigorously attacked him from the left. Károlyi wholeheartedly echoed the widespread view that by allowing Macartney to speak, the BBC "fosters the propaganda of official pro-Nazi Hungary,"[542] and he took particular offence at the fact that Macartney did not let him speak in his talks. Macartney, however had the absolute conviction that the best way to discourage Hungarianresistance to Germany was to appeal to pro-British circles by the sole ap-

---

[537] Macartney 1977, 7.
[538] Ibid.
[539] Macartney, "Voronyezs Again," January 24, 1943. BBC WAC; and "Pack of Lies," February 18, 1942. BBC WAC.
[540] Bán 162, 1998.
[541] PRO FO 371/34 383. C.3345.
[542] Mihály Károlyi, letter to BBC Overseas Section, March 1, 1942. PRO FO 371/30 965. C5358/G.

plication of the stick,[543] especially if it was done by that "unfortunate national scape-goat"[544] Károlyi.

The Czech emigrants in London, particularly Hubert Ripka, state minister in the Czechoslovak government-in-exile, made an even greater effort to discredit Macartney's talks[545] and constantly put forward the view that the broadcasts, by systematically appealing to "a small ruling minority" in Hungary actually served to shift the responsibility for Hungary's participation in the war. Frank K. Roberts, head of Foreign Office Central European Department, on the other hand, reacted to the "ill-founded, rather impertinent" accusations, maintaining the view that "we can hardly base our approach to Hungarians upon the ideas of the Czechs, who come only to the Roumanians in unpopularity with the Hungarians."[546]

The British Czechophile officers, among others Deputy Under-Secretary of State for Foreign Affairs and Director-General of Political Warfare Executive Bruce Lockhart, however, expressed a rather divergent view. In a minute dated August 3, 1942, he argued that Hungary should be "our lowest priority" as nothing can be achieved "except at the expense of our smaller allies." As being "the symbol of British softness to Hungary" and "a reminder of the era of the late Rothermere," he reasoned, Macartney should be silenced temporarily.[547] Though in his response Roberts opposed "the increasingly tough line" taken by Lockhart, the latter's point of view prevailed, and the broadcasts were indeed terminated for a few months.

---

543 Several Hungarian friends strengthened him in this belief. József Balogh, editor of the *Hungarian Quarterly*, argued in one of his letters dated January 24, 1941, that instead of abusing the Germans and the Germanophiles in Hungary it would be more effective "to state, imply or even hint that nothing will be taken away from Hungary, that she has nothing to fear from British victory." PRO FO 371/26 624 C4270. (Balogh's comment was understandable, though rather unrealistic, as the principle Great Britain followed early in the war was that no advance commitments should be made regarding frontiers. By 1943, however, not only Macartney but also the Foreign Office grew more and more impotent to oppose Russia's endeavours in the region.) Another Hungarian friend, Aladár Szegedy-Maszák, argued in line with Balogh when suggesting to Macartney that the talks "should not only scold and threaten, but praise and take into account the sensitivity of the [Hungarian] nation." (Aladár Szegedi-Maszák, *Az ember ősszel visszanéz..., Egy volt Magyar diplomata emlékirataiból* [One looks back in autumn..., from the memoirs of a former Hungarian diplomat], Budapest, 1996, Vol. I/295.) Macartney appeared to follow the above advice as "sensitive" issues, eg., landed interests, the Jewish question or communism were indeed omitted from the talks, and he did not criticise the Regent either. PRO FO 371/30964.
544 Macartney 1977, 9.
545 Hubert Ripka's letter dated July 1, 1942, to Philip Nichols, then minister to the Czechoslovak government in London. In line with Roberts, Philip Nichols also rejected Ripka's accusations as being based on arguments quoted out of context and the failure "to grasp Macartney's irony". PRO FO 371/30 965 C6701.
546 Frank K. Roberts to Bruce Lockhart, July 28, 1942, Ibid.
547 Bruce Lochardt's minute on August 3, 1942. Ibid.

In autumn 1942 Macartney was again allowed access to the microphone, though for a fairly short period, as the opponents intensified their activities. Pál Ignotus and Lajos Hatvani, employed by the Hungarian Section, together with the Czechoslovak exiles' campaign contributed to the growing suspicion concerning the usefulness of the broadcasts, which in July 1943 finally had to "cease forthwith."[548]

It is not impossible that Seton-Watson, who was known to have a strong aversion to his colleague and was well connected not only in Czech émigré circles, had a hand in silencing Macartney, however the extent of his influence was far below that of the First World War years. After his retirement in the autumn of 1942, the elderly historian became even more detached from British foreign policy makers: he returned to the Department of Eastern Europe at the University of London, and at Beneš's suggestion and with his financial backing, he began preparations for the establishment of an Oxford chair of Czechoslovak studies.[549] His commitment to the Czechoslovak cause was crowned by the hasty publication of his last major work, *A History of the Czechs and Slovaks*.[550]

Despite having lost one valuable public forum, Macartney, on the other hand, remained on the Foreign Office staff until the end of the war, hoping that as an expert on East-Central Europe, he could contribute to a more reasonable settlement.

## 2.22. Steed's BBC Broadcasts until Romania Changed Sides (August 25, 1944)

Unlike Macartney, Steed had been actively involved with radio propaganda from an earlier time and on a much bigger scale. Since early 1938 he had been commenting on world affairs in Empire and Overseas Services in the BBC, and

---

548 Macartney 1977, 8.
549 Rychlík, Marzik, Bielik (eds.) 1995, Vol. I/57.
550 Seton-Watson's 1943-book was dedicated to "the loyal and steadfast Czech people" and to Masaryk, the mythical figure who created the young Czechoslovak state. The XIV. Chapter on pre-1918 history consistently presented the Highlands as Slovakia, put the number of Slovaks in the dualism era at three million, and conflated Deák's and Eötvös's views on nationalism with those of Kálmán Tisza, which did little service to historiography. The whole endeavour was crowned by the argument that the former borders of the Turkish occupation and the Kingdom of Hungary "bear sufficient resemblance" to the later Trianon settlement as evidence of the geographical unity of the territory; clearly a step further away from an unbiased historical analysis. The book was thus more akin to a propaganda piece written at the height of a bitter military conflict - like his *German, Slav and Magyar* in 1916 - written in haste, in fact as „a timely warning," to promote the cause of a post-war settlement. Seton-Watson, *A History of the Czechs and Slovaks*. London, 1943, 275 and 5.

three months after the outbreak of World War II he was allowed to talk once a week—with only two minor interruptions—to the British Commonwealth and Empire on "World Affairs," and thus to build up an almost personal relationship with a great many listeners in Africa, India, in both Americas, Australia and New Zealand. During the Blitz in 1940–41 it was often not easy or safe to get to Broadcasting House; Steed had to grope through dark streets, but fortunately, he did not suffer any injuries. However, the BBC house was hit by bombs, which was followed by the staff's migration to underground dungeons, and Steed was awed by the courage and the high spirits of the hard-working BBC staff members who "shepherded and watched over" him.[551]

Steed's broadcasts' potential audience included not only influential and well-informed opinion-makers, but also many listeners whose distance from Europe prevented them from understanding the quality and the extent of "German falsehoods." "My victim was German propaganda," declared Steed and—much to his satisfaction—he was soon classed with Churchill and Foreign Secretary Anthony Eden by Dr. Goebbels, earning the following epithets: "one of the worst British warmongers," "a poisoner of the public mind about Germany," "a miserable hireling bribed and bought," or the more neutral "old fox of British journalism."[552]

After the German attack on the Soviet Union in June 1941, as we have seen, Romania alongside Hungary were quick to join the Nazi war effort, therefore BBC introduced the Romanian Service, and soon Steed found himself talking to Romanians, or at least about Romania, alternately in English and French.[553] In the first broadcast he greeted his listeners expressing great personal grief, as "her sons were fighting and dying on the wrong side for the wrong cause."[554] Further on, Steed was eager to comment on every significant event; upon Romania's signing the Anticomintern pact, Steed explained that Romania gave up territory at Hitler's bidding, which he identified as an "act of weakness." He warned that British patience and tolerance were exhausted, and British a declaration of war might follow, which would mean for Romania "irrevocable con-

---

551 Steed, "Impressions of an Empire Broadcaster," BBC Yearbook, December 19, 1944. Steed Papers MS 74 181.
552 Ibid.
553 It is all the more interesting as he had turned away from Romania in July 1937 after having met "His Erratic Majesty" King Carol II in London, who informed him about his plans for establishing a royal dictatorship in Romania. Steed stopped lecturing right after the experience: "of late I give Roumania as wide a berth as possible and stick to Central-Europe." Steed to Mr S.T. Shovelton, May 3, 1938. Steed Papers, MS 74131.
554 Steed, BBC Roumanian Service. Untitled. November 11, 1941. Steed Papers MS 74 178.

demnation"— unless it should arouse the people at the twelfth hour to take their fate into their hands.[555]

The subsequent broadcasts had a clear structure: Steed often addressed his Romanian listeners on the occasion of a sorrowful anniversary, e.g., that of entering the war, which was followed by an episode from the glorious past, e.g., the creation of Great-Romania, in order to establish the needed tension and contrast. Further on Steed enumerated some of the great Romanians he had known, King Carol I, King Ferdinand and Queen Marie, Nicolae Iorga, Titulescu, Ion and Vintilla Brătianu, Iuliu Maniu and other Transylvanian leaders who had honoured him with their friendship, as against "the faithless and unworthy bearers of Roumanian name," primarily Antonescu, a once "brilliant soldier and friend"[556] who "thought it safer and more profitable to join hands with the despoilers of Czechoslovakia, Poland, Greece and Yugoslavia and even to join the Magyars in fighting Hitler's battles than to stand with Romania's true friends."[557] The talks usually ended with the speaker's prophecy about the inevitable German defeat, his "earnest counsel" that the Romanians should take the "last opportunity to earn their own freedom,"[558] as well as the hope he vested in "Roumanian valour."[559]

On May 5, Steed greeted his listeners on the occasion of the National Day, which he believed was degraded to a "celebration of Servitude" and then continued, "If I am not among the friends of Roumania who think that the frontiers of Transylvania were perfectly drawn after last great war, I remember it was not the fault of Titulescu that a permanent and amicable settlement with the Magyars could not be reached." Steed once again came up with the idea that Titulescu offered Count Bethlen equitable territorial adjustments on condition that they should form the basis of a final Hungaro–Romanian agreement, which adjustments were rejected due to the Magyars' pursuit of the restitution of pre-1918 borders. [560]

From July 1943 Steed spoke alternately in French, hoping to reach even more people. His broadcasts followed the lines highlighted above but became even more tendentious and simplistic and largely focusing on "Romania's choice" to quit the German war effort. Every Allied victory, e.g., the beginning of the lib-

---

555 BBC Roumanian Service, Untitled. November 28, 1941. Steed Papers MS 74 178.
556 Antonescu was military attaché in London and Paris from 1922-1926. BBC Roumanian Service, Untitled. July 1, 1941. Steed Papers MS 74 178.
557 BBC Roumanian Service, Untitled, August 25, 1942. Steed Papers MS 74 178.
558 BBC Roumanian Service, Untitled, April 13, 1943. Steed Papers MS 74 178.
559 BBC Roumanian Service, Untitled, March 24, 1943. Steed Papers MS 74 178.
560 BBC Roumanian Service, "The National Day," May 5, 1943. Steed Papers MS 74 178.

## 2. From Versailles to Paris (1920–1947)

eration of Italy or the French resistance, offered ample occasion to warn the Romanian people to use their wits and face up to Nazism: "if they help allies break the German grip on their country," thus sounded Steed's encouragement, "they may come through tribulation without deadly loss."[561]

In January 1944 in the preface of a short book titled *Why Rumania Failed?* he drew a sharp contrast between King Carol I, "foremost among makers of modern Rumania," and Carol II, "the degenerate great-nephew versus an illustrious uncle" who introduced "unbridled personal rule."[562]

The broadcast right after the Nazi occupation of Hungary in March 1944 was primarily devoted to Hungary. After listing at length his Hungarian linguistic, historical and cultural background, Steed hoped to sound more professional and credible: with a fervour that belies post-World War II Stalinist Hungarian historiography he set out to prove that Horthy was nothing more than Hitler's "faithful friend and ally," thus "no tears need to be shed" over him, his prime minister Kállay, or "any of the clique," i.e., the real originators of the system "which took the name of Fascism in Italy and of Nazism in Germany," and he likened the Hungarian political leadership to "the jackals of the Nazi beast of prey since first went ravening in Europe." Logically, Steed was extremely critical of post-1920 revisionist policy, too. Austria-Hungary "blew up," and was not "wilfully and wickedly dismembered," and what Horthy and fellows wanted to restore was the oppressive power of a minority of Magyars in Hungary over a majority of non-Magyars—thus sounded his post-Trianon mantra. Towards the end of his talk, he addressed his Romanian listeners, again arguing that after the occupation of Hungary, the precious oil fields round Ploiești would be the next target for Hitler, the "desperado" who would "try to do as much damage as he can before he goes under."[563]

As the Soviet army approached Romania, Steed's broadcasts became increasingly assertive, even threatening. He issued several warnings to the Romanians that if they "obstruct and delay Allied victory over Hitler's Germany by continuing to resist Russian armies nothing will save them from being treated as a conquered enemy [...] if they cease to oppose Russian sources, or, still better, join them in driving the Germans from Roumania they will spare their country and themselves a hard and evil fate."[564]

---

561 BBC Roumanian Service, Untitled, January 19, 1944. Steed Papers MS 74 178.
562 Pavel Pavel, *Why Rumania Failed?* London, Alliance Press, 1944. Steed's Preface, 10, 7.
563 BBC Roumanian Service, Untitled. March 24, 1944. Steed Papers MS 74 180.
564 BBC Roumanian Service, "Counsel to Roumania," April 4, 1944. Steed Papers MS 74 180.

## 2.22. Steed's BBC Broadcasts until Romania Changed Sides

On August 25, 1944, Romania finally overthrew the Antonescu dictatorship and not only made peace with the Allies but actively joined the Allied war effort. All this was welcomed by Steed, who considered the events in part a personal victory: "I know Roumania, her people and most of her leading men fairly well; and when the Antonescu Government issued a booklet three months ago to answer my warnings, I guessed that some of them must have gone home."565

After the Romanian changeover, the advancing Red Army approached the Hungarian capital by mid-December. Steed took special interest in the military operations there, and in the radio broadcast on December 15 he recalled some figures from Hungarian history with uncharacteristic nostalgia—like a snapshot before its destruction: Empress Elizabeth of Austria, also Queen of Hungary in her favourite castle of Gödöllő (east of Budapest), the emperor's only son, Archduke Rudolph, "the gifted heir to the throne of Austria and to the Sacred Hungarian Crown," both with "real affection for Hungarians," and Franz Joseph, the emperor lacking in "vision or constructive wisdom." "If Budapest falls to the Russians," Steed continued, it will serve as a strange sequel to the events of 1849, when "the quixotic action of the Russian Tsar, Nicholas I," saved Franz Joseph.566

Within a month after Romania changed sides, Steed had turned away from the lofty principle of national self-determination he had fought so hard to lead to triumph in 1918. He claimed that

> liberated peoples of Europe [...] will not tolerate in their midst the German minority who in Poland, Czechoslovakia, Roumania, and Yugoslavia became centres of disloyal Nazism and pan-Germanism. Regarding the inclusion of large German minorities within future frontiers of non-German state, there are arguments for and against. All in all, as self-determination proved to be an abstract principle offering no solution, "it may therefore be well to give phrases like [it] a well-earned rest except nations which have suffered from German application of it may be recognized to have a prior claim to whatever benefits they confer.567

---

565 BBC Roumanian Service, Untitled, August 25, 1944. Steed Papers MS 74 180.
566 BBC World Affairs, December 15, 1944. Steed Papers MS 74181.
567 Steed, "Frontiers of Peace," *Times*, September 20, 1944.

## 2.23. The Foreign Office Research Department, Seton-Watson and Steed on the Future of East-Central Europe

Before the Hungarian capital was completely devastated, the British Foreign Office had not yet given up on making peace plans to bring a more lasting settlement to East-Central Europe, plans that were more than the one that followed the First World War. Its experts produced a number of fact-finding studies on the future of the eleven tension zones of the world, one of the most significant of which was the all-encompassing document "Confederations of Eastern Europe" compiled in August 1942.[568] A result of in-depth research to which practically all East-Central European experts of the Foreign Office contributed, the document stated the case for two confederations in the region, a northern and a southern one. The former would comprise Czechoslovakia, Hungary, Poland and possibly Austria, the latter the Balkan States (Greece, Yugoslavia, Bulgaria and Romania). Apart from membership, form and structure and in order to minimize conflicts between the states, the experts had to discuss territorial revision, exchange of population or minority issues in strict compliance with the ethnic principle. In relation to Hungary this would have meant the retention of the northern frontier—with the sole exception of Košice (Kassa) and Nitra (Nyitra)—and a revision of the southern one, together with the exchange of populations. Regarding Subcarpathia, experts were vacillating between the Czechoslovak, namely the status quo ante, and the Hungarian versions, the latter strongly advocated by Macartney. For Transylvania, one of the "Gordian knots" of the region, the document advocated an independent state as the ideal solution, but owing to the intransigence on both sides, it added that frontier rectifications in Partium, together with autonomy for the Szeklers appeared to be more realistic.[569]

By 1943 the centralization of government information and intelligence work within a single department came to be required, and in April, the professional staff of 177 rose in status after the merger of the FRPS, at that time already a "minor backwater," with the Political Intelligence Department (PID) of the Foreign Office, which meant unrestricted access to all documents and in-

---

[568] Since the outbreak of the war Toynbee had been convinced that control over "the belt of small and weak countries btw Germany and Russia" was the key to "predominance in Europe." Toynbee to Gerard Bailey, National Peace Council, April 2, 1940. Toynbee Papers BL Oxford MS13967/63/2

[569] Foreign Research and Press Service paper on the Confederations in Eastern Europe, PRO FO 371/31 500. Although Macartney's signature did not appear on the final version, it is almost certain that he, as one of the main experts on Central and Eastern Europe, was also involved in drafting the memorandum. Lojkó 1999, 45–46.

## 2.23. The Foreign Office Research Department

formation coming into the Foreign Office. Toynbee influenced the terms and conditions of the merger; the new body was called Foreign Office Research Department (FORD), and its officers were required to look after individual countries instead of entire regions. However, in contrast to what he had done during the First World War, Toynbee did not commit to concentrating on any one region. He edited others' reports instead, negotiated with high-ranking officials—including the foreign secretary—and took care of administrative duties. Although he was extremely busy, he enjoyed the work and thought it was vital because it directly affected the possibility of a just and long-lasting peace.[570] In May 1943 the Foreign Office even sped up policy: "There was general agreement that we should aim at a Central European or Danubian Group centred around Vienna [...] it might prove important that this large grouping should be established soon after the war ended, before there had been time for opinion to harden on other lines."[571]

By the time of the merger, Seton-Watson was no longer a member of the PID, having retired in September 1942. The main reason for this was that his official employment prevented him from publishing his *Masaryk in England*, and the Foreign Office did not contribute to the launch of *New World* either, which was to succeed the once so influential *New Europe*. But that was not all. The ageing professor did not take kindly to Macartney's ability to publish his short book *Problems of the Danube Basin*,[572] which analysed the past and pondered the future

---

[570] Simultaneously with the transfer of FRPS to become part of the Foreign Office, personal troubles hit Toynbee when his wife abandoned him. Toynbee was devastated: "Until three years run out, no door shut on Rosalind," he vowed. "My present civil Marriage with Rosalind is legally right in my eyes but not in hers, [...] I would remedy it legally," he promised, but she was unrelenting. As a result, he reluctantly filed a lawsuit on the grounds of desertion, and on May 27, 1944, the court awarded him a divorce. Importantly for Toynbee, however, cordial relations between him and his much-respected ex father-in-law survived up until Gilbert Murray's death. Toynbee to Father Columba, July 14, 1944, 13967/79/1 Correspondence.

[571] PRO, CAB 65/34, WM 86(43), 92–93, based on WP (43), 218 of 25 May 1943. Quoted in Keyserlingk, 558.

[572] The first seven chapters of Macartney's book provide a concise, to-the-point overview of the history of the Danube Basin from the Early Middle Ages to the outbreak of war. The seventh chapter deals in detail with the excesses and one-sidedness of the Versailles settlement, but offers little that is new after his previous works. The concluding chapters are all the more interesting. On the present, on East-Central Europe in 1938–41, the author stressed that the "new nationalism" which dominated the region was "exclusive and dissimilationist," making it almost impossible to establish any long-term economic and cultural cooperation, let alone any kind of political unity. Reflecting on the future, Macartney underlined in the final chapter that the independence and stability of the Danube Basin was "a vital interest of the whole world," and then identified Germany and the Soviet Union as "powerful and aggressive states" which rob the East European nations of their independence and "also threatens the safety of the world." In order to avoid subjugation, he argued, the transcendence of the nation-state would require defence-, economic- and even a degree of political cooperation among the countries concerned in some kind of Dan-

## 2. From Versailles to Paris (1920–1947)

of the region, without any difficulty in 1942. The Foreign Office explained this distinction by the fact that the staff of the Foreign Research and Press Service were not part of the Foreign Office staff and therefore could not be subject to the publication ban, and unlike the staff of the Intelligence and Analysis Department, they were not allowed to consult most official foreign documents.[573]

The confederal reorganisation of East-Central Europe was also essentially supported by Seton-Watson. He outlined his vision in a paper titled "The Zone of Small Nations in Eastern Europe," delivered at the RRIIA (Chatham House) in June 1943. In his view, the southern confederation, which he labelled the "Balkan Union," would have included Romania, Albania, Greece, decentralised Yugoslavia and finally Bulgaria, which, in his opinion held the key. Thereafter the speaker listed Poland, Czechoslovakia, Austria and Hungary as members of the northern confederacy, the latter being by far the most problematic: As "the last survival of feudalism in Central Europe, [it] is an obstacle to the formation of either a northern or a southern confederacy." Seton-Watson was convinced that the real bond between the eight states lay in the fact that they were predominantly peasant societies, and once Hungary was transformed from a feudal to a popular democratic basis, the main obstacle to cooperation in the whole region would be removed.[574]

What Seton-Watson exactly meant by the "democratic transformation" of Hungary was revealed in an earlier report to the PID, in which, to prevent a post-war communist takeover, he proposed "an extremely radical, but not Red-Revolutionary" land reform involving a reorganisation of property relations and a complete change of political elites. Such a reform, Seton-Watson argued, would automatically marginalize border disputes by bringing social and economic issues to the fore.[575]

Like Seton-Watson, Steed was an outsider in the formal planning of the future of Central- and Eastern Europe. In September 1943, in a letter to V.A. Voigt, he did, however, offer his support, albeit less enthusiastically, for the organisation of the region's states into confederations. When for example Poles approached him with the "madcap" concept that King George VI's younger brother should rule over a confederation uniting Poland, Lithuania, Slovakia and Hungary, he

---

ube confederation, which he did not, however, specify at the time. In: Macartney, *Problems of the Danube Basin*, Cambridge, 1942, 128,149.
[573] Hugh and Christopher Seton-Watson 1984, 430; and "Ban on Publication of Books on Political Subjects by Members of PID or FO." PRO FO 30 840 b/2358.
[574] Rychlík, Marzik, Bielik (eds.) 1995, Vol. I/ 629-630.
[575] Seton-Watson, Outline of Russian Policy, March 27, 1942. Seton-Watson Papers, SEW 12/4/3. See also his article in the *Manchester Guardian* (MG), December 1943. Seton-Watson Papers, SEW 19/4/3.

categorically rejected the plan since it was conceived "in an anti-Russian and in a Roman clerical spirit."[576]

In the same month as Steed's letter was dated, Macartney, already as member of FORD, compiled a lengthy study on the feasibility of the British plan, that is the confederative settlement in Eastern Europe. In his likely most significant wartime memorandum, "The Settlement of Eastern Europe," he envisaged four possible futures for that region. The first was permanent German or Russian control, in which case "Britain would *ex hypothesi* be reduced to the role of a spectator," or second, an independent Eastern Europe based on a comprehensive principle. The third, namely an independent Eastern Europe based on a selective principle was, in his opinion, a solution that bore strong resemblance to the Versailles Settlement,[577] therefore he warned: "If the selective solution is adopted, the losers will turn for help sooner or later to Germany or Russia, and sooner and later, Germany or Russia will be willing to help them. There will be result at best a division of spheres between them; otherwise, a fresh war into which we shall once again be drawn."

Macartney was convinced that the fourth version, namely a comprehensive solution, would be the most satisfactory for the region and the world. Macartney realistically assessed that the belief in the cooperation of the inhabitants of the region was illusory as long as the confederal reorganisation was not preceded by the "political satisfaction" of the peoples concerned: the establishment of political borders on the basis of the principle of equal treatment, strictly following the ethnic principle, leaving as few minorities as possible on the "wrong" side of the border. "Those who say," he argued with no little irony, implicitly taking aim at Seton-Watson, Steed and Czech émigré politicians, "that political appeasement will follow on the course of time, on the basis of a thoroughly unequal sellective [sic] solution, are either fools (the usual case when they are Britons) or hypocrites (if Central Europeans)."[578]

The question of the future Hungarian frontiers and that of the Hungarian minorities were not elaborated on in Macartney's above memorandum, though they were in many other documents he produced during the war. Concerning the 1920 Austrian–Hungarian frontier he seemed not to expect any changes;[579]

---

576 Steed to V.A. Voigt, September 16, 1943. Steed Papers, MS 74 148.
577 Here Macartney criticised the Versailles Settlement in a similar vein to Toynbee: "Many observers believe that no single factor has been so largely responsible for the present chaos in Eastern Europe as the attempt to foist upon it the West-European ideal of nation-state."
578 Macartney, The Settlement of Eastern Europe. PRO FO 371/34400.
579 "There seems in general little argument for altering in any respect the 1919-21-frontier"- claimed Macartney in "The Frontier between Austria and Hungary," September 27, 1944. MMs. Eng. c. 3286. Doc 11. (fols 84-87)

regarding the Hungarian-Slovak border, however, he advocated firm adherence to the ethnic principle. In order to counter allegations spread by several Czech authors and their British sympathisers he stated that Great Britain and France "took no part" in the negotiations preceding the First Vienna Arbitration, which rested on an ethnic line "practically unchanged" for centuries.[580] Macartney came to very similar conclusions in a later memorandum written already as FORD's expert on the Hungarian-Slovak frontier. After having collated the data of the Hungarian and Slovak censuses, he regarded the Vienna Arbitration as "following the ethnic line fairly closely, with small, but distinct bias in favour of Hungary." Therefore, apart from the Kassa-Košice region, he fiercely opposed any correction of that line, which in his opinion would inevitably increase the number of minorities on the wrong side.[581]

Regarding Hungary's southern frontier, Macartney suggested rectification in three possible zones. Owing to the ethnic principle and the narrow-minded nationality policy of the Yugoslav state, he maintained the view that the territory east of Lendva-Lendava, the Baranya-Drave triangle and the region in the Bácska-Voivodina lying north of Zombor should belong to Hungary, which amounted approximately to half of the territory reoccupied by Budapest in April 1941.[582]

For all experts of the region, Macartney not excepted, the future of Transylvania posed a much more complicated problem than the northern and southern frontiers of Hungary. As in his earlier writings on the subject, Macartney refused to take into account arguments based on historical precedence, as he regarded them as anachronistic as well as inconclusive, while once again characterising Romanian rule between the wars as "political, economic and social retrogression." In the case of Transylvania, but practically in all frontier issues, Macartney's first priority since the 1930s had been to diminish the number of ethnic minorities. On the other hand, he was equally aware of the economic absurdity of the Second Vienna Arbitration, which seemed most closely to comply with the above requirement. Therefore, in his memoranda–one of the most significant of which was his "Situation of Hungarians in Transylvania Since Roumania Changed Sides"—he argued strongly in favour of an independent Transylvania in the same confederation with Hungary and Romania; a concept that

---

580 Macartney, The Hungarian-Slovak Frontier, February 6, 1942. Macartney Papers MSS. Eng. c. 3287, Doc 7, (fols 176–179).
581 Macartney, The Hungarian-Slovak Frontier. Macartney Papers MSS. Eng. c. 3287, Doc 13, (fols 253–254.)
582 Macartney, The Magyar Minority in Yugoslavia," October 15, 1944. Macartney Papers MSS. Eng. c. 3288, Doc 46, (fols 308–312).

he had found "hardly feasible" back in 1937. Six years later, however, his ideal would have been a separate state comprising six autonomous cantons on a nationality basis, and Brasov-Brassó as a free city.[583] In any case, Macartney wanted to leave the narrow western strip (Partium) with Hungary, in accordance with the FORD expert staff (against, of course, Seton-Watson).

To gain Foreign Office backing for his independent Transylvania scheme, Macartney tried referencing Transylvania as the island of peace during the Western religious wars in the seventeenth century,[584] which turned out to be not quite ineffective: among others, the new head of the Foreign Office Central Department, Frank K. Roberts, also came to support the idea. In a record prepared for Anthony Eden before the Moscow meeting of foreign secretaries in September 1943, he presented the concept as the only possibly permanent solution for the long-standing Romanian–Hungarian feud.[585]

To counter Macartney's reports, Seton-Watson had already drafted a document for the Foreign Office in March 1942 on the future of Transylvania, "the most tangled of all that many knots"[586] in East-Central Europe. In December that same year, he further refined his ideas in a lecture at Sommerville College, Oxford, the material of which was published in 1943 in a pamphlet titled "Transylvania: A Key Problem."

In his short work, the ageing historian severely denounced pre-1918 Hungarian nationalism as "one of the causes of the Great War" (*sic*) as well as Hungarian revisionism after Versailles. However, he was also fiercely critical of the "rabid chauvinism" of the leaders of Great Romania: he was not sparing, first and foremost, of Brătianu, but also of his old acquaintance Octavian Goga, who had misled Maniu, not to mention "crooked and perverse" Marshall Antonescu.[587]

But more importantly, the author analysed all possibilities concerning the future of Transylvania: he depicted drawing a frontier on purely ethnographic lines as impossible and rejected Transylvanian independence as well. Instead,

---

583 Macartney, The Situation of Hungarians in Transylvania Since Roumania Changed Sides on 23 August 1944. Annex 5: Scheme for Transylvania as an Independent State. MMs. Eng. c. 3301. Doc 1, (fols 331–354).
584 Ambrus Miskolczy, Barát vagy ellenség? Scotus Viator és Macartney Elemér. Két vélemény Erdélyről, Magyarországról és Romániáról [Friend or Foe? Scotus Viator and Elemér Macartney. Two Opinions on Transylvania, Hungary and Romania], *Holmi*, October 1994, 1506.
585 Qtd. in Gyula Juhász, *Magyar-brit titkos tárgyalások 1943-ban* [Hungarian-British secret talks in 1943], Budapest, 1978, 247.
586 Pavel Pavel, *Transylvania and Danubian Peace*, London, 1943, 10. (With an Introduction by R. W. Seton-Watson.)
587 Seton-Watson 1943, 4, 8, 10 and 14.

## 2. From Versailles to Paris (1920–1947)

for the first time in his career, he advocated the exchange of populations as the only real solution that would "relieve Roumania's worst fears."[588]

In his 1943 book, Seton-Watson argued strongly for the restoration of the *status quo ante bellum*, i.e., against any adjustment in Hungary's favour, this time not on the basis of an "insatiable" Hungary, but on the basis of British interests. The *cordon sanitaire* that had been separating Germany from Russia, he argued, had come under German control. Therefore, it was vital for Britain to support these "Small Nations"; among them Romania, which had been forced into war by Germany to get its lost territories back. Thus, by nullifying the Second Vienna Arbtration in public, moreover, by "showing understanding" to Romania, the British government could undermine the fascist Romanian government. On the other hand, encouraging Hungary was, in the author's opinion, not desirable, since they hindered the reconstruction of the surrounding states, thereby "playing into hands of reaction in Europe."[589]

During 1943–1944, Seton-Watson's agenda of restoring Transylvania to Romania did not become official British policy: the Foreign Office flatly rejected any Hungarian revisionist claims against its allies, Yugoslavia and Czechoslovakia, whereas in the case of Romania it tended to accept a compromise. However, as the war proceeded, it gradually became evident that not only the Hungarian-Romanian frontier, but also the future of the whole of East-Central Europe depended on the fact of which power, after Germany and France, was going to prevail in the region.

As in November 1943 at the Conference of Teheran, the British and the Americans rejected the Balkans Debarkation Plan under Soviet pressure; they practically yielded to the Sovietization of the region. A year later, the infamous "percentage agreement" between Churchill and Stalin was in fact the British ac-

---

588 Ibid., 14. In contrast, in a report by the executive committee of the League of Union to the general council of the Union collated by Macartney et al, it was explicitly stated in 1942 that the transfer of populations "runs counter the spirit of tolerance and good neighbourliness for which League of Nations Union stands." Macartney et al, *The Minorities Problem*, June 19, 1942. Macartney LNU Miscellaneous Pamphlets Vol. 8. British Library 3685-3805.

589 Ibid., 19. Seton-Watson's last article on Hungarian history was published in July 1943 with the following, in a war situation unusually sober and rather nuanced conclusion: "The Magyars, unquestionably the torchbearers of constitutional liberty in all the Danubian countries, become at the same time advocates of racial uniformity and assimilation in its extreme form, and try to apply to the other races of the country, which still form a decided majority of the population, the very methods which they resent so intensely when applied by the Germans to themselves. This is the central tragedy of the year 1848, in which the Magyars might have assumed the leadership of south-eastern Europe, but showed themselves lacking in the necessary constructive statesmanship and breadth of outlook." Seton-Watson, The Era of Reform in Hungary, *The Slavonic and East European Review*, American Series, Vol. 2, No. 2 (November 1943), 145-166, 166.

## 2.23. The Foreign Office Research Department

knowledgement of Soviet dominance in Central and Eastern Europe; for example, 75 percent of Russian influence in Hungary "could easily be made to work out at 100-0," as Macartney aptly observed.[590] Thus, all British plans for confederations based on independence, equality and democracy were long relegated to pipe-dream status. This process was envisaged by many other specialists in the Foreign Office, one of whom, Denis Allen, had noted already in autumn 1943 regarding Macartney's "Settlement of Eastern Europe" that, "it is clear that any attempt on our part to impose a solution in face of Soviet opposition would be fruitless. The Soviet Government have made it pretty clear that they have no intention of agreeing to anything approximating to what Mr. Macartney describes as the 'comprehensive' settlement."[591]

Macartney's memorandum was thus written against the background of a world increasingly dominated by the growing influence of the Soviet Union. He, on the other hand, proceeded to write memoranda on the East-Central European- and especially the Hungarian situation, though with diminishing effect.[592] As both Hungary and Romania had been Hitler's allies, he still entertained some hope for an unprejudiced settlement, particularly in Transylvania. It can be asserted that his influence led to the use of the following formula in the terms of armistice given to Romania in September 1944: Romania would be given "Transylvania, or the greater part of it, subject to confirmation at the peace settlement."

Meanwhile, Macartney was busy with two Hungary-related projects. First, he played a significant part in the creation of the Handbook on Hungary (1944–1955), which was intended for the British military in the event of a British invasion. The original text had been complied by A.J.P Taylor, a young Oxford historian and friend of both exiles, Beneš and Mihály Károlyi. Taylor was employed by the Political Warfare Executive (PWE) as an expert on Central Europe. Macartney found his text so biased and personal that he believed it might

---

590 Macartney 1977, 11.
591 PRO FO 371/34 400. 10967.
    At the same time the bombardment of further Axis territory, including Hungary, was proposed in the Foreign Office, which Macartney vigorously opposed. Ránki György, Találkozásaim Macartney Elemérrel [My encounters with C.A. Macartney], Élet és Irodalom, 1978/ 27, 6.
592 Macartney wanted to be of use in other ways, too. For example, in February 1944 he wrote to the head of FO Central Department, Frank K. Roberts, contesting the usefulness of the Allied plan of bombing Budapest. He recommended that a new message should be sent to Hungary with the concrete steps the Kállay government was expected to take and a warning that failure to act would immediately entail the bombardment of the capital. However, Roberts was convinced that the only way to dispel the Soviet charge of undue British tenderness towards Hungary was to carry out acts of war, that is, air raids against Budapest. Juhász 1979, 276.

have results contrary to what had been intended. Having fully endorsed Macartney's view, the Foreign Office Central Department requested that Taylor rewrite the text, which—after its pro-Hungarian tone was somewhat modified by the PWE—went into print in March 1944. [593]

Second, in collaboration with the PID and the Warfare Executive Committee Macartney interrogated former Hungarian regent Miklós Horthy, then a POW in Luxembourg, during July 17-18, 1945. "I do not think that on any he told me a conscious lie," reported Macartney to his superiors. "This was partly because he does not feel that he has anything with which to reproach himself—quite the contrary; and his mind, unsharpened by any sense of guilt, is not subtle." [594]

In the meantime, after having occupied the whole of the region, the Soviets vigorously demanded the restoration of all 1920 Hungarian frontiers. Having learned this, Macartney proposed in 1946 that the Foreign Office should recommend an international conference consulting on the future of Transylvania. His proposal was rejected by the Foreign Office as was the idea of his intended visit to Budapest in early 1946, organised by the British Council. Moreover, Mr. Thwaites, while minuting the arrangements for the lecture tour, described Macartney rather unfairly as "strongly pro-Horthy" and also as "openly antisemite" who was regarded by all progressive Hungarians as "an enemy." Macartney reluctantly accepted the refusal and retorted with pride: "I can only cast aside modesty and say that I am at present such a popular figure in Hungary that the plain fact of my being there forms encouragement [...] to the pro-British element." Having realised the true intentions of his government to follow the second course of appeasement, this time in favour of the Soviet Union, he added, "It was precisely this which made the BBC shut off."[595]

Having recognized that, by the end of the war, not only the aggressive biological-racial notion of Pax Germanica had been crushed, but the Foreign Office was also squeezed out of the reorganisation of Central and Eastern Europe, Ma-

---

593 Taylor came to resent Macartney, the "right-wing historian," and, as his letter to his wife, Hungarian historian Éva Haraszti, reveals, he had destroyed his original text. Kathleen Burk, *Troublemaker: The Life and History of A.J.P. Taylor*, New Haven and London, Yale University Press, 2000, 180 and 441. Tibor Frank, *Britannia vonzásában* [Attracted by Britain], Budapest, 2018, 152; Attila Pók, *The Politics of Hatred in the Middle of Europe. Scapegoating in Twentieth Century Hungary. History and Historiography*, Savaria University Press, 2009, 53–54.

594 Macartney, Memorandum of an Interview with Admiral Horthy. MMs. Eng. c. 3287. Doc. 18. National Archives, War Office WO204/12489) "Egy angol professzor beszélgetései Horthy Miklóssal" [An English professor's conversations with Miklós Horthy], *Élet és Tudomány*, 1993/36-37. 1128-1130, and 1160-2.

595 PRO FO 371/ 59026. 9938.

cartney bitterly noted that his six years of expert activity, his 143 memoranda and 186 radio broadcasts on the Danube Basin, and especially on Hungary, had been completely fruitless. So, in May 1946, following Seton-Watson, he left the Foreign Office Research Department and returned to All Souls College, Oxford, to devote himself once more to academic work.

After the Allied victory, Seton-Watson watched developments in Central and Eastern Europe from a distance. He praised the Yugoslav government, particularly Marshall Tito, who, having been "inspired by real statesmanship," instituted decentralization.[596] Beneš's return to Prague notwithstanding, the aging historian continued to maintain a close relationship with him, while also moving to Oxford as the new chair of Czechoslovak studies, founded and financed by the Czechoslovak government. In his inaugural lecture at the University of Oxford in February 1946, he praised the president as follows:

> Attempts have sometimes been made to distinguish between Masaryk, the Father of his country, and Beneš, the supple opportunist: in reality there never was a closer alliance of heart and head, a more unqualified mutual trust and loyalty than that between the two Czechoslovak statesmen. They stand or fall together.[597]

Seton-Watson naturally welcomed the annulment of the first Vienna Arbitration and the restoration of the 1937 borders. In his interpretation, the Munich Agreement could only have come about because the Western democracies had sacrificed Czechoslovakia in order to avoid war. Following in his footsteps, most of his Czech and Slovak contemporaries, who looked back on their coexistence with a critical but also nostalgic eye, came to the conclusion that the pre-war governments had made a mistake in granting rights to the German and

---

[596] Seton-Watson, Caxton Hall Speech on the Fifth Anniversary of Yugoslavia's Entry into the War. Seton-Watson Papers, SEW 15/1/5.
[597] Seton-Watson, "Czechoslovakia in its European Setting." An Inaugural Lecture on February 6, 1946, Oxford, 1946.
Masaryk is still portrayed as a liberal, understanding and open-minded leader who even advised his son Jan to learn Hungarian because "Beneš is learning it too."; someone who demanded that "justice and humanity" become „the guiding principle for all official conduct" in his state, where "nationalism remains, but national resentment does not." (Masaryk, *Cesta demokracije*, II, Ústav T.G. Masaryka, 2007, 122 and 298.) At the same time, it is an interesting contradiction that Hájková, too, mentions that the president regarded Czechoslovakia as a nation-state with one Czechoslovak nation, and although himself an ethnic Slovak, he considered a separate Slovak ethnicity a fiction. Hájková, T. G. Masaryk and his Stances on Minority Issues after the Establsihment of Czechoslovakia, 61–74. In: Eiler-Hájková (eds.), 2009, 72–73 and 285.

Hungarian minorities. Indeed, it became a widespread belief that national minorities had ruined the republic.[598]

As Czech historian Zbyněk Zeman argues, the First World War created the Czechoslovak state and World War II offered Beneš a chance to make it a homogenous entity.[599] "In a national state there is no room for minority problems,"[600] argued the exiled president. In fact, out of the many laws bearing his name,[601] Decree no. 33 not only stripped 2.5 million Sudeten Germans and tens of thousands of Hungarians of their citizenship as well as of their lands after World War II, but also aimed "at all costs" to expel them. Using the 1923 population exchange between Greece and Turkey as a precedent, the following arguments were cited: the Sudeten Germans had ruined Czechoslovakia as a fifth column; it was in the Germans' best interests to leave, given Czech public animosity; and the departure was required to thwart future German territorial aspirations, too.[602] Interestingly, there is not a single mention of the Beneš decrees, let alone Nr. 33, in any of the British historian's papers.

Not knowing this, after long years of silence, Seton-Watson's old friend, Oszkár Jászi wrote to the Oxford historian asking him to use his influence to help the cause of disenfranchised Hungarians, claiming that "the new Czechoslovak policy against the Hungarian minority was one of the worst episodes of my life which has shaken my belief in the intelligence and morality of men [...] The road [the Czech leaders have] taken will lead to disaster and create an unbearable atmosphere in the whole Danube Basin.[603] Seton-Watson's bequest contains no trace of a response to this letter, but in his inaugural lecture at Oxford University, he stated that in his opinion, after six years of war atrocities, the Sudeten Germans' "plea for mercy is not very convincing."[604] Jászi's letter's last, hand-

---

598 László Szarka, Gergely Sallai, Önkép és kontextus Magyarország és a magyarság történelme a szlovák történetírásban a 20. század végén [Self-image and context: The history of Hungary and Hungarians in Slovak historiography at the end of the 20th century], *Regio*, 2000. 2. sz. 71–107.80.
599 Zeman 2009, 80.
600 Beneš, Postwar Czechoslovakia, *Foreign Affairs* 24, No. 3, 1946, 400.
601 The decrees had been drafted by the Czechoslovak government-in-exile between July 21, 1940, and October 27, 1945, and retroactively ratified by the Czechoslovak Interim National Assembly. On August 2, 1945, the day the Potsdam conference came to a close, Beneš signed decree 33/1945 SB depriving the majority of Czechoslovak Germans and Hungarians of Czechoslovak citizenship.
602 Glassheim 2000, 471–472. Moreover, after Stalin's seizure of Eastern Poland, expulsion as a solution was also legitimised as a compensation for the Polish, with German territory cleared of Germans. Bradley F. Abrams, Morality, Wisdom and Revision: The Czech Opposition of the 1970s and the Expulsion of the Sudeten Germans, *East European Politics and Societies*, 9, No. 2, 1995, 236.
603 Oszkár Jászi to Seton-Watson, November 9, 1945. Seton-Watson Papers, SEW 17/11/12. See also Rychlík, Marzik, Bielik (eds.) 1995, Vol. I/ 635–6.
604 Seton-Watson, "Czechoslovakia in its European Setting," an Inaugural Lecture. February 6, 1946. Oxford, 1946, 19.

written sentence reads: "[...] the situation in Czechoslovakia has become even worse." Meanwhile, in the summer of 1946, during his last trip abroad, Seton-Watson and his family spent two joyous weeks in beautiful, undamaged Prague hosted by the presidential couple.[605]

Seton-Watson's intimate relationship with the increasingly dominant and left-leaning Beneš stood in sharp contrast to his hostility to the strongman of Hungarian politics between the two world wars, the economic reconstructor, István Bethlen. The former prime minister had opposed unilateral German orientation, Jewish laws and his country's entry into the World War II. His anti-Habsburg restoration-, anti-Nazi and anti-Bolshevik stance, and the fact that he remained staunchly pro-British even at the height of Hitler's conquest of Europe, were not enough for Seton-Watson to revise his earlier scathing views.

In October 1946, István Bethlen died in a Moscow prison.

## 2.24. BBC Broadcasts Continued: Steed and the Second Appeasement
## The Paris Peace Conference 1946

From the late 1930s onwards, Steed, the man of strong anti-Nazi sentiments, who spoke with unconcealed frankness about his dislike of Hitler, calling him a "murderer," became increasingly tolerant and understanding of Stalin, the Soviet Union and its ideology. "The Russian Bolshevist threat to property," Steed wrote in December 1938, "suffice[s] to make ignorant and obstinate 'business' men like our bankers, millionaire newspaper proprietors and Chamberlains fear and hate any association with Soviet Russia." It never occurs to them, he continued, that Nazism and Fascism are simply "Bolshevism of the Right, [ ...] more dangerous to human freedom [...] than Stalinism is likely to be."[606] Unlike Churchill, Steed seemed in fact to have profoundly misread Stalin's true intentions about East-Central Europe, too: he was convinced, for instance, that the Anglo–Russian and Franco–Russian treaties would be a useful safeguard against the spread of the "short-sighted and not particularly progressive" idea of organ-

---

605 More on this in Rychlík, Marzik, Bielik (eds.) 1995, Vol. I/58.
　　Upon being interviewed, the former Czech minister of foreign affairs, Karel Schwarzenberg, an heir of a well-to-do Bohemian family, himself a victim of the Decrees reacted: "The expulsion was a grave violation of human rights. Measured by today's standards, the government, including President Beneš, would probably be in the Hague." Arnold Suppan, *Hitler–Beneš–Tito: National Conflicts, World Wars, Genocides, Expulsions, and Divided Remembrance in East-Central and Southeastern Europe, 1848–2018*, Austrian Academy of Sciences Press, 2019, 803.
606 Steed to Dr Roman, FW, December 9, 1938. Steed Papers MS 74131.

ising a kind of protective zone against Russian influence."[607] Late in 1944, in a tone of praise, he further explained that the Soviet Union had been engaged on a vast programme of social and economic development, and, siding with the prevailing British opinion, he stated that it was "none of our business to check or interfere with these inevitable transformations [in other countries], even should they appear to be influenced, directly or indirectly by the example or the *support* of Soviet Russia."[608]

D-Day in Europe further strengthened the position of the Soviet Union, and Steed, showing no little naivety, put forward in 1945 the idea that it would be "unwise" to be frightened by the social and economic ideology which the great majority of Russians cherished "with almost religious faith." Russian political and social systems need to be studied instead, he advised, "with all the understanding and goodwill that the Western democracies can muster"; only this way could suspicions be "gradually dispelled," and the "basis for cooperation found."[609] Even in the autumn of 1945, Steed's optimism did not fail him and he was convinced that "things may go a good deal better" in that year compared to 1918–1919, the sudden end of the First World War, with Allied solidarity lost, followed by each, non-French delegation entrenching itself in a big Paris hotel while "mortally afraid to contact each other."[610]

In late September 1945 the US and British delegates in the Council of Ministers declined to prepare peace treaties with the "enemy countries" of Hungary,[611] Romania and Bulgaria, the governments of which, they argued, had been set up under Russian influence, thus were not sufficiently representative and democratic. Soon the London meeting of the Foreign Ministers Council broke down, too; yet Steed was ready to excuse the representatives of the participating nations, the Soviet Union in particular, as the deadlock in his opinion was due to lingering uncertainty about the influence of atomic energy upon external and internal security of even the most powerful nations.[612]

Further on, double standards coupled with the exculpation of Soviet aggression remained an important element of Steed's speeches: the Soviet obsession with the idea of security was perhaps "alleged" and their actions should be assessed "in the light of Russian history;"[613] while referring to the Nuremberg Tri-

---

607 BBC World Affairs, December 15 1944. Steed Papers MS 74181.
608 BBC World Affairs, December 15 1944. Steed Papers MS 74181.
609 BBC World Affairs, June 8 1945. Steed Papers MS 74182.
610 BBC World Affairs, September 14, 1945. Steed Papers MS 74182.
611 The Government of Hungary soon obtained British and US recognition.
612 BBC World Affairs, October 5, 1945. Steed Papers MS 74182.
613 BBC World Affairs, November 2, 1945. Steed Papers MS 74182.

als, he stated proudly that "the rule of law distinguished civil from barbarian."[614] It is hard to imagine that Steed, who had previously been exceptionally well informed about East-Central European affairs, had not heard about the atrocities committed by the Red Army at the end of and after World War II, so it seems realistic to assume that he simply ignored them as "groundless fear."[615]

Despite the total exploitation of economic and human resources by the occupying Red Army, Steed's appeasing attitude did not abate. Upon detecting Moscow's rigidifying attitude concerning the upcoming peace treaties, he advised that the meeting of the Council of Five should take place in the Soviet capital.[616] Moreover, in his talk on December 28 he offered a lengthy explanation of the Russian outlook, making a genuine effort to understand the Russian point of view: he identified Russian Communism as "a form of Orthodox Eastern civilization," in line with liberalism and humanism. Russian fears and suspicions, he argued, derived from the Western threat to overthrow the dictatorship of the proletariat that had toppled the Tsarist autocracy. Therefore, he warned, the Western Powers should always be careful "to give no grounds for suspicion that they are working against Russia."[617]

By the spring of 1946, on the first anniversary of total Allied victory in Europe, Steed acknowledged that the outlook was "by no means unclouded": due to the persistent deadlock between the Great Powers' foreign ministers and their governments, which had impeded the drafting of peace treaties with Italy, Hungary, Romania and Bulgaria, the Peace Conference of twenty-one states, originally fixed for May 1, had to be postponed to some uncertain later date. Steed, however, quickly offered an explanation: after many years of violent shock, he argued, "the process of recovery is bound to be slow." Moreover, behind the failure to reach agreement lay "a fundamental misunderstanding": the Western democracies assumed from the outset that the peace treaties with the enemy countries drafted by the victorious powers would be negotiated and concluded in agreement with the nations concerned, which would gradually establish representative democratic governments. The Soviet Union, on the other hand, assumed that Bulgaria, Hungary and Romania, if not in Italy, must become "proletarian democracies" [sic] organised by communist parties under the auspices of Moscow. Given the differences of opinion, Steed concluded, it was not quite easy to see how the Paris meeting of the foreign ministers could yield "harmo-

---

614 BBC World Affairs, November 23, 1945. Steed Papers MS 74182.
615 BBC World Affairs, November 30, 1945. Steed Papers MS 74182.
616 BBC World Affairs, December 14, 1945. Steed Papers MS 74182.
617 BBC World Affairs, December 28, 1945. Steed Papers MS 74182.

## 2. From Versailles to Paris (1920–1947)

nious and satisfactory results."[618] A few months later, however, he was content to share that the main features of a peace treaty with the former enemy countries had been drafted and that unlike in 1919, the Conference started to work upon them "without delays."[619]

Deadlock, nevertheless, reoccurred, or rather, continued. By late August 1946, one month after the opening, Steed noted with disappointment the tendency toward Soviet curtailment of influence of the smaller states.[620] He noted as well that no formal intercourse had been taking place between Molotov and his British, American and French colleagues, "as if they been sitting in their Washington, London or Paris offices." Yet, he immediately set out to find the real causes of the problem: due to "unconfessed hostility," he argued, only a few Westerners realised the immense damage done to Soviet Union, the "burning grievance" of the terrific losses due to invasion by Nazis and their German satellites, thus "all [that Moscow] can lay hands upon in ex-enemy countries [is] a mere fragment of what they have to make good before they again reach the degree of relative well-being that they had won themselves in 1941."[621]

Macartney's address to Chatham House offers an exciting counterpoint to Steed's either lack of awareness or ignorance of the East-Central European reality. After his visit to Hungary in January 1946, Macartney claimed that though they "were tending [sic] to leave, a million Soviet soldiers who needed to be fed constituted a heavy burden for the nation as well as the poorly organized, frequently wasteful requisitioning, the arrest and internment of between forty and fifty thousand people[622] in the street as POWs, the ongoing looting, and rape cases"—were matters trivialized by the Soviets. According to Macartney, the outcome, "deep-seated dread and hatred," particularly among women and peasants, was predictable. However, he believed the short-term political situation to be "hopeful" since, while polling between 50 percent and 60 percent, the Smallholders "very rightly had not had enough confidence to form a government," and he praised the Communists for being "the most energetic and intelligent" in restoring communication and supplying food. The speaker must have erred

---

618 BBC World Affairs, April 19, 1946. Steed Papers MS 74183.
619 BBC World Affairs, July 23, 1946. Steed Papers MS 74183.
620 Steed, Articles for Ministry of Information, August 7, 1946. Steed Papers MS 78 189
621 BBC World Affairs, August 30, 1946. Steed Papers MS 74184. In his weekly Intelligence Report, he stated that the "world situation is one of hopeless confusion and inextricable muddle." Steed Articles for Ministry of Information, August 21, 1946. Steed Papers MS 78 189
622 According to most recent research, the number of POWs, or rather people, women and children, too, whom the Soviet authorities interned as POWs, amounts up to at least 6-700,000 people. Zalán Bognár, *The Fate of Hungarian, German, Austrian, Slovak, Polish, French, Italian and Other POWS in HUngary Occupied by the Red Army, 1944-1945*, Budapest, Kairosz, 2017, 11.

in this regard; what he meant by "some reallocation of ministries" actually implied the Communist takeover of the Ministry of Inferior and the secret police, which marked the onset of a communist takeover backed by Soviet weapons.[623]

By October 1946, the Paris Peace Conference was drawing to its close, which due to utmost Soviet pressure rejected the compromise solution, among others, regarding the Hungarian–Romanian border. The Soviet position was justified by the relative weakness of the indigenous Hungarian and Romanian communist movements. However, while the communist-dominated Romanian Petru Groza government needed a national cause in order to gain support, the failure of the Smallholder-led Hungarian government to keep Northern Transylvania served the interests of the communists. Thus, very much like Hitler, the Soviets utilized the Transylvanian question to control both Romania and Hungary. In the meantime, the Hungarian delegates made valiant attempts in Paris to win Western backing for both minority protection and territorial issues. Without these, they argued, the treaty would be a national catastrophe that their still largely pro-Western government would not be able to survive.[624] According to the contemporary US State Department specialist on Eastern Europe, John C. Campbell, who had prepared draft treaties with Romania, Bulgaria, and Hungary:

> The new territorial settlement is open to serious criticism. It leaves intact many of the 1919 frontiers which, on the basis of experience, should have been changed, and it establishes others which go far beyond any of the more cynical decisions of 1919. [...] In eastern Europe the crucial question was not where the western frontier of the Soviet Union was to be fixed, but how far into Europe the zone of Soviet control would extend.[625]

Steed, the former "spiritual godfather" of the post-Habsburg states, four of which went under Soviet yoke, found the wide divergence between the Western democracies and "those of Russian group of States" [sic] "certainly unpleasant,"[626] but he accepted the new modus vivendi, adding that "if we realise that Russian

---

623 Macartney, "Conditions in Hungary," Address on May 18, 1946. RIIA. RIIA Archives, 8/1209. Macartney Papers MMs. Eng. c. 3287. Doc 19.
624 John C. Campbell, The European Territorial Settlement, *Foreign Affairs*, October 1947, Vol. 26, No. 1, 196–218, 211–214.
625 Ibid., 217.
626 BBC World Affairs, October 18, 1946. Steed Papers MS 74184.

habits of thought and expression are totally different from our own, discussion may still be difficult but will not be impossible."[627]

The outrageous conduct of the occupying Red Army was resented not only by the former enemy countries, like Hungary or [East-]Germany that Steed had long shunned, but by Poland, Romania or Czechoslovakia, too. Yet, by 1945-6, Steed's utmost compassion was suspended with respect to Moscow's doings, and he turned a blind eye to the new oppressed states, former victors or vanquished alike. But there was nothing surprising about it. While at the end of the First World War he had subordinated the ethnic principle to the interests of the British Empire, that is the creation of a new *cordon sanitaire* against German expansion, in 1945 he disregarded national self-determination in East-Central Europe, by accepting the Sovietization of the region: the price of peace with the Soviet Union as a superpower.

As Winston Churchill aptly put it in the House of Commons: "It is better to have a world united than a world divided. But it is also better to have a world divided than a world destroyed."[628] Thus, owing to the incapacity of the British Empire to dominate decision-making regarding Central and Eastern Europe, Steed, Seton-Watson as well as Toynbee and Macartney ceased to be part of the British foreign-policy-making elite. They were not alone. Upon recognising that the West had very little influence in the region, the U.S. representative in Romania, Burton Berry, for example, invested his time on expanding his collection of vintage coins and rugs.[629]

Toynbee arrived in Paris in April 1946, but the opening plenary session of the Peace Conference occurred almost three months later; the delegation of the United Kingdom was offered twenty seats for its prominent politicians, among them Foreign Secretary Ernest Bevin,[630] who did act on Toynbee's advice, very much unlike David Lloyd George some twenty-seven years earlier. Peace-making, however, soon proved to be a "glacial" experience for the former FORD director.[631] Midway through July, when the conference broke down for the second

---

627 BBC World Affairs, October 11, 1946. Steed Papers MS 74184.
628 "Foreign Affairs." Churchill in the House of Commons, June 5 1946. https://api.parliament.uk/historic-hansard/commons/1946/jun/05/foreign-affairs#S5CV0423P0_19460605_HOC_329 (Accessed May 29, 2023)
    Qtd. in Articles for Ministry of Information, June 12, 1946. Steed Papers MS 78 189.
629 Csaba Békés, László Borhi, Peter Ruggenthaler, Ottmar Traşcă, (eds.), *Soviet Occupation of Romania, Hungary, and Austria 1944/45–1948/49*, CEU Press, 2015, 19.
630 Toynbee Papers BL Oxford MS13967/137 Miscellaneous 1946.
631 Toynbee Papers BL Oxford MS13 967/128/1 Reviews and Correspondence 1915-1970.

time, Toynbee left the Foreign Office to return to Chatham House as director of studies. The conference's general failure meant that Toynbee would not be able to round off his professional career by assisting in bringing about a just and lasting peace.

Unlike Steed, a junior peacemaker in 1919, by 1946 a senior diplomat, Harold Nicolson, was crystal-clear about the role of the Soviets in the break-up of the conference earlier:

> The rigid doctrinal orthodoxy of the Russian delegation, and their immediate associates, rendered them dogmatic in the assertion of their own opinions and impervious to the opinions of others. Their mechanical repetition of the same catchwords and phrases, the fixity of their vocabulary, precluded that elasticity of intercourse through which alone conflicting national interests can be brought within the area of compromise.[632]

In March 1947, the Truman Doctrine offered substantial financial and political support to Greece and Turkey with the primary aim of containing Soviet geopolitical expansion during the Cold War. Around the same time, Steed's attitude to the Soviet Union finally underwent a major transformation, too. He welcomed the US president's "frankness" as well as Foreign Secretary Ernest Bevin's "outspoken language,"[633] yet he was more critical of Churchill's United Europe-scheme, which the former prime minister had devised in Zurich, as he understood that by 1947 United Europe would be confined to a Western Europe "united without Russia," and probably "without any of the states accepting [sic] her leadership."[634]

In contrast to Steed's portrayal of the British foreign secretary as someone with strong anti-communist rhetoric, the fact was that as Hungary and Romania had no bearing on the British position in the Eastern Mediterranean according to the Foreign Office, they tolerated Soviet influence in that region, even if it meant the implementation of communist regimes. It was equally important that a few months later, the political situation in Hungary would make it quite clear to Steed that the adoption of the Soviet political-economic model was not

---

632 Harold Nicolson, Peacemaking at Paris: Success, Failure or Farce? *Foreign Affairs*, January 1947, Vol. 25, No. 2, 190–203, 198. After April 1947, BBC broadcast Steed's "World Affairs," in rotation with Nicolson, among others. J. Bolark to Steed, August 1, 1947. Steed Papers, Correspondence with the BBC 1928–1953 MS 74 116.
633 Steed, BBC World Affairs, March 14, 1947. Steed Papers MS 74 185.
634 Steed, BBC World Affairs, May 16, 1947. Steed Papers MS 74 185.

at all a matter of choice for the countries of East-Central Europe. He was closely following and assessing the events in his weekly radio broadcasts, and regarded the removal of Hungarian prime minister Ferenc Nagy by communists as a "conspiracy," and even asserted that ousting the prime minister had persuaded the US secretary of state, George Marshall, to put forward "without delay" his proposal for further aid to European countries.[635] A week later, he criticised the Soviet intervention in Hungarian affairs with even harsher words, calling it a "flagrant interference" and highlighting the fact that the British ambassador to Moscow had reminded Molotov that the Soviet government "had recognized the British right to share in the control of Hungary during armistice period and receive all information." Steed also acknowledged that events in Hungary were matched by Communist doings in Bulgaria, Romania and Yugoslavia, too, adding, somewhat naively, that one of the puzzles of the situation was "why Soviet Russia should persistently estrange by her political methods"[636] [...] the very countries which might afford her the material aid she sorely needs."[637]

On December 1947 Steed delivered the last of his BBC talks, which praised the US's Marshall aid and its "strong sense of responsibility." He also added that further Soviet military advance was "not probable" and offered a sound conclusion that all his East-Central European friends had long been waiting for: "Soviet Russia and communism go wrong in hankering after absolute stability by the universal application of what I firmly believe to be unsound and fallacious doctrine of economic materialism which leaves moral factors of human life entirely out of account."[638]

---

635 Steed, BBC World Affairs, June 6, 1947. Steed Papers MS 74 185.
636 Steed, BBC World Affairs, December 4, 1947. Steed Papers MS 74 185.
637 Steed, BBC World Affairs, June 13, 1947. Steed Papers MS 74 185.
638 Steed, BBC World Affairs, December 4, 1947. Steed Papers MS 74185.

# 3. In a Bipolar World 1947–78

## 3.1. Lives in Full: Seton-Watson, Steed, Macartney and Toynbee

After his returning to office from exile in 1946, President Beneš received A.J.P. Taylor. As they gazed out at the breath-taking view from the president's office in magnificent Prague Castle, Beneš allegedly noted that at Munich he "saved Prague" and his people "from destruction." Given that more Poles perished in World War II as a result of Poland's entry into the conflict in 1939 than Czechs had perished after the Czechoslovak decision to abstain from hostilities in 1938, Taylor argued in his book that Beneš had indeed been the real winner at Munich (and in World War II).[1] The expulsion of millions of Germans and thousands of Hungarians from Czechoslovakia, based on the Western powers' Munich guilt, however, did not create an ideal Czechoslovak nation state free of minority problems, as was envisioned by Beneš or endorsed by Seton-Watson and Steed. The methods used to get rid of the minorities, or at least a good part of them, with Stalin's blessing, mirrored as well as predicted the Soviet-style strategy of eliminating rivals and taking their property.

The Communist Klement Gottwald's takeover in Prague in late February 1948 meant not only Beneš's second humiliation but also the abrupt end of the newly founded Oxford Chair. Seton-Watson was overcome by a "poignant grief,"[2] which only deepened with the deaths of his friends Jan Masaryk[3] and the for-

---

[1] A.J.P Taylor, *The Troublemakers*, London, Hamish Hamilton. 1957, 296–297.
[2] In Steed's wording. Tributes to R.W. Seton-Watson: A Symposium, *Slavonc and East European Review*, June 1952, 336.
[3] After the communist coup, Masaryk was one of the few non-communists left in office. In less than three weeks, he committed suicide by jumping out of a third-story window at the Foreign Ministry.

mer president. In an obituary written for *Slavonic Review*, the ageing historian depicted Czechoslovakia between 1918 and Munich as a true success story and Beneš as the apostle of democracy and freedom.[4] Seton-Watson commemorated the late president by quoting his address to the Caroline University (April 7, 1948): "[...] 'liberty, based upon respect of man for man, and upon the wide tolerance of which our university has always been the traditional home, will guide it once more and, please God, all of us with it, to another blossoming and a truly happy future.' That is the Beneš whom we know, and whose memory we shall always cherish."[5]

From then onwards, Seton-Watson's only joy came with his appointment to the Royal Historical Society and the rising career of his sons, Hugh and Christopher, as historians. In 1949 he was diagnosed with Parkinson's Disease and his health gradually deteriorated. As his wife recalled, on his deathbed, in near delirium, he returned to the Political Intelligence Department which had been set up in the last years of the First World War, and demanded that an important document be handed over to his old comrade-in-arms, Steed...[6]

Robert William Seton-Watson passed away at his home in his beloved Scotland on July 25, 1951. He died during the darkest period of Stalinist terror. His friends and colleagues, including Henry Wickham Steed and the Romanian friend Viorel Tilea, paid tribute to him as a "legendary figure" in the pages of the *Slavonic and East European Review*, which he had founded. In contrast to his opponent Edith Durham's cult in Enver Hoxha's Albania, communist Czecho-

---

After World War II, Steed remained loyal particularly to his Czechoslovak friends and also took part in the BBC Czechoslovak Programme (in order to somewhat counter communist propaganda). In his opinion, Jan Masaryk had lent his name to the communist government "in the hope of restraining it," which he labelled "self-sacrifice." "Steed in the BBC Czechoslovak Programme," March 7, 1954. Steed Papers MS 74 186. See also A. Anderson, BBC Czechoslovak Programme Organizer's letter in which he requested Steed to send a message to the people of Czechoslovakia on the thirtieth anniversary to counter communist propaganda, "this absurd reading of history." Anderson to Steed, October 18, 1948. Steed Papers, Ms 74 104.

4   Seton-Watson, Edward Beneš, *Slavonic Review*, October 1948, 359–362.
5   Seton-Watson, Edvard Beneš, *Slavonic and East European Review*, May 1949, 359–362, 362.
    Interestingly, Seton-Watson's and Steed's high regard of the Czechoslovak president was not fully in line with several British politicians' opinions: for instance, Sir George Russel Clerk (1874–1951), a special envoy to the Peace Conference to Bucharest and Budapest in 1919, was sceptical about Beneš's goodwill regarding the minorities: he had expressed "a desire to conciliate them," claimed Clerk, "but he really in the back of his mind would like to humiliate them on every occasion." Qtd. in Zbyněk Zeman, Antonín Klimek, *The Life of Edvard Beneš 1884–1948*, Oxford, Oxford University Press, 1997, 60. Lloyd George also dismissed him as "a fussy little man who trots around the world running errands for French Ministers of state." Qtd. in Robert Bruce Lockhart, *Retreat from Glory*, London, Putnam 1934, 76.
6   Marion Esther [May] Seton-Watson acknowledged that Steed's knowledge of Scotus had been even greater than hers. May Seton-Watson to Steed, August 4, 1951. Steed Papers MS 74134

slovakia, Romania or Yugoslavia ignored his death, while eagerly imprisoning all kinds of opponents of communism: academicians, journalists, military officers, priests, politicians, professors, economists, and historians. Having been convicted in the June 1947 trial of the leaders of the National Peasants' Party, for instance, Seton-Watson's once close friend, former Romanian prime minister Iuliu Maniu died in February 1953 in the notorious Sighetu Marmatiei (Máramarossziget) prison.

Seton-Watson's other, lifelong friend Henry Wickham Steed wrote in 1950 that he detested the "intellectual and economic abominations" of Marxism-Leninism-Stalinism and set out at the age of 79 to promote a propaganda offensive against them.[7] What that entailed, he unfortunately did not elaborate on. As part of his 1953 BBC reminiscences,[8] on the other hand, he gave three talks, the last of which focused on Munich. In it he developed the following theory: "If we had decided to stick to our guns, Germany would have been beaten, the German generals would have revolted against Hitler, who would have been smashed within a fortnight, and the problem of Russia would have taken an entirely different aspect.[9] In other words, he argued that the reason for the Soviet subjugation of Central and Eastern Europe after World War II had been the lenient attitude of post-1933 British governments, most notably the policy of appeasement. If His Majesty's government had taken a harder line against Nazi Germany, he opined, there would have been nothing to justify Moscow crossing the borders of the Soviet Union and conquering more territory.

However, others saw things differently. By weakening the region, it was the very disintegration of Austria-Hungary in 1918 that created the conditions for Soviet intervention, they opined,[10] so in 1954, Steed took the effort to once again defend his life's work: the break-up of the Dual Monarchy, he retorted, had on the one hand been a military necessity, and on the other hand, a logical outcome of events, as none of the nationalities, "Poles, Czechoslovaks, Yugoslavs, Rumanes" [sic] had been willing to continue to live "under Habsburg rule." "The peace treaties, unsatisfactory in many respects though they were, reg-

---

7 Steed to L.F. Behrens, December 27, 1950. Steed Papers MS 74134. Leonard Frederick Behrens (1890– March 12, 1978). a British Liberal Party politician.
8 "The Reminiscences of Wickham Steed: Vienna and the Hapsburgs," interview by Steven Watson, April 18, 1953, 10 pm, BBC Home Service. Steed Papers MS 74 186.
9 "The Reminiscences of Wickham Steed: Between The Wars: The Troubled Thirties," interview by Steven Watson, January 26 1954, BBC Home Service. Steed Papers MS 74 186.
10 George Edinger, letter to the editor, Times, April 9, 1948.

istered these facts,"[11] he concluded, reiterating almost verbatim the position he had taken for more than three decades.

In his lifelong support for the small state system, as well as his distrust of Germany or Hungary, Steed never wavered, earning him the epithet "Wicked Steed."[12] He also preferred to shut out voices and events that challenged his view. His increasing deafness might be an interesting physical manifestation of this. He did not live to see the 1956 revolution or the Suez crisis, as he died in January of that year, while lying on his bed among his beloved books and maps.

Twenty-four years younger than Steed, Carlile Aylmer Macartney's academic career peaked in the post-war years. In October 1946 he was elected a full member of the Hungarian Academy of Sciences and reacted with the words: "Nothing I have received from Hungary in thirty years has given me so much pleasure."[13] Five years later, he was first appointed to the Department of International Relations at the University of Edinburgh, a post he held until 1957. Afterwards, from 1951 to 1966, he became a research fellow then a fellow emeritus, while authoring a number of his major works, though due to his conservative views he was in fact "a political pariah" in leftist Oxford.[14] The year 1957 saw the publication of the two-volume *October Fifteenth, A History of Hungary 1929–1945*, which in Hungary is still the best known among his books. The author assembled a vast amount of material based on thirty years of personal experience and supplemented by a scrupulous reading of written press and official documents. Conversations with the political elite of the Horthy era, including the Regent, Prime Minister Miklós Kállay and others, enriched the volume and made it an indispensable source work, even for the Marxist historiography of the time.[15] "No other writer, Hungarian or foreign, has done this job," wrote Hugh Seton-Watson, "or is or ever will be in a position to do it."[16] Then *Independent Eastern Europe* (1962), co-authored with Alan Palmer, was followed by a short summary,

---

11  *Times Literary Supplement*, August 13, 1954. Qtd. in Liebich 2018, 338.
12  Liebich 2018, Steed, 54.
13  Macartney to the Hungarian linguist Gyula Németh, October 20, 1946. OSZK KT 121/1076.
14  Péter László. Qtd. in Miklós Lojkó, C.A. Macartney and Central Europe, *European Review of History*, Vol. 6, 1 (Spring 1999): 37–57, 44.
15  See Robert John Weston Evans, The Making of October Fifteenth: C.A. Macartney and his Correspondents. In: Péter, Rady (eds.) 2004, 259–271.
16  Hugh Seton-Watson 1981, 424.
    While in Budapest, on February 3, 1940, Macartney gave a talk in Hungarian discussing the origins of the term "Pasca Romanorum." Professor István Hajnal thanked Macartney for citing sources that had not yet been dealt with in detail by Hungarian historians. In: *Magyar Országos Tudósító* [Hungarian National Correspondent] 1929–1944, Vol. XXII, No. 33, February 3, 1940.

*Hungary*, "a calm study of the past by unrivalled Magyar scholarship which helps us understand the passions of the present."[17] The little book was an apparent success, becoming a textbook at Western universities. Returning in 1969 to the topic of Austria where his career began some fifty years earlier, Macartney wrote the internationally acclaimed *Habsburg Empire 1790–1918*, which he considered his major work.

In the latter work, Macartney paid particular attention to the creation of Austria-Hungary as a semi-great power made possible by the Settlement of 1867, which he analysed in a separate chapter in more than seventy pages. In the foreword to the work, he stressed that "tribal [that is, national] histories [...] cannot be completely satisfactory even for their own tribes [nations], for the political, social and economic development of each people was bound up with and largely conditioned by that of the others, without some knowledge of which it does not even make a sense." Therefore, the ideal book in his opinion, which remains to be written, is a transnational, *gesamtmonarchisch* history, seen from Vienna, and not that each part described the "sufferings of his own people in the Babylonian captivity of the Habsburgs."[18]

Macartney was not particularly surprised by the communist takeover in East-Central Europe, which he described with an unusual amount of indignation as "Asiatic brutality" manifested in "mass judicial murders, imprisonments or internment under wretched conditions, often accompanied by vile torture, of the opponents of the new order."[19] At the height of the Cold War, in 1949 together with scientists who were labelled anti-regime, his membership in the Hungarian Academy of Sciences was withdrawn on the orders of the Hungarian Communist Party, which he remembered bitterly until his death. (Meanwhile, in 1965 he was elected a Fellow of the British Academy of Sciences.)

In his private life Macartney remained concerned about the fate of the peoples of the Danube Basin, especially the Hungarians. In 1951, the year Seton-Watson passed away, he founded and became the first president of the British-Hungarian Fellowship. The 1956-revolution filled him with hope and eventually shocked him: "A nation asks the West for help and does not get it. One percent [i.e., the Stalinist leadership] asks the East and gets it," he reportedly commented on the events on Radio Free Europe.[20] Following the 1956 revolution, he left for Vienna with Cambridge- and Oxford scholarships at hand for students flee-

---

17 Gordon Brook-Shepherd, "Troubled Magyars," *Daily Telegraph*, January 11, 1963, 1.
18 Macartney 1971, xii. (Revised edition)
19 Macartney, *Hungary, A Short History*, Edinburgh, 1962, 239.
20 Zoltán Balassa, 1956 is an Ethnic Visa in Politics, *Erdélyi napló*, 1996, Vol. 51, 12.

ing reprisals, and from then onwards, around October 20 each year, his letters to the editor of the *Daily Telegraph* would appear, intending to call attention to the annual meeting held jointly by the British–Hungarian Fellowship and Hungarian Freedom Fighters in memory of the 1956 Revolution.

After World War II, Macartney travelled extensively. During his American tour in 1962, for instance, he lectured on Central Europe at eighteen colleges and universities. In Texas, it was reported that the man "who speaks Hungarian with a better accent than Zsazsa Gabor" provided lessons for all contemporary and future researchers/politicians with an interest in the region: "The things they [behind the Iron Curtain] write in English aren't worth reading"— sounded his clarification, "You have to read the Hungarian books and newspapers, the things they write for their own people to know what's going on."[21] While abroad, Macartney paid attention to meeting members of the 1956 Hungarian emigration: in Canada, at the age of seventy-five, he was entertaining Winnipeg Hungarians with his endless Hungarian memories of the 1930s, sometimes singing along with them and suddenly toasting, "I raise my glass to Hungarian freedom!" Those around him were then shocked to discover that "Hungarian History itself" was drinking wine with them, "in the person of a smiling old Englishman."[22]

As the regime changed from totalitarian to authoritarian, Macartney also visited Hungary several times, last in 1973, as a guest of the Hungarian Academy of Sciences. At a garden party a week before he passed away, he made a commitment to begin writing his autobiography soon, but he did not have the time.[23] He died on June 18, 1978, shortly after his membership of the Hungarian Academy had been restored. It is a noble gesture that the only appreciation of him to have appeared in English to date was written in 1983 by Seton-Watson's elder son Hugh, who was usually polemical with his father on the Hungarian question.

As far as Macartney's memory in Hungary is concerned, it is worth quoting from a somewhat sentimental article published in the emigrant newspaper *Magyar Élet* in the summer of 1978:

In Budapest, unfortunately, too many people have been given statues and monuments, who perhaps did not deserve them in their lifetime. Too

---

21 Marj Whiteman, "C.A. Macartney, Oxford Hungary Expert," *Austin American*, December 4, 1962, 1.
22 Endre Haraszti, "Meghalt a legmagyarabb szívű Ánglius" [The most Hungarian-hearted Englishman has died], Winnipeg, *Magyar Élet [Hungarian Life]*, August 5, 1978, 9.
23 On the later part of his life, see Lojkó 1999, 51; Ránki 1978; Hugh Seton-Watson 1982, 425–426; and Czigány 1995.

many streets are named after people who died long ago, who perhaps did not know or love Hungary. I wonder if anyone at home will think of naming a street after this great English scholar with a Hungarian heart? Will the Hungarian nation express its gratitude–in the form of a statue, a monument–to C.A. Macartney, who has just died [...]?[24]

Thirty-four years after the end of communism, one can only hope that the Hungarian academic community will finally erect a worthy memorial to Macartney, not so much because of his "Hungarian heart," but rather as an outstanding and–compared to Seton-Watson or Steed-unbiased expert on East-Central European history.

In July 1946, Macartney's former chief both at FRPS and FORD, Arnold Joseph Toynbee, left the Paris Peace Conference and diplomatic service for good and re-joined the London School of Economics as well as Chatham House, which he hoped to transform into a center "for a new way of looking at history as a whole."[25] In this very spirit he released a condensed version of his *Study of History*, the masterful abridgement of the first six volumes by an American history teacher, David Churchill Somervell.[26] Still a door-stopper, the new book catapulted him to overnight fame in the USA.

During his 1947 visit, Toynbee met the US magazine magnate Henry Luce, the head of the world's largest media empire at the time. As much as British media-mogul Lord Northcliffe had assisted Steed's career, Luce made Toynbee famous almost overnight. The historian's idea of the United States as the successor in world leadership of dwarfed Britain, put forward in his Chatham House talk, among others,[27] greatly impressed Luce, an adherent of US missionary nationalism. Thus, only five days after the declaration of the Truman Doctrine, Toynbee appeared as the cover story on *Time Magazine*. The narrative was written by Whittaker Chambers, a former Marxist who came to see Toynbee as a replacement for Marx, a new spiritual leader to defend civilization against the

---

24 Haraszti 1978, 9.
25 Toynbee to Ivison Macadam, December 13, 1948. RIIA Archives 4 /TOYN/3, 6.
26 Many years later Somervell confessed in a letter to Toynbee: "I have derived much more fame and fortune from missing [leaving] out parts of your book than from writing any of my own." Toynbee, Janus at 75. Toynbee papers MS 13967/40. General miscellaneous correspondence 1931-1964
27 Unification would come, Toynbee hoped, through a peaceful federation under "a co-operative world government." Toynbee, The International Outlook, *Survey of International Affairs*, Vol. 23, No. 4 (October 1947), 463-476. 474-476.

Soviet threat.²⁸ With many radio and television appearances, Toynbee was one of the few serious academics to enter the public eye in the USA. *Time* declared him "undoubtedly the most eminent historian of our time."²⁹

Having arrived home from the USA, in another Chatham House-talk Toynbee addressed communism again, viewing its Eastern European dominance with "shock."³⁰ However, he did not expect a third world war for a great many years to come, but predicted "a long period of cold war,"³¹ one of the most obvious manifestations of which on the European map was the division of Germany. When German historian, folklorist (and former *SS-Hauptsturmführer*) Professor Hans Beyer approached Toynbee on the problem of partition, the director explained that in his view it was the inevitable consequence of deliberate acts, committed by Germans. "No human rights are inalienable," stressed Toynbee, and nations, like individuals, "can forfeit rights by abusing them [...]. Germany has forfeited at least the right to live in unity." Toynbee was nevertheless optimistic in the long term and predicted the three major milestones "the native political spirit of West-Germany" that would reach into the future: the integration of the country into a united Western Europe, the education of East German refugees in West German political affairs and, eventually, peaceful reunion.³²

---

28  *Time*, March 17, 1947. The article and the abridged bestseller became mutually reinforcing: *Time* received no fewer than 14,000 requests for reprints of the article, while the book was sold 129,471 times in its first year of release by Oxford University Press, New York. Of the numerous expressions of approval *Time* received, the following very well illustrates the kind of reaction the editors hoped for in publishing the Toynbee-story: "In these days when Americans are called upon to make decisions of direct consequence to the whole world, they should understand something of the nature and course of civilization. *Time* and Toynbee have helped to fill that need." A Letter from the Publisher," *Time Magazine*, April 28, 1947. See also: Richard Crockatt, Challenge and Response: Arnold Toynbee and the United States during the Cold War. In: *War and Cold War in American Foreign Policy, 1942-62*, Dale Carter, Robin Clifton (eds.), Palgrave Macmillan, 2001, 108-130; McNeill 1989, 215.

29  Toynbee influenced Henry Kissinger, too, whose Harvard undergraduate paper was titled, "The Meaning of History: Reflections on Spengler, Toynbee, and Kant." (Nash K. Burger, Books of the Times, *New York Times*, September 25, 1958. Toynbee Papers 13967/30 Reviews.) No wonder he soon developed an addiction to the spotlight and granted interviews to practically everyone upon request. What did not help either, was that Toynbee continued to write too much and that too quickly, taking great pride in his speed. McNeill, Toynbee Revisited, 14, 23.

30  Toynbee, "The Study of History in the Light of Current Development." Address at Chatham House, June 8, 1948, MS 13967/3 Toynbee Lectures 1926-1948.

31  Toynbee, "Russian Catfish and The Western Herring," Herald Tribune Book and Author Luncheon Talk, Hotel Astor, April 12, 1949. Toynbee Papers, MS 13967/3 Lectures 1949-67.

32  Toynbee to Prof. Hans Beyer, *Nordfriesische Nachrichten*, February 21, 1950. Toynbee Papers BL Oxford MS13967/76/2 Germany: Correspondence and papers 1933-50.
Less than two years after the Berlin Wall was built, Toynbee proposed nothing less than that the US should offer to guarantee the current western borders of Poland, Czechoslovakia and the Soviet Union in exchange for the Soviet government's agreement to reunify the two current Germanies. Toynbee to Prof. Larski, December 20, 1963. Toynbee Papers BL Oxford MS13967/63/2.

While Toynbee gathered many admirers in West Germany due to his comprehensive worldview,[33] in the USA, what he had to say and what Americans wanted to hear were becoming more and more at odds. By the mid-1950s, he abandoned his former vision of a USA as the defender of civilization (against communism), and labelled the American view of Communism as the ultimate evil as "pathological,"[34] calling attention to the "importance of being willing to admit failure, to have a second thought, and to change one's policy," as against "American history taught as an unbroken success story."[35] Soon he went so far as to denounce Americans for feeling "automatically privileged" and for leading a "rather pampered and intellectually indolent" life.[36] From the second half of the fifties, his disillusionment with the American way of life grew more pronounced with each passing year.

At the age of sixty-five, Toynbee retired and soon found enough time for one of his favourite pastimes, travelling. News of the 1956 Hungarian Revolution and the Suez Crisis reached him in Japan. Alarmed, he wrote to the RIIA-secretary:

> My gloomiest forebodings [...] have been far surpassed. Half my friends, and about a third of my children's friends, have given their lives to resist suppression, and now our country has been turned into an aggressor by Eden [...]. It is frightful being ashamed of one's own country when one is abroad. I never thought that I should have this experience. It is a lesson against the sin of pride. we are now in the same dock with the Germans, Italians, and Japanese. [...] M[ussolini]. and H[itler] have conquered other countries and this is what <u>we</u> are doing in Egypt and the Russians in Hungary. [...]

---

Half a year later he wrote: "I myself hope for a united Europe in which the past bitterness of the British against the Germans will be forgotten." Toynbee to Paul Krellmann, May 27, 1964. Toynbee Papers BL Oxford MS13967/ 76/1 Germany 1926-68.

33 Jürgen Osterhammel, "Arnold Toynbee and the Problems of Today," Toynbee Lecture, delivered at the Annual Meeting of The American Historical Association, Denver, January 6, 2017. *Bulletin of the GHI*, Spring 2017, 77.

34 Toynbee to Robert W Masoner, New Cumberland, USA, May 7, 1968. Toynbee Papers MS 13 967/63/1 Correspondence 1931-74.

35 Toynbee to Mr Galbraith, Indianapolis, Indiana, Office of the National Commander, February 28, 1968. Toynbee Papers MS 13 967/63/1 Correspondence 1931-74.

36 Toynbee to David Davies, March 2, 1958. Toynbee papers MS 13967/80 Individuals: D 1919-1973. See McNeill 1989, 241-246.
A few years before his death Toynbee's contribution to scholarship was assessed in a rather contradictory fashion: "a fascinating and incredible mixture of profound insight and fanciful hogwash" or "many brilliant truths [...] offset in too many cases by observations of an almost infantile thoughtlessness." J.G.Harrison, "A Prophet to Profit from," *Christian Science Monitor*, October 28, 1971. Toynbee Papers 13967/31 Reviews.

Nasser has broken an important commercial content, but he has not made war and not shed blood. It is we who have done that. [...]. We boast of being "the Free World." Oughtn't the Arab peoples to be free?[37]

On November 3, the rector and seventeen professors of the University of Szeged drew up a letter to Nobel-laureate biochemist Albert Szent-Györgyi to the USA: "Support the Hungarian people in their fight for freedom!"[38] Toynbee sympathized with the Hungarian cause as much as he did with Egyptian self-determination: in a private letter he confessed to being "as dead against Russia in Hungary as [...] against Britain in Egypt," meanwhile seriously fearing the outbreak of a third world war. In the best-case scenario, he expected, with no little naivety, that the United Nations, led by the USA, "may be able to get us and the French out of the Arab countries and Cyprus, and get the Russians out of Eastern Europe. These are formidable jobs."[39]

His former father-in-law, in fact his "second father,"[40] Gilbert Murray, however, assented to the British–French attack on Egypt. Toynbee reacted with regret: "It is strange how, having the same fundamental principles, we can see the same events in such different lights."[41] Sadly, Murray passed away the following May, leaving no time to rekindle their old relationship.

After the suppression of the Hungarian Revolution and the joint British–French fiasco at Suez, but still on his world tour, Toynbee concluded in a private letter that the events of autumn 1956 could be interpreted as a double watershed. First, the facts demonstrated not only that the Soviet Union would never be able to lead the world but also "the beginning of the end of Russian Imperialism in Eastern Europe." Moreover, by deploying tanks to Budapest against everyday Hungarians, the Kremlin abandoned an inexpensive weapon, that is, their claim to be allies against imperialism. Second, the events in October–November could be interpreted as "the Fall of Britain" and that of France, the two "mid-sized powers," as well as the end of French and British imperialism in Asia and Africa. "We and the French are now finding our true level," Toynbee continued, like Japan, Italy, and Germany, a process which he believed would be

---

37 Toynbee to Miss Norah Williams. RIIA (From the International House of Japan, Tokyo) Nara (Nava), November 5, 1956. Toynbee Papers BL Oxford MS13967/63/2.
38 Ibid.
39 Toynbee to Miss Norah Williams. RIIA (From the International House of Japan, Tokyo) Nara (Nava), November 27, 1956. Toynbee Papers BL Oxford MS 13967/63/2.
40 Toynbee to David Davies, May 29, 1957. Toynbee Papers MS 13967/80 Individuals: D 1919–1973.
41 Toynbee to Gilbert Murray, November 27, 1956. Toynbee Papers MS. 13967/72/1 Family correspondence 1914–1957.

"painful." Finally, returning to his favourite subject, he stated that the United Nations might serve as the foundation of a global government under American leadership, to which he had given his full support, acknowledging that they could not have attempted to expel the Russians from Hungary without "igniting a third world war."[42]

Thus, the year 1956 became a double turning point in Toynbee's thinking, forecasting the fall of communism and that of traditional Western imperialism, too. A few years before his death, he expressed the view he had long held that Russia had been "singularly unsuccessful in having any cultural impact on Eastern European countries" and, as a consequence, Eastern Europe "will emerge un-Russified."[43] Despite his strong convictions, nevertheless he refused to propagate this perspective much. On the sixth anniversary of the Hungarian Revolution, Tibor Tollas wrote a letter to Toynbee on behalf of the Vienna-based journal Nemzetőr [National Guard], asking him to express his views on the impact of the events of 1956. The journal aimed to publish the statements of the public figures it contacted as a message to the millions of people living behind the Iron Curtain. Toynbee's response was nevertheless dismissive: it would not serve "a useful purpose," he claimed, adding: "My answer would be the same if I were asked to make a declaration concerning the contemporary Egypt, about which my feelings are no different."[44]

As for the decline of Western imperialism, Toynbee returned to that subject in a lecture at a meeting of the Siam Society in late 1956. After 1914 one could witness the gradual decline of Western predominance, he opined, claiming that once Western history was reduced "to its proper position and proportion," which he believed was timely—all the more so, since the West had not been a cradle of any "higher" (that is, monotheistic) religions— humans would learn

---

42 Toynbee to Father Columba Cary-Elwes OSB, December 4, 1956, Rangoon(?). MS 13967/78. Correspondence.
Eleven years later Toynbee added yet another layer of interpretation to 1956: Superpowers "America and Russia" bore great responsibility: they happened to have the same policy and stopped the aggression in three days in 1956, and "if you worked together, what *couldn't* you do towards putting the world in order?" Conversations with A Toynbee, September 1967. Toynbee Papers, MS 13967/7 Broadcasts 1929-1955.
43 Toynbee on Toynbee, Conversation between Arnold J. Toynbee and G.R.Urban, Oxford University Press, former director of broadcasting for Radio Free Europe. 1972? Toynbee Papers BL Oxford MS13967/31/1.
44 Tibor Tollas (Nemzetőr, newspaper of the Authors and Poets of the Hungarian Fight for Freedom, Vienna) to Toynbee, September 10, 1962. Toynbee to Tibor Tollas, September 17, 1962. Toynbee Papers BL Oxford MS13967/63/2.

more about humanity's history.⁴⁵ He felt he was bored by Westerners' "seeing and judging everything from a Western point of view,"⁴⁶ As his gradual disenchantment with them had deeper, primarily religious, roots, we turn to religion in the next chapter.

## 3.2. Toynbee on Religion and Secular Religions:⁴⁷ Nationalism, the Great Modern Heresy⁴⁸

> *"I was brought up as a Protestant, but have not become a Catholic."*⁴⁹

> *"Since 1870, political nationalism has become a disintegrating instead of a unifying force, in Europe, in the British Empire and in the East, too."*⁵⁰

During the First World War, while investigating the Armenian genocide in the field and writing other pamphlets exposing the atrocities of the Central Powers, Toynbee saw the horrors of war at close quarters. Having been devastated by the senseless brutality in the summer of 1920, he borrowed Oswald Spengler's *Der Untergang des Abendlandes* from his friend, Lewis Namier. The German author's conclusions mirrored his own: first, the smallest "intelligible units" of histor-

---

45 Toynbee, "The Value of Oriental History for Historians." Lecture at the meeting of Siam Society. Reprinted from the journal of Siam Society, Vol. XLV, Pt 2, October 1957, 73-79, December 4, 1956. Toynbee Papers, MS 13967/3.
46 Interview with Prof Toynbee, July 7, 1961, *German Feature*. Toynbee Papers BL Oxford MS13967/7 Broadcasts 1929-1955.
47 Initially used to describe contemporary totalitarian ideologies, the phrase "secular religion" quickly spread to include various political, socioeconomic, and cultural concerns. The use of terms like "secular," "false," "pseudo," "ersatz," "lay," "quasi," etc. in connection with "religion" has been hotly debated: many scholars tend to use the term "new religion" instead. As Tamás Nyirkos explains, religion ceases to be secular in any meaningful sense of the word the moment that the nation, the race, the human self, the market, money, nature, history, etc. become absolute points of reference, reflecting an ultimate concern even to the point of becoming deified. Moreover, "the proliferation of the literature of secular religions despite all definitional problems reinforces the suspicion that with some creativity, everything can be called a religion, which is, however, almost the same as saying that nothing can be called as such." Though only "an empty signifier" for some thinkers, no widely accepted alternative exists for the term religion, thus the terminological difficulties linger on. Nyirkos 2021, 78-79. See also Emilio Gentile, *Politics as Religion*, Princeton, Princeton University Press, 2006, and Tara Isabella Burton, *Strange Rites: New Religions for a Godless World*, New York, Public Affairs, 2020.
48 McNeill, Toynbee Revisited 14.
49 Toynbee, *A Study of History*, Vol. I, London, Oxford University Press, 1934, 212.
50 Toynbee, "Nationalism in Politics," Broadcast Talks Pamphlets: Britain and the Modern World Order by Toynbee and J.L Hammond, June 2, 1932, BBC. Toynbee Papers BL Oxford MS13967/43: Diaries and offprints.

## 3.2. Toynbee on Religion and Secular Religions

ical study were civilizations rather than arbitrarily isolated fragments, such as modern nation-states in the West; second, Western civilisation had reached the end of its development and it was in decline greatly owing to its enlightened-rationalist tradition that had rejected religion and Christianity per se.[51] Thus, we need to take a closer look at the complex role religion played in the great historian-diplomat's life in order to understand his post-First World War attitude on nationalism.

Toynbee's preoccupation with religion is revealed in his long letters of 1937-55 to Father Columba, a Dominican monk who he later called "the most direct door to God."[52] Throughout his life, he was torn between attraction and aversion to Catholicism and faith in general. The years in Oxford alienated him from the ordinary Anglicanism of his home and of his early schooling; and the two "revelations" during his 1929-30 journey to Japan, as well as many years later, around the death of his first-born son in 1939, recalled in him a belief in the existence of "some kind of transcendent reality," but no personal God.[53] By the second half of the thirties, partly due to the influence of his wife, Rosalind Murray, he was on the threshold of Catholicism,[54] and was then discouraged by intel-

---

51  Toynbee, *Civilization on Trial*, Oxford University Press, 1948, 9-10. Qtd. in McNeill 1989, 98-99.
52  Toynbee to Father Columba, (Cary Elwes, 1903-1994), September 30, 1939. Toynbee Papers 13967/79/1 Correspondence
53  In Japan he experienced the presence of the transcendent reality when withstanding a strong (sexual) temptation. In his own assessment, tension between his classical and Christian education never abated, and he remained an agnostic until the very end, neither a committed Christian nor a universal humanist. (Toynbee, 1969, 91.) This is somewhat contradicted by the fact that Toynbee considered it important to have his second marriage consecrated in the Church of England (which did not happen) and have the first annulled by the Holy See. (Archbishop's Office to Toynbee, original undated, [December 13, 1946]. Toynbee Papers BL Oxford MS13 967/39 General Miscellaneous Correspondence 1911-1956.) McNeill 1989, 323.
54  " I do not believe I ever could become a Catholic myself," confessed Toynbee in 1944. "If I am not, and perhaps never could be, a Catholic, I certainly am, and shall remain a philo-Catholic—for Rosalind's sake, for your sake [...] for sake of my Catholic friends [...] and the Catholic saints whom I reverence and admire.[...] I did not follow in her wake, though temptation was very strong, because being married to her was my most precious possession in this life." Toynbee to Father Columba, July 14, 1944. Toynbee Papers 13967/79/1 Correspondence.
Rosalind's flirtation with Catholicism and her eventual conversion in 1929 was a way to emerge from her agnostic father's shadow. What followed was an almost decade-long struggle to convince the intellectually independent Toynbee to convert. Even his mother-in-law advised quite against putting his "historical genius in blinkers." Marry Murray to Toynbee, August 3, 1933. Toynbee Papers, MS 13967/72/2 Family correspondence 1910-1939 and Correspondence [1890s-1940s].
Greatly owing to Rosalind's new orientation and domineering attitude, after a number of attempts to get a spiritual reconciliation "on the basis of the normal relation btw husband and wife," Toynbee divorced her for desertion on May 27, 1946, and started life "from beginning again" with his secretary, Veronica Boulter. Toynbee to Father Columba, June 13, 1946. Toynbee Papers 13967/79/1 Correspondence.
Along with Rosalind's fading influence, his inclination toward Catholicism decreased, and Toynbee began to value the more inclusive Indian religions. "I was brought up to believe that Christi-

247

lectual, anthropological and professional considerations: although he believed it not impossible that Catholicism was *a* revelation, he found it most improbable that it was *the* revelation of God. Likewise, if he converted to Catholicism, he argued, the pagan intellectuals would immediately dismiss him as someone who had "gone soft-headed" and should no longer be regarded seriously. Being afraid of losing all credibility in their eyes, he rather declared himself "still on the way."[55] Columba was non-interfering: "I wait patiently for God to call you into it in his own good time, to be a leader of your generation, someone who will dare to face the fact of our ancestors' sin [that is English Reformation(s)] and counteract it."[56] From the second half of the 1930s onwards, the historian was a regular visitor to Ampleforth Monastery in search of inner peace and clarity, however, no conversion occurred.[57]

Meanwhile, Toynbee began to view contemporary historical phenomena, and above all emerging ideologies in a religious framework, however, unlike the overtly pessimistic Spengler, he believed that Western civilization could be capable of continuous renewal. The Japanese attack on Manchuria (1932) and the Italian aggression against Abyssinia (1935), and especially the failure of the League to address the crises properly by checking the dictators, were interpreted by him as a failure of Western Christianity: "The spirit of man abhors a spiritual vacuum," he opined, "and if it loses sight of God as He is revealed in Christianity it will inevitably relapse into the worship of [...] militant State cults—whether Fascist or Communist—which have been most successful in gaining converts during these post-war years."[58] He approached World War II with the same religious orientation, regarding the worldwide conflict as an opportunity: the severe hardships, he believed, that Britain and the whole world would face, would, in a very compelling manner, dispel the illusion that "an earthly paradise" (cap-

---

anity was a unique revelation of the whole truth. I have now come to believe that all the historic religions and philosophies are partial revelations of the truth in one or other of its aspects," he came to acknowledge in 1954. Toynbee, A Study of History: What I am Trying to Do, *International Affairs* (Royal Institute of International Affairs 1944-), Vol. 31, No. 1 (January, 1955), 1-4. (Published by Oxford University Press on behalf of the Royal Institute of International Affairs, 4.) Interestingly, in 1929 Toynbee's sister, Jocelyn also became a Catholic. More in John A. O'Brien, *The Road to Damascus, the spiritual journey of fifteen converts to Catholicism*, Vol. II, London, W.H. Allen, 1950, 195-201. Despite these conversions, in the first volume of *Study* Toynbee used the secular "élan vital" instead of God, *Study of History*, Vol. I, Oxford University Press, 1934, 249.

55 Toynbee to Father Columba, August 5, 1938. Toynbee Papers 13967/79/1 Correspondence.
56 Father Columba to Toynbee, September 22, 1939. Toynbee Papers 13967/79/1 Correspondence.
57 In 1944 Columba censured Toynbee for intellectual arrogance and severed ties with him for two years.
58 Toynbee, letter to the editor of the *Manchester Guardian*, April 9, 1935. McNeill 1989, 185.

italist, Marxist, Fascist, etc.) was "just around the corner."[59] In his Burge address prior to the French capitulation, he referred to Christianity as "the heir of all higher religions." His shift in perspective was astounding, as outlined by McNeill: whereas a 1920 Toynbee lecture defined religion as a "chrysalis" for civilizations, passing wisdom and knowledge from one generation to the next, in 1940, civilizations came to serve religion by providing a chance for spiritual development amidst the misery their collapse had brought about.[60] As is generally known, the end of World War II and especially the ensuing Cold War did not lead to spiritual advancement but to further suffering, and Toynbee's religious outlook only broadened: in contrast to its growing popularity in the West, he looked at Marxism as "western heresy,"[61] and viewed the cold war as "missionary" warfare, "a spiritual struggle between rival religions."[62]

However, besides having dismissed Marxism-Leninism in extraordinarily religious language, Toynbee grew increasingly hostile towards nationalism, too. As touched on earlier, already in his excellent book *Western Question in Greece and Turkey* (1922) he labelled it the "fatal Western idea" that may have caused the misery of Greeks and Turks (and Armenians) who had formerly cohabited peacefully in the same area. In the following decades, quite in contrast to the often "studiously colourless" *Surveys*, Toynbee's "Nonsense-books," as he came to call his volumes of *Study of History*, vehemently castigated nationalism. In the first volume it was defined as "a spirit which makes people feel and act and think about a part of any given society as though it were the whole of that society," that is couched in neutral enough terms. However, a page later the author turned critical: nationalism next to industrialism *de facto* dominated Western society and as an exclusive worship of local community, "indeed a regression to tribalism," it undermined humanity's spiritual development by fuelling fratricidal conflict.[63]

In the subsequent *Study* volumes, especially from the 1930s onwards, Toynbee turned even more censorious, further scourging nationalism: it was depicted as a false religion as it intensified "the brutal and irrational side of human nature." Whereas Christianity advocated the brotherhood of humanity under the

---

59  Toynbee to Father Columba, January 14, 1940. Toynbee Papers 13967/79/1 Correspondence.
60  Toynbee, "Christianity and Civilization," Burge Memorial Lecture, May 23, 1940. Toynbee Papers BL Oxford MS13967/29/2. McNeill 1989, 187-188.
61  Toynbee, The World and the War (1953). Toynbee Papers MS 13967/31/2
62  Toynbee, "Democracy in the Atomic Age," the *Dyason Lectures*, under the Auspices of the Australian Institute of International Affairs, Oxford: Oxford Universty Press, 1956. Toynbee Papers BL Oxford MS13967/3 Lectures 1926-1970.
63  Toynbee, *A Study of History*, Vol. 1, Oxford University Press, 1946, 9. (first edition in 1934)

fatherhood of God, nationalism was nothing other than "the lamentable victory of parochialism over ecumenicalism."[64]

Retaining this negative tone about nationalism, Toynbee developed his theory further in subsequent volumes of the *Study*: ethnocentrism was harmful to humanity not only because it was exclusionary and hate mongering, but also as it destroyed the fundamental ideals of democracy, "Nationalism is a cuckoo in the democratic nest. [...] Democracy imprisoned in parochial states degenerates into Nationalism."[65] As his celebrated contemporary, German historian Friedrich Meinecke put it: In the first half of the nineteenth century, liberal nationalists believed that a unitary state free from foreign subjugation was consistent with the principle of natural rights, and argued that patriotism led to love of humanity. However, by the end of the nineteenth century nationalists denounced liberalism as the primary threat to national greatness. Dissociated from liberalism, nationalism started to embrace mysticism: the cult of heroes, the cult of the leader and that of force. "Just and unjust, good and bad, true and false, lose their meaning; what men condemn as disgraceful and inhuman when done by others, they recommend in the same breath to their own peoples as something to be done to a foreign country."[66]

Around the outbreak of World War II, and particularly after the surrender of France, Toynbee not only envisaged an opportunity for spiritual renewal, as touched upon above, but also the end of the nation state and the coming of a "world state," created either by Hitler or by the English-speaking peoples.[67] In a private letter he concurred that one of the reasons the League had failed was because the West attempted to maintain their local sovereignty while also gaining all the benefits that would result from renouncing it. In the histories of many civilizations, this conflict between political parochialism and spiritual and economic interconnectedness has led to their demise. It is inevitable that our planet would become politically united into a single state. Historically, this had only ever been accomplished through force—one Great Power eliminating the competition at the expense of the spiritual and economic exhaustion of the entire population. He put forward the idea of a real federation of the democratic states of Western Europe and North America plus Australia, "so preponderant"

---

64   Toynbee, *A Study of History*, Vol. VII/b, Oxford University Press, 1954, 443. Qtd. in Marvin Perry, Arnold Toynbee, Nationalism as a "false god", *Interpretation, A Journal of Political Philosophy*, Vol. 4/1, Winter 1974, 51.
65   Toynbee, *A Study of History*, Vol. IV, Oxford University Press, 1939, 163.
66   Meinecke, *The German Catastrophe*, Boston, 1963, 23-24. Qtd. in Marvin Perry AT: Nationalism as a "false god," *Interpretation, A Journal of Pol Philosophy*, Vol. 4/1, Winter 1974, 54.
67   Toynbee to Father Columba, June 23, 1940. Toynbee Papers 13967/79/1 Correspondence.

a power, "virtually a World Government." This would achieve global peace with the least amount of violence and injustice.⁶⁸

In October 1941, a delegation of American clergy visited Balliol under the auspices of the World Council of Churches to discuss peace goals with Toynbee and a group of Anglican clergy and laity. A second American delegation, led by future secretary of state John Foster Dulles, arrived at Balliol after the United States entered World War II. In these meetings, Toynbee played both an official and an informal role. He had access to official British documents pertaining to the terms of the peace, which he was not allowed to disclose to the World Council of Churches. However, he was free to express himself as a private person. When the New York-based Rockefeller Foundation invited Toynbee to come to the USA "to consult on post-war challenges," his function as a go-between with Americans took on a new dimension. He received permission to accept this invitation and, as a result, left Great Britain on August 23 via air and did not return to London until October 20, 1942. Toynbee attended a meeting at Princeton with Dulles and other representatives of the Commission on a Just and Durable Peace, an organization connected to the World Council of Churches, whose representatives had previously contacted him at Oxford. Toynbee argued that the only effective answer to the primary issues with the current world order was a global government: The world has become a community, and its members no longer have the moral right to exercise "sovereignty" or "independence," which is now nothing more than a legal right to act without regard to the harm which is done. His specific proposal was a reconstruction of a World Association of Nations, to which all of the United Nations would initially belong, and the Axis powers as soon as possible. The time has arrived for nations to give up their freedom to act immorally.⁶⁹

After World War II he came to believe that the abrogation of national sovereignty and the unification of Western Civilization were the two major challenges and once met, universal peace could be established. In a world armed with atomic weapons, Toynbee claimed, "our choice now lies between co-existence or non-existence,"⁷⁰ with tremendous responsibility on all sovereign governments and on the electorates. The UN will only work, he continued, if all concerned

---

68  Toynbee to Lionel Curtis, February 16, 1939. RIIA Archives, 4/TOYN/6E. See also Toynbee, *Experiences*, 91-92.
69  Memorandum re Toynbee visit to the United States, no date. Toynbee Papers MS 13967/92 Journeys-Correspondence 1928-48 McNeill 1989, 184-185.
70  Toynbee, *The Ultimate Choice*, Chichester, Sussex, R.J. Acford Ltd., 1961 reprint.

"make great voluntary sacrifices of national sovereignty and interests."[71] The future therefore should lie in extensive devolution; however, he was convinced that nation states could not be abolished but rather subordinated to world purposes. As long as it does not include the right to wage war, he believed, the national state's variety of culture and language is good in and of itself [...] levels of loyalty need not be exclusive. It is perfectly possible to maintain a loyalty to the local community while the paramount loyalty is given to the world.[72]

Interestingly, around the late 1960s, besides Nazism communism and nationalism, Toynbee also included liberal democracy among his targets as "new paganism." While preparing a volume of documents on the diplomatic relations between Britain and Nazi Germany, the eminent Churchill-biographer-historian Martin Gilbert approached Toynbee to include one of his 1935 letters on "Nazism as a serious moral challenge to Christianity." Toynbee agreed on condition that a short footnote was inserted stating that he

> [...] still holds the view [...] that we have to choose between the new paganism and non-pagan religion, but he now thinks of the new paganism as including all forms of religion (e.g. nationalism, communism, and liberal democracy) in which some human community or institution is taken as having ultimate value, and he thinks of non-pagan religion as including all forms of religion (e.g. Buddhism, Judaism, Islam, as well as Christianity) which stand for an ultimate spiritual reality beyond man.[73]

In 1967 Toynbee argued that once great religions break down, communism, individualism and nationalism would be worshipped and would become pseudo-religions, that is, new forces for unification. Out of the three, Toynbee believed nationalism was the strongest, which always won in case of conflict. This triumph, nevertheless, was harmful for humanity:

---

71 Toynbee to Reverend D.E. Richard, June 17, 1955. Toynbee Papers BL Oxford MS13967/96. Journeys: correspondence.
"The UN will only work if all concerned nations make great voluntary sacrifices of national sovereignty and interests." Toynbee to the Bishop of Albany, June 17, 1955. Toynbee Papers BL Oxford MS13967/85.
72 Donald Keys, Transcript of Interview with Arnold Toynbee, National Committee for Sane Nuclear policy, July 1961. Toynbee Papers BL Oxford MS13 967/63/2.
73 Toynbee to Martin Gilbert, March 18, 1968. Toynbee Papers BL Oxford MS13 967/63/1 Correspondence 1931-74.

The devotion that has been transferred from Christianity to Nationalism has detached itself from what is good in Christianity but has clung to what is evil in it. It has repudiated the ideas of love, self-sacrifice, and concern for mankind as a whole [but] retained the fanaticism that is the common vice of the religions of the Judaic family [...]. [74]

However, towards the end of his life, Toynbee's contempt for nationalism was somewhat tempered, at least he took a more pragmatic view:

Nationalism [...] is the real religion today of the majority of the people. Nationalism has been superseded only nominally by the "higher" religions, each of which aims at converting the whole of mankind to its own prescription for putting the individual into touch with ultimate reality. Whether we profess to be followers of one of the historic higher religions or not, almost all of us are nationalist under the skin.[75]

### 3.3. "A Prophet to Profit from"? Toynbee's Assessment in Britain and Beyond

Toynbee once declared: "I had thought I was a cosmopolitan by grace but after all I am only an English-man."[76] Indeed, he was one, whose fame in his home country had never been equal to his world-wide renown.[77] He often faced brutal attacks, especially after World War II, when Marxist-liberal discussions dominated British academia, which tended to overlook ages unrelated to liberty and regarded Eastern Europe, let alone the Far East as *terra incognita*. A.J.P. Taylor and historian and former intelligence officer Hugh Trevor-Roper came to dominate the scene: Toynbee's critical attitude towards the West as well as his

---

74 Toynbee, *Change and Habit*, 110. See also: Conversation with Toynbee (Thomas Davies), November 27, 1955, Vol. 21, No 3, 189th Broadcast. Bulletin of America's Town Meeting of the Air, ABC Network. Adapted from A Town Hall Lecture by Dr. Toynbee. Toynbee Papers, MS 13967/43 Diaries and offprints. See also Toynbee, *Surviving the Future*, Oxford University Press, 1971. Toynbee Papers 13967/31 Reviews and MS 13 967/128/1 Reviews and Correspondence 1915-1970.
75 Toynbee, *Surviving the Future*, NY, 1971, 65.
76 "Encounters between Civilizations," a talk by Toynbee, May 12, 1949. Toynbee Papers, MS 13967/43 Diaries and offprints.
77 "Toynbee appears in a historian's disguise as a religious prophet [...] he hopes to be canonised. That he does not directly identify himself with Jesus, or rather announce himself as a new and modern Christ, seems only due, after all, to a fear of making a fool of himself. [...He] has never had any prestige among English historians." Herbert Tingsten, "Finished with Toynbee," *Dagens Nyheter*, Dec 6, 1954. RIIA Archivees 4/TOYN/4

assertion that religion might resolve global issues became the targets of his critics' anger in the 1950s.[78]

In a series of annual BBC radio lectures given by leading figures of the day, the British Broadcasting Corporation asked Toynbee to deliver the 1952 Reith Lectures.[79] In his lecture, titled "The World's Encounter with the West," Toynbee attempted to do his very best: he duly attacked the good old-fashioned patriotism of his fellow Britons by denouncing the Western aggression inherent in past colonisation while ignoring its benefits. He also defended Turkey in defiance of the liberal notion that Balkan nations had been oppressed, which was the direct antithesis of his First World War propaganda.[80] For many, this was the last straw: the ageing Steed also joined the choir of critics by claiming that Toynbee, who had suffered severely "from red-tapeworm during the war," seemed a ridiculous "sort of Billy Graham with an ecclesiastic-hierophantic complex."[81] In fact, ten days after Steed's letter, Toynbee did emphasize that he should "steer clear of theology," on which he was "only an amateur"[82]—which, nevertheless, he failed to follow.[83]

In 1954 he resigned as director of studies, and soon not only the idea of the *Annual Surveys* was abandoned but also Toynbee's global approach, his interest in civilizations, etc.[84] Interestingly, apart from the Stevenson Chair at the London School of Economics in 1948 (which was rather a formality), Toyn-

---

78  In a letter to his father-in-law, Gilbert Murray, Toynbee talked about his "Copernican" denial of the centrality of national and West European history for the human past as a whole. Toynbee to Gilbert Murray, November 21, 1953. Toynbee papers, MS 13967/72/1 Family correspondence 1914-1957. More in Ian Hall, *Dilemmas of Decline: British Intellectuals and World Politics, 1945-75*, Berkeley, CA, University of California Press, 2012, 131-151.
Another staunch Toynbee-critic was the Dutch historian Pieter Geyl (1887-1966), who in a lecture delivered at the University of Utrecht in November 1946 reproached the English professor, "a hater of nationalism," for on the one hand distrusting national independence and discarding national ambitions, specifically those of the Boer Republics, and on the other hand for praising South Africa, a peaceful multi-national state. All these errors, Geyl argued, derived from Toynbee's "lack of understanding for the reality of the national factor in history." Qtd. in: Pieter Geyl, Arnold J. Toynbee and Pitrim Sorokin, *The Pattern of the Past: Can We Determine It?* Boston, Beacon Press, 1949, 68-69.
79  These lectures, which bear the name of the BBC's first director, were created with the goal of capping the broadcast year by addressing a crucial issue facing the British people.
80  Toynbee Papers, MS 13967/128/1 Reviews and correspondence: various works 1915-1970.
81  Steed to Gooch, October 14, 1954. Steed Papers MS 74134.
82  Toynbee to Rev David Emrys Richard, Suffragan Bishop, October 24, 1954. Toynbee Papers, MS 13967/96. Journeys: correspondence 1955.
83  As a result, his later, synthetizing, rather intuitive works were subjected to even harsher criticism: "Every man for its trade: [...] no one can wonder at a historian, however great his genius, uttering enormities on psychology, morality and religion, if these subjects are not his speciality." Toynbee's *The Present-Day Experiment in Western Civilization*, (OUP, 1962), Reviewed by L. Lauwers in *World Justice*, vol 6., 99. Toynbee Papers BL Oxford MS13967/31/1.
84  Christopher Brewin, Arnold Toynbee and Chatham House. In: Bosco-Navari 1994, 137.

bee was never assigned to a significant chair in the British university system or a top position in an Oxbridge college, probably as he had not thought his job as a professor required him to teach. "I myself happen to be devoted to research and writing, while I do not much care for teaching and positively dislike administrative work," he confessed in 1953.[85] He had been appointed as a Knight Commander of the Most Distinguished Order of St Michael and St George (only) in recognition of his wartime services to the State,[86] which appointment he turned down eventually. With or without acknowledgement, Toynbee masterfully anticipated today's concerns: global responsibility in the atomic age,[87] worldwide ecological problems,[88] the hazards of technology,[89] the economic "take-over" of Europe by the USA,[90] the decline of the West and the rise of China,[91] and many more...

McNeill rightly claims that Toynbee never identified himself as a prophet, but insofar as he set out to expose God to all of humanity, he did in fact become one.[92] At least by offering spiritual support for many. Béla Kapótsy, the former secretary of the Hungarian-American Society of Budapest (1945-1949) and former political prisoner, who spent 28 days on death-row wrote to Toyn-

---

85 The Stevenson Research Chair: notes on the Chair and the work involved by Dr. A.J. Toynbee, Princeton, New Jersey, June 23, 1953. Toynbee Papers, MS 13967/40 General Miscellaneous Correspondence 1931-64. In 1970 Toynbee confessed that he disliked politics, too. Arnold Toynbee, "Was Britain's abdication folly?" The Round Table, 1970. 60:238, 219-228, DOI: 10.1080/00358537008452875, 228.
86 Toynbee declined the knighthood because he believed it would harm his relationship with "other nationalities, including Americans," which seems a rather feeble excuse. Foreign Office to Toynbee & Toynbee to Foreign Office, May 28, 1945. Toynbee Papers BL Oxford MS13967/83/2 Correspondence.
87 Here Toynbee was mainly thinking about atomic energy. "We are like children armed with atomic weapons- a most dangerous thing. This is really the religious question; so it requires a change of heart." Will Businessmen Unite the World? (Three international business leaders' discussion with A. J. Toynbee), Center Magazine, September 23, 1970. Toynbee Papers, MS 13967/7 Broadcasts 1929-1955. See also Conversations with A. Toynbee, September 1967. Toynbee Papers, MS 13967/7 Broadcasts 1929-1955.
88 Ibid.
89 Marvin Perry, Arnold Toynbee, Nationalism as a "false god," Interpretation, A Journal of Political Philosophy, Vol. 4/1, Winter 1974, 61.
90 Toynbee to Herve Lavenir, Brussels, Belgium, July 10, 1967. Toynbee Papers BL Oxford MS13 967/63/1 Correspondence 1931-74. "Personally I wish she would come closer." [GB to ECSC], Toynbee to Madame Micheu, March 16, 1953. Toynbee Papers BL Oxford MS13 967/128/1 Reviews and Correspondence 1915-1970.
91 Toynbee and Daisaku Ikeda, Choose Life, Bloomsbury Academic, 2007, 231-33.
Already in his 1915 Nationality and the War, Toynbee foresaw that China would make an effort to reorganize her national life and to use all of her untapped potential strength to gain her "place in the Sun," which, according to his prediction, would result in "a more titanic struggle than Germany is currently engaged in." Toynbee 1905, 333.
92 McNeill 1989, 220-221.

bee in 1964. He explained that the Hungarian Secret Police did not burn his copy of Toynbee's *Study*, but gave it back to him to read while still in prison.[93]

> Your boundless references to God, the general way of your writing [...] History as but a manifestation of God's will on earth and your constant quotations from the Holy Bible and from Sacred Writings supplied us—my cellmates and myself, all condemned to death—with a truly life-sustaining force and with deepest consolation and trust in God which we were so greatly in need of at our plight [...] you have helped rescue our souls from desperation [....][94]

The "much touched" Toynbee responded: "My book could have no better use than to give some consolation to fellow human beings in extremis."[95]

Another instance of spiritual guidance was in Japan in the late 1960s, when Toynbee enjoyed enormous popularity, concurrent with his condemnation in Britain. A substantial group of intellectuals turned to Toynbee for guidance when Marxism failed to fill the moral gap created by the rejection of the nationalist Shinto faith. When the seven-day conversation between Toynbee and Kai Wakaizumi, a professor of international affairs at Kyoto Industrial University, was published in 1971, the response from the general public was as overwhelmingly positive as it had been in the USA in 1947. Toynbee's guidance on how to feel and live filled the void left by the rejection of Shinto tradition and the defeat in World War II.[96] Right after Toynbee's death, Professor Wakaizumi praised him in the *Times*: "It was his non-Europe-centred stance, with heavy emphasis on the future potential of East Asia, that made such a great appeal to Japanese scholars as well as the thinking public."[97]

In August 1974, Toynbee suffered a stroke that left him bedridden, unable to speak or write. Fourteen difficult months passed until he died, at last.

---

93 Dr. Béla Kapótsy to Toynbee, March 28, 1964. Toynbee Papers BL Oxford MS13967/40. Kapótsy wrote an article in the journal *Magyar Szabadság* [Freedom of Hungary], too, titled Mr Toynbee is not for Burning.
94
95 Toynbee to Béla Kapótsy, April 27, 1964. Toynbee Papers BL Oxford MS13967/40.
96 McNeill 1988, 25-26.
97 Kei Wakaizumi, letter to the *Times*, November 30, 1975. McNeill 1989, 271.

# Conclusion

"The search for truth ought to be disinterested"[1]

In 1937, in *Black Lamb and Grey Falcon*, journalist and travel-writer Rebecca West (1892–1983) wrote:

> English persons [...] of humanitarian and reformist dispositions constantly went out to the Balkan peninsula to see who was in fact ill-treating whom, and, being by the very nature of their perfectionist faith unable to accept the horrid hypothesis that everybody was ill-treating everybody else, all came back with a pet Balkan people established in their hearts as suffering and innocent, eternally the massacree and never the massacrer [...] The problems of India and Africa never produced anything like the jungle of savage pamphlets that sprang up in the footsteps of the Liberals who visited Turkey in Europe under the inspiration of Gladstone.[2]

West's brilliant argument might be extended to all smaller peoples of East-Central Europe, or even somewhat beyond, who from the late nineteenth century up to 1945 also had their share of prominent British *philes* (and *phobes*); that inexhaustible list contains Albanophile Edith Durham, Bulgarophile Noel Buxton, pro-Romanian Allen Leeper or the pro-Ruthene Lewis Namier, all of whom have been touched on only superficially and who could be the subjects of (an) other book(s). The main protagonists of the present work all had their favourites, too: Seton-Watson was captivated by the Slovaks but came into closer, and more

---

1 "One World, One History," presentation by Toynbee at Princeton University Bicentennial Conference "The University and its World Responsibilities," February 20, 1947. Toynbee Papers, MSS 13967/3 Lectures.
2 Rebecca West, *Black Lamb and Grey Falcon*, Penguin Classics, 2007, 20–21.

enduring contact with the Czechs; Steed was engrossed in South-Slav matters,[3] Macartney, intrigued by Hungary,[4] as well as Toynbee who extended Christian do-goodism the farthest, to the Armenians and the Greeks (joining other philhellenes, most notably Ronald Burrows and Sir Arthur Evans).

Distance offers fresh perspective. In his 1922 inaugural lecture Seton-Watson claimed that, "the British Historian who does not belong to any of the rival nationalities which jostle each other throughout the wide area of central Europe, is doubtless saved from the worst pitfall that threatens his continental colleagues."[5] But was it really so? Even with his pro-Hungarian bias taken into account, Macartney was clearly less prejudiced and more detached than Seton-Watson, let alone Steed. Macartney was a "cool brain free from 'pro' and 'anti'-complexes, according to G. P. Gooch.[6] His early work at the LNU was already characterised by "scholarly temper and scrupulous accuracy" by his superior at LNU, Professor Gilbert Murray, not incidentally also Toynbee's father-in-law. Steed's, Seton-Watson's and some of Toynbee's papers and correspondence, on the other hand, rather reveal, albeit to varying degrees, that they tended to glorify or denigrate entire peoples by applying strong labels such as "civilized" or "barbaric" and other labels like "natural" or "artificial" to their often-would-be borders and states. As a moralistic, self-righteous liberal, Seton-Watson, for instance, was described by Permanent Under-Secretary William Strang as "a notorious energumen with passionate prejudices in foreign affairs and a keen desire to influence foreign policy."[7]

The truth is that the way of using such labels often disclosed less about the observed and more about the observers. Upon arriving in Austria-Hungary, Seton-Watson noted that "the vital question of Nationality" met him at every corner, clamouring for a "solution."[8] Thus, as a lifelong idealist, he was convinced that social issues not only have to be addressed, but could be solved too, and national self-determination would be such a "one cure for all." He also swallowed

---

3   "Mr. Steed was, however unjustifiably, regarded by the majority of opinion in that country as so ardent a partisan of the Southern Slavs that it would be difficult for him to take a wholly impartial view of certain issues, over which conflicts of interest were sure to arise." Sir James Rennell Rodd, G.C.B., *Social And Diplomatic Memories 1902–1919*, London, Edward Arnold & Co., 356–357.
4   In 1955, when Arnold Toynbee, learned that Macartney was writing a book about Hungary, he said, "Oh, Macartney is more Hungarian than the good Hungarians themselves." Miskolczy added: „Perhaps it was not up to us that we failed to make an enemy of him." Qtd. in Miskolczy 1994, 1512.
5   Seton-Watson 1922, 11.
6   Chaired by G.P Gooch. Macartney, "The Situation in Hungary," Address at RIIA, October 12, 1931. RIIA Archives 8/161.
7   Rychlík, Marzik, Bielik (eds.) 1995, Vol. I/62.
8   Seton-Watson 1908, vii.

the popular pre-war idea that the application of the right of self-determination would result in democratic regimes in the region, together with the notion that just because a nation is small, once freed it would necessarily become liberal.[9] In this respect, Steed was no different. In his then-newly-purchased monthly, *The Review of Reviews*, he argued that the Great War had been "an immense act of faith in democracy."[10]

However, unlike Seton-Watson, as we have seen, Steed was focusing primarily on the European balance of power from the perspective of the British Empire, even at times by sacrificing or completely ignoring little nations. A prime example of this was his reaction to the Bulgarian–Serbian–Greek and Montenegrin attack on the Ottoman Empire in October 1912. Nine days later, he wrote to Geoffrey Robinson, his successor as the *Times* Vienna correspondent:

> When war between the Balkan States and Turkey has once fairly broken out, England will have every interest to see Turkey smashed and humiliated. A victorious Turkey [...] would gain such prestige in Egypt and India that Pan-Islamism would receive a tremendous impulse. A beaten Turkey would be far less dangerous for us. [...] but if Turkey comes out of this war with prestige, we shall feel the pinch of it everywhere.[11]

Some twelve years later, Steed disclosed his priorities: "In the little work I did, it was not so much the idea of helping any individual people as in that of trying to save Europe as a whole from pan-German military domination and thus open the way for a freer life to Europe."[12]

Steed was also proud enough to declare that the sense of duty he owed to the public was "sufficiently keen" to prevent him "from foisting upon it merely partial or one-sided views.[13] But that was nothing more than wishful thinking. He was also prejudiced, or rather, he was the most prejudiced of the four. Besides his anti-Semitism,[14] his visceral Germanophobia was legendary and long-

---

9  Ibid., 52.
10 *The Review of Reviews*, August 15, 1924.
11 Steed to Goffrey Robinson (later Dawson), October 17, 1912. PHS Papers. Steed Papers.
12 Steed to Václav Klofáč, January 9, 1924. Steed Papers MS 74103. Klofáč was a Czech journalist, politician, and after 1919, the first Czechoslovak minister of national defence.
13 Steed to Lord Northbourne, January 2, 1930. Steed Papers MS 74128. He continued: "My confidence in my judgement is strong enough to make me hold to an opinion when once I have formed it."
14 More on this in Liebich 2012.

lasting; the French minister in Vienna, Gabriel Puaux, referred to his *"austrophobie notoire,"*¹⁵ as late as 1938.

Unlike Steed or Seton-Watson, Macartney was convinced that the sense of nationality was of all "great political feelings the most subjective and the most variable."¹⁶ Therefore, as put forward by Miklós Lojkó, for him as a Conservative, the aim of politics was not an abstract policy of satisfying national ambitions, but rather to provide for the well-being of its citizens, *both* culturally and economically.¹⁷ Given the inherent weakness of nationality, he was looking for federative solutions for East-Central Europe, transforming the Danube Basin into a kind of "Eastern Switzerland"¹⁸ based on "complete national equality." As this was violated in Versailles, he opined, frontier rectifications were a necessary. Macartney, on the other hand, was no classic appeaser: revision was the precondition for long-term political consolidation in the region to serve primarily cultural and economic reasons, and not to please the strong (Germany) at the expense of the weak (Czechoslovakia).

Though not closely attached to the New Europe circle, Toynbee initially approached East-Central Europe and Turkey through the lens of Seton-Watson, thus with a similar indignation and sense of justice rooted in the Gladstonian missionary spirit. As we have seen, he proved to be an excellent student, producing one denouncing propaganda leaflet after another during the First World War. However, he soon came to reconsider his earlier stance as post-World War I events proved the weakness of the small nation-state system that Seton-Watson and Steed were instrumental in bringing to life. First, upon visiting war-torn Turkey in 1922, Toynbee witnessed the occupying Greeks demonstrating the same unfitness as the Turks for governing a mixed population. Second, he remained equally sceptical about the new states of East-Central-Europe as well. For example, in 1934 he wrote:

> Let us try to imagine ourselves writing the history of the Western Society round one of those national states which have attained statehood since 1918 [...] whether a Czechoslovak or a Jugoslav national consciousness yet ex-

---

15 As well as "aversion marquae a l'egard du regime habsbourgeois." Documents diplomatiques francais, 2nd series, Vol. VIII, doc. No. 14. Qtd. in Thomas Angerer, *Henry Wickham Steed, Robert William Seton-Watson und die Habsburgermonarchie, Ihr Haltungswandel bis Kriegsanfang im Vergleich*. Mitteilungen des Instituts für Österreichische Geschichtsforschung, MIÖG Bd. 99/3-4, Vienna, Bühlau Verlag, 1991, 472.
16 Macartney 1937, 13.
17 Lojkó 1999, 42.
18 Macartney 1937, 496.

ists has hardly ceased to be a debatable question. Certainly, such consciousnesses were non-existent as recently as fifty years ago; [...] Short of writing a Slovako-centric or a Croato-centric history of the West, we should find it impossible to write even a Slovako-centric history of Slovakia or a Croato-centric history of Croatia. [...] the emergence of new national states like Czechoslovakia and Jugoslavia which have no history at all and whose component parts have no history that is intelligible in isolation. [...] began to implant a separate consciousness in peoples of so small a calibre that these were incapable not only of forming Great Powers but even of forming minor states of political, economic and cultural independence.[19]

Thirteen years later, Toynbee referred to the break-up of Austria-Hungary after the First World War as the "outstanding example of the potency of history," The war provided the occasion, but it was the popularisation of the findings of academic historians that brought about the nation-states of East-Central Europe, he opined, adding that he was "not sure whether these effects have been altogether good."[20] Given their support for the national-states, which was dubious at best, Toynbee as well as Macartney advocated a supranational settlement. As regards the remaining minorities, Toynbee argued, the ideal would have been "an enlarged Habsburg Monarchy with a democratic federal constitution." This would have been the only way of creating a "neutral belt" that was truly independent of both Germany and Russia.[21]

Thus, the underlying factor that further distanced Toynbee from his earlier self and the New-Europe group was his infatuation with the "big picture," manifested in his "Nonsense Book," the twelve volumes of *The Study of History*, and its underlying idea that the nation-state could not function as an intelligible unit of historical study compelled him from early on to look beyond, or rather above historical dimensions. Even regarding the much and rightly cursed Nazism, he wrote the followings in the late 1950s: "The moral is that civilization is now here and never secure. It is a thin cake of custom overlying a molten mass of wickedness that is always boiling up for an opportunity to burst out. Civilization cannot ever be taken for granted. Its price is eternal

---

19  Toynbee, *A Study of History*, Vol. 1, Oxford University Press, 1946, 12-14. (first edition in 1934)
20  ] Toynbee, "One World, One History," a presentation at Princeton University's Bicentenial Conference "The University and its world responsibilities," February 20, 1947." Toynbee Papers, MSS 13967/3 Lectures.
21  "The territories, he argued, could not have remained included in Poland without keeping many times their number of Byelo-Russians and Ukrainians in Pol too." Toynbee to Prof Larski, December 20, 1963. Toynbee Papers BL Oxford MS13967/63/2.

vigilance and ceaseless spiritual effort."[22] Thus Toynbee, who by education, temper, concern and personal relationships, not the least by its own definition, had been an adherent of the classical liberal humanist tradition,[23] became a thinly-veiled conservative. This was manifest in, among others, his anthropological realism (or pessimism),[24] as well as the fact that, though often not consciously, in critical boundary situations (facing death would be one, according to Karl Jaspers), he always preferred order and security above freedom: for instance, he skipped military service in the First World War and hurriedly left London during the Blitz.[25]

It seems, then, that it was Toynbee's much derided flirtation with transcendence that prevented him from becoming permanently obsessed with anything that he saw as less dignified, be it a nationality, the nation-state or the drawing of any kind of border. As a result, he found it easier to reassess some of his earlier arguments: in his 1934 *Survey* he asserted for example that by 1918, Serbs and Croats had been living "in cultural isolation from one another for the best part of a thousand years." He also admitted that it was difficult to go back more than fifty years before the Yugoslav nation-state was founded before the idea first emerged that having a single language was the cause of political cooperation.[26] In his opinion, the best settlement was when the stronger party was careful not to humiliate the weaker one to an extent that the weaker party would be left with a desire for revenge[27]—the exact opposite of what had happened in Versailles in 1919, which was dominated by two ambitions: the desire to establish democratic nation-states and, from a geopolitical perspective, the simultaneous containment and weakening of Germany and Bolshevik Russia. Both failed: German and Hungarian leadership's unwillingness to accept the postwar settlement—just as its neighbours' unwillingness to alter it—determined much of the region's future fate.

Due to his post-1930 focus on the transcendent, Toynbee was also more willing or at least more compelled to resort to self-scrutiny:

---

22 Toynbee, *The World and the West* [Civilization on Trial], Cleveland, Ohio, 1958, 280.
23 Toynbee Papers BL Oxford MS13 967/128/1 Reviews and Correspondence 1915-1970.
24 "I am sadly convinced of the perversity of human nature," he claimed in 1972. Toynbee to Dr. Franz Rauhut, (Würzburg) June 23, 1972. Toynbee Papers BL Oxford MS13967/63/1 Correspondence 1931-1974.
25 See McNeill 1989, 190 and 321.
26 Toynbee, *Survey* 1934, Oxford University Press, 1935, 540.
27 Toynbee, Answers to the Questions in Dr. Eurich's Letter of August 15, 1972. Toynbee Papers, MS 13967/81/1 Correspondence.

[...] while we must do our best to keep our feelings and our moral judgments within limits, we cannot expect to be able to eliminate them altogether, and ought not even to hope to achieve this. What we can and must do all the time is to strive to be aware of what our own personal bias is, and to make our readers aware of it as far as we know it. To recognize our human limitations is less misleading than to flatter ourselves that we have transcended them. Whether the historian's subject is the more recent or the less recent past, the historian himself is a human being who is studying his fellows. This is a situation from which he cannot escape, and, the more frankly he acknowledges it, the greater the chance that he will be giving himself of doing, in his line of work, the best job that is practicable for human nature.[28]

The architects of the "New Europe," Henry Wickham Steed and Robert William Seton-Watson, on the other hand, did not even question any aspect of their work of having created a New Europe, i.e., the reorganisation of the continent on the basis of the principle of national self-determination. Regarding their two darlings at least, history has proved them wrong. Despite Czechoslovakia providing millions of its (non)national residents with rights that were more comprehensive than those provided by its neighbours, very few identified themselves with Czechoslovakism in a country where no language group made up 50 percent of the population. Eagle Glassheim thus rightly described Czechoslovakia as "oxymoronic country," with the Prague elite ruling a multinational nation-state "in the name of a single (or here artificially double) nationality."[29]

Steed's and Seton-Watson's other pet-state was even more complicated. To start with, there was no consensus among the justice warriors on how to spell the new creation's name (Jugoslavia according to Seton-Watson, Yugoslavia, in Steed's opinion, or perhaps Yougoslavia or Jugo-Slavia), but they had been all the more adamant to bring it about ever since 1914, quite from "behind the desk" while ignoring the differences and individual characteristics of the Balkan peoples. (For example, though a talented linguist, Steed, the great partisan of Yugoslavism, knew no Slavic languages.) Conflicts and hostilities between the South Slavic political groups during the First World War were passed on to the inter-war period. After 1920, the country was further destabilised by the

---

28  Toynbee & Veronica Toynbee, Problems of Research in International Relations, *International Studies*, Vol. 3(1), January 1960, 1–5, 5.
29  Eagle Glassheim, National Mythologies and Ethnic Cleansing: The Expulsion of Czechoslovak Germans in 1945, *Central European History* 33, No. 4 (2000): 463–486, 467.

fact that six of its seven neighbours challenged its borders, due to the excess of minorities it had acquired. Ironically, it was the originally Croatian-Slovenian partisan Josif Broz Tito who in 1943 actually implemented the long-awaited federal state structure in Yugoslavia, but he did that at the expense of democracy.[30]

Despite Steed's and Seton-Watson's endeavours regarding Czechoslovakia or Yugoslavia, the spirit of interwar Europe was not supranational but ultranational,[31] claimed Géza Paikert, and rightly so, as, even more than in Czechoslovakia, the post-1920 history of the united South Slav state was nothing but that of a protracted struggle of ethnic groups. Certainly, neither Steed nor Seton-Watson could know that after the fall of communism, the South Slav conflicts would escalate into a Yugoslav civil war, or that Yugoslavia would eventually become no more than an state experiment, with the highest percentage of people calling themselves "Yugoslav" never rising above 7 percent.[32] More recently, Croat social scientist Ivo Pilar argued that the Monarchy had been the only appropriate solution for the interests of Croatians, emphasizing that attempts to integrate Croatians and Serbs on the ruins of Austro-Hungary were unnatural and ahistorical.[33] In a similar vein, Bulgarian historian, Maria Todorova explains in *Imagining the Balkans* that the Habsburg–Ottoman frontier has become an essential element in the hierarchy of self-identification among the East-Central European peoples, in which every society has seen itself as more "Western" and less "Balkan" than their immediate eastern and southern neighbours. Once having been a subject of Austria-Hungary is still referred to as cultural superiority.[34]

Both Seton-Watson and Steed lived long enough to witness many of the Central and Eastern European politicians they had once so loudly celebrated becoming unworthy of praise, and to see the political systems of the nation-states these politicians represented often go irreparably wrong. Although Steed, and even more so Seton-Watson were prepared to issue friendly warnings and even use open blackmail to reverse undesirable developments, they were incapable, until the end of their lives, of fundamentally reassessing the Versailles-system they had helped create.

---

30 Szegő 2024, 270.
31 G.C. Paikert, Hungary's National Minority Policies, 1920-1945, *American Slavic and East European Review*, Vol. 12, No. 2 (Apr., 1953), 201-218, 204.
32 Brian Hall, *The Impossible Country: A Journey Through the Last Days of Yugoslavia*, Oxford University Press, New York, 1995, 6.
33 Stjepan Matković, Ivo Pilar, R.W. Seton-Watson. Dva pogleda na južnoslavensko pitanje, *Croatian Journal of Social Sciences and Humanities*, Vol. 1/1 (2006): 21-45.
34 Maria Todorova, *Imagining the Balkans*, Oxford University Press, NY, 1997, 38-61.

## Conclusion

As a matter of fact, Seton-Watson's preoccupation with Central and Eastern Europe consisted of three successive periods: first, from 1905–14, he was a Wandering Scot as well as an *investigator*, "bent on the study of History," collecting data and then, drawing on his vast body of knowledge he gave advice and issued (friendly) warnings, while bowing to constructive criticism. In this respect, 1914 was the year of the great caesura, his second period, which transformed the by then distinguished historian into a committed *propagandist* for the causes of, above all, Czechoslovakia, Yugoslavia and Greater Romania. His new task stifled his original academic sensitivity, which he could never recover in full.

The difference between Seton-Watson's first and second periods is clearly illustrated by the "outline" of a weekly journal under the name "Interpreter" or "The European Review" drawn up between 1913 and July 1914 and its realisation in 1916 as *The New Europe*. According to plan, "The European Review" would have been a "survey of nationality" and its manifestations in arts and culture, with the lofty aim "to interpret and encourage national individuality all over Europe," with all articles signed and, what is more, devoid of party labels and political propaganda.[35] As is well-known, *The New Europe* was everything but this, and together with his 1916 book *German, Slav and Magyar*, it was another imprint of this change.

Finally, after Versailles, Seton-Watson became an *apologist*, less in favour of the new creations than of the territorial status quo he had helped create: he was busy "perfecting" or "adjusting" the peace settlement by formulating reform proposals and political guidelines for the leaders of the successor states. He was convinced all along that the new order was a *sine qua non* for lasting peace in Europe. Thus, while it was still possible to fine-tune his ideas up to 1914, which the Hungarian political leadership stupidly missed, his post-Sarajevo position was one of academic hibernation, at least in one aspect. As literary historian, and not incidentally the librarian of the British Embassy in Budapest, István Gál explained in 1946: "Seton-Watson ceased to take note even of the achievements of Hungarian scholarship. He looked at the Hungarian question from the outside, through the history of his neighbours. He wrote the history of the South Slavs, the Romanians and, most recently, the Czechs and Slovaks, [and] he cited no recent Hungarian scholarly work."[36]

---

35 Seton-Watson (ed.), *The European Review, A Survey of Nationality*, London: Constable & Co. Ltd., 1914. Seton-Watson Papers, SEW/2.
36 István Gál, "Magyarország világhelyzete angol szemmel nézve" [Hungary's Situation in the World Seen from the English perspective], *Új Magyarország*, January 30, 1946, No. 4, 4.

In an interview, Macartney, quite harshly, called Seton-Watson "an upright and conscientious Puritan, who knew everything and understood very little,"[37] referring to his inability on the one hand to differentiate between "forcible" and "event-driven/ spontaneous" assimilation;[38] and on the other to accept that his friends were not beyond corruption and prejudice. The same contemporaries who easily overlooked the blunders of Seton-Watson (and also of Steed), were busy condemning Toynbee, mainly for questioning or rejecting almost all of the conventional wisdom associated with the British liberal perspective of the twentieth century, including the unchanging belief in progress, the nation-state as the optimum form of government, and ultimately the primacy of the West and its principles. "Most probable of all is to suppose that Toynbee's reputation will recover somewhat from the unjust dismissal he suffered at the hands of small-minded critics in the 1950s," McNeill concluded his Toynbee biography back in 1989.[39] Looking at the past twenty-four years, one could probably agree with that.

Given the varying emotional investments in their causes, what, above all, unites these four distinguished Britons? Having reviewed their work and careers in the context of (East-Central European) nationalism(s), one cannot help but conclude that Steed, Seton-Watson, Toynbee and Macartney all disdained intellectual restrictions and labels of any kind, while at the same time respecting academic or intellectual independence to the utmost. This could often manifest itself in small things: for example, Steed's proud rejection of ten packets of Romanian cigarettes offered in return for his services during 1918,[40] but more importantly, his steady refusal of decorations and returning them back to Romania, Serbia or Belgium to keep himself above suspicion. He even declined British knighthood in 1918 as well as refused the *Legion of Honour* in France three times in order that he might be free to criticize the French.[41] In a letter to the essayist and journalist Arthur Clutton Brock in 1917, Steed explained that candida-

---

In contrast, both Steed biographer Andre Liebich (2018, 54) and Mark Cornwall (2020, 28) argue for a less static post-1919 Seton-Watson image.
37 "The great war is a hideous proof that the policy of racial dominance and forcible assimilation is morally bankrupt, [...], and that those racial minorities whose separate existence reasons of geography and economics render impossible, will attain guarantees of full linguistic and cultural liberty." Seton-Watson, *What is at Stake in the War*, Humphrey Milford, Oxford University Press, 1915, 70.
38 As in the following statement: "There never was in all modern history a more fanatical and unnatural concentration of effort upon a policy of assimilation than in Hungary from, say, 1840 to 1918." Seton-Watson 1934, 55.
39 McNeill 1989, 288.
40 Koszta 2010, 65 and 239.
41 Steed to Wilson Harris, November 30 and Steed to WH, December 21, 1934. Steed Papers MS 74 130

ture for Parliament was out of question, as he had "never belonged to any party, Conservative, Liberal or Socialist," "never worn any label," and hoped "never to wear one."[42] He considered his independence from party affiliation so important that he regularly gave voice to it.[43]

Similarly, Steed's close friend Seton-Watson was equally adamant to prove his independence by flatly refusing accusations of partisanship. His first major work, and probably the most significant one, too, *Racial Problems in Hungary* begins with a chapter in which he defends himself: the author was "neither "an emissary of British Finance," nor 'an agent of the press bureau of the Ballplatz in Vienna," nor "to be found in the neighbourhood of the Roumanian Court." Rather he was a travelling Scotsman, "bent on the study of History and politics."[44] A year later, when Seton-Watson turned his attention more and more to the South Slav cause, the Croatian emigrant journalist Ivo Lupis-Vukić sent him a letter of gratitude: "I, in fact, we, all Croats, cannot pay your work, but with gratitude."[45]

This was undoubtedly the case in 1909, but after the First World War, it rarely held true. As was previously discussed, the School of Slavonic Studies had been established during the First World War to help the lofty cause of national self-determination to triumph by supplying the intellectual foundation for the new European order with a proportion of its income contributed by the three governments of the Successor States. In 1922, Seton-Watson became the Masaryk Chair in Central European History and Steed was soon given the opportunity to give lectures on East-Central European, primarily Romanian, history. Additionally, from 1945 to 1949, Seton-Watson served as the first chair of Czechoslovak Studies at Oxford University, too, a position that was not only created but also financially supported by Beneš's Czechoslovakia. And that was not all; following the concerned Madame Rose's request in 1927, Jan Masaryk, and through

---

42  Steed to Arthur Clutton Brock, July 26, 1917, PHP Papers, Printing House Papers?
43  "I never belonged or supported the organisation of any political party [...] I have voted for the candidates of all three parties when personally or the political principles he, she represented appealed to me . I belong to [...] the non-party vote." Steed to Mr Patrick Early, liberal candidate, December 20, 1937. Steed Papers MS 74131.
"I have never belonged to any pol party. If I am anything politically, I am anti-despot, anti-bureaucrat, anti-clerical, but pro-everything that makes for responsible freedom." Steed to H.G. Wells, July 31, 1940. Steed Papers MS 74133.
Steed on the June 1945 British elections: "I never belonged to any pol party and am, to that extent, unbiased." BBC World Affairs, June 8, 1945. Steed Papers MS 74182.
On standing for parliamentary elections see: Steed to Thomas Ogilvy, July 25, 1925. Steed Papers MS 74 126.
44  Seton-Watson 1908, xi.
45  Ivo Lupis-Vukić to Seton-Watson, November 1, 1909. *Korespondencija*, Vol. 1., 56. Hugh and Christopher Seton-Watson 1983, 66.

him the Prague government stepped in to save Steed's monthly journal, *The Review of the Reviews*, from bankruptcy. From then onwards, Czechoslovakia became the journal's most generous sponsor, purchasing more advertising space than ever before in addition to paying for the publication's new Czechoslovak supplement.[46]

Not only interwar Czechoslovakia but also, mainly through its Foreign Secretary, Nicolae Titulescu, Romania also "subsidized" Western political and public figures, as well as journalists, among them Seton-Watson, from a "secret fund of the Foreign Ministry," or so claimed Romanian-Canadian historian Dov. B. Lungu in his *Romania and the Great Powers 1933-1940*.[47] To this, Holly Case added that when in the fall of 1940 Romanian foreign minister Mihai (Mihael) Sturdza requested the termination of Seton-Watson's Romanian government stipend (owing to the fact that he had been a "democrat" working for British intelligence), Ion Antonescu intervened in person: "Seton-Watson has been a good friend of Romania. He always supported us in the matter of Transylvania. His democratic activities don't interest me."[48]

The two other Britons were more cautious to avoid even the appearance of becoming a mouthpiece for any propaganda. This ambition is evident very early on in Toynbee, despite his pro-New Europe stance: as a result, from early on in his career he was attacked with equal ferocity by Greeks, Turks and Armenians, which he often took as a confirmation of his former reservedness. He directed the RIIA and the *Surveys*, the two forums for the scientific study of international relations, having explained what he meant by *scientific:* "objective, unbiased, un-partisan, un-emotional."[49] On the wartime role of Chatham House, the director was resolved not to join the ranks of propaganda organizations: "We would throw away our reputation for disinterestedness in the study of international affairs," he contended, "together with our own self-respect."[50] The same inde-

---

46 These facts were retrieved from the Prague archives after Hitler's invasion of the Czech capital in 1939 and were offered as proof that Steed, "with the appearance of a perfect gentleman," had permitted himself to be bought in order to avoid his personal financial problems. The truth was, however, that Steed really did not know about Madame Rose's move, claiming that no money had gone into his pocket. Despite Czechoslovak subsidies, he eventually had to sell the paper in 1930. Dr. Rudolf Urban, *Demokratenpresse in Lichte Prager Geheimakten*, Prague, Orbis, 1943, 94. Qtd. in Liebich 2018, 225-227.
47 Having returned from Canada, Lungu was granted access to Bucharest Archives in 1989. Dov. B. Lungu, *Romania and the Great Powers 1933-1940*, Durham–London, Duke University Press, 1989, 15-16.
48 ANIC, Fond Președentia Consiliului de Miniștri Cabinetul Militar Ion Antonescu, Dosar 194/1940, Factura de subvenții pentru Seton-Watson, f.100. Qtd. in Case 2009, 40.
49 Toynbee 1969, 61.
50 Toynbee to Geoffrey M. Gathorne Hardy, March 31, 1938. Toynbee Papers MS 13 967/39 General Miscellaneous Correspondence 1911-1956.

pendence of mind he claimed to possess as an individual scholar, too. In a letter to the Institute's co-founder, Lionel Curtis, in February 1939, he rather loftily claimed to see the pros and cons of all points of view more clearly than some, partly because of his temperament and partly because of his professional self-education, adding that "it would be a pity if I in any way identify myself with one particular view."[51] However, quite unconsciously, Toynbee stopped being unpartisan or un-emotional when it came to religious- or related topics, and he was duly attacked for using "history as religious propaganda."[52]

In a similar vein, in one of his BBC talks on Hungary, Macartney naturally had to touch upon the most significant factor in the country's interwar foreign policy: revisionism. He proudly proclaimed that he "was never one of those so-called Magyarophile foreigners who used to come to Hungary, have themselves [...] feasted, and, in return, act more or less conscientiously as mouthpieces of the Hungarian Revision League."[53]

After all, there is a common point among the four Britons: they all were critical of interwar Hungary, and its Horthy regime. Interestingly, Steed and Seton-Watson scourged it the most for its rigidity and refusal to implement genuine reforms, whereas they were the least willing to take a self-critical view of their earlier positions. Certainly, this does not excuse, for example, the attitude of most of the pre-First World War Hungarian politicians towards foreign critics, let alone the blasphemous reactions[54] of the majority of the Hungarian press.

As part of his 1953 BBC reminiscences,[55] Steed gave three talks. He gladly recalled "charming, witty, lovely" Hungary, retelling the story of his encounter with Apponyi exactly half a century earlier with the same tone of resentment, while providing a fairly accurate description of the high-handedness of the Hungarian ruling elite:

> Splendid people at first, until you began to see that some of the explanations they so willingly gave you did not quite rhyme with what you have

---

51  Toynbee to Lionel Curtis, February 13, 1939. RIIA Archives, 4TOYN/6E General Correspondence 1939.
52  Herbert Tingsten,"Finished with Toynbee," *Dagens Nyheter*, December 6, 1954. RIIA 4/TOYN/4.
53  Macartney, "Don't Miss the Bus," September 7, 1941. BBC WAC.
54  More about this in Jeszenszky 2020b; and Ágnes Beretzky, *Scotus Viator és Macartney Elemér: Magyarország-kép változó előjelekkel (1906–1945)* [Scotus Viator and C.A. Macartney: Changing Views on Hungary, 1906–1945], Budapest: Akadémiai kiadó, 2005.
55  "The Reminiscences of Wickham Steed: Vienna and the Hapsburgs," interview by Steven Watson, April 18, 1953, 10 pm, BBC Home Service. Steed Papers MS 74 186.

observed. Then you'd ask for explanations, readily given, even those explanations didn't fit facts and then you'd ask for further explanations, and then you'd be treated as an inquisitive foreigner, almost an enemy, and you'd gradually be frozen out.[56]

Ultimately, we East-Central Europeans must also look back at our history, but with a dispassionate eye, preserving what has stood the test of time and rejecting without mercy what has been proven wrong. With their brilliant insights and major blunders alike, Steed, Seton-Watson, Toynbee and Macartney *together* can lend a helping hand, in John Stuart Mill's spirit:

> He who knows only his own side of the case knows little of that. His reasons may be good, and no one may have been able to refute them. But if he is equally unable to refute the reasons on the opposite side, if he does not so much as know what they are, he has no ground for preferring either opinion.[57]

---

56 "The Reminiscences of Wickham Steed: on Versailles," interviewed by Steven Watson, September 19, 1953, 10 pm, BBC Home Service. Steed Papers MS 74 186.
57 John Stuart Mill, *On Liberty*, London, Longman, 1864, 67.

# Bibliography

Archives and Manuscript Collections

Official Papers and Publications of Documents
The National Archives (TNA), London-Kew, Foreign policy files. Foreign Office files, FO/371/2300-5900.
The Hungarian Problem in the British Parliament: Speeches, Questions and Answers thereto in the House of Lords and the House of Commons from 1919 to 1930. London: Grant Richards, 1933.
Woodward, Edward-Butler, Rohan, Documents on British Foreign Policy, 1919-1939, London, First Series, Vol II, London, 1948, 289-293.
The Hungarian Question in the British Parliament. Speeches and Answers thereto in the House of Lords and the House of Commons from 1919 to 1930. London: Grant Richards, 1933.
Rogers P. Churchill, George V. Blue, Shirley F. Landau (eds.), Foreign Relations of the United States, Diplomatic Papers, 1933, General, Volume I, Washington: United States Government Printing Office, 1950.

Private Papers

Archive of the *Times*, Printing House Square Papers
  Steed Papers
University College London School of Slavonic and East European Studies (SSEES) Library
  Robert William Seton-Watson Collection
Bodleian Library-Weston Library, Oxford, United Kingdom: Western Manuscripts
  Carlile Aylmer Macartney Papers, Ms. Eng. c. 3280-3316. Box 1-37.
  Arnold Joseph Toynbee Papers, MSS. 13967/1-18, 25-131, 136-137.
  Alfred Zimmern Papers, Western Manuscripts, MSS. Zimmern 1-183.
The British Library (BL) London
  Correspondence and Papers of Henry Wickham Steed, British Library Archives, Western Archives and Manuscripts, Catalogue: 74101-74208
  League of Nations Union (LNU), LNU Leaflets, Miscellaneous, Pamphlets. Vol. 1-10. 1923-1942.

Library and Archives of the Royal Institute of International Affairs, (RIIA Archives), London
Arnold Joseph Toynbee, Correspondence
Macartney, C.A. 1931. The Situation in Hungary. October 12, 1931. 8/161.
Macartney, C.A. 1931. Political Relations in the Balkans. February 2, 1931. 8/120.
Macartney, C.A. 1931. Hungary and the Present Crisis. October 11, 1938. 8/551.
Macartney, C.A. 1936. Ruthenia: A Problem of the Future. February 27, 1936. 8/399.
Macartney, C.A. 1937. Some Aspects of Present-Day Hungary. December 2, 1937. 8/475.
Macartney, C.A. 1946. Conditions in Hungary. March 18, 1946. 8/1209.
BBC Archives, Reading
Macartney Broadcasts to Hungary
McGill Library Archival Collections
Noel Buxton Correspondence
Széchenyi National Library, Budapest Manuscript Collection. OSZK KT
Balogh, József correspondence
Jászi, Oszkár correspondence
Pulszky, Polixénia correspondence
Allen Leeper Papers, University of Cambridge, Churchill Archives Centre

Books and articles

"Egy angol professzor beszélgetései Horthy Miklóssal" [An English professor's conversations with Miklós Horthy] *Élet és Tudomány*, 1993/36-37.
"Londoner Momentaufnahmen", *Pester Lloyd*, December 11, 1924, 2.
"Magyarország hivatása a Dunamedencében". [Hungary's Vocation in the Danube Basin]. Bethlen István gróf beszédei és írásai [Count István Bethlen: Speeches and Writings], Budapest, Genius, 1933, Vol II.185.
Ablonczy, Balázs, *A visszatért Erdély 1940-1944* [Transylvania Regained, 1940-1944], Budapest, Jaffa, 2011.
Abrams, Bradley F. "Morality, Wisdom and Revision: The Czech Opposition of the 1970s and the Expulsion of the Sudeten Germans," *East European Politics and Societies*, 9, no. 2, 1995.
Ádám, Magda. *The Little Entente and Europe (1920-1929)*, Budapest: Akadémai, 1993.
Anderson, Benedict. *Imagined Communities*, London: Verso, 2006.
Antonescu, Mihai. *Warum wir kämpfen*, Bucharest, 1942.
Arday, Lajos. *Térkép csata után, Magyarország a brit külpolitikában (1918-1919)* [Map After the Battle: Hungary in British Foreign Policy (1918-1919)], Budapest: Magvető, 1990.

Balassa, Zoltán. "1956 is an ethnic visa in politics," *Erdélyi napló*, 1996 Vol. 51.

Balogh, Béni L. *Küzdelem Erdélyért - A magyar-román viszony és a kisebbségi kérdés 1940-1944 között [Struggle for Transylvania - Hungarian-Romanian Relations and the Minority Question Between 1940-1944]*, Budapest, Akadémiai, 2013.

Balogh, József. "Scotus Viator pálfordulása." In *Magyar Szemle*, March, 1930.

Balogh, József. *A magyar revízió angol előharcosa: Lord Bryce születésének századik évfordulójára* [The English Pioneer of Hungarian Revisionism: On the Centenary of the Birth of Lord Bryce]. Budapest: Franklin-Társulat, 1939.

Bán D., András, "Seton-Watson és a csehszlovákiai magyar kisebbség" [Seton-Watson and the Hungarian Minority in Czechoslovakia]. *Valóság*, 1997/6

Bán D., András. "Dokumentumok a csehszlovákiai magyar ellenzéki politikusok R.W. Seton-Watsonnal folytatott megbeszéléseiről" [Documents on the Discussions of Hungarian Opposition Politicians in Czechoslovakia with R.W. Seton-Watson], 1923, *Regio*, 1992/1, 143.

Bán D., András. *Illúziók és csalódások, Nagy-Britannia és Magyarország 1938-1941, [Illusions and Disappointments Great-Britain and Hungary 1938-1941]*, Budapest, 1998.

Barta, Róbert. *A magyarság vonzásában. Válogatás Carlile Aylmer Macartney írásaiból és beszédeiből* [Attracted by the Hungarians: A selection of Carlile Aylmer Macartney's writings and speeches], Debrecen, 2011.

Bátonyi, Gábor, *Britain and Central Europe, 1918-1933*, Oxford:Clarendon Press, 1999.

Beazley, Charles. *The Road to Ruin in Europe 1890-1914*, J. M. Dent & Sons Ltd, 1932.

Becker, András, The Dynamics of British Official Policy towards Hungarian Revisionism, 1938-39 *The Slavonic and East European Review*, Vol. 93, No. 4 (October 2015), pp. 655-691.

Becker, Peter. and Wheatley, Natasha. (eds.), *Remaking Central Europe. The League of Nations and the Former Habsburg Lands*, Oxford: Oxford University Press, 2020, 283-314.

Beneš, Edouard. "Postwar Czechoslovakia," *Foreign Affairs* 24, no. 3, 1946.

Beneš, Edouard. *Souvenirs de guerre et de révolution*, Paris, 1928.

Beretzky, Ágnes. "Twin Champions of the Slovak Cause: Bjørnstjerne Bjørnson and Robert William Seton-Watson," *Central Europe*, 2023, 1–15.

Beretzky, Ágnes. *Scotus Viator és Macartney Elemér: Magyarország-kép változó előjelekkel (1906-1945),* [Scotus Viator and C.A. Macartney: Changing Views on Hungary, 1906-1945]. Budapest: Akadémiai kiadó, 2005.

Bethlen, Stephen. "The Transylvanian Problem", *IA*, May-June 1934, 362-367.

Birn, Donald S. *The League of Nations Union*, Oxford: Clarendon Press, 1981.

Bolsover, G.H. "R. W. Seton-Watson, 1879-1951, From the *Proceedings of the British Academy*, vol. XXXVII", London, 1952.

Bosco, Andrea and Cornelia Navari (eds.). *Chatham House and British Foreign Policy 1919-1945*. London: Lothian Foundation Press, 1994.

Buckler, W.H. "A Study in the Contact of Civilizations" *New Republic*, December 6 1922.
Burk, Kathleen. *Troublemaker The Life and History of A.J.P. Taylor*, New Haven and London: Yale University Press, 2000.
Burton, Tara Isabella. *Strange Rites: New Religions for a Godless World*. New York, Public Affairs, 2020.
Campbell, John C. "The European Territorial Settlement", *Foreign Affairs*, October 1947, Vol. 26, No. 1, 196-218.
Caples, Matthew. "Et in Hungaria Ego: Trianon, Revisionism, and the Journal Magyar Szemle (1927-1944)," *Hungarian Studies* 19, no. 1, 2005.
Carr, Edward H. *The Future of Nations, Independence or Interdependence*, London, 1941.
Chamberlain, Austen. "Great Britain As a European Power," *International Affairs*, March 1930, 185.
Cieger, András. Horvát képviselők a magyar országgyűlésben (1868-1918) [Croatian Representatives in the Hungarian Parliament], In: Pál Fodor-Dénes Sokcsevits, *A horvát-magyar együttélés fordulópontjai. Intézmények, társadalom, gazdaság, kultúra*, [The Turning Points of Croatian-Hungarian Coexistence. Institutions, Society, Economy, Culture,], MTA Bölcsészettudományi Kutatóközpont Történettudományi Intézet, Horvát Történettudományi Intézet, [Centre for Humanities Research Institute of History, Croatian Institute of History] Budapest, 2015, 426-435, 2015.
Cline, Catherine Ann. "British Historians and the Treaty of Versailles", *Albion: A Quarterly Journal Concerned with British Studies*, Vol. 20, No. 1 (Spring, 1988), pp. 43-58.
Clissold, Stephen (ed.). *A Short History of Yugoslavia*. Cambridge, 1966.
Cornwall, Mark. "R.W. Seton-Watson And Nation-Building Clashes in Late Habsburg Space." *The Slavonic and East European Review*, 100 (1), 2022.
Cornwall, Mark. "Robert William Seton-Watson and Nation-Building Clashes in Late Habsburg Space." *Slavonic and East European Review*, Vol 100, Number 1, January 2022, 65-94.
Coudenhove-Kalergi, R. *The Totalitarian State against Man*, Glarus, Switzerland: Paneuropa Editions, 1939.
Crockatt, Richard. *Challenge and Response: Arnold Toynbee and the United States during the Cold War. War and Cold War in American Foreign Policy, 1942-62*. editor Dale Carter; Robin Clifton. Palgrave Macmillan, 2001. pp. 108-130.
Crozier, A. J. *Appeasement and Germany's Last Bid for Colonies*, Basingstoke, 1988, 99-206.
Csaba Békés, László Borhi, Peter Ruggenthaler, Ottmar Trașcă (eds.). *Soviet Occupation of Romania, Hungary, And Austria 1944/45-1948/49*, CEU Press, 2015.
Dawson, W. H. "The Urgency of Treaty Revision." *Contemporary Review* 144 (July 1933), 15-23.
Deák, Francis. *The Hungarian-Rumanian Land Dispute*, Columbia University Press, 1928.

Dreisziger, N.F. "New Twist to an Old Riddle: The Bombing of Kassa (Košice), June 26 1941." *The Journal of Modern History*, 1972/June, 232-242.

Fazakas, Zoltán József. "The Romanian Agrarian Reform Following World War I – a tool for building the nation-state." *Journal of Agricultural and Environmental Law*, 2022 Vol. XVII No. 33 pp. 32-50.

Frank, Tibor. "C'est La Paix!' – The Sixtus Letters and The Peace Initiative of Emperor Karl I." *Hungarian Review*, Vol. VI, No. 5, September 2015.

Frank, Tibor. "Editing as Politics: József Balogh and The Hungarian Quarterly," in *Ethnicity, Propaganda. Myth-Making: Studies on Hungarian Connections to Britain and America, 1848-1945*, Budapest, Akadémiai Kiadó, 1999.

Frank, Tibor. "Luring the English-Speaking World: Hungarian History Diverted", *Slavonic and East European Review*, 1991/1.

Frank, Tibor. "Patronage and Networking The Society of The Hungarian Quarterly 1935-1944." *The New Hungarian Quarterly*. 50, 2009. 3-12.

Frank, Tibor. "To Comply with English Taste: The Making of The Hungarian Quarterly,1934-1944". *The Hungarian Quarterly*, 2003, No. 171), 112-124.

Frank, Tibor. *Britannia vonzásában* [Attracted by Britain], Budapest, 2018.

Friedjung, Heinrich. *Geschichte in Gesprächen, Aufzeichnungen 1898-1919*, Band II, 1904-1919, Wien: Böhlau Verlag, 1997.

Gál, István, "Magyarország világhelyzete angol szemmel nézve" [Hungary's Situation in the World Seen from the English perspective], *Új Magyarország*, January 30 1946, No 4, 4.

Gentile, Emilio. *Politics as Religion*, Princeton, Princeton University Press, 2006.

Geyl, Pieter, Arnold J. Toynbee and Pitrim Sorokin, *The Pattern of the Past: Can We Determine It*. Boston, Beacon Press, 1949.

Gheorghe, Ion. *Rumäniens Weg zu Satellitenstaat*, Heidelberg, Kurt Vorwinckel Verlag, 1952.

Gibson, Hugh. (ed.), *The Ciano Diaries, 1939-1943: The Complete, Unabridged Diaries of Count Galeazzo Ciano, Italian Minister of Foreign Affairs, 1936-1943*, Simon Publications, 1945.

Glassheim, Eagle. "National Mythologies and Ethnic Cleansing: The Expulsion of Czechoslovak Germans in 1945," *Central European History* 33, no. 4 (2000): 463-486.

Glassheim, Eagle. *Noble Nationalist: The Transformation of The Bohemian Aristocracy*. Cambridge, Massachusetts, Harvard University Press, 2005.

Goldstein, Erik and Igor Lukes (eds.). *The Munich Crisis, 1938: Prelude to World War II*, Routledge, 1999.

Gooch, G.P. *Studies in Diplomacy and Statecraft*. London: Longmans, 1942.

Gooch, J. P. "Recent Revelations of European Diplomacy." *Journal of the British Institute of International Affairs*, Vol. 2, No. 1 (January 1923), pp. 1-29.

Gooch, J. P. *Recent Revelations of European Diplomacy*, Longmans, 1928.

Gordon Brook-Shepherd, "Troubled Magyars." *Daily Telegraph*, January 11 1963.
Gower, Robert. et al, "Middle Europe, Treaties by Agreement," *The Times*, July 5, 1933.
Gower, Robert. et al., "The Treaty of Trianon, Frontier Rectification," *The Times*, June 27 1934, 12. See also Gower, "The Treaty of Trianon," *The Times*, June 9, 1934.
Griffiths, Richard. *Fellow Travellers of the Right: British Enthusiasts for Nazi Germany, 1933–1939*. London: Faber and Faber, 2011.
Hajdú, Tibor and György Litván. *Károlyi Mihály levelezése* [The Correspondence of Mihály Károlyi], Vol. 3, Budapest, 1991.
Hájková. "T. G. Masaryk and his Stances on Minority Issues after the Establishment of Czechoslovakia" 61–74. In: Eiler-Hájková (eds.), 2009.
Hall, Brian. *The Impossible Country: A Journey Through the Last Days of Yugoslavia*, Oxford University Press, New York, 199.
Hall, Ian. *Dilemmas of Decline: British Intellectuals and World Politics, 1945–75* (Berkeley, CA, University of California Press, 2012, 131–151.
Hanak, Harry. *Great Britain and Austria-Hungary during the First World War*, London, 1962.
Haraszti, Endre. "Meghalt a legmagyarabb szívű Ánglius", [The most Hungarian-hearted Anglican has died]. Winnipeg, *Magyar Élet [Hungarian Life]*, August 5 1978.
Hardy, Henry (ed). *Isaiah Berlin: Letters*, Vol 1, 1928–1946, Cambridge University Press, 2004.
Herczeg, Ferenc. "Scotus Viator és a budapesti radikálisok" [Scotus Viator and the Budapest radicals], *Magyar Figyelő*, December 15, 1911.
Herczeg, Ferenc. *Hűvösvölgy*, Budapest: Szépirodalmi, 1993.
Horváth, Jenő. "Magyarország és utódállamai" [Hungary and Her Successors]. *Budapesti Szemle*, April, 1938, 79–93.
Howard, Christopher H. D. (ed.). *Diary of Edward Goschen*, London, Offices of the Royal Historical Society, 1980.
Inge, William Ralph. *The End of an Age: and Other Essays*, Putnam, 1948.
Iorga, Nicolae. *A History of Anglo-Romanian Relations,* Bucharest: Societate Anglo-Română, 1931.
Iorga, Nicolae. *A History of Roumania. Land, People, Civilisation*. London, 1925.
Iorga, Nicolae. *My American Lectures*, Bucharest: State Printing Office, 1932.
Janek, István. "Magyar törekvések a felvidék megszerzésére 1938-ban" [Hungarian Aspirations to Obtain the Highlands in 1938]. *Történelmi Szemle*, 2010/ 1.
Jászi, Oszkár. "Scotus Viator Magyarországról" [Scotus Viator on Hungary], *Huszadik Század* 2 (1909-II): 60–72.
Jászi, Oszkár. *Revolution and Counterrevolution*, London: P. S. King and Son, 1924.
Jeszenszky, Géza. A történelmi Magyarország egyik sírásója: H. W. Steed. [One of the gravediggers of historical Hungary: H. W. Steed], *Emlékirat és Történelem*, Budapest:

Magyar Történelmi Társulat Nemzetközi Magyarságtudományi Társaság, [Memoirs and History, Hungarian Historical Society International Society for Hungarian Studies], 2012, 18-35.

Jeszenszky, Géza. *Lost Prestige: Hungary's Changing Image in Britain 1894-1918*, Helena History Press, 2020.

Joll, James (ed.). *Britain and Europe, Pitt to Churchill, 1793-1940*, Oxford: Oxford University Press, 1967, 174. See also Cornwall 2017, 329-333.

Jones, Tom. *A Diary with Letters*, Oxford: Oxford University Press, 1954.

Judson, Pieter. *The Habsburg Empire: A New History*, Belknap Press: An Imprint of Harvard University Press, 2016.

Juhász, Gyula, *Magyar-brit titkos tárgyalások 1943-ban [Hungarian-British Secret Talks in 1943]*, Budapest, 1978.

Juhász, Gyula. Hungarian Foreign Policy, Budapest: Akadémai Kiadó, 1979.

Kadar Lynn, Katalin, "Strange Partnership: Lord Rothermere, Stephanie Von Hohenlohe and the Hungarian Revisionist Movement." The Independent Scholar [Quarterly] 25.4 (November 2012): 1–13. Reprinted in Independent Scholar Vol. 5, August 2019.

Károlyi, Mihály. *Faith without Illusion*, London: Jonathan Cape, 1956.

Kaufman, David. The "One Guilty Nation" Myth: Edith Durham, R.W. Seton-Watson and a Footnote in the History of the Outbreak of the First World War, *Journal of Balkan and Near Eastern Studies*, Volume 25, 2023 - Issue 3.

Kaufman, David. The "One Guilty Nation" Myth: Edith Durham, R.W. Seton-Watson and a Footnote in the History of the Outbreak of the First World War, *Journal of Balkan and Near Eastern Studies*, Volume 25, 2023, Issue 3., 297-321.

Keyserlingk, R.H. "Arnold Toynbee's Foreign Research and Press Service, 1939-1943 and its Post-war Plans for South-east Europe", *Journal of Contemporary History*, London, Vol 21, 1986, 539-558.

Koszta, István: *"Nemcsak Erdély volt a tét"- Kései tudósítás a párizsi konferenciáról: Alexandru Vaida-Voevod levelei, feljegyzései, levéltári okmányok, emlékezések, naplórészletek a párizsi békekonferenciáról*. ["It was not only Transylvania at stake" - Late coverage of the Paris Conference: letters, notes, archival documents, memoirs, diary excerpts of Alexandru Vaida-Voevod from the Paris Peace Conference.] Miercurea Ciuc-Csíkszereda–Budapest, 2010, 238-239.

Laffan, R. G. D., Arnold and Veronica M. Toynbee et al. *Survey of International Affairs*, 1938 Vol III, Oxford University Press, 1953.

Laffan, R. G. D., *The Guardians of the Gate: Historical Lectures on the Serbs*. Oxford: Clarendon, 1918.

Leeper, Allen. *Justice of Rumania's Cause*, London, Hodder and Stoughton, 1917.

Liebich, Andre. *Henry Wickham Steed, Greatest Journalist of His Times*, Peter Lang AG, 2018.

Liebich, Andre. *The Antisemitism of Henry Wickham Steed*, Patterns of Prejudice, Vol. 46, 2012.

Litván, György (ed.). *Jászi Oszkár naplója*, [Oszkár Jászi's Diary]. Budapest: MTA Történettudományi Intézet, 2001.

Litván, György. "Oscar Jászi (1875-1957), A Biographical Essay", Manuscript, Budapest, 1984.

Lockhart, Robert Bruce. *Retreat from Glory*. London, Putnam 1934, 76.

Lojkó, Miklós. "C.A. Macartney and Central Europe." *European Review of History*. Vol. 6, 1. (Spring 1999): 37-57.

Lojkó, Miklós. *Meddling in Middle Europe. Britain and the 'Lands Between' 1919-1925*, Central European University Press, 2005.

Lord Bryce [Arnold Toynbee]: *Armenian Atrocities: The Murder of a Nation*, London: Hodder and Stoughton, 1915.

Lorman, Thomas. *The Making of the Slovak People's Party. Religion, Nationalism and Culture War in Early 20th-Century Europe*, London, Bloomsbury Academic, 2019.

Lungu, Dov. B. *Romania and the Great Powers 1933-1940*, Durham-London: Duke University Press, 1989.

Lyde, L.W. "The Frontiers of Hungary." *The Times*, March 18, 1926, 17.

Macartney, C.A. "Grievances of Minorities. The Case of Hungary." *The Times*, October 7, 1938.

Macartney, C.A. "Hungaria Aeterna," *The Hungarian Quarterly (HQ)*, 1936/1.

Macartney, C.A. "Hungary in February" 1940, *Hungarian Quarterly*, Spring 1940.

Macartney, C.A. "Hungary since 1918." *Slavonic and Eastern European Review (SEER)*, 1929/3.

Macartney, C.A. *Hungary and Her Successors: The Treaty of Trianon and Its Consequences*, Oxford University Press, 1937.

Macartney, C.A. "Magyar and Slovak. The Rival Claims. An Opportunity for Just Revision." *The Times*, October 26, 1938.

Macartney, C.A. Aims of British Propaganda to Hungary. 17 February 1942. FO 371/30965. Macartney, C.A. British Policy Towards Hungary in the Second World War. Anglo-Hungarian Conference of Historians, 1977. Manuscript.

Macartney, C.A. *Hungary, A Short History*. Edinburgh, 1962.

Macartney, C.A. *Hungary*, London: Ernest Benn Ltd., 1934.

Macartney, C.A. *National States and National Minorities*, London, 1934.

Macartney, C.A. *Poems*, Erskine Macdonald, London, 1915.

Macartney, C.A. *Problems of the Danube Basin*, Cambridge, 1942.

Macartney, C.A. *Social Revolution in Austria*, reviewed by Seton-Watson. *Slavonic Review*, 1927/March.

Macartney, C.A. *The Danubian Basin*, Oxford, 1939.

Macartney, C.A. *The Social Revolution in Austria,* Cambridge: Cambridge University Press, 1926.

Marczali, Paula [Póli]. *Apám [Marczali Henrik] pályája, barátai* [My father's Career, and Friends], Auróra könyvek, München, 1973.

Masaryk, Tomáš. *Cesta demokracije,* II, Ústav T. G. Masaryka, 2007.

Masaryk, Tomáš. *The Making of a State,* London: George Allen and Unwin Ltd, 1927.

Mason, John W. *The Dissolution of the Austro-Hungarian Empire, 1867-1918.* London-New York: Longman,1997.

Matković, Stjepan. "Ivo Pilar i R.W. Seton-Watson (Dva pogleda na južnoslavensko pitanje)." *Croatian Journal of Social Sciences and Humanities,* vol. 1/1 (2006): 21-45.

May, Arthur J. "R. W. Seton-Watson and British Anti-Hapsburg Sentiment." *The American Slavic and East European Review,* February 1961, Vol. 20, No. 1 pp. 40-54.

McKercher, B.J.C. *Esme Howard: A Diplomatic Biography,* Cambridge University Press, 1989.

McNeill, William H. *Arnold J. Toynbee: A Life,* Oxford: Oxford University Press, 1989.

McNeill, William. "H. Toynbee Revisited." *Bulletin of the American Academy of Arts and Sciences,* Vol. 41, No. 7 (Apr., 1988).

Medlicott, William Norton. *Contemporary England 1914-1964.* London: Longmans, 1967.

Michela, Miroslav. *Trianon labirintusaiban Történelem, emlékezetpolitika és párhuzamos történetek Szlovákiában és Magyarországon* [The labyrinths of Trianon History, memory politics and parallel histories in Slovakia and Hungary], Magyarországi Szlovákok Kutatóintézete Magyar Tudományos Akadémia Bölcsészettudományi Kutatóközpont Történettudományi Intézet Békéscsaba-Budapest, 2016.

Miller, David. *Political Philosophy, A Very Short Introduction,* Oxford: Oxford University Press, 2003.

Miskolczy, Ambrus. "Barát vagy ellenség? Scotus Viator és Macartney Elemér. Két vélemény Erdélyről, Magyarországról és Romániáról." [Friend or Foe? Scotus Viator and Elemér Macartney. Two Opinions on Transylvania, Hungary and Romania.] *Holmi,* October 1994, 1506.

Monger, David. "Networking against Genocide during the First World War: the international network behind the British Parliamentary report on the Armenian Genocide". *Journal of Transatlantic Studies,* 2018 Vol. 16, No. 3, 295-316.

Móricz, Kálmán, "Magyarország és az utódállamok" [Hungary and Her Successors]. *Külügyi Szemle,* April 1938, 182-191.

Motta, Giuseppe. "The Birth of Yugoslavia: A Vision from Italy, 1918-20." In: Rudić, Srđan - Biagini, Antonello (eds.): *Serbian-Italian Relations: History and Modern Times.* Požega: The Institute of History Belgrade and Sapienza University of Rome, 2015.

Murádin, János Kristóf. "Minority Politics of Hungary and Romania between 1940 and 1944. The System of Reciprocity and Its Consequences." *Acta Univ. Sapientiae, European and Regional Studies*, 16 (2019) 59-74.

Nagy, Elek. *Magyarország és a Népszövetség*, Franklin Társulat, 1930.

Nagy, Zsolt. *Grand Delusions: Interwar Hungarian Cultural Diplomacy, 1918-1941*. A dissertation submitted to the faculty of the University of North Carolina at Chapel Hill, Department of History.Chapel Hill, 2012.

Newman, Bernard. *Danger Spots of Europe*, London, The Right Book Club, 1939.

Nicolson, "Allen Leeper", *The Nineteenth Century and After, Annual Bulletin of Historical Literature*, October 1935.

Nicolson, Harold. "Peacemaking at Paris: Success, Failure or Farce?", *Foreign Affairs*, January 1947, Vol. 25, No. 2, pp. 190-203.

Nicolson, Harold. *Peacemaking 1919*, London, Constable, 1934.

Nyirkos, Tamás. The Proliferation of Secular Religions: Theoretical and Practical Aspects, *Pro Publico Bono, Public Administration*, 2021/2, 68-85.

O'Brien, John A. *The Road to Damascus, The: Fifteen Converts to Catholicism*, Vol. II, W. H. Allen, 1951

O'Sullivan, John. "Making a Virtue of Nationalism." In: *Hungarian Review*, Vol XI, no. 3, May 2020.

Orzoff, Andrea. *Battle for the Castle the Myth of Czechoslovakia in Europe, 1914-1948*. Oxford: Oxford University Press, 2009.

Osterhammel, Jürgen. "Arnold Toynbee and the Problems of Today", Toynbee Lecture, Delivered at the Annual Meeting of The American Historical Association, Denver, January 6, 2017. Bulletin of the GHI, Spring 2017.

Paikert, G. C. "Hungary's National Minority Policies, 1920-1945", *The American Slavic and East European Review*, Vol. 12, No. 2 (Apr., 1953), pp. 201-218.

Pavel, Pavel. Transylvania and Danubian Peace, London, 1943.

Pavel, Pavel. *Why Rumania Failed?*, London: Alliance Press 1944 .

Perry, Marvin. "Arnold Toynbee: Nationalism as a 'false god'." *Interpretation, A Journal of Pol Philosophy*, Vol 4/1, Winter 1974, 51.

Péter, László, "The Army Question In Hungarian Politics 1867-1918." *Central Europe*, Vol. 4, No. 2, November 2006, 84-110.

Péter, László. "Scotus Viator és a magyar kérdés az első világháború előtt" [Scotus Viator and the Hungarian Question before the First World War], in Éva Saáry-Judit Steinmann (eds.): *Gesta Hungarorum III*, Swiss Hungarian Literature and Fine Arts Society, Zurich, 1990.

Péter, László. "The Political Conflict between R. W. Seton-Watson and C. A. Macartney over Hungary." In: Péter, László - Rady, Martyn, *British-Hungarian Relations Since*

*1848*, London, Hungarian Cultural Centre and School of Slavonic and East European Studies, University College London, 2004. 167-193.

Peterecz, Zoltán. "The visit of the most popular American of the day: Theodore Roosevelt in Hungary." *Hungarian Studies*. 28 (2): 2014, 235-254.

Picks, Hella. *Guilty Victims: Austria from the Holocaust to Haider*, I.B. Tauris, 2000.

Pók, Attila. *The Politics of Hatred in the Middle of Europe. Scapegoating in Twentieth Century Hungary. History and Historiography*, Savaria University Press, 2009.

Pritz, Pál. *Magyar diplomácia a két háború között*, [Interwar Hungarian Diplomacy]. Budapest, 1995.

Raffay, Ernő. *Mr. Trianon, Scotus Viator a magyarok legnagyobb ellensége* [Mr. Trianon. Scotus Viator, the Greatest Enemy of Hungarians], Budapest: Kárpátia Stúdió, 2023.

Ránki, György. "Találkozásaim Macartney Elemérrel" [My Encounters with C.A. Macartney]. *Élet és Irodalom*, 1978/ 27.

Richard Clogg *Politics And The Academy: Toynbee And The Koreas Chair*, London: Routledge, 2013.

Roberts, Andrew. *The Holy Fox: Biography of Lord Halifax*, London, Weidenfeld & Nicolson, 1991.

Rodd, Sir James Rennell, G.C.B., *Social And Diplomatic Memories 1902-1919*, London: Edward Arnold & Co., 356-357.

Romsics Ignác (ed.) *Integrációs törekvések Közép- és Kelet-Európában a 19. és 20. században*, [Integration Efforts in Central and Eastern Europe in the 19th and 20th Centuries], Budapest, 1997, 63-103.

Romsics, Ignác, *Hungary in the Twentieth Century*, Budapest, Corvina-Osiris, 1999.

Romsics, Ignác. "A brit külpolitika és a „magyar kérdés". 1914-1946 [British foreign policy and the "Hungarian question"1914-1946]. *Századok*, (130) 1996/2.

Romsics, Ignác. *Bethlen István. Politikai életrajz* [István Bethlen. Political Biography,] Budapest: Magyarságkutató Intézet, 1991.

Rónai, András, *Térképezett történelem* [History Mapped], Budapest: Püski, 1993, 103.

Rychlík, J., T. Marzik and M. Bielik (eds.). *R. W. Seton-Watson and His Relations with the Czechs and Slovaks, Documents 1906-1951*, Praha - Martin: Ústav T. G. Masaryka and Matica Slovenská, 1995, I/433.

Rychlík, Jan. "The Situation of the Hungarian Minority in Czechoslovakia 1918-1938", 27-38. In: Ferenc Eiler-Dagmar Hájková et al., *Czech and Hungarian Minority Policy in Central Europe 1918-1938*, Prague-Budapest, 2009.

Sakmyster, Thomas L. *Hungary, the Great Powers and the Danubian, Crisis*, University of Georgia Press, 1980.

Sallai, Gergely. *Az első bécsi döntés* [The First Vienna Award]. Budapest, 2002.

Schumpeter, Joseph A. "The Social Revolution in Austria by C.A. Macartney." *The Economic Journal*, Vol. 37, No. 146 (June 1927), pp. 290–292.
Scotus Viator. "A Monster Trial in Hungary", Spectator, March 28, 1908.
Seton-Watson (ed.). *The European Review, A Survey of Nationality*, London: Constable & Co. Ltd., 1914.
Seton-Watson, Christopher (ed.). *Confidential Print*, Series F, Vol. 2, (1923–June 1930).
Seton-Watson, Hugh and Christopher. *The Making of a New Europe, Robert W. Seton-Watson and the Last Years of Austria-Hungary*, University of Washington Print, 1981.
Seton-Watson, Hugh-Bodea, Cornelia. (eds.), *R.W. Seton-Watson and the Romanians 1906–1920*, Bucharest, 1988.
Seton-Watson, Hugh. "Carlile Aymler Macartney 1895–1978." The Proceedings of the British Academy, London, LXVII (1981).
Seton-Watson, Hugh. "Robert William Seton-Watson and the Trianon Settlement." in K. Király, Béla-Pastor, Peter-Sanders, Ivan (eds.). *War and Society in East-Central Europe, Essays on Word War I.: Total War and Peacemaking, A Case Study on Tranon*. New York, 1982.
Seton-Watson, Hugh. *Nations and States an Enquiry into the Origins of Nations and the Politics of Nationalism*, Methuen-London, 1977.
Seton-Watson. "Allen Leeper," *Slavonic and East Eu Review*, April 1935, 684–685.
Seton-Watson. "Austria and Her Neighbours", *Slavonic and East European Review*, 1935 April, 554.
Seton-Watson. "Danubian States, Steps to Economic Agreement." *The Times*, March 16, 1932, 10.
Seton-Watson. "Edvard Beneš", *The Slavonic and East European Review*, 1949 May, 359–362.
Seton-Watson. "Hungary and Rumania: The Land Dispute." *The Times*, 1928 March 12.
Seton-Watson. "Hungary in the Grip of Reaction." *The New Europe*, October 14, 1921.
Seton-Watson. "Obituary: Louis Eisenmann, International Affairs (Royal Institute of International Affairs 1931–1939)." Vol. 16, No. 4 (Jul., 1937), 601–602.
Seton-Watson. "President Wilson and Europe." *The New Europe* Vol. II. No. 16. February 1, 1917 pp.77–82.
Seton-Watson. "The Fall of Béla Kun," *The New Europe* 12, no. 148, August 14, 1919, 100.
Seton-Watson. "The German Dilemma," *Fortnightly*, CXXXIX (May, 1936), pp. 519–530. In: Historiography and British Appeasement In 1936 Judith S. Libby Butler University.
Seton-Watson. "The German Minority in Czechoslovakia." *Foreign Affairs*, Vol. 16, No. 4 (Jul., 1938), 651–666.
Seton-Watson. "The Middle Way in Europe, Tasks for British Statesmanship". *The Times*, June 30, 1933.
Seton-Watson. "The Problem of Revision and the Slav World." *The Slavonic and East European Review*, Vol. 12, No. 34 (Jul., 1933), pp. 24–35.

Seton-Watson. "The Problem of Small Nations and European Anarchy". Montague Burton International Relations Lecture, 1939.
Seton-Watson. "The Problem of Treaty Revision and the Hungarian Frontiers". In: *IA*, July 1933, 481-499.
Seton-Watson. "The Question of Minorities." *The Slavonic and East European Review*, Vol. 14, No. 40 (Jul., 1935), pp. 68-80.
Seton-Watson. "The Question of Minorities." *The Slavonic and East European Review*, Vol. 14, No. 40, Jul., 1935.
Seton-Watson. "The Question of Minorities". In: *SEER*, 1935 July.
Seton-Watson. "Transylvania in the 19th Century." *The Slavonic Review*, Vol. 3, No. 8 (Dec., 1924), 313-314.
Seton-Watson. "Transylvania since 1867." *The Slavonic Review*, Vol. 4, No. 10, Jun., 1925.
Seton-Watson. "Transylvania since 1867." *The Slavonic Review*, Vol. 4, No. 10., Jun., 1925.
Seton-Watson. "Transylvania. (I)." *The Slavonic Review*, Vol. 1, No. 2, Dec., 1922.
Seton-Watson. "Transylvania. (II)." *The Slavonic Review*, Vol. 1, No. 3 Mar., 1923.
Seton-Watson. "Yugoslavia and Croatia." A Lecture in the Royal Institute of International Affairs. January 29, 1929. *The Journal of International Affairs [IA]*, 1929/3.
Seton-Watson. *A History of the Czechs and Slovaks*. London, 1943, 275.
Seton-Watson. *A History of the Roumanians. From Roman Times to the Completion of Unity*, Cambridge: Cambridge University Press, 1934.
Seton-Watson. *Britain and the Dictators*, Cambridge University Press, 1938.
Seton-Watson. *Corruption and Reform. A Study of Electoral Practice*, London: Constable and Co., 1911.
Seton-Watson. *Czechoslovakia in its European Setting*. An Inaugural Lecture on February 6, 1946, Oxford, 1946.
Seton-Watson. *Czechoslovakia in its European Setting*. An Inaugural Lecture. February 6, 1946. Oxford, 1946.
Seton-Watson. *King Alexander's Assassination. Its Backgrounds and Effects*. International Affairs, January/February 1935.
Seton-Watson. *Maximilian, Holy Roman Emperor, (Stanhope Historical Essay 1901)*. London, A. Constable & Co. Ltd., 1902, 4.
Seton-Watson. *Munich and the Dictators - Munich and Danzig*, London, Methuen, 1939.
Seton-Watson. *Munich and the Dictators. Methuen*, 1939.
Seton-Watson. *Political Persecution in Hungary: An Appeal to British Public Opinion*, A. Constable, 1908.
Seton-Watson. *Roumania and the Great War*. London: Constable and Company Ltd., 1915.
Seton-Watson. *The Historian as a Political Force in Central-Europe*. An Inaugural Lecture Delivered before the University of London, November 22 1922.

Seton-Watson. *The New Slovakia*, Prague: F. Borový, 1924.
Seton-Watson. *The Problem of Small Nations and European Anarchy.* Montague Burton International Relations Lecture, 1939.
Seton-Watson. The Spirit of the Serb, in Low, Sydney (ed.): *The Spirit of the Allied Nations.* London, 1915.
Seton-Watson. *Transylvania: A Key Problem*, Oxford, 1943.
Seton-Watson. *Treaty Revision and Hungarian Frontiers*, London: Eyre & Spottiswoode Ltd., 1934.
Seton-Watson. *Treaty Revision and Hungarian Frontiers*, London: London: Eyre and Spottiswoode, 1934
Seton-Watson. *War and Democracy*, London: MacMillan & Co, 1919.
Seton-Watson. *What is at Stake in the War*, Humphrey Milford, Oxford University Press, 1915, 70.
Seymour, Charles. *Letters from the Paris Peace Conference*, (edited by Harold B. Whiteman), Yale University Press, 1965.
Sherwood, Peter. "Magyar stúdiumok Londonban" [Hungarian studies in London]. *Hungarológia* 1, 1993, pp.111-121.
Smith, Anthony D. "Memory and Modernity: Reflections on Ernest Gellner's Theory of Nationalism," *Nations and Nationalism*, 3, 1996, 371-388.
Smith, Wilfred Cantwell. *The Meaning and End of Religion*, First Fortress Press Edition, 1991.
Steed, Henry Wickham. "From Frederick the Great to Hitler: The Consistency of German Aims". *International Affairs*, Vol XVII, 1938.
Steed, Henry Wickham. "Frontiers of Peace" To the editor of The Times, September 20 1944.
Steed, Henry Wickham. "Hungarian Land Dispute, Rumanian Motives", April 11, 1928.
Steed, Henry Wickham. "Hungary and Rumania, To the Editor of the Times", March 24, 1928, 10.
Steed, Henry Wickham. "Hungary and Rumania: A Settlement by Equity", The Times, March 16, 1928.
Steed, Henry Wickham. "Revision of the Peace Treaties", *The Times*, March 27, 1933.
Steed, Henry Wickham. "The Frontiers of Hungary." *The Times*, March 19,15.
Steed, Henry Wickham. "The Great War 1914-1918." In: Stirling Taylor (ed.), *Great Events in History*, London: Cassell and Company, Ltd., 1934.
Steed, Henry Wickham. "The Great War, 1914-1918", In: *Great Events in History*, ed. Stirling Taylor, London: Cassell and Company, Ltd., 1934.
Steed, Henry Wickham. "The Map of Europe". The Times, July 18, 1933, 10.
Steed, Henry Wickham. *The Doom of the Hapsburgs*, Arrowsmith, 1936.
Steed, Henry Wickham. *The Hapsburg Monarchy*, London: Constable and Company, 1913.

Steed, Henry Wickham. *Through Thirty Years 1892-1922*, London: William Heinemann Ltd, 1924.
Steed., Henry Wickham. *Fifth Arm*. London: Constable and Company, 1940.
Stourton, Edward. *Auntie's War: The BBC during the Second World War*, London: Doubleday, 2017.
Suppan, Arnold. *Hitler–Beneš–Tito: National Conflicts, World Wars, Genocides, Expulsions, and Divided Remembrance in East-Central and Southeastern Europe, 1848–2018*, Austrian Academy of Sciences Press, 2019.
Szarka, László and Gergely Sallai, "Önkép és kontextus. Magyarország és a magyarság történelme a szlovák történetírásban a 20. század végén" [Self-image and context. The history of Hungary and Hungarians in Slovak historiography at the end of the 20th century], *Regio*, 2000. 71–107.
Szász, Zsombor. *M. Seton-Watson et l'histoire des Roumains*, Nouvelle Revue de Hongrie, 1934/november.
Szegedi-Maszák, Aladár. *Az ember ősszel visszanéz..., Egy volt Magyar diplomata emlékirataiból* [One Looks Back in Autumn..., From the Memoirs of a Former Hungarian Diplomat], Budapest, 1996.
Taylor, A.J.P. *The Course of German History*, New York: Capricorn Books 1962.
Taylor, A.J.P. *The Troublemakers*, London: Hamish Hamilton 1957.
Tilea, Ileana. (ed). *Envoy Extraordinary: Memoirs of a Roumanian Diplomat*, London, 1998.
Tingsten, Herbert. "Finished with Toynbee", *Dagens Nyheter*, Dec 6 1954. RIIA 4/TOYN/4
Todorova, Maria. *Imagining the Balkans*, Oxford University Press, NY, 1997.
Toynbee, Arnold J. "A Turning Point in History", *Foreign Affairs* January 1939, 305–320.
Toynbee, Arnold J. "After Munich: The World Outlook". *International Affairs* (Royal Institute of International Affairs 1931–1939), Vol. 18, No. 1 (January – February, 1939), pp. 1–28.
Toynbee, Arnold J. "Peaceful Change or War? The Next Stage in the International Crisis," *International Affairs* (Royal Institute of International Affairs 1931–1939), Vol. 15, No. 1 (January–February 1936.
Toynbee, Arnold J. "The International Outlook", *Survey of International Affairs*, Vol. 23, No. 4 (Oct., 1947), pp. 463–476.
Toynbee, Arnold J. "Trends of International Affairs Since the War." Fourth Conference of Institutions for the Scientific Study of International Relations, Copenhagen, June 8–10, 1931. In: *Pacific Affairs*, Vol 4, No 9 (September 1931), pp. 753–778.
Toynbee, Arnold J. "Trends of International Affairs Since the War", Fourth Conference of Institutions for the Scientific Study of International Relations, Copenhagen, June 8–10, 1931. In: Pacific Affairs, Vol 4, No 9 (September 1931), pp. 753–778.
Toynbee, Arnold J. "Was Britain's abdication folly?" *The Round Table*, 1970, 219–228.

Toynbee, Arnold J. "Was Britain's Abdication Folly?" *The Round Table*, 1970. 60:238, 219–228.
Toynbee, Arnold J. *A Study of History*, Vol I, London: Oxford University Press, 1934.
Toynbee, Arnold J. *A Study of History*, Vol III, Oxford, 1934.
Toynbee, Arnold J. *A Study of History*, Vol IV, Oxford University Press, 1939.
Toynbee, Arnold J. *Acquaintances*, Oxford University Press, 1967.
Toynbee, Arnold J. and Daisaku Ikeda, *Choose Life*, Bloomsbury Academic 2007.
Toynbee, Arnold J. and Veronica Toynbee. "Problems of Research in International Relations." *International Studies*, vol. 3(1), January 1960.
Toynbee, Arnold J. *Change and Habit, The Challenge of our Time*, Oxford: One World, 1966.
Toynbee, Arnold J. *Civilization on Trial*, Oxford University Press, 1948.
Toynbee, Arnold J. *Experiences*, London: Oxford University Press, 1969.
Toynbee, Arnold J. *Murderous Tyranny of the Turks*, London: Hodder & Stoughton, 1917.
Toynbee, Arnold J. *Nationality and the War*, London: J.M. Dent & sons Limited, 1915.
Toynbee, Arnold J. *Subject Nationalities of the German Alliance*, 1-4. Cassel &Company Ltd, London, 1917.
Toynbee, Arnold J. *Survey of International Affairs 1924*, Oxford University Press, 1926.
Toynbee, Arnold J. *Survey of International Affairs 1926*. Oxford University Press, London. Humphrey Milford, 1928.
Toynbee, Arnold J. *Survey of International Affairs 1927*. Oxford University Press for the Royal Institute of International Affairs, 1929.
Toynbee, Arnold J. *Survey of International Affairs 1928*, Oxford University Press, 1930.
Toynbee, Arnold J. *Survey of International Affairs 1931*. Oxford University Press, 1932.
Toynbee, Arnold J. *Survey of International Affairs, 1934*, Oxford University Press, 1935.
Toynbee, Arnold J. *Survey of International Affairs, 1935*. Vol II, London 1936.
Toynbee, Arnold J. *Survey of International Affairs, 1936*. London: Oxford University Press, 1938.
Toynbee, Arnold J. *Surviving the Future*, NY, 1971.
Toynbee, Arnold J. *The Ultimate Choice*. R.J. Acford Ltd, Chichester, Sussex, 1961 reprint.
Toynbee, Arnold J. *The World After the Peace Conference, Issued under the auspices of the British Inst of International Affairs*, Humphrey Milford, Oxford University Press, 1926.
Toynbee, Arnold J. *The World and The West* [Civilization on Trial], Cleveland, Ohio, 1958.
Toynbee, Viscount Cecil of Chelwood, Marquess of Lothian and R. A. Butler. "The Issues in British Foreign Policy." *International Affairs* (Royal Institute of International Affairs 1931-1939), Vol. 17, No. 3 (May - Jun., 1938), pp. 307-407.
Traşcă, Ottmar. *Relațiile româno-ungare și problema Transilvaniei, 1940–1944* (I) [Romanian-Hungarian Relations and the Transylvanian Question, 1940–1944]. Anuarul Institutului de Istorie D. A. Xenopol. 2004.

Trommer, Aage. "MacDonald in Geneva in March 1933." *Scandinavian Journal of History*, 1(1-4), 1976, 293-312.

Urban, Rudolf. *Demokratenpresse in Lichte Prager Geheimakten*, Prague: Orbis, 1943.

Vangelis Kechriotis-Maciej Górny-Ahmet Ersoy (eds.), *Discourses of Collective Identity in Central and Southeast Europe, Vol. 3/1: Modernism: The Creation of Nation-States*, CEU Press, 2009.

Vansittart, Robert. *Black Record: Germans Past and Present*. Hamish Hamilton, 1941.

Vansittart, Robert. *In his Lessons of My Life*. New York: A. Knopf, 1943.

Viscount Rothermere. *My Campaign for Hungary*. London: Eyre and Spottiswoode, 1939.

West, Rebecca. *Black Lamb and Falcon*, Penguin Classics, 2007.

Whiteman, Marj and C.A. Macartney, "Oxford Hungary Expert." *The Austin American*, December 4, 1962.

Wilson, Jim. *Nazi Princess: Hitler, Lord Rothermere and Princess Stephanie von Hohenlohe, The History Press*, 2011.

Wilson, Trevor. "Lord Bryce's Investigation into Alleged German Atrocities in Belgium, 1914-15". *Journal of Contemporary History*. 14 (3), July 1979: 369-383.

Wiskemann, Elizabeth. *Czechs and Germans: A Study of the Struggles in the Historic Provinces of Bohemia and Moravia*, Oxford: Oxford University Press, 1938.

Zeidler, Miklós. *Ideas on Territorial Revisionin Hungary, 1920-1945*. Columbia University Press, New York, 2007.

Zeman, Zbyněk and Antonín Klimek. *The Life of Edvard Beneš 1884-1948*. Oxford, Oxford University Press 1997.

Zeman, Zbyněk. "Edvard Beneš's foreign policy and the minorities" 75-84. In: Eiler, Ferenc, Hájková, Dagmar, et al., (eds.). Czech and Hungarian Minority Policy in Central Europe, 1918-1938. Prague: Masarykův ústav a [Archiv] Akademie věd ČR; Budapest: MTA Etnikai-nemzeti Kisebbségkutató Intézete, 2009.

Zlatar, Zdenko. The Yugoslav Idea and the First Common State of the South Slavs. In: *Nationalities Papers* 25/2, 1997: 387-406.

Gallery

1. The bust of RWSW erected in October 1937 on the 20th anniversary of the Chernivtsi tragedy, in Rozsahegy. Sculpture by Vojtech Ihriský (Wikimedia Commons)

2. Toynbee in 1900. George Grantham Bain Collection, United States Library of Congress's Prints and Photographs division (Wikimedia Commons)

Gallery

3. Lieutenant C A Macartney
Royal Field Artillery ©Imperial
War Museums HU_117317.tif

4. Home of Steed and Madame
Rose, the famous Saturday tea
parties Lansdowne-House W11
London (Wikimedia Commons)

5. Robert William Seton-Watson around the time of the Versailles Treaty (Wikimedia Commons)

6. The Hungarian delegation leaving Grand Trianon Palace at Versailles, after the treaty was signed on 4 June 1920 (Wikimedia Commons)

7. Steed on the cover of the 1924 Czech edition of his Through Thirty Years *(Třicet let novinářem)* (©Alamy 2KEW69E)

8. Robert William Seton-Watson with Masaryk during his tour of Czechoslovakia in 1928, in the Lány Castle of the Head of State (©Archives of Masaryk Institute, fund T. G. Masaryk, sign. 1928-2-19.)

Gallery

9. Carlile Aylmer Macartney at the BBC microphone (©BBC Archives 338251)

10. Henry Wickham Steed at the BBC microphone (©BBC Archives 111615)

11. Macartney after 1948 (©Bodleian Library-Weston Library, Oxford, Ms. Eng. c. 3316. Photogr. C. 19. fols. 35-36.)

12. Arnold J. Toynbee on January 1 1953 (© Alamy G6AAJM)

13. Toynbee with his second wife Veronica Toynbee on 29 June 1967, the year of the publication of his memoir Acquaintances *(Wikimedia Commons)*

14. Arrival to London (Victoria St.) on June 13 1938.
On the left side of the picture is Barcza Györgyné Alexa Jeszenszky, with György Barcza, diplomat and Hungarian Minister to England on her right, as well as Robert William Seton-Watson, the host of the couple, in the background (©FTB 861 FAlbum 1226 National Széchényi Library, Historical Photographs and Interview Gallery)

# Index

*Names in italics refer to photo captions*

Alexander I of Yugoslavia, 76, 110, 146, 147
Allen, Denis, 223
Allen, Lord Reginald Clifford, 166, 167
Anderson, Benedict, 9
Andrew II of Hungary, 21
Antonescu, Ion, 1n4, 198, 199, 213, 215, 221, 268
Apor, Vilmos, 151
Apponyi, Albert, 16, 17, 21, 87, 269
Árpád, Hungarian Prince, 21
Atatürk, Kemal, 64

Balogh, József, 98, 100n179, 115, 129, 138, 139, 151, 175, 210n543
Barclay, Colville, 105
Barcza, György, 191, 198, 296
Bárczy, István, 115
Barker, Ernest, 65
Barthou, Louis Jean, 146
Bartlett, Charles Vernon Oldfield, 44
Bátonyi, Gábor, 83
Bauer, Otto, 70
Beazley, Charles, 141
Bell, Moberly, 17, 18
Beneš, Edvard, 1, 19, 59, 82n115, 84, 85, 103n185, 113, 115, 170, 173, 178, 182, 189, 201n512, 223, 225–27, 235, 236
Berber, Fritz, 148
Berry, Burton Y., 232
Bethlen, István, 62, 82, 84–88, 90, 93, 97, 98n173, 100, 113–15, 125–29, 133, 136, 150, 151, 160, 161, 205, 209, 213, 227
Bevin, Ernest, 232, 233
Beyer, Hans, 242
Bjørnson, Bjørnstjerne, 23
Bliss, Tasker Howard, 51

Bortnowski, Władysław, 175
Brătianu, Vintilla, 213, 221
Brenier, Henri, 144
Bryce, James, 34, 36n88, 42n117, 98n172
Buckmaster, Lord Stanley, 105
Bunsen, Maurice de, 76
Burrows, Ronald Montagu, 39, 58–60, 62, 258

Cadogan, Alexander Montagu George, 191
Campbell, John Charles, 231
Carr, Edward Hallett, 154n374, 155, 192, 193
Case, Holly, 268
Chamberlain, Austen, 88n140, 112
Chamberlain, Neville, 145n338, 162, 165, 171, 181, 184, 185, 188, 191
Chambers, Whittaker, 241
Charles II of Romania, 198
Chirol, Valentine Ignatius, 18, 23, 68, 69
Churchill, Winston, 39, 118, 119n234, 143, 202, 203, 212, 222, 227, 232, 233, 252
Ciano, Galeazzo, 196
Ciotori, Dimitrie, 1
Clemenceau, Georges, 5
Clutton Brock, Arthur, 267
Columba, Father Cary-Elwes, 247, 248
Coudenhove-Kalergi, Richard von, 95
Cromer, Lord Evelyn Baring, 32n72, 39
Crowe, Eyre Alexander Barby Wichart, 47
Curtis, Lionel George, 51, 68, 69, 76, 192n484, 269
Curzon, Lord George Nathaniel, 52n149, 84

Davies, David, 193
Dawson, Jeoffrey, 87, 96n166
Dawson, William Harbutt, 141
Deák, Ferenc, 134, 211n550
Disraeli, Benjamin (1st Earl of Beaconsfield), 10
Drummond, Eric James, 107
Dulles, John Foster, 251
Durham, Edith Mary, 44, 76, 77, 79, 80, 146n343, 236, 257

Eden, Robert Anthony, 119, 145, 149, 150, 165, 212, 221, 243
Edward VII of the United Kingdom, 5
Eisenmann, Louis, 69, 87, 88
Elisabeth of Austria
Evans, Arthur John

Ferdinand, Romanian king, 213
Festetich, György, 151
Fisher, Allan George Barnard, 140
Fisher, H. A. L. (Herbert Albert Laurens Fisher), 5, 136
Foch, Ferdinand, 180
Frank, Tibor, 129
Franz Ferdinand, 31, 51, 76, 78, 147
Franz Joseph, 17, 27, 40, 70, 92, 215
Friedjung, Heinrich, 20, 29
Friedrich the Great, King of Prussia, 169

Gaj, Ljudevit, 29
Gál, István, 265
Garami, Ernő, 85
Garibaldi, Giuseppe, 7
Garnett, Maxwell James Clerk, 155
Garvin, James Lewis, 81, 96
George VI of the United Kingdom, 5, 218
Gilbert, Martin, 252
Gladstone, William Ewart, 10, 11, 34, 63, 69, 257
Glassheim, Eagle, 236
Goebbels, Joseph, 212
Goga, Octavian, 109, 221

Goldis, Vasile, 22
Gooch, George Peabody, 76, 132, 133, 141, 258
Goschen, Edward William, 5
Gottwald, Klement, 235
Gower, Robert, 96n166, 120, 128
Graham, Billy, 254
Grigg, Edward William Macleay, 57

Halifax, Lord Edward Frederick, 169
Hamid, Abdul II, 34
Harmsworth, Esmond Cecil, 93, 94
Harmsworth, Harold Sydney (1st Viscount Rothermere), 90, 92, 93
Hatvany, Lajos, 95, 96
Headlam-Morley, James, 43, 51, 67, 76, 77, 104
Heinlein, Konrad, 146, 152
Hitler, Adolf, 119n234, 141–46, 149, 150, 152–54, 166, 169, 172, 173n435, 174, 175, 178, 182, 184–86, 188–90, 192, 195, 196, 199, 200, 202, 206, 212–14, 223, 227, 231, 237, 250, 268n46
Hlinka, Andrej, 23n44, 73, 168
Hoare, Samuel John Gurney (1st Viscount Templewood), 144, 167
Hodža, Milan, 94, 201n512
Hohenlohe-Waldenburg, Stephanie, 92, 153
Hóman, Bálint, 115
Horthy, Miklós, 62, 80–82, 87, 100, 114, 123, 137, 139, 159, 162–64, 195, 206, 208, 214, 224, 238, 269
Horváth, Jenő, 163
House, Edward Mandell (Colonel House), 51
Howard, Esmé William, 25n53, 57
Hoxha, Enver, 236
Hunyadi, János, 134, 157
Hus, John (Jan), 19

Ignotus, Pál, 211
Imrédy, Béla, 140, 175, 178, 191n478
Inge, William Ralph, 9

Iorga, Nicolae, 133, 134, 158, 213
Iványi-Grünwald, Béla, 206

Jaspers, Karl, 262
Jászi, Oszkár, 62, 79, 81–83, 86, 90, 136, 226, 227
Jeszenszky, Géza, xii, 15, 24, 33
Jones, Tom, 150
Jovanović, Ljuba, 76, 77
Judson, Pieter, 26

Kállay, Miklós, 208, 214, 223n592, 238
Kállay, Tibor, 84
Kánya, Kálmán, 150, 176, 181n459
Károlyi, Gyula, 115
Károlyi, Mihály, 19n23, 80–82, 86–90, 95, 136, 143, 182, 209, 210, 223
Kerr, Philip Henry (11th Marquess of Lothian; see also Lord Lothian), 51, 141
Khuen, Karl, 152
Knox, Geoffrey George, 140, 191n478
Kornfeld, Móric, 115, 151
Kornis, Gyula, 151
Korošec, Anton, 75
Kossuth, Lajos, 17, 20, 134
Kun, Béla, 80, 127

Lampson, Miles, 77, 86, 87
Láng, Lajos, 21
Laval, Pierre, 144
Law, Bonar, 84
Lázár, Miklós, 95
Leeper, Allen, 43, 47–49, 60, 85, 133, 136, 257
Leeper, Rex, 43, 192n484, 200, 201n512, 202n516
Liebich, Andre, xi, 4, 15, 99
Lloyd George, David, 44, 51, 64n35, 91, 142, 232, 236n5
Lockhart, Bruce, 210
Lojkó, Miklós, xi, xii, 260
Lothian, Lord (Philip Kerr), 141, 142n320, 154

Luce, Henry, 241
Lungu, Dov B., 268
Lupis-Vukić, Ivo, 267
Lyde, Lionel William, 89, 90

Macadam, Ivison, 147, 149
MacDonald, Ramsay, 113, 119, 120, 133
Madame Rose (Clémence Rayer-Rose de Corps-Billoux), 19, 20, 92, 169n419, 268, *290*
Mamarchev, Dimitri, 52
Mamarchev, Nedella, 52
Maniu, Iuliu, 74, 109, 113, 213, 221, 237
Manoilescu, Mihail, 196
Marshall, George, 234
Marx, Karl, 241
Masaryk, Jan, 169, 171, 235, 268
Masaryk, Tomáš Garrigue, ix, 19, 29, 30, 32, 33, 39, 58, 59, 71, 72, 74, 103, 104, 152, 211n550, 225, 235, *292*
Maximilian, Holy Roman Emperor, 5
McNeill, William, 15, 50, 141, 187n470, 255, 266
Medlicott, William, 55
Mikes, George (György), 206
Mișu, Nicolae, 47n133, 58
Molotov, Vyacheslav Mikhaylovich, 230, 234
Monckton, Walter, 201
Móricz, Kálmán, 163, 164
Murray, Gilbert, 56, 57, 65, 140, 150, 151, 170, 217n570, 244, 254n78, 258
Murray, Rosalind (Rosalind Toynbee), 217n570, 247
Mussolini, Benito, 118, 119, 144, 145, 147, 154

Nagy, Ferenc, 234
Nagy, Zsolt, 61
Namier, Lewis Bernstein, ix, 43, 246, 257
Newman, Bernard, 138
Newton, Lord (Thomas Legh), 83, 105, 107, 108n200

Nicolas I of Russia, 215
Nicolson, Harold George, 44, 47–49, 60, 233
Noel-Buxton, Noel Edward, 57, 190n476
Norman, Montagu Collet, 84
Northcliffe, Lord (Alfred Harmsworth), 30, 37, 41, 44, 90, 92, 142n325, 241

O'Malley, Owen St Clair, 191, 194, 205
Orlando, Vittorio, 40
Ottlik, György, 151

Paikert, Géza, 264
Palmer, Alan, 190, 238
Palmerston, Lord (Henry John Temple), 4n14, 10
Pares, Bernard, 59
Pašić, Nikola, ix, 38, 46
Peidl, Gyula, 85
Péter, László, xi, xii, 13, 15, 18
Phillimore, Lord Francis Stephen, 83n122, 105
Phipps, Eric, 150
Pilar, Ivo, 264
Pitt, William, Jr, 55
Pollock, Frederick, 105
Ponsonby, Frederick Edward Grey, 84
Puaux, Gabriel, 260

Radić, Stepan, 79
Rajniss, Ferenc, 113
Ribbentrop, Joachim von, 92, 145n338, 148, 196
Richmond, Herbert William, 57
Ripka, Hubert, 210
Roberts, Frank Kenyon, 194, 210, 221, 223n592
Robinson, Geoffrey, 259
Roosevelt, Theodore, 16
Ruppeldt, Fedor, 181, 182n460
Rutter, Owen, 129
Rychlík, Jan, 72

Sargent, Orme, 171, 173

Schumpeter, Alois, 71
Scott, C. P. (Charles Prestwich Scott), 63
Seton-Watson, Christopher, 15, 236
Seton-Watson, Hugh, 15, 236
Smith, Frederick Edwin (Earl of Birkenhead), 108
Smith, Jeremias, 85
Somervell, David Churchill, 241
Spengler, Oswald, 246, 248
Štefánek, Anton, 1, 22
Stephanie von Hohenlohe Waldenburg-Schillingfürst, 92, 153
Stevenson, Daniel, 67
Strang, William, 194n489, 258
Strossmayer, Josip Juraj, 29
Sturdza, Mihai (Mihael), 268
Supilo, Frano, 19, 33, 46
Szász, Zsombor, 136
Szekfű, Gyula, 53, 100
Szent-Györgyi, Albert, 244
Stalin, Joseph Vissarionovich, 208, 222, 226n602, 227, 235

Tardieu, André, 113
Tarján, György, 206
Taylor, A. J. P. (Alan John Percivale Taylor), 142n322, 223, 224, 235, 253
Teleki, Pál, 115, 151, 178, 191, 194n492, 195, 196, 198, 206–09
Thomson, Lord Christopher Birdwood, 108
Thwaites, John Anthony, 224
Tilea, Viorel, 75, 94, 104, 236
Tiso, Josef, 176, 192
Tisza, István, 17, 28, 78, 134, 211n550
Titulescu, Nicolae, 1n4, 84, 85, 135, 178, 213, 268
Todorova, Maria, 264
Tollas, Tibor, 245
Tolstoy, Lev, 74
Torday, Emil, 77
Trevor-Roper, Hugh, 253
Trócsányi, Zoltán, 138
Troubridge, Ernest Charles Thomas, 45

Trumbić, Ante, 19, 46
Tyrell, William George, 68, 87

Vámbéry, Rusztem, 16n1, 85
Vansittart, Robert Gilbert, 203
Victoria, Queen of the United Kingdom, 6, 84n124

Wakaizumi, Kai, 256
Watson, Cameron, 109
West, Rebecca (Cicily Isabel Fairfield), 257

White, Henry, 51
Whitman, Walt, 74
Whyte, Alexander Frederick, 39
Wilson, Thomas Woodrow, 40, 44, 55, 64, 71, 186
Wiskemann, Elizabeth Meta, 155
Woodward, E. L. (Ernest Llewellyn Woodward), 184

Zeman, Zbyněk, 103n185, 226
Zimmern, Alfred Eckhardt, 24, 43, 201, 204